Praise for *Thinking the Twentieth Century*

"There are so many ways that *Thinking the Twentieth Century* is a remarkable book. The lifetime of scholarship and intellectual engagement lying behind that verb 'thinking' in the title. The way ideas crackle in the interplay between the authors. The passionate involvement with issues political and controversial. That the book could have been written at all, given the tragic circumstances surrounding it . . . Judt proceeds to take the reader on a wild ride through the ideological currents and shoals of twentieth-century thought." —*Los Angeles Times*

"Provocative and inspiring . . . For sheer human courage as well as intellectual brilliance, the result is impressive. . . . *Thinking the Twentieth Century* is a substantial achievement." —*Financial Times*

"In this marvelous book, two explorers set out on a journey from which only one of them will return. Their unknown land is that often fearsome continent we call the twentieth century. Their route is through their own minds and memories. . . . Brilliantly eloquent, and apparently recalling every book they have ever read, the two historians find something striking and original to say about almost everything." —Neal Ascherson, *The Guardian* (London)

"A brilliant compilation of [Judt's] ideas on history and politics." —Ian Buruma, *The New York Review of Books*

"It is essential reading for all who want to know what contemporary historians have to tell us. It is also a model of civilized discourse in the academic global village. It shows that historians can inquire into their own assumptions, examine their own certainties, and see the ways in which their own lives are shaped and reshaped by their century. And not least, it is a worthy memorial to a remarkable person and the life he contrived to live." —Eric Hobsbawm, *The London Review of Books*

D0050424

"An important achievement of a scholar and intellectual whose premature passing we should all regret."

—Francis Fukuyama, *The New York Times Book Review*

"Fans will find plenty to sustain them in this poignant coda to a life marked by great feats of penmanship, scholarly insight, and contemporary polemic. . . . [Judt's] bravery is ever-present, but rightly understated. As Mr. Snyder notes in his introduction, the book is both about the life of the mind and a mindful life. Judt exemplified both." —*The Economist*

"It is Judt's carefully considered and passionately held *non serviam* that makes this volume so invaluable and that places him among the great independent voices of our culture like Orwell and Camus." —*The Denver Post*

"Judt was a provocateur, but maybe an accidental one, and after reading this remarkable, impassioned book, it's hard to doubt his sincerity. . . . *Thinking the Twentieth Century* is Judt's final salvo against what he saw as a culture of historical ignorance and political apathy, and it's every bit as brilliant, uncompromising, and original as he was." —NPR.org

"Incandescent on every page with intellectual energy."

—Pankaj Mishra, *Prospect Magazine* (London)

"[*Thinking the Twentieth Century*] is in many ways the book Judt was meant to write, and a fitting swan song to an incendiary intellectual life. . . . Timely and inspired, *Thinking the Twentieth Century* is a prescient look at the ideas that shaped the last hundred years." —*The Vienna Review*

"Most moving for the reader are Judt's fierce commitment to history as an indispensable key to understanding the present and his ability, even when speaking his final thoughts through a breathing tube, to express himself in clear, forthright language. . . . The result is a volume filled with memorable insights that any educated person will enjoy." —*Foreign Affairs*

"This marvelous précis, vibrantly alive, rich, and piquant, is one last gift from an exceptional public intellectual. Not only academics and fans of Judt, but also those who enjoy the *New York Review of Books* and *The New Yorker* will flock to read it. Highly recommended."

—*Library Journal* (starred review)

"Scintillating . . . Interweaving autobiographical sketches with fluent, free-wheeling discussions of history, politics, and culture, Judt revisits crucial twentieth-century intellectual currents: the impact of two world wars and the Great Depression on politics and philosophy; the development of and rivalry between communist and fascist dogmas; the success of social democracy and Keynesian economics in bringing liberal government, broad-based growth, and social equality to the postwar world; and the retreat from those achievements prompted by free-market fundamentalism's attack on the activist state. . . . Judt's ability to distill heaps of erudition into lucid, pithy conversation, even when on a breathing apparatus, is astonishing; he's as engaging on the religious dimensions of Marxism and Freudianism as on Obama and the Iraq War. Snyder, a historian and former student of Judt's, contributes probing interjections that stimulate and test his mentor's ideas. The result is a lively, browsable, deeply satisfying meditation on recent history by a deservedly celebrated public intellectual."

—*Publishers Weekly* (starred review)

"Two brilliant scholars parse the politics and economics of the past one hundred years. That could be a dry task, but for the quiet passion of Judt (*The Memory Chalet*, 2010, etc.) and Snyder (History/Yale Univ.; *Bloodlands: Europe Between Hitler and Stalin*, 2010, etc.). . . . Social democracy has rarely had better informed, more ethically rigorous advocates than these two distinguished men. For readers who like to be challenged, this searching look at our recent history provides a firm intellectual and moral foundation for understanding the dilemmas of our time." —*Kirkus Reviews*

ABOUT THE AUTHORS

Tony Judt was educated at King's College, Cambridge, and the École Normale Supérieure, Paris, and taught at Cambridge, Oxford, and Berkeley. He was the Erich Maria Remarque Professor of European Studies at New York University, as well as the founder and director of the Remarque Institute, dedicated to creating an ongoing conversation between Europe and America.

The author or editor of fourteen books, Professor Judt was a frequent contributor to *The New York Review of Books*, *The Times Literary Supplement*, *The New Republic*, *The New York Times*, and many journals across Europe and the United States. Professor Judt is the author of *The Memory Chalet*, *Ill Fares the Land*, *Reappraisals: Reflections on the Forgotten Twentieth Century*, and *Postwar: A History of Europe Since 1945*, which was one of *The New York Times Book Review*'s Ten Best Books of 2005, the winner of the Council on Foreign Relations Arthur Ross Book Award, and a finalist for the Pulitzer Prize. He died in August 2010 at the age of sixty-two.

Timothy Snyder is the Housum Professor of History at Yale University and the author of five award-winning books, most recently *Bloodlands: Europe Between Hitler and Stalin*, which has won eight prizes and been translated into twenty-four languages. He lives in New Haven, Connecticut.

THINKING THE TWENTIETH CENTURY

TONY JUDT

with Timothy Snyder

PENGUIN BOOKS

PENGUIN BOOKS

Published by the Penguin Group

Penguin Group (USA) Inc., 375 Hudson Street, New York, New York 10014, U.S.A. •
Penguin Group (Canada), 90 Eglinton Avenue East, Suite 700, Toronto, Ontario M4P 2Y3,
Canada (a division of Pearson Penguin Canada Inc.) • Penguin Books Ltd, 80 Strand, London
WC2R 0RL, England • Penguin Ireland, 25 St Stephen's Green, Dublin 2, Ireland
(a division of Penguin Books Ltd) • Penguin Group (Australia), 707 Collins Street, Melbourne,
Victoria 3008, Australia (a division of Pearson Australia Group Pty Ltd) • Penguin Books
India Pvt Ltd, 11 Community Centre, Panchsheel Park, New Delhi – 110 017, India • Penguin
Group (NZ), 67 Apollo Drive, Rosedale, Auckland 0632, New Zealand (a division of Pearson
New Zealand Ltd) • Penguin Books (South Africa), Rosebank Office Park, 181 Jan Smuts Avenue,
Parktown North 2193, South Africa • Penguin China, B7 Jiaming Center,
27 East Third Ring Road North, Chaoyang District, Beijing 100020, China

Penguin Books Ltd, Registered Offices:
80 Strand, London WC2R 0RL, England

First published in the United States of America by The Penguin Press,
a member of Penguin Group (USA) Inc. 2012
Published in Penguin Books 2013

5 7 9 10 8 6 4

THE LIBRARY OF CONGRESS HAS CATALOGED THE HARDCOVER EDITION AS FOLLOWS:
Judt, Tony.
Thinking the twentieth century / Tony Judt, with Timothy Snyder.
p. cm.
Includes bibliographical references and index.
ISBN 978-1-59420-323-7 (hc.)
ISBN 978-0-14-312304-0 (pbk.)
1. Judt, Tony—Interviews. 2. Judt, Tony—Political and social views. 3. Political
science—Philosophy—History—20th century. 4. History—Philosophy—History—20th century.
I. Snyder, Timothy. II. Title. III. Title: Thinking the 20th century.
JC257.J83J8 2012
320.092—dc23
2011031473

Printed in the United States of America
DESIGNED BY AMANDA DEWEY

CONTENTS

For Daniel and Nicholas

FOREWORD

This book is history, biography and ethical treatise.

It is a history of modern political ideas in Europe and the United States. Its subjects are power and justice, as understood by liberal, socialist, communist, nationalist and fascist intellectuals from the late nineteenth through the early twenty-first century. It is also the intellectual biography of the historian and essayist Tony Judt, born in London in the middle of the twentieth century, just after the cataclysm of the Second World War and the Holocaust, and just as communists were securing power in Eastern Europe. Finally, it is a contemplation of the limitations (and capacity for renewal) of political ideas, and of the moral failures (and duties) of intellectuals in politics.

To my mind, Tony Judt is the only person capable of writing such a broad treatment of the politics of ideas. As of 2008, Tony was the author of intense and polemical studies of French history, essays on intellectuals and their engagement, and a magnificent history of Europe since 1945, entitled *Postwar*. He had allowed his gifts for moralization and for historiography to find distinct outlets in brief reviews and longer scholarly studies, and had brought both forms very close to perfection. This book arose, however, because at a certain point that November I understood that Tony would be incapable of any further writing at all, at least in the conventional sense. I proposed to Tony that we write a book together the day after I realized that he could no longer use his hands. Tony had been stricken with ALS (amyotrophic lateral sclerosis), a degenerative neurological disorder that brings progressive paralysis and certain and usually rapid death.

This book takes the form of a long conversation between Tony and myself. On Thursdays during the winter, spring and summer of 2009, I took the 8:50 train from New Haven to New York's Grand Central Station, then the subway downtown to the neighborhood where Tony lived with his wife, Jennifer Homans, and their sons, Daniel and Nick. Our meetings were scheduled for eleven in the morning; usually I had about ten minutes in a café to collect my thoughts about the day's subject and make a few notes. I washed my hands in very hot water in the café and then again in Tony's apartment; Tony suffered terribly from colds in his condition, and I wanted to be able to grasp his hand.

When we began our conversation in January 2009, Tony was still walking. He could not turn the knob to open the door to his apartment, but he could stand behind it and greet me. Soon he was welcoming me from an armchair in the sitting room. By spring his nose and much of his head were covered by a mechanical breathing apparatus, doing the work that his lungs no longer could. In summer we met in his study, surrounded by books, Tony looking down at me from an imposing electric wheelchair. Sometimes I would work its controls, since of course Tony could not. By now Tony was largely unable to move his body at all, save his head, eyes and vocal chords. For the purposes of this book, that was enough.

To watch the course of this destructive illness was a great sadness, especially in moments of rapid decline. In April 2009, having seen Tony lose the use of his legs and then his lungs in a matter of weeks, I was convinced (as were, I had the impression, his doctors) that he had no more than a few weeks to live. I was and am thus all the more grateful to Jenny and the boys for sharing Tony with me during such a time. But the conversation was also a great source of intellectual sustenance, bringing the pleasure of concentration, the harmony of communication and the gratification of good work achieved. Attending to the subjects at hand, and keeping pace with Tony's mind, was an absorbing labor, and also a happy one.

I am a historian of Eastern Europe, where the spoken book enjoys a proud tradition. The most famous example of the genre is the Czech writer Karel Čapek's series of interviews with Tomáš Masaryk, the philosopher-president of interwar Czechoslovakia. This happens to be the first book that Tony read in Czech from cover to cover. Perhaps the best spoken book is *My Century*, the magnificent autobiography of the Polish-Jewish poet Aleksander Wat, as extracted from him over tape recorders by Czesław Miłosz in California. This I read for the first time on a train from Warsaw to Prague, just as I was beginning doctoral studies in history. I wasn't thinking of these examples as such when I proposed a spoken book to Tony, nor do I regard myself as a Čapek or a Miłosz. As an east Europeanist who has read many such books, I just took for granted that something enduring could arise from conversation.

My questions to Tony arose from three sources. My original and rather general plan was to talk through Tony's books from beginning to end, from his histories of the French Left through *Postwar*, seeking general arguments about the role of political intellectuals and the craft of historians. I was interested in themes that are indeed prominent in this book, such as the elusiveness of the Jewish question in Tony's work, the universal character of French history and the power and limits of Marxism. I had the intuition that Eastern Europe had broadened Tony's ethical and intellectual outlook, but had no idea just how profoundly true this was. I learned about Tony's east European connections, and much else, because Timothy Garton Ash and Marci Shore suggested, and Tony agreed, that we devote some of our sessions to Tony's life rather than to his work. Finally, Tony revealed that he had been planning to write a history of intellectual life in the twentieth century. I used his chapter outline as the basis for a third round of questions.

This book's conversational character required that its authors be familiar with thousands of other books. Because Tony and I were speaking to each other in person, there was no time to check references. Tony did not know in advance what I would ask, and I did not know in advance what he would answer. What appears in print here reflects the spontaneity, unpredictability, and sometimes playfulness of two minds purposefully engaged through speech. But everywhere, and especially in its historical sections, it depends upon our mental libraries, and in particular upon Tony's improbably capacious and well-catalogued one. This book makes a case for conversation, but perhaps an even stronger case for reading. I never studied with Tony, but the card catalogue of his mental library overlapped considerably with my own. Our previous reading created a common space within which Tony and I could venture together, noting landmarks and vistas, at a moment when other kinds of movement were impossible.

Still, to speak is one thing, and to publish is another. How exactly did that conversation become this book? Each session was recorded, then saved as a digital file. The young historian Yedida Kanfer then undertook the transcription. This was itself a demanding intellectual task, since to puzzle out what we were saying from imperfect recordings Yedida had to know what we were talking about. Without her dedication and her knowledge, this book would have been far harder to achieve. From summer 2009 through spring 2010 I edited the transcripts into nine chapters, according to a plan approved by Tony. In October and December 2009 I flew to New York from Vienna, where I was spending the 2009–2010 academic year, so that we could discuss progress. From Vienna I sent Tony draft chapters by e-mail, which he then revised and returned.

Each of the chapters has a biographical and a historical component. Thus the book moves through Tony's life and across some of the most important loci of twentieth-century political thought: the Holocaust as a Jewish and a German question; Zionism and its European origins; English exceptionalism and French universalism; Marxism and its temptations; fascism and anti-fascism; the revival of liberalism as ethics in Eastern Europe; and social planning in Europe and the United States. In the historical sections of the chapters, Tony appears in plain text and I in italics. Although the biographical sections also arose from conversation, I have removed myself entirely from these. Thus each chapter begins with a bit of Tony's biography, in Tony's voice in plain text. At a certain point I appear with a question, in italics. Then the historical section proceeds.

The point of uniting biography and history is not, of course, that Tony's preoccupations and achievements can be drawn in any simple way from his life, like so many buckets of water from a well. We are all more like vast subterranean caverns, uncharted even by ourselves, than we are like holes dug straight into the ground. The urge to insist that the complex is just a disguise for the simple was one of the plagues of the twentieth century. In asking Tony about his life, I wasn't looking to quench a thirst for a simple explanation, but rather tapping on walls, seeking after passages between underground chambers whose existence, at the beginning, I only dimly sensed.

It is not the case, for example, that Tony wrote Jewish history because he is Jewish. He never really has written about Jewish history. Like many scholars of Jewish origin of his generation, he evaded the manifest centrality of the Holocaust to his own subjects, even as his personal knowledge of it motivated, at some level, the direction of his research. Likewise, it is not that Tony writes about the English because he himself is English. With a few exceptions, he has never written much about Great Britain. Englishness, or rather his particular English education, gave him a taste for literary form and a set of references that has seen him through (as I understand matters) the turmoil of his intellectual affections and of the politics of his generation—the generation of 1968. His strong association with France had less to do with origins than with a yearning (in my opinion) for a single key to universal or at least to European problems, for a revolutionary tradition that might yield truth when embraced or spurned. Tony is east European chiefly by his association with east Europeans. But it was these friendships that opened to him a continent. Tony is American by choice and by citizenship; his identification with the country seems to be with a great land in constant need of critique.

My hope is that this particular form, with biography introducing themes of intellectual history, will allow the reader to see a mind at work over the course of a life, or perhaps even a mind developing and improving. In some sense the intellectual history is all inside Tony: a reality that each week, speaking with him, I absorbed in a starkly physical way. Everything on these pages had to be in his mind (or in mine). How the history came to be inside the man, and how it came out again, are questions that a book of this kind can perhaps address.

T ony once told me that the way to repay him for his help to me over the years was to assist young people when the time came. (Tony is twenty-one years my senior.) At first, I saw this book as a way to ignore his advice (not for the first time) and repay him directly. But the conversation was so gratifying and fruitful that I find myself unable to consider the labor of producing this book a repayment of any kind. In any event, whom exactly would I be repaying? Either as a reader or as a colleague I have known Tony in all of the guises in which he figures here. Throughout our conversation, I was personally interested (although I never raised the issue explicitly) in how Tony became a better thinker, writer and historian over time. In general, his preferred answer to related questions was that, in all of his various identities and in all of his various historical methods, he was always an outsider.

Is he? Is to be a formerly committed Zionist to be an insider or outsider among Jews? Is to be a former Marxist to be an insider or outsider among intellectuals? Is to have been a scholarship student at King's College, Cambridge, to be an insider or an outsider in England? Does doctoral study at the École Normale Supérieure make of one an insider or an outsider on the European continent? Does friendship with Polish intellectuals and knowledge of Czech make one an insider or an outsider in Eastern Europe? Is directing an institute for the study of Europe in New York the mark of an insider or outsider to other Europeans? Is being the scourge of fellow historians in the *New York Review of Books* an indication of insider or outsider status among scholars? Does suffering from a terminal degenerative illness without access to public health care make of Tony an insider or an outsider among Americans? One can answer each question both ways.

The truth, I think, is more interesting. Wisdom seems to come from being both an insider and an outsider, from passing through the inside with eyes and ears wide open and returning to the outside to think and to write. As Tony's life makes clear, this exercise can be repeated any number of times. Tony did brilliant work while thinking of himself as an outsider. The outsider implicitly accepts the terms of a given dispute, and then tries very hard to be right: to dismount the old guard and penetrate the sanctuaries of the insider. What I found more interesting than the many times that Tony was right (on his own terms) was his increasing capacity for what the great French historian Marc Bloch called understanding. To understand an event requires the historian to release any one framework and to accept the validity of several frameworks simultaneously. This brings much less immediate satisfaction but greater enduring achievement. It is from Tony's acceptance of pluralism in this sense that his best work, above all *Postwar,* arose.

It is also here, around this question of pluralism, that Tony's own intellectual path met the intellectual history of the twentieth century. The temporal trajectory of the two parts of this book, the biographical and the historical, meet in 1989, the year of the revolutions in Eastern Europe, the final collapse of the Marxist framework, and the year Tony began to think about how to write what became his unmatched, and perhaps unmatchable, history of postwar Europe.

It is also at about this time when Tony and I first met. I read a long draft version of an article of his on the dilemmas of east European dissidents in spring 1990, in a course on east European history taught by Thomas W. Simons, Jr. at Brown University. Shortly thereafter, thanks to the initiative of Mary Gluck, Tony and I met in person. Thanks in large measure to Professors

Gluck and Simons, I had become fascinated with east European history, which I would study in earnest at Oxford. I was beginning then the two decades of reading and writing that would allow me to carry out this conversation. Tony was reaching in 1989 (as I see matters now) a crucial turning point. After one last polemic with another great polemicist (Jean-Paul Sartre, in *Past Imperfect*), and despite the occasional one-sided essay still to come, he was turning to a more gentle, and a more fruitful idea of truth.

The intellectuals who contributed to the east European revolutions of 1989, people such as Adam Michnik and Václav Havel, were concerned with living in truth. What does this mean? Much of this book, as a history of intellectuals and politics, is concerned with the difference between the big truths, the beliefs about great causes and final ends which seem to require mendacity and sacrifice from time to time, and the small truths, the facts as they can be discovered. The big truth might be the certainty of a coming revolution, as with some Marxists, or it might be the apparent national interest, as with the French government during the Dreyfus Affair or the Bush administration during the Iraq War. But even if we choose the small truths, as Zola did during the Dreyfus Affair and Tony did during the Iraq War, it remains unclear in just what truth might consist.

An intellectual challenge of the twenty-first century might be this: to endorse truth as such, while accepting its multiple forms and bases. The case that Tony makes for social democracy at the end of this book is an example of how this might look. Tony was born just after the catastrophe brought by National Socialism, and lived through the slow-motion discrediting of Marxism. His adulthood was the time of several attempts to regenerate liberalism, none of which finds universal acceptance. Amidst the wreckage of a continent and its ideas, social democracy survived as a concept and was realized as a project. Over the course of Tony's life social democracy was built, and then sometimes dismantled. His case for its reconstruction depends upon several different kinds of argument, appealing to several different intuitions about different kinds of truth. The strongest argument, to use a word that Isaiah Berlin favored, is that social democracy enables a decent life.

Some of these different sorts of truth dart across the pages of this book, often in pairs. The truth of the historian, for example, is not the same as the truth of the essayist. The historian can and must know more about a moment of the past than an essayist can possibly know about what is happening today. The essayist, far more than the historian, is obliged to take into account the prejudices of his own day, and thus to exaggerate for emphasis. The truth of authenticity is different from the truth of honesty. To be authentic is to live as one wishes others to live; to be honest is to admit that this is impossible. Similarly, the truth of charity is different than the truth of criticism. To call forth the best in ourselves and others requires both, but they cannot be practiced in the same moment. There is no way to reduce any of these pairs to some underlying truth, let alone all of them to some ultimate form of truth. Thus the search for truth involves many kinds of seeking. This is pluralism: not a synonym of relativism, but rather an antonym. Pluralism accepts the moral reality of different kinds of truth, but rejects the idea that they can all be placed on a single scale, measured by a single value.

There is one truth that seeks us rather than the other way around, one truth that has no complement: that each of us comes to an end. The other truths orbit around this one like stars around a black hole, brighter, newer, less weighty. This final truth helped me to give this book its final shape. This book could not have arisen without a certain effort at a certain time, little more than a companionable gesture on my side, but an enormous physical campaign on Tony's. But it is not a book about struggle. It is a book about the life of the mind, and about the mindful life.

Prague, 5 July 2010

A study of the history of opinion is a necessary preliminary
to the emancipation of the mind.
—John Maynard Keynes

1.

THE NAME REMAINS: JEWISH QUESTIONER

These are two ways to think about my childhood. From one perspective, it was an utterly conventional, somewhat lonely, very lower-middle-class London childhood of the 1950s. From another perspective, it was an exotic, distinctive, and therefore privileged, expression of mid-twentieth-century history as it happened to immigrant Jews from East Central Europe.

My full name is Tony Robert Judt. Robert is an English twist, chosen by my mother Stella, so let me begin with her. My mother's father, Solomon Dudakoff, grew up in St. Petersburg, the capital of the Russian Empire. I remember him (he died when I was eight) as a huge, bearded Russian military type, a bit like a wrestler crossed with a rabbi. In fact he was a tailor, though he probably learned the trade in the army. My mother's mother, Jeannette Greenberg, was a Romanian Jew from Moldavia, whose family was rumored to have had inappropriate liaisons with gypsies at some point. She certainly *looked* like a gypsy soothsayer off the back of a wagon: tiny, mischievous, slightly frightening. Because there were many families of that name from the same region of Romania, some of whom must have come from the same town and been related, my sons have long traded on the plausible but unlikely claim that we are related to the great Jewish slugger Hank Greenberg.

My mother's parents met in London, where Jeannette Greenberg and her family had come after the 1903 pogrom in Chisinau. Like thousands of Jews, they fled what was for its time an event of unparalleled violence: the murder of forty-seven Jews in the nearby Bessarabian province of the Russian Empire. They made it to London no later than 1905. My mother's father Solomon Dudakoff had fled Russia for England, but for different reasons. According to family legend, in defending his father from hooligans he accidentally beat one of them to death. He then hid in the oven of a baker uncle for the night before fleeing the country. This account is probably somewhat romanticized, since the timing suggests that Solomon left Russia at much the same time and probably for the same reasons as hundreds of thousands of other Jews. In any case, he made directly for England. So my mother's parents were in England by 1905, and were married that year. My mother, Stella Sophie Dudakoff, was born just south of the Jewish East End of London in 1921, the youngest of eight children. She always felt a little out of place in her cockney, working-class neighborhood near the London docks; but then it was my impression that she was never quite at home in her own family or community either.

Like my mother, my father came from a Jewish family with roots in Eastern Europe. In his case, though, the family made two stopovers between the Russian Empire and Britain: Belgium and Ireland. My paternal grandmother, Ida Avigail, came from Pilviskiai, a Lithuanian village just southwest of Kaunas: now in Lithuania, then in the Russian Empire. Following the early death of her father, a carter, she worked in the family bakery. Sometime in the first decade of the century, the Avigails decided to make their way west to the diamond industry in Antwerp, where they had contacts. There in Belgium Ida met my paternal grandfather. Other Avigails settled in Brussels; one started a dry-goods store in Texas.

My father's father, Enoch Yudt, was from Warsaw. Like my maternal grandfather, Enoch too served in the Russian Army. He seems to have deserted around the time of the Russo-Japanese War of 1904–1905, making his way west in stages, reaching Belgium before World War I. He and my grandmother, together with their extended families, then made their way to London in anticipation of the German armies' advance on Belgium in August 1914. They both spent the First World War in London, where they married and had two children. In 1919 they returned to Antwerp, where my father, Joseph Isaac Judt, was born in 1920.

My first given name, Tony, comes from the Avigail side of the family. Growing up in Antwerp, my father was close to his cousins, his maternal uncle's three daughters: Lily, Bella and Toni—presumably short for Antonia. My father saw a lot of these girls, who lived in Brussels. The youngest, Toni, was five years my father's junior, and he was very fond of her, though they lost regular contact once my father left Belgium in 1932. A decade later, Toni and Bella were transported to Auschwitz and killed. Lily survived, interned by Germans as a London-born Jew: in contrast to her Belgian sisters—one of the minor mysteries of Nazi categorization.

I was born in 1948, about five years after Toni's death. It was my father who insisted that I be named after his cousin; but this was postwar England and my mother wanted me to have a good English name so that I could "blend." Accordingly, I was provided with Robert as a backup and insurance, though I have only ever been known as Tony. Almost everyone I meet assumes that my first name must be Anthony, but few inquire.

My father's father Enoch Yudt was a Jewish economic marginal in a state of permanent migration. He had no particular skill except selling, and not much of that. In the 1920s he apparently got by on the black market between Belgium, Holland and Germany. But things must have got a bit warm for him around 1930, probably because of debt and perhaps on account of the impending economic collapse; he was obliged to move on. But whither? Enoch had been assured that Eamon de Valera's newly self-governing Ireland was a welcoming place for Jews and in some measure he had been well-informed. De Valera was very keen to attract commerce to the new Ireland; being a conventionally anti-Semitic Irish Catholic, he naturally assumed that Jews were good at buying and selling and would be an asset to the economy. Accordingly, Jewish immigrants were welcome in Ireland with almost no restrictions, as long as they were willing to work or could find employment.

Enoch Yudt turned up in Dublin, initially leaving his family behind in Antwerp. He set himself up in business, making ties, ladies' underwear, stockings: *schmutters*. In time, he managed to bring over his family, the last two of whom, my father and his older brother Willy, arrived in Dublin in 1932. My father was one of five children. The eldest was a girl, Fanny; then came four boys—Willy (for Wolff), my father Joseph Isaac, Max and then Thomas Chaim (known as Chaim in Antwerp, Hymie in Dublin and then Tommy in England). My father was Isaac Joseph in Belgium and Ireland, and then Joseph Isaac, in England, or finally just Joe.

He recalls Ireland as idyllic. The family were tenants in a big house just south of Dublin, and my father had never seen so much space or greenery. Coming from a Jewish tenement in Antwerp, he and his family had landed in what must have seemed the lap of luxury, an upstairs apartment in a small manor house, overlooking a field. His memories of Ireland are thus entirely colored by this sense of ease and space, and almost completely unclouded by recollections of prejudice or hardship. My father came to Ireland with no English, of course, but with three other languages from his first twelve years of life in Belgium: Yiddish from home; French from school; and Flemish from the street. Slowly he lost the Flemish, which had gone completely by the time I appeared; he no longer speaks active Yiddish, though the language remains there as a passive presence. Curiously, he retained a lot of French, which prompts the thought that the language you are forced to study is the one that you retain longest when you lack any motive to use the native tongues.

In 1936, after the family business had failed in Dublin, my grandfather's brother, who had settled in London, invited him to England. And thus my Yudt grandfather transposed his economic incompetence back across the Irish Sea. My father joined him, leaving school at fourteen to work odd jobs. Thus while both of my parents spent their late teens in London, my mother was and remained far more English in her soul than my father, having been born there. Both of them left school upon turning fourteen, but unlike my father Stella had a defined skill and trade. Despite her misgivings, she was apprenticed to a ladies' hairdresser, then a respectable and reliable trade for ambitious girls.

It was World War II that brought Stella Dudakoff and Joe Judt together. Upon the outbreak of war, my father sought to join the army but was told that he was not acceptable: his lungs were scarred with tuberculosis, a sufficient justification for exemption. In any case, he was not a British subject. In fact, my father was stateless. Though born in Belgium, he was only a Belgian resident, but never a citizen: Belgian citizenship laws in those days required that your parents be citizens of the country before you could claim citizenship, and Joe's parents were, of course, immigrants from the Russian Empire. Thus my father had come to London on a "Nansen passport," the travel document for stateless people in those days. In the autumn of 1940, the Luftwaffe began to bomb London in the course of what became known as the Battle of Britain. The bombing—the *blitz*—brought my parents to Oxford, where they were to meet. My father's older sister, enamored of a Czech refugee (probably Jewish though I'm not sure) had followed the young man to Oxford. After their house in North London was bombed, most of the rest of the family, including my father, followed her there, where my father lived for two years on the Abingdon Road, working for a coal yard and for the Co-op, making deliveries—in a van he was permitted to drive despite having no license; the requirement was suspended during the war. My mother also spent the war years in Oxford. The area of East London where she grew up was now under permanent attack, thanks to its proximity to the docks, and her home and the hairdressing salon where she worked disappeared in the bombing. Her parents moved to Canvey Island on the east coast, but she went to Oxford, a town she grew to love and always describes in a warm glow of nostalgic recall. My parents were married there in 1943 and would return to London shortly thereafter.

After the war, my mother established herself again in London as a hairdresser; between them my parents set up a small hairdressing establishment which supported the family in a limited but sufficient manner. The first years after the war were hard, as my parents remember them. My father even thought of emigrating to New Zealand in 1947, but had to abandon the plan since he still had no British passport and his stateless condition precluded easy acceptance in the British Dominions (he finally got a passport in 1948).

I was born in 1948 in a Salvation Army hospital in Bethnal Green, East London. The first thing I remember is walking along what must have been Tottenham High Road. In my memory we go into a tiny hairdressing establishment, with a staircase leading to the flat we lived in over the shop. I once described the scene to my mother, and she said, yes, that's exactly how it was. I was then somewhere between eighteen months and two years old. I have other memories of North London life, including looking at trucks and buses out of my parents' bedroom window. I also have very early memories of seeing, meeting, being introduced to young men who were camp survivors taken in by my grandfather Enoch Yudt. By then I must have been about four or five.

I cannot recall a time when I did not know about what was not yet called the Holocaust. But it was confused in my mind by its misleading representation in England, as exemplified by my very English mother. She used to stand up when the Queen gave her Christmas greeting, on radio and then television—my father, by contrast, would stay firmly sitting down, both on political grounds and because he did not feel particularly English: all of his tastes were continental, from cars to coffee. In any event, my mother, when she thought of the Nazis, always referred to Belsen—images of which she had first seen on British Movietone News at the time of the camp's liberation by British forces.

She was thus typically English in those days in her unfamiliarity with Auschwitz, Treblinka, Chełmno, Sobibór and Bełżec, camps where Jews were killed in very large numbers, in contrast to Bergen-Belsen which was not primarily a Jewish camp. And so the image that I had of the Holocaust combined my familiarity with young survivors from the eastern camps with visual images of skeletons at Belsen. As a small child, I knew little more than that. I learned who Toni was, and why I bore her name, only much later, although I myself cannot remember the precise moment. My father insists that he told me when I was young, but I don't believe he did. He spoke often of Lily (who lived in London and whom we occasionally saw) but rarely if ever of her sisters Bella and Toni. It was as if the Holocaust penetrated everything—like a fog, ubiquitous but inchoate.

The stereotypes of course remained, not only about gentiles but about Jews. There was a clear pecking order among us *Ostjuden*, Jews from Eastern Europe (who were all of course despised by the cultivated German-speaking Jews of central Europe). Broadly speaking, Lithuanian and Russian Jews saw themselves as superior, in culture and social standing; Polish (particularly Galician) and Romanian Jews were lowly creatures, to put it politely. This ranking applied both within my parents' marital antagonism and across their extended families. My mother in moments of anger would remind my father that he was nothing but a Polish Jew. He would then point out that she was Romanian.

Neither of my parents was interested in raising a Jew, even though there was never any genuine question of complete assimilation; after all, I had a foreign father, even though his spoken English was more or less perfect and he had no accent that you could place. I always knew we were different. On the one hand, we were not like other Jews because we had non-Jewish friends and lived a decidedly anglicized life. Yet we could never be like our non-Jewish friends, simply because we just were Jewish.

My mother in particular seemed to me to have no friends at all, except for a German Jewish lady, Esther Sternheim, whose sadness I sensed even as a child. Her parents had been shot by the Germans. Her older brother was killed in action as a British soldier. Her sister escaped to Palestine, but later committed suicide. Esther herself had escaped Germany by train with her younger brother. The two of them survived, but he was mentally disturbed in some way. In postwar England such immigrant family tragedies were commonplace and somehow familiar; yet they were typically treated and referred to in isolation from the larger catastrophe which had produced them. But to grow up knowing such people was to imbibe unawares a certain sort of experience.

Even as a boy I always felt that we were so different that there was little point in trying to understand how and why. This was true even in a self-consciously un-Jewish family like ours. I was bar-mitzvahed because it would have been inconceivable—and very hard—to deal with the grandparents had I not been. But other than that, there was nothing Jewish about our household. In 1952 my parents escaped the stifling, *ersatz mitteleuropeisch* ghetto of North London Jewry and moved south, across the river to Putney. In retrospect I can see that this was an assertive act of ethno-self-rejection: there were almost no Jews in Putney—and such Jews as there were would probably have shared my parents' perspective, actively disposed to put their Jewishness behind them.

So I was not brought up Jewish—except of course that I was. Every Friday evening we would get into the car and drive across London to my grandfather Enoch Yudt's house. Enoch had chosen, characteristically, to live at the very edge of Stamford Hill, in inner North London. Stamford Hill was where the religious Jews lived—"cowboys" as my father called them for their black hats and kaftans. Thus my grandfather kept his distance from the orthodox world of his childhood, while cleaving close enough to be observant when he felt the need. Since we arrived by car on the Sabbath eve, we had to park around the corner in order not to offend my grandparents (who knew perfectly well that we had driven but who did not wish to share this information with their neighbors).

Even the very car in which we drove suggests a certain non-Jewish Jewishness on my father's part. He was a big fan of the Citroën car company, though I don't believe he ever once mentioned to me that it had been established by a Jewish family. My father would never have driven a Renault, probably because Louis Renault was a notorious wartime collaborator whose firm had been nationalized at the Liberation as punishment for his Vichyite sympathies. Peugeots, on the other hand, got a favorable pass in family discussions. After all, they were of Protestant extraction and thus somehow not implicated in the Catholic anti-Semitism of Vichy-era France. No one ever said a word about the background to all this, and yet it was all somehow quite plain to me.

Well into the mid-1950s, the other guests at my grandfather's Friday-evening meals were often the Auschwitz survivors my grandfather referred to as "the boys." He had first met some of them, overhearing them speak Polish or Yiddish, in a London West End cinema in 1946. These boys, young men by now, joined the Primrose Jewish Youth Club, where my father and his brothers were active. At one point, my father, two of his brothers, and two of the "boys" were among the eleven starters on the football team. In the team photos you can see the tattoos on the arms of the young men.

My Lithuanian-Jewish grandmother would mount the complete Jewish Friday meal, with marvelously soft, sweet, salty, highly-flavored food in seemingly endless quantities (a striking contrast to the rather etiolated Anglo-Jewish cuisine of my culinarily-challenged mother). And thus I would fall into a warm bath of *yiddishkayt*—because of course Yiddish was spoken on those Friday evenings, at least among the older generation. This was an utterly Jewish milieu—and therefore also a very east European one. Forty years later I was to experience a similar sense of homecoming when I started to visit and make friends in east-central Europe: there I found people drinking tea from glasses, dunking little bits of cake into them, while energetically talking across one another through cigarette smoke and brandy fumes. My private *madeleine*? Apple cake dripping sweet lemon tea.

My family experienced its own brief simulacrum of postwar prosperity, from about 1957 to 1964. Ladies' hairdressing was a profitable trade then; it was the age of big hair. My parents had acquired a larger women's hairdressing salon and were making decent money. They could even afford, in those years, to have a series of au pair girls, hired to care for me and my sister

Deborah (born in 1956). Most au pairs in Britain in those days came from Switzerland, France or Scandinavia. But by a curious accident we had one au pair girl from Germany, though her stay with us was brief: my father fired her after finding in her room a prominent photo of her father in Wehrmacht uniform. The last au pair girl to grace our home was just sixteen years old, and I remember her primarily for the very attractive anatomy she used to reveal while performing handstands in front of me. She too did not last long.

Thus my family could now afford some comforts, including foreign travel. My father was always seeking ways to return to the continent—from the early postwar years he would travel back and forth on brief vacation sorties. My mother, characteristically English in this as in so many other respects, would doubtless have been content to go to Brighton. In any event, in the summer of 1960 we found ourselves in Germany thanks to an invitation from a former Danish au pair. Agnes Fynbo, from the little town of Skjern, had invited us to spend a couple of weeks with her family in Jutland. Quite why we did not take the boat directly from Harwich to Esbjerg I don't know. But my father is a person of habit, and we had always gone to Europe via the Dover-Calais ferry: so we took that route, driving into Belgium and thence Holland, where I remember we visited some relatives of my father who lived in Amsterdam.

It is remarkable that these Amsterdam relatives had survived the war. My grandfather Enoch Yudt had an older sister called Brukha, who had married in Poland and had two children there. She left her first husband in Poland and came to Belgium, where she married husband number two, Sasha Marber (a relative of the playwright Patrick Marber). Brukha had brought her two children with her; her second husband already had two children of his own, and then they had two more children together. This sort of thing was much more common in the old Jewish world than we sometimes suppose. Brukha was murdered at Auschwitz, together with much of her family.

But Paulina, one of Brukha's daughters from her first marriage, survived. In 1928 Paulina had married a Belgian Jew; my father, her first cousin, remembers the wedding well: he traveled to Brussels in order to take part in the celebrations. Paulina's husband could find no work at home and took his young family to Indonesia where he secured employment as a manager on a Dutch rubber plantation. Thus Paulina found herself in Indonesia, then a Dutch colony. The couple had three children, all girls: Sima, Vellah and Ariette. During the war Paulina and her daughters were interned in a camp in Indonesia by the Japanese: not as Jews of course, but as enemy subjects. According to family legend, which seems to be true, her husband was beheaded by the occupying Japanese after attempting to defend the rights of his indigenous employees. But Paulina and the girls survived the war, returning to Holland in 1945. When the Netherlands recognized Indonesian independence in 1949, the four women were offered the choice of Indonesian or Dutch citizenship, and thus became Dutch. And so we found them in Amsterdam.

From the Netherlands, you have to cross Germany in order to reach Denmark. My father had bought as much gas as he could in Holland, so as not to have to stop in Germany, and indeed we made it two-thirds of the way across. But everyone was tired in those pre-freeway days, and we were obliged to pass the night in Germany. Had he so wished, my father could doubtless have made his way in German via Yiddish, but he simply could not bring himself to communicate with Germans. Nevertheless, there we were in a hotel in Germany and communication was unavoidable. I was twelve, and was duly primed to do all the talking. I already had passable French—thanks to school classes together with visits to French-speaking family members—but I had not yet started German. So I had basically to invent my German, with my father pre-instructing me in Yiddish equivalents. And thus I, a little boy named after a child gassed at Auschwitz just seventeen years earlier, went downstairs to the reception in this provincial German hotel and announced: *Mein Vater will eine Dusche*—my father wants a shower.

The world of my youth was thus the world that was bequeathed us by Hitler. To be sure, twentieth-century intellectual history (and the history of twentieth-century intellectuals) has a shape of its own: the shape that intellectuals of right or left would assign to it if they were recounting it in conventional narrative form or as part of an ideological world picture. But it should be clear by now that there is another story, another narrative that insistently intervenes and intrudes upon any account of twentieth-century thought and thinkers: the catastrophe of the European Jews. A striking number of the *dramatis personae* of an intellectual history of our times are also present in *that* story, especially from the 1930s forwards.

In some sense it is my story, too. I grew up and read and became a historian and, I like to think, an intellectual. The Jewish question was never at the center of my own intellectual life, or indeed my historical work. But it intrudes, inevitably, and with ever greater force. One of the aims of this book is to allow such themes to encounter each other, to permit the intellectual history of the twentieth century to meet the history of the Jews. This is a personal as well as a scholarly effort: after all, many of us who have, in our work, kept these themes distinct are ourselves Jews.

> *One starting point from which to grasp the complexities of Jewish and intellectual history in our time is Vienna, a place that you and I have in common. One image of the city we have inherited from Stefan Zweig: a tolerant, cosmopolitan, energetic central Europe, a republic of letters with an imperial capital. But the tragedy of the Jews impinges upon that story. Zweig's memoir,* The World of Yesterday, *is backward-looking description of the twentieth century, uniting the horrors of the Second World War with nostalgia for the world before the First.*

For Zweig and his Jewish contemporaries, that world of Habsburgia before the First World War was limited to the urban oases of the empire: Vienna, Budapest, Cracow, Czernowitz. Intellectuals of his generation were as unfamiliar with rural Hungary, Croatia or Galicia (if they were Jews) as those other worlds were unacquainted with them. Further west, the Habsburg monarchy extended to Salzburg, Innsbruck, Lower and Upper Austria and the mountains of the South Tyrol, where the Jews of Vienna, or Viennese cultural life in general, was either a mystery or an object of hate, or both.

So one must be careful when reading Zweig and others as a guide to the lost world of central Europe. In 1985, I visited an exhibition in the Historical Museum of the City of Vienna, "*Traum und Wirklichkeit: Wien 1880–1930.*" In one room the curators had pasted enlarged pages from a Viennese right-wing paper. The article, in German of course, was about the horrors of cosmopolitanism: the Jews and the Hungarians and Czechs and Slovaks and others who were polluting Vienna and creating crime. The curators had highlighted this text in different colors according to the words and their roots, to show how very little of it was in literary German: much of this characteristically nativist rant was, unbeknown to its author, written in words of Yiddish, Hungarian or Slavic origin.

The Habsburg monarchy, the old Austrian empire thus had a double identity. More than anywhere else in Europe at that time, it was here that one was most likely to encounter overt prejudice on the Freudian principle of the narcissism of small differences. At the same time, people and languages and cultures were utterly intertwined and indissolubly blended in the identity of this place. Habsburgia was where a Stefan Zweig or a Joseph Roth could feel most completely at home—and it was from there that they were the first to be expelled.

> *Let's press this irony a little further. It was precisely the Roths and the Zweigs and other assimilated central European Jews writing in German—what else?—who were to play such a prominent role in creating the high literary German which marks the literature of the age. I wonder whether this is sufficiently emphasized in Carl Schorske's classic account,* Fin-de-Siècle Vienna. *Schorske seems to underplay the distinctively Jewish qualities and origins of the*

> *Austrian protagonists in his story, adoringly grounded in a*
> *German culture which was to reject and abandon them within a*
> *generation.*

Yes. The East European Jews of my own background had no such grounding in a local high culture to which they had assimilated and whose value they acknowledged: they could hardly identify with the language and culture of the hostile Poles, Ukrainians and Romanians who surrounded them and with whom there was for the most part a relationship based exclusively upon antagonism, ignorance and mutual fear. As for their own Jewish heritage of religion and *yiddishkayt*, by the twentieth century a growing number of younger *Ostjuden* were disposed to reject that too. Thus the very idea of a unified history of European Jews is itself problematic, to say the least: we were divided and splintered by region, class, language, culture and opportunity (or its absence). Even in Vienna itself, as the Jews of the provincial empire poured into the capital so the culture of the German-speaking Jews faced dilution and division. But well into the 1920s, Jews who had been born in Vienna or Budapest, even if their families were of eastern rural extraction, were brought up to think of themselves as "German." And therefore they had Germanness to lose.

On her mother's side, my first wife's family were prosperous Jewish professionals from Breslau: representative types from a long-established Jewish German bourgeoisie. Although they had escaped Nazi Germany and settled comfortably in England, they remained profoundly German in everything they did: from the décor of the household, to the food they ate, to the conversation, to the cultural references with which they identified one another and newcomers. Whenever one of the aunts wished to put me in my place, she would politely inquire as to whether I had read such and such German classic. Their sense of loss was palpable and omnipresent: the German world that had abandoned them was the only one they knew and the only one worth having—its absence was a source of far greater pain than anything that the Nazis had perpetrated.

My father, from a very different, *Eastern* European Jewish background, was unfailingly astonished to learn that his in-laws returned year-in, year-out to Germany for their vacations. He would just turn to my mother in utter bewilderment and ask, silently, but how could they? To tell the truth, my first mother-in-law remained rather fond of Germany—both the Silesia of her childhood and the prosperous, comfortable new Bonn Republic with which she was increasingly familiar. Both she and her sister remained convinced that it was Hitler who was the aberration. *Deutschtum* for them remained a living reality.

German civilization was one Jewish ideal of universal values; international revolution—its polar opposite—was another. In some ways, the tragedy of our century lies in the discrediting of both these universals by the 1930s, with the implications and horrors of that unraveling rippling outwards for decades to come. Yet the place of anti-Semitism in this story is not always as straightforward as people fondly suppose. When Karl Lueger was first elected mayor of Vienna in 1897 on an overtly anti-Semitic platform, the culturally confident Jews of Vienna by no means conceded to him an authority to define national or cultural identity. They were at least as secure in their own identity and would probably, if asked, have preferred that he choose (as he claimed to do) who was and was not Jewish rather than who could and could not be German. Lueger for them, like Hitler for a later generation, was a passing aberration.

In the Habsburg monarchy, anti-Semitism was a new form of politics that Jews and liberals found distasteful but which they thought they could accommodate. It was in these years, at the turn of the nineteenth and twentieth centuries, that Austrian socialists spoke of anti-Semitism as the "socialism of fools," of workers who could not yet recognize their own class interest, and so instead blamed Jews—as factory-owners or department store magnates— rather than capitalism for their exploitation. After all, if the problem is just foolishness, then it can be addressed

by education: when workers are properly self-aware and informed,
they will not blame Jews. Imperial liberalism *in the central urban*
zone of Europe had allowed Jews to migrate to great cities and rise
upward in status: why should Jews (or socialists) abandon it, or lose
faith in its promise?

Take the case of Nicholas Kaldor, the prominent Hungarian economist. He had grown up in interwar Hungary and thought of himself first and above all as an educated member of the upper middle class of his native Budapest: his world was that of cultivated, German-speaking, German-educated Hungarian Jews. By the time I first met him, in the early 1970s, he was being visited by a younger generation of Hungarian economists and intellectuals whom he regarded with, at best, a sympathetic distance: newly promoted provincials, shorn of the culture and language of their parents and reduced to life in one small communist outpost. Whereas in my own English Jewish childhood, Jews were always and obviously parvenus or pariahs, to apply Arendt's categories. Nicki Kaldor had clearly never acquired either identity in the course of his Budapest youth.

Budapest was an even more distinctive instance of elective
assimilation than Vienna. The Hungarians, having attained
something very much like state sovereignty within the Habsburg
monarchy in 1867, set about building their capital as a kind of
model modern city, importing architectural and planning
templates from elsewhere to raise a remarkable urban world of
squares, cafés, schools, stations and boulevards. In this new city
they managed to achieve, to a striking degree and without any very
deliberate intention, the integration of many urban Jews into
Hungarian society.

Such integration, even if inevitably imperfect, would not have been available even to the best assimilated Polish or Romanian Jew. In the space assigned to the Pale of Settlement of the Russian Empire, and those regions just to its west, Jews were constrained to work against the prevailing assumption: that whatever the admirable or assimilable qualities of any given individual, the community itself was by definition and long-standing practice alien to the national space. Even in Vienna, Jews were restricted in practice to membership of the German *cultural* space which had been opened up by the empire, especially after the constitutional reforms of 1867; after 1918, once German Austria was redefined as a nation, the place of Jews within it became far more problematic.

To put the matter schematically: the linguistic divisions and institutional insecurity of Europe's eastern half made the region peculiarly inhospitable for multiple outsiders like Jews. Since Ukrainians, Slovaks, Belarusians and others faced their own challenges in defining and securing a national space distinct from that of their neighbors, the presence of Jews could only complicate and antagonize, offering a target for expressions of national insecurity. Even in the Habsburg monarchy, what Jews had really been part of was an urban civilization contained within a rural empire; once the latter was broken up after World War I and redefined by national spaces in which towns and cities were isolated islands in a sea of agrarian life, Jews lost their place.

Early on, I think, I came to appreciate in the context of my own family something that I would only later discover in the course of reading Joseph Roth: my parents and grandparents, for all that they originated there, knew nothing of Poland and Lithuania, Galicia or Romania. What they knew was *empire*: in the end, all that mattered for most Jews were decisions taken at the center, and protections afforded them from above. Jews might live at the periphery, but they were bound by ties of interest and identification to the imperial center. People like my paternal grandmother, growing up in her *shtetl* in Pilviskiai in southwestern Lithuania, knew nothing of the world around them. Like her, they knew the *shtetl*, they knew the imperial regional capital Vilna, a largely Jewish city—and then the world (to the extent that this meant anything to them). Everything else—the region, the surrounding population, local Christian practices and the like—were little more than an *in addition*

empty space in which their lives were fated to be played out. It is frequently
observed today—and true, withal—that their Christian neighbors (Ukrainians, Belarusians, Poles, Slovaks etc.) were miserably ill informed about the
Jewish communities in their midst. They cared little for them and harbored
ancient prejudices in their regard. But the same was largely true of Jews in
their feelings towards "the *goyim*." The relationship, to be sure, was profoundly unequal. But in this respect at least there was a certain symmetry.

Indeed, it was precisely that interdependence of mutual ignorance which
would account for the ease of ethnic cleansing and worse in central and Eastern Europe over the course of the twentieth century. This emerges very clearly
when one reads survivor testimonies from, e.g., Ukraine or Belarus: when
Jews recall what it was that gave them away as Jews—beyond incontrovertible
physical markers such as circumcision—they typically list the things that they
(we) could simply not do, because they lived in a hermetically separated social
space. Jews did not know the Lord's Prayer; it was a rare Jew in this part of the
world who could saddle a horse or plough a field. Jews who did survive were
characteristically from that minority within the community who for some
chance reason knew about such things.

This speaks to something that we can read, for example, in Franz
Kafka's tormented trajectory back and forth across the boundary markers of
ethnic exclusivism: the "horrors" of Jewish narrowness and the "glories" of
Jewish culture. To be a Jew was at one and the same time to belong to a constrained, circumscribed, ill-educated and often poor little world—and yet,
by the standards of the surrounding population, this claustrophobic Jewish
world was at the same time unusually well educated and literate, and although
its culture was inward-looking it was a culture for all that; moreover, it was
attached to a universal civilization extensive in time and space. Out of this
paradox were born both the much-remarked-upon Jewish sense of over-
weening pride—we are the chosen people—and the profound sentiment of
vulnerability that marked a perennially insecure micro-society. Understandably enough, many young Jews in the late nineteenth and early twentieth
centuries strove hard to turn their back on both dimensions of this culture.

In Vienna or Budapest or even Prague (not to mention
cosmopolitan cities further west), professional integration,
upward economic and social mobility and linguistic assimilation
were all open to ambitious young Jews. But there was a glass
ceiling; politics. It was one thing for Jews to make their way
to the center of the Christian world: to know its streets, to share
its topography, to understand its high culture and make it
their own. In the days of empire, this sufficed. "Politics," the
business of government and rule, was beyond the reach of most
Jews; it was less an activity than a shield against society.
But in post-imperial spaces in nation-states, politics worked
quite differently, making the state a threat rather than
a patron.

Yes. Odd as it may sound today, democracy was a catastrophe for Jews, who thrived in liberal autocracies: notably in the window that opened up between the eighteenth-century Austrian Empire under Joseph II and its curious apotheosis in the long reign of Emperor Franz Joseph II, from 1848 to 1916, an era of ongoing political constraint but cultural and economic liberation. Mass society posed new and dangerous challenges: not only were Jews now a serviceable political target, but they were losing the increasingly ineffectual protection of the royal or imperial figurehead. In order to survive this turbulent transition, European Jews had either to disappear altogether or else change the rules of the political game.

Hence the emerging Jewish proclivity, in the early decades of the twentieth century, for non-democratic forms of radical change with an accompanying insistence upon the irrelevance of religion, language or ethnicity and a primacy attached to social and economic categories in their place; hence too the much-remarked presence of Jews in the first generation of left-wing authoritarian regimes that emerged from the revolutionary upheavals of the age. Looking forward from 1918, or back from the present day, this seems to me perfectly comprehensible: short of an active commitment to Zionism or else departure for other continents, the only hope for the Jews of Europe was either perpetuation of the imperial status quo or else radical, transformative opposition to the nation-states that succeeded it.

The obvious exception, in the interwar decades at least, was the truly democratic and relatively tolerant Czechoslovakia of Tomáš Masaryk. Here, at least by comparison with neighboring Romania, Hungary or Poland, was a multinational state in which all minorities were at least tolerated: to be sure, there was no "Czechoslovak" majority community—even the Czechs themselves constituted only a relative majority, such that Germans, Slovaks, Hungarians, Ruthenes and Jews could all find their place, although the Germans especially were susceptible to <u>irredentist</u> sentiments imported from their neighbors.

> *It is striking that you read Kafka as migrating uncomfortably*
> *back- and forward across his various identities—Jewish,*
> *Czech, German. It seems just as reasonable to interpret his*
> *subject as the sheer terror that one faces when the state, hitherto*
> *a distant protector, advances into dangerous proximity and*
> *becomes the source of oppression, forever observing, assessing,*
> *judging.*

Indeed so, and it is altogether understandable that his readers would absorb that lesson above all from Kafka's best-known writings. But it has often struck me that the issue of authority in Kafka is richly inlaid with a mix of the personal and the political: while there is much to be said for reading him in the shadow of his tormented communications with his father, it does not hurt to locate him in the broader context of Czech, Jewish and central European history. Authority and power, in that time and place, were at once oppressive and ambivalent. The ambiguity in, for example, *The Trial* and *The Castle*, regarding the protagonist's feelings towards the "authorities" echoes and illustrates an ambiguity we can find in Jewish history and indeed in the response of many in the region towards serial dictatorship and occupation.

> *When thinking about the 1890s and the 1900s, a lot perhaps*
> *hangs on whether one understands the father is a symbol of*
> *authority, or authority as a symbol of the father . . .*

> *I'd like to develop a little the categories we've been discussing. The*
> *other pattern to which you've alluded is Poland, where assimilation*
> *proceeds but not nearly so far as in Hungary, and so where many*
> *though not most Jews do come to feel that they're part of the nation.*
> *And thus you have the phenomenon of the quite remarkable Jews of*
> *Łódź or Warsaw who, beginning in the last years of the old Russian*
> *Empire, elected quite consciously to assimilate into Polish civilization*
> *and culture, regarding themselves unproblematically as both Poles*
> *and Jews. That said, the Polish language and culture suffered from*
> *a fatal characteristic (and fatal not just for Jews): it was and is*
> *substantial and attractive enough to provincialize those who partook*
> *of it, drawing them away from cosmopolitan allegiances; but it*
> *was not large or self-confident enough to absorb and shield minorities.*

I've never detected in German, or Hungarian, or Austrian Jews, the same complex mix of familiarity, attraction and *ressentiment* that you get among educated Jews of Polish background.

I once saw the distinguished medieval historian and Solidarity activist and foreign minister Bronisław Geremek interviewed on French TV. The well-intentioned interviewer kept asking: what have you read that gives you great personal pleasure and succor in hard times? Geremek would then stream off a series of unpronounceable (Polish) names that the guy had clearly never heard of; the audience, similarly mystified, reacts with polite silence. You could see that the French interviewer, primed for a central European intellectual—Jürgen Habermas as it might be, or Gershom Scholem, has nothing to say. Poland is big enough for educated Jews within it to be highly sophisticated and yet, to the otherwise well-informed outsider, to appear utterly obscurantist when speaking of their own culture. I don't believe this is true of any other European Jewish community.

> *It always seems to me that Jewish Poles, Polish Jews, Jews who are Poles, have a problem of scale which is like the one that Poles have in general—that it's a mid-sized country, and therefore proudly awkward in its existence and at the same time uncomfortably non-existent to others.*

Poles and Jews have a lot more in common than that. There is this Polish-Jewish propensity—Polish and Jewish propensity—to feel that unless you overstate your centrality, you are always at risk of marginalization. In Norman Davies's *Europe*, the introductory map of Europe has been adjusted such that Warsaw is at the epicenter. And, indeed, in Davies's account of Europe, Poland itself manages to be at the heart of its own history and everything else. This seems to me patently silly: Warsaw is not, and for most of European history never was, the center of very much at all.

But Jews do this too: placing their own history, for example, at the center of the twentieth century and its meaning. It can be very difficult, particularly when teaching here in the United States, to convey how far the Holocaust was from the center of people's concerns or decisions during World War II. I don't mean by this that it did not matter, much less that it does not matter today. But we cannot, if we wish to give a fair account of the recent past, read back into it our own ethical or communitarian priorities. The harsh reality is that Jews, Jewish suffering and Jewish extermination were not matters of overwhelming concern to most Europeans (Jews and Nazis aside) of that time. The centrality that we now assign to the Holocaust, both as Jews and as humanitarians, is something that only emerged decades later.

*But in a certain important sense Poland is in the center of
everything. European history, so far as Jewish life is concerned,
passed through three stages. Its medieval center was clearly in
Western and Central Europe. Then came the great Plague and the
expulsions, after which Jews and Jewish life moved eastward to the
Polish-Lithuanian Commonwealth and the Ottoman Empire.
Finally we have the modern period—beginning, let us say, in the
late eighteenth century with the revolution in France and the
Polish partitions—as a consequence of which a very significant
part of European Jewry, living in Galicia, falls under the
Habsburg monarchy for the first time. Their children and
grandchildren move to Moravia and finally Vienna, where they
create European modernism. These are the people we have been
talking about, indeed the people who invented many of the concepts
we are using, so in any conversation about Jewish integration,
assimilation and participation in modernity, we have to begin
with Poland.*

If you stop the clock in 1939, I would have nothing to object to in what
you say. Both the narrative and its significance would have to be keyed to a
process which culminated in the urbanization and liberation of the Jews of
Polish-speaking Europe and the consequences of that narrative for Europe at
large. But what happens then? Poland is brutally extruded from the picture:
first by World War II, then by the communist takeover, then—in coming
decades—by a growing appreciation for what happened to the Jews; this
restoration of memory and increased sensitivity to the recollection of Jewish
suffering not only reduces Poland's place in the Jewish narrative, but crucially recasts it in a negative light. Poland, once a Jewish homeland, becomes
the bystander and occasional participant in the destruction of the Jews.

This bleak image is then, as it seems to me, cast backward across the
history of Jews in Poland: beginning in the 1930s and working its way back
through into earlier centuries. The Poland that emerges—certainly this was

the Poland I grew up with in our family—was a bad place to be Jewish. The history of the Jews becomes instead a forward-looking narrative of geographical emancipation: escaping the wrong places and finding our way to better ones. The latter in this modern narrative might be Western Europe, Canada, the U.S. or, more problematically, Israel. But it is never Eastern Europe. Conversely, the wrong places are almost always located in a real or (more commonly) imagined Eastern Europe, stretching from the Leitha to the Bug. This version of Jewish geographical victimhood now so completely overlays earlier accounts that it is very hard to disentangle them.

I think that's utterly right. But what I'm trying to do is connect your two lines of Jewish history, the provincial East European and the cosmopolitan Central European.

Let's look again at the static, asynchronic image of Jewish life in fin-de-siècle Vienna. This is the beautiful portrait that one gets through Zweig and Roth and Schorske. You look along the horizon of Jewish achievement, and you see something which is tactile, firm, coherent, and then you wait for it to break because you know it's going to break. But it was never so firm and coherent. The Jews were one generation away from Moravia and two generations away from Galicia, and so not far at all from that older Polish world that was itself destroyed at the end of the eighteenth century.

What that account does is reify the youth of a certain generation of Jews at the end of the nineteenth century, who rather than inherit this Viennese world, in fact made it, and then modestly in old age give credit to history for their own achievements, rather than blame history for breaking them.

Zweig doesn't just write about it, he kills himself because of it. And because of what is going to happen—first after 1918, then in 1934 with the

Nazi coup attempt and civil war in Austria and of course above all from 1938 to 1945 when Austria was part of Nazi Germany—his version acquires retroactively a plausibility that it would otherwise have lacked: in short, that this was a peculiarly poignant catastrophe because something unique was undone and lost forever.

I wonder whether much the same could not be said of the fin-de-siècle wonderland of post-impressionist Paris? After all, France (and Paris above all) was in actuality a profoundly divided society, riven by competing political memories and abrasive disagreements over religion and social policy. In retrospect, however, and within just a few years, the French themselves had come to explain and understand these decades—à la Zweig—as a glorious dawn, overshadowed and displaced by war and politics—the former and perhaps even the latter self-servingly credited to others.

An echo of this nostalgic account can be heard even in the writings of the outstanding British economist John Maynard Keynes, in his *Economic Consequences of the Peace*. As early as 1921, we find him speaking with palpable longing and loss of the misplaced world of his pre-war youth. This is very much a trope of the generation born in the last decades of the Victorian era. Old enough to recall the confidence and security of the last years of the nineteenth century and the optimistic first decade of its successor, they would live long enough to see the utter collapse of what had once seemed not just a permanent condition of prosperous well-being, but a new and promising world in the making.

Naturally we think of Keynes above all as the economist who created an entire school of economic thought, based upon the argument that the state can intervene during times of economic downturn. But of course you're right that he arrives at this conclusion from personal experience. We'll focus on that a bit later. But for now in the most general terms: Keynes has the wonderful sentence about the world before the First World War as being one where, in order to travel, one didn't need a passport, one simply had one's man go to the bank

and get the appropriate amount of gold bullion and then book
passage across the channel, and one was on one's way.

Keynes and others may indeed have been right that things were
getting better at the turn of the nineteenth and twentieth centuries,
and not just in Britain. Global trade was on the increase. The
Austrians were making their way southward into the
Mediterranean; even in Russia, agrarian reform appeared at last
to be making serious inroads on the rural economy.

This was indeed an age—economically, not politically nor ideologically—of enormous self-confidence. That confidence took two forms. There was the view—of neoclassical economists and their followers—that capitalism was doing very well, would continue to do well, and indeed bore within it the sources and resources of its own indefinite renewal. And then there was the parallel and no less modernist perspective which saw in capitalism—whether or not it was thriving in the present—a system doomed to decline and collapse under the weight of its own conflicts and contradictions. From very different starting points these were both, so to speak, forward-looking perspectives, and both more than a little self-satisfied in their analysis.

The two decades following the end of the late-nineteenth century economic depression were the first great age of globalization; the world economy was truly becoming integrated in just the ways Keynes suggested. For precisely this reason, the scale of the collapse during and after the First World War and the rate at which economies contracted between the wars is difficult for us to appreciate even now. Passports were introduced; the gold standard returned (in 1925 in the British case, reinstated by Chancellor of the Exchequer Winston Churchill over Keynes's objections); currencies collapsed; trade declined.

One way to think of the implications of all this is the following: it took until the mid-1970s for even the core economies of prosperous Western Europe to get back to where they had been in 1914, after many decades of contraction and protection. In short, the industrial economies of the West (with the exception of the United States) experienced a sixty-year decline, marked by two world wars and an unprecedented economic depression. More than anything else, this constitutes the background and context for everything we have been discussing and indeed for the history of the world in the last century.

When Keynes came to write his *General Theory of Employment, Interest and Money* (first published in 1936), he was concerned—obsessed might be a better word—with the problem of stability and disruption. In contrast to the classical economists and their neoclassical heirs (his own teachers) he was convinced that conditions of uncertainty—with the attendant social and political insecurity—should be treated as the norm rather than the exception in capitalist economies. In short, he was proposing a theory of the world he had just lived through: far from being the default condition of perfect markets, stability was an unpredictable and even scarce byproduct of unregulated economic activity. Intervention, in one form or another, was the necessary condition for economic well-being and, on occasion, for the very survival of markets themselves. In a distinctively English key, this conclusion amounted to a version of Zweig: we once thought everything was stable, now we know that all is in flux.

> *Yes, it is very striking, isn't it—the very first chapter in Zweig's* World of Yesterday *is about security, as the thing which has been lost. By this Zweig does not merely mean that there was a war and things changed. Everything of his young life that he recalls with such nostalgia and precision—his father's household, the predictability of the roles that people performed—entailed and required a broader economic security which was never to return.*

> *It seems to me that there's a negative way of putting the point, as well. In the absence of reassuring and real global trade after the First World War, the project of making national economies*

self-sufficient is the dark side of the European twentieth century.
After all, both the Nazis and the Soviets were consumed by the
attraction of scale as the condition for well-being: with enough
space, productive capacity and workers you could become self-
sufficient and thereby recapture the security of global trade and
exchange—on your own terms.

Thus, if you have, as Stalin put it, socialism in one country, it
matters less that the world revolution has been indefinitely
postponed. If you have sufficient Lebensraum, *as Hitler believed,*
you can achieve something comparable: autarchy for the benefit of
the master race.

So there is a desire to create new sorts of empire, combined with the
sense that postimperial nation-states were just too small. The
Austrians of the 1920s were obsessed with economic
Lebensunfähigkeit, *the assertion that having lost everything, and*
being reduced to so small and impoverished an alpine space,
Austria could not possibly exist as an independent entity. The word
itself illustrates the mood of those years: "incapacity for life."

Recall, however, that interwar Austria, for all its reduced size and capacity, was blessed with an unusually sophisticated and well-established socialist movement, which was only defeated and ultimately destroyed as the result
of successive reactionary coups: first in 1934 and then again in 1938. Austria
was the distilled essence of everything that World War I had brought to continental Europe: the risk and even the likelihood of revolution; the longing
for (and the impossibility of) a self-sufficient nation-state; the increased difficulty of peaceful political coexistence within a civic space unsupported by
economic resources.

One is struck by the great historian Eric Hobsbawm's comment regarding his childhood and youth in 1920s Vienna: you felt, he writes, as if

suspended in limbo between a world that had been destroyed and one that was yet to be born. It was in Austria too that we find the origins of the other great current of economic theorizing in our times, running sharply counter to the conclusions associated with the work of Keynes and identified with the writings of Karl Popper, Ludwig von Mises, Joseph Schumpeter and, supremely, Friedrich Hayek.

The three quarters of century that followed Austria's collapse in the 1930s can be seen as a duel between Keynes and Hayek. Keynes, as I was saying, begins with the observation that under conditions of economic uncertainty we would be imprudent to assume stable outcomes and therefore had better devise ways to intervene in order to bring these about. Hayek, writing quite consciously against Keynes and from the Austrian experience, argues in the *The Road to Serfdom* that intervention—planning, however benevolent or well-intentioned and whatever the political context—must end badly. His book was published in 1945 and is most remarkable for its prediction that the post–World War II British welfare state already in the making should anticipate a fate similar to that of the socialist experiment in post-1918 Vienna. Starting with socialist planning, you would end with Hitler or a comparable successor. For Hayek, in short, the lesson of Austria and indeed the disaster of interwar Europe at large boiled down to this: don't intervene, and don't plan. Planning hands the initiative to those who would, in the end, destroy society (and the economy) to the benefit of the state. Three quarters of a century later, this remains for many people (especially here in the U.S.) the salient moral lesson of the twentieth century.

> *Austria is so full of content that one could extract contradictory lessons without even trying. The historical achievement of the socialist Viennese city planners was not replicated in the country as a whole. It was not, after all, the central Austrian government but rather the municipal government of Vienna which was controlled by the socialists after World War I (as it is today), and which successfully built up the famous new housing stock, attractive little*

urban communes etc. It was the public housing that, for the rest of
the country, became a symbol of the dangers of planning: precisely
because the communes worked quite well, they served the "Jews"
and the "Marxists" as a power base. And then in that first crisis of
which you spoke, the Austrian civil war of 1934, the central
government (controlled by conservative Christian parties) lined its
artillery pieces up on the hills above Vienna and set about quite
literally shelling socialism: firing down upon the Karl-Marx-Hof
and all those other nice working-class Hofs, *with their*
kindergartens, daycare centers, swimming pools, shops and so on—
municipal planning in action and despised for just that reason.

Quite so. Ironically, the Austrian experience—which was always and
above all a political encounter between the urban Marxist left and provincial
Christian rightists suspicious of Vienna and all its works—has been elevated
to the status of economic theory. It is as though what had taken place in Austria was a debate between planning and freedom, which was never the case,
and as though it were self-evident that the course of events which led from a
planned city to authoritarian repression and ultimately fascism can be summarized as a necessary causal relationship between economic planning and
political dictatorship. Relieved of its Austrian historical context and, indeed,
even of the very historical reference, this set of assumptions—imported to the
U.S. in the suitcases of a handful of disabused Viennese intellectuals—has
come to inform not just the Chicago school of economics but all significant
public conversation over policy choices in the contemporary United States.

We'll return to that. But before we take our leave of Jewish Vienna:
hasn't the Austrian lesson of the twentieth century also taken a
psychic form?

Sigmund Freud arrived just in time to influence a whole generation of
central European thinkers. From Arthur Koestler to Manès Sperber the logi-

cal stepping-stone out of a youthful Marxist commitment was psychology: Freudian, Adlerian, Jungian, according to taste. Like Marxism itself, which we'll also return to, Viennese psychology offered a way of demystifying the world, of identifying an all-embracing narrative with which to interpret behavior and decisions according to a universal template. And also, perhaps, a comparably ambitious theory of how to change the world (albeit one person at a time).

Psychology, after all, and in this respect it bore distinct similarities to both Marxism and the Judeo-Christian tradition, proposes a narrative of self-delusion, necessary suffering, decline and fall, followed by the onset of self-awareness, self-knowledge, self-overcoming and ultimate recovery. I am struck, in the memoirs of central Europeans born around the turn of the century, by the number of people (Jews above all) who comment on the contemporary vogue for analysis, for "explaining," for the categories of the new discipline (neurosis, repression etc.). This fascination with digging beneath the surface explanation, with unpicking mystifications, with finding a story which is all the truer for being denied by those it describes—surely this is uncannily reminiscent of the procedures of Marxism as well.

> *There's another similarity. One can also extract a three-part, optimistic story from Freudianism, just as one can from Marxism. Rather than being born into a world where property has destroyed our nature, we're born into a world where some original sin was (or was not) committed, a father was (or was not) killed, a mother was (or was not) slept with—but we're born into a world where we feel guilty about that, and we don't have the nature that we would have had, perhaps purely theoretical. We can return to something like that "natural" condition if we understand the family structure and undergo therapy. But as with Marx, so with Freud: it's a bit unclear just what that utopia would actually be like if one were to get there.*

In the Freudian story, as in the Marxian narrative, the crucial consideration is unstinting faith in the inevitable success of the outcome if the process itself is correct: in other words, if you have correctly understood and over-come the earlier damage or conflict, you will necessarily reach the promised land. And this guarantee of success is itself sufficient to justify the effort needed to get there. In Marx's own words, he was not in the business of writing recipes for the cookbooks of the future; he merely promised that future cookbooks there will be, if only we correctly deploy today's ingredients.

Let me use a Freudian term to ask about something that I see as a displacement in your own work, or about the great rupture in the history of the century: the Holocaust. The title of your history of Europe is Postwar. *Which is itself, of course, a claim about a new quality. But beginning your book in 1945 allows you not to write about the mass murder of the Jews. And indeed very little of your historical work poses Jewish questions, even when they are there to be posed. And so my question is: when (if yet) did what we now call the Holocaust start to inform the way that you personally were thinking about history?*

If I have any special insight into the history of the historiography of the Holocaust, it is because it tracks my life quite closely. As I mentioned earlier, I was unusually well-informed on this subject for a ten-year-old child. And yet, as a student at Cambridge University in the 1960s, I have to confess that I was remarkably uninterested in the subject—not only the Holocaust, but Jewish history in general. Moreover, I don't believe that I was in the least taken aback when we studied, e.g., the history of occupied France without any reference to the expulsion of the Jews.

I did, as a matter of fact, undertake a specialized research paper on the subject of Vichy France, but the questions I posed (which faithfully reflected the scholarship of the time) had nothing to do with French Jews. The problem that obsessed historians in those years was still the nature of the right-wing politics of the era: what kind of a regime was Vichy? Reactionary? Fascist? Conservative? I don't mean by this that I knew nothing of the fate of the Jews of France in those years; quite the contrary. But somehow that private knowledge was never integrated into my academic interests, not even into my study of Europe. Only in the 1990s did the subject move to the center of my scholarly interests.

> *Maybe this would be a good place to introduce Hannah Arendt,*
> *who early and influentially treated the Holocaust as a problem for*
> *everyone, not just its perpetrators and victims. She makes three*
> *claims which—although she is herself both a German and a Jew—*
> *suggest that the Holocaust should not be confined to Germans and*
> *Jews. First, she says that Nazi policies are best understood in the*
> *light of the broader category of "totalitarianism," a problem and*
> *product of mass societies. Second, mass societies in turn reflect a*
> *pathological interaction between "mob" and "elite," a distinctive*
> *dilemma of what she calls modernity. Arendt goes on to claim*
> *that another characteristic of modern society is the paradox of*
> *distributed responsibility: bureaucracy dilutes and obscures*
> *individual moral responsibility, rendering it invisible and thus*
> *producing Eichmann and, with Eichmann, Auschwitz. Third,*
> *Arendt asserts—in a letter to Karl Jaspers in, I believe, 1946—*
> *that what Jaspers, called implicit, metaphysical guilt, has to be the*
> *foundation for any new German republic. In this way Arendt has,*
> *so to speak, closed the historical conversation about the Holocaust*
> *even before it begins.*

That's well summarized. I find myself at odds with most of Arendt's other admirers. Overwhelmingly, they tend to be fascinated with her ambitious reflections on the nature of modernity, on the prospects for the Republic, on the goals of collective action, and other para-philosophical speculations of the kind presented in, e.g., *The Human Condition.* Conversely, many readers are troubled and even angered by what Arendt has to say on Jews and what she termed "the banality of evil."

I, by contrast, find Arendt irritatingly elusive and metaphysical in many of her speculative texts, precisely in those arenas where epistemological precision and historical evidence are called for. Yet what she has to say about the Jewish condition in modern society—from her biographical study of Rahel Varnhagen through her report on the Eichmann trial—seems to me absolutely spot on. I don't mean by this that she has everything right. She is far too readily disposed to condemn the *Ostjuden* for passivity or even *de facto* collaboration: in other words, to blame them for aspects of their own suffering. This insensitivity has authorized some of her critics to assert that she just doesn't understand the circumstances of Jews in places like Łódź, because all that she—an exemplary product of German-Jewish *Bildung*—can imagine is the circumstance of Jews in Frankfurt or Königsberg, where they would have been much better connected, would have a far more sophisticated grasp of events, and would have had the luxury of more choice between staying, leaving or resisting.

And yet, she gets one thing absolutely right. Think, for example, about that controversial phrase: "the banality of evil." Arendt is writing in terms that reflect a Weberian grasp of the modern world: a universe of states governed by administrative bureaucracies themselves subdivided into very small units where decisions and choices are exercised by, so to speak, individual non-initiative. Inaction, in such an institutional environment, becomes action; the absence of active choice substitutes for choice itself, and so forth.

Recall that Arendt published *Eichmann in Jerusalem* at the beginning of the 1960s. What she was arguing had yet to become conventional opinion but would do so within a couple of decades. By the 1980s it was a commonly held view among specialists in the field that the history of Nazism, and indeed of totalitarianism in all of its forms, could not be fully grasped if it was reduced to a tale of malevolent persons consciously and deliberately engaging in criminal acts with harm in mind.

From an ethical or a legal perspective of course, the latter makes more sense: not only are we uncomfortable with notions of collective responsibility or guilt, but we require some evidence of intention and action in order to arrange to our satisfaction issues of guilt and innocence. But legal and even ethical criteria do not exhaust the terms available to us for historical explanation. And they certainly provide insufficient purchase for an account of how and why otherwise nondescript persons, undertaking decidedly nondescript actions (like the management of train schedules) with untroubled consciences, can yet produce very great evil.

In Christopher Browning's *Ordinary Men,* a history of a battalion of German Order Police in occupied Poland, the same issues arise. Here we have men who would otherwise be anonymous and invisible committing, day by day, week by week, actions which by any standard constitute crimes against humanity: the mass shooting of Polish Jews. How should we even begin to think about what they are doing, why they are doing it and how we are to describe it? Arendt at least offers a starting point.

> *What Arendt is doing is seeking out your kind of universal account of what just happened. And, of course, Jean-Paul Sartre was after the same thing in those years; he too set out to propose a universal psychological portrait of what had happened in Europe during the Second World War. The existentialist idea of moral creativity and responsibility is an answer to the lonely world free of immanent values. That all comes from Martin Heidegger, of course; we'll return to that connection later.*

> *Let us say that Arendt is right and that the significance of the Holocaust is not parochially confined to Jewish victims and German criminals but can only be grasped in universal and ethical terms. It seems as though an existentialist who had been inspired by war would be bound to consider its loneliest victims. This prompts the question of Sartre's own relative unconcern with the problem of French responsibility in the Holocaust.*

I don't think that Sartre's worst shortcoming was his failure to see straight in World War II. However, I do think that his political myopia during the occupation years should be understood in the light of his completely apolitical worldview hitherto. This is a man, after all, who managed to live through the 1930s with no apparent political engagement or response of any kind, notwithstanding a year spent in Germany and the remarkable upheaval of the Popular Front in France. There can be no doubt that, in retrospect, Sartre—like many of his friends—felt uneasy about all this. Some of his later moral writings, on the subject of good faith, bad faith, responsibility and the like, are perhaps best understood as retroactive projections of his own bad conscience.

However, what has always troubled me about Sartre was his continuing failure to think straight, long after the ambiguities of the 1930s and 1940s had dissipated. Why, after all, did he so insistently refuse to discuss the crimes of communism, even to the extent of remaining conspicuously silent about anti-Semitism in Stalin's last years? The answer, of course, is that he made a deliberate decision not to think of those crimes in ethical terms, or at least in a language which would engage his own ethical commitment. In short, he found ways to avoid a difficult choice—while insistently claiming that avoiding hard choices was precisely the exercise of bad faith which he so famously defined and condemned.

It was this unforgivable confusion—or, more bluntly, dissemblance—that I find unacceptable in precisely Sartre's own terms. It is not as though his generation was unusually confused or mystified: Jean-Paul Sartre was born within a year of not just Hannah Arendt but also Arthur Koestler and Raymond Aron. That generation, born around 1905, was without question the most influential intellectual cohort of the century. They reached maturity just as Hitler was coming to power and were drawn willy-nilly into the historical vortex, confronting all the tragic choices of the age with little option but to take sides or have their side chosen for them. After the war, young enough in most cases to avoid the discredit that fell upon their seniors, they exercised precocious intellectual and literary influence, dominating the European (and American) scene for decades to come.

Martin Heidegger himself became all but unacceptable in the
States as a result of his Nazi sympathies, so much so that many
American intellectuals believe that his phenomenology is itself
inherently National Socialist. Meanwhile Sartre's existentialism,
which comes from Heidegger, becomes and remains very popular
in American university departments. But returning to our
concerns: Not just Arendt and Sartre but a whole generation of
European intellectuals were connected to Heidegger, directly or
otherwise.

The larger story here is the unprecedented impact of post-Hegelian, post-idealist German thought on European intellectuals from the 1930s through the 1960s. From one perspective, that of German philosophical influence, this story should be understood to include the rise (and later fall) of Marxist thought in Western Europe; the intellectual attraction of Marx— as distinct from the political influence of parties operating in his name— cannot be divorced from the growing scholarly familiarity with his early writings and his roots in Young Hegelian debates and exchanges. But at least from a more parochial French perspective, it is clear that part of the charm of the great nineteenth-century Germans and their successors was the contrast with the indigenous philosophical heritage, which by the 1930s was spectacularly irrelevant to the concerns of a rising generation. Phenomenology, coming first from Husserl and then from his student Heidegger, offered the appealing idea that the self was something deeper than the Freudian psychological self. It proposed a notion of authenticity in an inauthentic world.

Thus even Raymond Aron, by no means a slave to fashion then or since, observed in his (1938) doctoral dissertation that German thought offered the only way to think intelligently about the century and about the age. Indeed, I cannot recall any significant thinker in those years—outside of the Anglo-American context, already influenced by Austrian empiricism—who would not have seconded Aron's remarks. Neither in France nor in Italy, not to mention points east, was there any serious competition for the existentialist reading of German phenomenology which was to colonize much of continental thought in the post–World War II years. Indeed, following the defeat of Nazism and the utter devastation of German cultural life, it is more than a little ironic that in this one arena the country should have preserved its early-twentieth-century predominance.

With the collapse of Nazi Germany, Arendt, Jaspers, and then— following them—the political philosopher Jürgen Habermas, had a place to go: history. "We"—I'm speaking here of Arendt and Jaspers—"have experienced the abyss and now we are going to sublimate it into a political ethics. And we're going to do it with a grab bag of philosophical tools and terms, at our disposal thanks to the heritage of a German education. We may not be systematic in the way we set about this new approach, but we shall be articulate and convincing. And what we are really about, of course, is articulating a way to translate the German historical experience into a justification for constitutionalism."

I wonder whether Habermasian constitutionalism, with its emphasis upon the burden of history, is exactly comparable to the ethics of republicanism as articulated by Arendt, for example. The latter seems to me something rather different from "republicanism" as conventionally understood in English or American thought. It is founded, I think, not upon an account of history, nor even a theory of natural arrangements or the artifices of human nature (as in Enlightenment exchanges), but approximates rather more closely to what the late Judith Shklar called "the liberalism of fear." Arendt's is, to coin a phrase, the republicanism of fear. In this way of thinking, the foundation for a modern, democratic politics must be our historical awareness of the consequences of *not* forging and preserving a modern, democratic polity. What matters, to put it bluntly, is that we understand as well as possible the risks of getting it wrong, rather than devoting ourselves over-enthusiastically to the business of getting it right.

*The Arendtian, or the Jaspersian, or the Habermasian solution is
so fragile. If the Second World War was a special moment in
history from which we are to derive a certain metaphysical or at
least meta-political lesson, this implies a kind of taboo regarding
how we talk about it. This must surely cause problems of another
kind: eventually historians and others are going to have things to
say about the past—if only because we know more than we used
to—which will not sit well with the uses to which the
constitutionalists have sought to put our uncomfortable history.*

You might be right, but we need some sense of the setting. It's important to remember, today, that the republic that Arendt or Jaspers or Habermas had in mind was West Germany. There was more than one Germany
after the war, and more than one German question. After its establishment in
1949, communist East Germany appeared far more serious in its efforts to
come to terms with Nazism. And indeed it really was more aggressive in its
public prosecution of Nazism, to obvious ideological advantage. In West
Germany, by contrast, there were very large numbers of people who were still
sympathetic to the Nazi regime—a stance which was not actively frowned
upon by the authorities of the new Federal Republic. Nazism might have
failed them, by provoking catastrophic defeat, but it was not otherwise perceived as guilty of any very distinctive crime.

This perspective remained alive in German minds, reinforced by a
sense of victimhood: the expulsion of masses of ethnic Germans from Eastern and Central Europe and the continuing imprisonment of German soldiers in the Soviet Union contributed to such sentiments. And thus there
emerged an ever-more salient schism between a West Germany apparently
unable fully to integrate the significance of its own defeat and moral humili-
ation, and an East Germany which (at least under its own account of things)
had thoroughly incorporated that story and, indeed, now presented itself as
part of the anti-fascist resistance, rather than as a defeated fascist country.

By the beginning of the 1950s, the Americans, the British and, obviously, the West German Chancellor Konrad Adenauer had redrawn not just the political but also the ethical lines: the issue now was the Cold War to be conducted against totalitarian communism. The Germans had been the problem; now they were the solution, a frontline ally against the new foe. Arming Germany would strengthen the Western alliance against the Soviet Union. In France, there was a certain amount of reluctance to switch gears with quite such speed, but the process moved rapidly and smoothly in England and above all in the United States. But for just that reason, a significant segment of the Left was provided with a pretext for re-casting the United States as an after-the-fact associate of unreconstructed German nationalism and even Nazism. This sentiment, which first surfaced in the mid-'60s, would become part of the core rhetorical strategy for New Left and extra-parliamentary politics in the Federal Republic.

The Cold War certainly suppressed discussions of the Holocaust in the West. But it's not as though the Soviets were eager to promote such discussions, either. One of the reasons why we haven't known what we haven't known about the Holocaust is the way the Soviets treated it. During the war, Stalin very consciously used the Jewish question as a way to raise money from his western allies; later, he pulled sharply back, turning against Jews who had helped him in this public relations exercise, killing some, purging others.

As a consequence, Treblinka all but disappears from the Soviet history of World War II. The Soviet novelist Vasily Grossman was at Treblinka as a Soviet war correspondent during September 1944. Grossman was perfectly well-informed about the Great Famine, about Stalin's Terror, about the Battle of Stalingrad; he knew that his mother had been killed by the Germans in Berdichev, and when he turns up in Treblinka and finds this mysterious field, he has little difficulty figuring out what happened

there. The Germans had gassed to death hundreds of thousands of
Jews. And so Grossman writes a very long article about it, called
"Treblinka Hell."

But this kind of writing, with its emphasis upon the specificity of
Jewish experience, could only be published for a very short time.
Within a few years of the end of the war there came Stalin's abrupt
reversal—in the USSR, but also, of course, in communist Poland
and throughout communist Eastern Europe. The consequence,
which would prove enduring, was the imposition of a sort of
universalization of Nazi victimhood: all of these people, massacred
in Treblinka or other camps whose sites had been recovered, were
just simple human beings, peaceful Soviet (or Polish) citizens.

The wartime favor accorded Yiddish actors and Jews who could go to
New York and raise money was certainly the exception rather than the rule in
the Soviet story. And obviously it was far easier for anyone raised in the Marxist tradition to think in terms of class when explaining fascism. Above all, it sat
easily with the Soviet leadership in those years to describe and promote "the
Great Patriotic War" as an anti-fascist struggle, rather than presenting the conflict with Stalin's recent ally as an anti-German undertaking, much less a war
against racists. Reasonably enough, therefore, Jews disappear from the story.

It was not that the suffering of Jews was denied or even minimized in
the course of the war. Ironically, the Jews of Eastern Europe and the Soviet
Union achieved in the course of their extermination the equality that they
had long since been promised by enlightened Europeans: they became citizens, just like everyone else and not distinguished from everyone else. They
thus got the worst of both worlds; killed as Jews, they were memorialized
and officially remembered merely as the citizens of whichever country they
happened to be in at the time of their death.

Even today there are many who are much more comfortable with the
Soviet version of German mass murder, without themselves being in the least

bit sympathetic to Marxism or the Soviet Union. Because postwar Soviet historiography and propaganda emphasized the persecution of nationals rather than ethnics, it authorized and even encouraged the playing up of *national* suffering and *national* resistance.

My friend and colleague Jan Gross would probably argue in addition that this version of events had a special appeal in certain places: Poland and Romania certainly, perhaps also Slovakia. By conflating victims of all kinds, whether murdered for their religion, their "race," their nationality or just in the course of an unprecedentedly violent war of occupation and extermination, the Soviet narrative effaced the embarrassing extent to which the destruction of Jewish Romanians, Jewish Poles etc. was not typically a matter of deep local regret. When all the victims are thrown together, there is less danger of retrospective score-settling or historiographical revision. The dead might of course wish to object to this re-description of their experience, but then the dead don't vote.

Well, if you are a Polish Jew and you live your adult life in postwar Polish society and somehow assimilate and have a more or less successful career, as some people did before the communists' anti-Semitic campaign of 1968 and even thereafter, it is difficult to separate yourself from that history. But we cannot assign the whole story and subsequent mystifications to Stalin alone; much of the responsibility belongs to Hitler. There weren't nearly as many ethnic Poles killed in the Second World War as Poles think, but there were still an awful lot. You know, surely not the three million usually cited, probably not even two million but closer to one million; but that's still a horrible figure.

And then there's the blurriness of the experience itself where, for example, you might have two people who worked for the information service of the Polish Home Army which, like the equivalent organ of the French Resistance, was disproportionately

Jewish. One of them might die—be killed for a political reason or just by chance; the other executed as a Jew, since they could easily have been denounced for quite different reasons. Or recall that the Warsaw Ghetto, once it had been thoroughly obliterated, became the site for German executions of Poles by the thousands. Their bodies were then burned in just the sort of improvised crematoria that the Germans had been using until recently for the Jews— sometimes, indeed, along with surviving Jews who were rounded up at the same time. The ashes, of course, were intermingled.

The problem with historical events which are intricately interwoven is that, the better to understand their constituent elements, we have to pull them apart. But in order to see the story in its plenitude, you have to inter-weave those elements back together again. Much of the historiography of the Jews of Eastern Europe, and indeed of Eastern Europe itself, has regrettably consisted either of an exercise in forced separation or else in a determined refusal to make any distinctions whatsoever. Separation falsifies one part of the story; its absence has a comparably distorting impact on something else.

This dilemma, a genuine one for the sensitive historical scholar, does not present itself in so troubling a form in Western Europe; indeed, this is one reason why the Second World War is so much harder to recount and understand in Europe's eastern half. West of Vienna we understand quite well, I think, the ambiguities with which we are faced. They concern resistance, collaboration and their nuances and consequences—often a matter of pre-war political conflicts playing out under the guise of wartime choices. In Western Europe the so-called "gray zone," the moral complexity of the alternatives and opportunities facing occupied populations, has been much debated, as have the lies and self-serving delusions that protagonists offered after the war. In short, we understand the constituent elements on which any comprehensive history of those years must draw. But deciding just how to identify the constituent elements themselves is still a primary task of the historian of those years in *Eastern* Europe.

But then the absence of East European history can be a problem
beyond Eastern Europe. Without clear accounts of what happened
there, the Germans can slip back to national history, or the history
of national victimhood. It strikes me, and I wonder if you agree,
that there's a difference between the German discussions of the
1980s and those of the 1990s and the first decade of this century.
The distinction has to do with the contrast between historicization
and victimization. In the 1980s, the debate that preoccupied West
Germany was still about how to locate the thirteen years of Hitler's
Reich in the national story. The terms of this difficult conversation
had already been set by Arendt and Jaspers nearly four decades
earlier. Habermas's objective, when he triggered the
Historikerstreit of the late 1980s, was to re-emphasize the morally
distinctive character of the Nazi epoch. His critics of course
countered that history cannot be written in such a moral key; one
way or another we just have to find a way to narrate German
history, even at the risk of "normalizing" it. Within ten years,
however, in the aftermath of the revolutions of 1989, the debate
had shifted to contentious claims and counter-claims: who suffered,
at whose hands and how much? That is a rather different kind of
question.

I agree. Until very recently in Germany, the very question of competitive
suffering would not have been regarded as a legitimate way to frame the historical question—except, of course, in circles that were not themselves politically legitimate. And then too you would not have expected to encounter
Germans writing books about German victims of allied bombings. Above all,
one would hardly have supposed that Günther Grass, of all people, would
produce a bestseller commemorating the German refugees who drowned on
the *Wilhelm Gustloff*, sunk by the Soviets in the Baltic Sea at the very end of
the war. It was not that these were in themselves inappropriate historical
subjects; but the very idea of emphasizing German suffering, and implicitly

comparing it with the suffering of others at German hands, would have sailed dangerously close to a relativizing of Nazi crimes.

As you say, all of this did indeed change in the course of the 1990s. The interesting question is why. One answer is that there was a generational transition. As late as the mid-1980s, Habermas could still claim, uncontentiously for many of his readers, that his fellow Germans had not earned the right to "normalize" their history: this option was simply not open to them. Ten years later, however, when history itself had normalized Germany—thanks to the revolutions of 1989, the disappearance of the GDR and the country's subsequent unification, normalization had become . . . normal.

Germany today is not only a reunited country, it is no longer occupied in even the most residual sense. The Second World War is thus legally as well as historically over, having lasted some five decades. The normalization of Germany has, predictably enough, precipitated a recasting of its history, and with it that of Europe as a whole. Today, Germans and others engage their past in terms closely comparable to those familiar to us from historiography elsewhere. Since this shift in perspective occurred in exactly the decade when "victimhood" was taking center stage in historical and political debates across the West, we should not be surprised that questions of comparative suffering, apology and commemoration—familiar from American identity politics to the South African truth commissions—have their place in German conversations as well.

"Telling the truth"—which for so long was itself a problematic exercise thanks to competing "truths" and the cost of airing them publicly—now became a virtue in itself. And the bigger the truth you have to tell, the greater your claim upon the attention of fellow citizens and sympathetic observers. Thus, despite the obvious risk of appearing to compete with the ultimate truth of Jewish genocide, speaking openly about hitherto uncomfortable episodes in the recent German past opens the possibility of encouraging the telling of many stories.

The real problem, of course, is that when one community speaks of "telling the truth," they don't just mean proposing a maximal version of their own suffering, but also the implicit minimizing of the suffering of others.

2.

LONDON AND LANGUAGE:
ENGLISH WRITER

For me, school was neither home nor an escape from home. The other kids, my friends included, had grandparents without accents. In its small way, this was mystifying and perhaps a little alienating. In my world, all grandparents had accents. That's what a grandmother or a grandfather was: someone whom you didn't quite understand because they would unpredictably slip into Polish or Russian or Yiddish. At my elementary school, the head teacher, in an ill-advised burst of philo-Semitic enthusiasm, once used me as an example of how clever Jews are, permanently assuring the envious dislike of half my classmates. This followed me for the rest of my school days.

At the age of eleven, I was admitted to Emanuel School, the local Direct Grant establishment, in essence a non–fee-paying selective school later forced into the private sector by the misguided comprehensivisation of British education. In a school of one thousand plus boys, I don't believe there were more than half a dozen Jews. I encountered quite a lot of anti-Semitism, from boys whose parents were no doubt anti-Semitic as well. Among the South London lower middle class and working class whom this school served, anti-Semitism in those years was neither rare nor remarkable.

We forget how much anti-Semitism there was in England, at least until the radical shifts of the 1960s and the emerging awareness of the Holocaust. Winston Churchill certainly did not forget. His wartime intelligence services had kept him appraised of widespread suspicion of Jews, and persistent mutterings to the effect that the war was being fought "for them." For this reason, he suppressed discussion of the Holocaust during the war and censored public debate over whether or not the Royal Air Force should bomb the camps.

I grew up in an England where Jews were still among the rare conspicuous outsiders: there were few Asians and even fewer blacks in those days. If Jews were an object of suspicion, particularly in the catchment area of Emanuel School, it was not because we were regarded as overachieving scholars, nor even because we were thought to be commercially predisposed or overly successful. We were simply alien: because we did not believe in Jesus whereas most people in those days still did, and because we came or were thought to come from strange foreign places. The number of boys who were overtly anti-Semitic was actually quite small, but they were loud and without shame.

Although rugby probably helped me some, for such boys I was always the stereotypical Jewish kid with glasses. Once or twice I got into fights provoked by anti-Jewish taunts, and this ambience of occasional hostility significantly detracted from the charms of my secondary school years. I attended school, studied and played sports, watching out for the bad kids on the way home; but I was otherwise utterly indifferent to the whole experience, recalling very little of pleasure from those years.

What I did *not* get from school was any sense of collective identity. I was and remained a solitary child. My sister was eight years younger, so we didn't spend much time together. My preferred pastimes from the age of seven through fifteen were reading in my bedroom, riding my bike, and traveling on trains. In the late nineteenth century Emanuel had been moved to a triangular plot of land in Battersea, just south of Clapham Junction Station. The site lay between two sets of railway lines: the southbound tracks from Victoria Station ran to the east, the southwest route from Waterloo to the Atlantic ports bounded the school to the west. Every class, every conversation, was punctuated by the sound of trains. School, a major source of my adolescent loneliness, did at least suggest an avenue of escape.

All the same, school exposed me to the same upbringing and influences as any Christian child. If nothing else, this furnished me with a better quality of English, thanks to the incomparable King James Bible. But I think that the influences run deeper still. If you asked me even today where I would feel more at home, in an Orthodox synagogue or a rural Anglican church, I would have to say that I feel at home in both, but in different ways. I would immediately be able to identify, recognize and share what was going on in the Orthodox synagogue, but I would not feel at all part of the world of the people around me. Conversely, I would feel completely at ease in the world of an English rural church and its surrounding community, even though I don't share the beliefs nor do I identify with the symbols of the ceremony.

School made me English in another way: we read good English literature. Emanuel followed the Cambridge high school syllabus, which was rightly held to be the most rigorous. We read poetry: Chaucer, Shakespeare, the metaphysical poets of the seventeenth century, the Augustan poets of the eighteenth. We read some prose as well: Thackeray, Defoe, Hardy, Walter Scott, the Brontë sisters, George Eliot. I won a prize for English, appropriately enough a book by Matthew Arnold. My schoolmasters in those days were under the influence of F. R. Leavis, and promoted a rigorously conservative vision of English literary culture.

This perspective, quite widespread at the time, meant that a child of the 1960s could still benefit from an education that was little different from, and perhaps even better than, that offered to previous generations. It was probably this range of traditional cultural reference, this sense of being at home in English if not exactly in England, that allowed people like me to swing comfortably back from radical youthful politics towards the liberal mainstream in later life.

However that may be, school gave me an appreciation for English as a language and for English writing that has stayed with me in spite of my foreign interests and connections. Many of my historian contemporaries became continental Europeans, by force of fashion, elective affinity and professional focus. I suppose I did too. But more than most of them, I think I felt and remained deeply English, curious as that may sound. I don't know whether I write better English than others, but I know that I write it with genuine pleasure.

We've spoken already about the spiritual significance of the First World War in Europe. The collapse that followed the First World War on the continent seems to follow in England after a decade of delay. Whereas in other empires—in land empires like the Habsburg monarchy for example—the break was clear and immediate: war, defeat, revolutions made or unmade, but in any case a new world in very short order. True, these changes were resisted all across central and Eastern Europe for some years, and indeed in the east there were armies still engaged in combat well into 1920. But something new was in the making: Keynes was doubtless right in the grander scheme of things. In little England, in contrast, it was possible for a while to dream of a return to the prewar world.

The characteristic voice of the 1920s is Evelyn Waugh's *Vile Bodies*: combining a sort of insouciant, post–World War I, live-it-up-now attitude with class-conscious carelessness about the looming shadow of social change. The privileged, at least for a while, continued to enjoy their privileges: the forms of their prewar life and resources, if not quite the content. Recall that Stephen Spender, a representative left-winger (and poet) of those times, looks back at the '30s as a crucial politicizing decade; but like so many others, he remembers the '20s in contrast as a time of striking political quiescence. Within a few years, English thinkers, writers and scholars were suddenly to awaken to the realities of interwar political strife; but they had few domestic references with which to make sense of this newfound world of commitment and engagement.

Indeed, in England, the Great Depression was not the latest in a series of crises, as it was across much of Europe; it *was* the crisis. The economic slump destroyed the political Left: the Labour government elected with such fanfare just two years earlier was to fall ignominiously in 1931 over the challenge of unemployment and deflation. The Labour Party itself split: a significant element, including most of the leadership, entered into a coalition with the Conservatives, the so-called "National Government." From 1931 until Churchill's defeat in the election of 1945, political conservatives governed the United Kingdom, with a sprinkling of renegade Labourites and survivors from Lloyd George's once-great Liberal Party.

Thus for much of this period, the political Left was not just out of office but utterly separated from the exercise of power. All political debate within the Left, and indeed any conversation dissenting from the conventions of the status quo, was thus forced outside of conventional parliamentary politics. If intellectuals in interwar England came to matter more than they ever had before in the 1930s, this was not because the country suddenly woke up to their cultural significance, nor because they became in the aggregate more politically aware and thus more "European," but simply on account of the absence of any other public space or conversation in which radical dissent and opinion could be formulated and debated.

*I can't remember which wife, I think it was Inez, and I can't
remember whether Spender wrote it to her, or she wrote it to him,
but I think it was her to him, the line, "First you love too little, then
you love too much," after their divorce. And the contrast between
the 1920s and the 1930s in England is—*

—exactly that—

*—because having spent the 1920s homebound in England,
Spender—just to take him as a case in point—goes first to Berlin
with Christopher Isherwood and W. H. Auden, but then to Vienna,*

*where he witnesses the failed Nazi coup and the civil war of 1934.
He also spent some time in revolutionary Spain. All of this is
described in* World Within World, *his memoir of that decade, as
the experience of being "hounded by reality": as though reality was
this thing which ought not to bother one, but now that it has
bothered one, it needs to be acknowledged.*

Curiously, both the geography of Spender's wanderings and the remark
that they prompt are reminiscent of observations made by Raymond Aron, who
was a young post-graduate student teaching in Germany exactly at the moment
of Hitler's coming to power. Aron returns to France and tries desperately to
convince colleagues and contemporaries—including Sartre, utterly uninterested
in those years—of the reality snapping at their heels. To be sure, the French case
was different in a number of ways, but there is a parallel with the British experience. In France too the 1920s was a relatively de-politicized decade, at least for
intellectuals, whereas the 1930s, of course, was an era of frenetic engagement.

That said, the "too little, too much" syndrome—the oscillation between
political indifference and angry commitment—is perhaps more marked in England than elsewhere. It was there, in the crucial years from 1934 to 1938, that
the Communist Party was able to seduce a generation of upper middle class
Oxbridge undergraduates into sympathy, apologias, activist fellow-traveling or,
in a handful of cases, outright spying for communism.

*I wonder if you would agree that the attraction to the Left has a lot
to do—at least in certain cases, though not for the Cambridge
group, who came along a decade later—with the experience of
Weimar Germany. Because I think that for some of these
characters—for Auden, Isherwood, Spender—Weimar Germany
was the most attractive democracy of all: it had the nicest young
men and the best architecture.*

It is certainly the case that, between Otto Wagner and the transvestites,

Germany *looked* much more interesting than England; and, to tell the truth, it was. In both Berlin and Vienna, there was indeed something unusual and interesting going on. To young Englishmen arriving fresh from Oxford in this intense cultural hothouse, the contrast must have seemed striking indeed. But the same holds even for the French. It was self-evident to the young Aron that he should live and study in Germany if he wished to complete his philosophical and sociological education; and in this respect, at least, the same was true of Sartre, who also spent a year in Germany, learning German (though nothing about German politics). They, like so many others, were attracted and electrified by the sheer energy of the place—including, of course, the negative energy emanating from the squabbling political sects.

Weimar echoes down the decades. Think of our colleague Eric Hobsbawm—who should be regarded for these purposes as a sort of transnational English intellectual, displaced from his Austro-German childhood to the intelligentsia of Cambridge in the course of the 1930s. In the dying years of Weimar, Hobsbawm—living in Berlin—was just old enough (fifteen) to be intensely affected by the mood and events of the time. There is a moment in his memoirs when he speaks movingly and with utter conviction of his feelings in those months: the sensation of being more alive, more engaged, more culturally and even sexually energized than at any point in the rest of his long life. Much later in his memoirs he writes approvingly and even apologetically about the GDR and East Berlin: gray and inefficient it may have been, but it had a certain charm and he is sorry to see it go. It is hard to resist the thought that he has conflated the East Germany of Eric Honecker with the Weimar of his youth. For Hobsbawm as for Spender and company, there is an unmistakable affection for a democracy so seductive and louche, so threatened and incapable of self-defense, but never boring. This memory would prove crucial in the making of a significant cusp generation of Englishmen, and would inform their politics for decades to come.

The Soviet Union, not as lived reality but as cultivated myth,
hangs in the distant background. For those English intellectuals

who were attracted to Weimar Germany and then to
communism, the appeal may have had something to do with
the communists' success in blending the categories of
"bourgeois" and "democracy." Their Weimar was scarcely
democratic bourgeois.

The notion that what is wrong with bourgeois democracy is the adjective rather than the noun was a truly brilliant innovation on the part of Marxist rhetoricians. If the problem with western democracies is that they are bourgeois (whatever that means), then internal critics constrained to live in such places may offer criticism risk-free: taking your distance from a bourgeois democracy costs you little and hardly threatens the institution itself. Whereas a critical stance towards democracy in pre-1933 Germany represented all too often an active commitment to its collapse. In short, Weimar intellectuals, whether they liked it or not, were constrained to live out the political logic of their discursive affinities. No one in England faced or faces comparable choices.

The bourgeois-democracy association always seems to me a
brilliant Freudian adaptation on the part of the Marxists: it
means that you can be against the lawyer-father or the banker-
father while remaining at liberty to enjoy the privileges of
childhood and childish rebellion.

Well, I suppose that you can shift readily enough from infantile Oedipal considerations to full-fledged Hegelian accounts of the logical template binding you to the history of the species. However, a sensitive, intelligent adult can only indulge such thoughts if they never overtly clash with his own self-interest. But they do so clash if you find yourself a child of bourgeois parents in a country where the bourgeoisie is truly threatened or has been radically dismembered. Because in that case, merely taking your distance from your class of origin is not much help: being the heir to a guilty class

suffices to condemn you. In the Soviet Union or communist Czechoslovakia, the outcome for two generations of "bourgeois" was decidedly unpleasant, at just the moment when their counterparts in New York or London,
Paris or Milan, were elevating themselves to the status of spokesmen for
History.

Politics does not quite seem to keep people apart in England as it
might on the continent. T. S. Eliot publishes Spender, for example.

Until the 1930s, the various overlapping circles of English writers and
thinkers were brought together not by shared politics, but rather through
common roots and their elective affinities and tastes. Bloomsbury, the Fabians, the Catholic networks around Chesterton, Belloc and Waugh were all
self-contained worlds of aesthetic or political conversation, engaging at most
a tiny self-selected sub-group of the English intelligentsia.

However, the educated elite in England was and perhaps still is very
small by American or continental European standards. Sooner or later, most
English intellectuals were bound to know one another. Noel Annan, a contemporary of Eric Hobsbawm at King's in Cambridge, would go on to be
elected provost of his own college and then of University College, London,
serving on practically every public committee of significance in English
institutional and cultural life for decades to come. His memoirs are entitled
Our Age. Notice that it is not "Their Age," but "Our Age": everyone knows
everyone else. Implicit in Annan's title and text is the assumption that his
generation collectively ran the affairs of their country.

As indeed they did. Until the late 1960s, the percentage of schoolchil-
dren going on to university in England was smaller than that of any other
developed country. Within that small cohort of the well-educated, only those
who attended Oxford or Cambridge (or, but to a much lesser degree, a couple
of the London colleges) could expect to gain entry to the inner circle of the
intellectual and political establishment. Further distill that tiny cohort, removing the considerable number of reasonably stupid "legacy" students—those

admitted to Oxbridge by virtue of their class or their parentage—and it will be clear that the socio-genetic pool from which English culture and the English intellectual scene was drawn is tiny indeed.

> *But didn't Oxford and Cambridge begin to admit people from the empire?*

Yes and no. On the one hand, recall that until the late 1950s you could live a lifetime in London without ever encountering a black or brown face. In the event that you did indeed meet a dark-skinned person, they were almost certainly drawn from the restricted elite of Indians who had been siphoned upwards into the British educational system: either through Indian replicas of British boarding schools or else English public schools to which the Indian aristocracy traditionally sent their sons, thence securing them entry into the elite universities of the empire. So yes, there were indeed Indians of various provenance in both Oxford and Cambridge from the late nineteenth century. Some of them would go on to lead their country into independence from Great Britain. But I hardly think that we should consider their presence significant, except in notable individual instances.

> *Another way in which the small pool of English intellectuals was expanded, surely, was by the addition of political émigrés: Isaiah Berlin at Oxford being perhaps the best-known example. Berlin certainly knew most if not all of the people we have been discussing thus far, despite being a thorough-going outsider: a Russian Jew from Latvia.*

But Isaiah Berlin was unique: Jewish and foreign to be sure, but the consummate insider. He was perceived in the British cultural establishment as exotic, but for just that reason exemplary evidence of the integrative function and capacity of the system. This was, of course, misleading: Isaiah Berlin was undoubtedly an outstanding instance of successful integration, but it was his very exoticism that rendered him, if not more acceptable, then at any rate altogether unthreatening. From an early stage, his critics were saying of Berlin that his success was in large measure due to his reluctance to take a stand, his unwillingness to be "awkward." It was this emollient capacity for accommodation that made Berlin so acceptable to his peers: as an undergraduate, as president of the British Academy and founder of an Oxford college.

In contrast, most outsiders are awkward by nature. The same was true of insiders who found a role as critics of their own community—George Orwell being perhaps the best known case. Whether they are born awkward, or become so over time, such men are difficult: they have sharp edges and prickly personalities. Berlin suffered no such defects. This was undoubtedly part of his charm; but over the years, it also encouraged in him a certain reticence on controversial matters, a reluctance to speak out which may, in the course of time, diminish his reputation.

The "system" could unquestionably integrate the right sort of people. It could induct an Eric Hobsbawm: an Alexandria-born, Vienna-raised, Berlin-dwelling, German-speaking Jewish communist. Within a decade of his arrival in London as a refugee from Nazi Germany, Hobsbawm had been elected secretary of the Apostles, a self-selecting secret society of the cleverest young men in Cambridge: it was hardly possible to become more of an insider than that.

On the other hand, to become an insider at Cambridge or Oxford does not in itself require conformity, except perhaps to intellectual fashion; it was and is a function of a certain capacity for intellectual assimilation. It entails knowing how to "be" an Oxbridge don; understanding intuitively how to conduct an English conversation that is never too aggressively political; knowing how to modulate moral seriousness, political engagement and ethical rigidity through the application of irony and wit, and a precisely-calibrated appearance of *insouciance*. It would be difficult to imagine the application of such talents in, say, postwar Paris.

That may have the consequence that for political choices, matters
of private life and especially love, end up mattering more for
British than for French intellectuals. French intellectuals are
divided by political discussion and they tend less, I think, to follow
their lovers around to various political commitments.

Arthur Koestler and Simone de Beauvoir had one bad night of sex. This, so far as we can judge from their correspondence and memoirs, was neither the cause of their political breakup nor an impediment to it. De Beauvoir was indubitably attracted to Albert Camus, which is perhaps one reason why Sartre was so jealous of the younger man. Nevertheless, this circumstance really is not relevant to their political disagreements one way or the other.

Conversely, through the 1970s at least, sexual relations among British intellectuals—both homosexual and heterosexual—were surely at the epicenter of their elective social affinities. I don't wish for one minute to suggest that the sex life of British intellectuals was in any salient respect more interesting or, indeed, more active than that of continental Europeans. Still, when you think of the relative quiescence and passivity of most other areas of their existence for much of the century, their emotional entanglements do acquire a certain prominence if only by default.

Even if people from the Empire don't yet matter much in British
intellectual life, surely the Empire mattered as a source of
experience? Think of George Orwell in Burma.

Orwell served in a low-level but locally senior administrative capacity for the Burma imperial police from 1924 to 1927. Reading him, one never feels that he developed much of an interest in the Empire per se; his writings from those years suggest the emergence of a set of moral and political considerations—deriving to be sure from his criticisms of Imperial rule—which will in the fullness of time permeate his observations on England itself.

Orwell's awareness that the Burmese (or Indian) question transcended issues of local injustice and concerned above all the impropriety and impossibility of imperial domination, would certainly color his political stance back home.

It seems fair to add that Orwell was one of the first commentators to grasp that issues of justice and subordination, no less than the traditional themes of class and politics, must be taken up by the Left—indeed, they *were* henceforth part of what it meant to be Left. We forget that well into the interwar decades it had been perfectly possible to combine social reformism and even political radicalism at home with liberal imperialism. Until quite recently it had been possible to believe that the key to social improvement in Britain lay in retaining, defending and even expanding the empire. By the 1930s, this position had begun to sound ethically as well as politically incoherent, and Orwell can take some credit for this shift in sensibilities.

> *Do you think it's the case that literature—the publications of the time but above all the novels that the generation of the 1930s would have been reading—serves as a way to consider the world of empire? Think of Joseph Conrad or later Graham Greene—with the characters who go elsewhere, often in the Empire, to perceive things, of course in the case of the espionage novels because they've been* trained *to perceive things.*

The popular literature of Empire is really about moral issues: who's good, who's bad, and who's right (usually us) and who's wrong (typically them). The literature about spies and about Germans that emerges in these years, for example, is very much imperially structured. And you see this as well in the cinema of the 1930s, with its focus on spies, vanishing ladies and so on. But it's my impression that these themes are more often set in "Central Europe": a sort of mythical territory, a place of mystery and intrigue, reaching roughly from the Alps to the Carpathians and getting more mysterious the farther south and east you go. Whereas the exotic for the British in the late nineteenth century was India and the Near East, it's curious that the exotic by the 1930s is just a train ride away from Zurich. In its way, this is an updating of imperial literature, with Bulgarians standing in for Burmese. So in an interesting way the British are at home in the world, and what is exotic are European lands not very far away but forever beyond Empire.

Sherlock Holmes has a mystery to solve in Bohemia, where everyone speaks German and no one speaks Czech. And of course the political corollary of this is that Bohemia is a far-away country of which we know little. Which, paradoxically, one could not have said about Burma.

Indeed so; Burma is a very far-away country about which we know something. But of course the sense of distance and mystery in central Europe has distant roots: think of Shakespeare and the "coast of Bohemia" in *The Winter's Tale*. This English sense that Europe is more mysterious than the Empire (once you get past Calais) is old and established. For the English, at least in their self-image, the wider world has meaning as a reference; but Europe is not something with which we wish to be too closely associated. You can go to Burma, or Argentina, or South Africa and speak English and run an English-owned company or an English-style economy; ironically, you can't do that in Slovenia, which is therefore much more exotic.

And in imperial India or the Indies you'll run into people—whether they are white school chums or brown, educated subordinates—who have the same references as you do. It's quite striking even today how much the educational baggage of a Caribbean, West African, East African or Indian university-educated man or woman over the age of fifty sat comfortably with that of their British contemporaries. When I meet people of my own generation from Calcutta or Jamaica, we are immediately comfortable with one another, swapping references and memories from literature to cricket, in ways that do not work nearly so well with casual acquaintances in Bologna or Brno.

*In the 1930s there began a very distinctive English romance with
the unknown east: that of the Soviet spies, "the Cambridge Five."*

Note that three of the five communist spies of that decade were intimately linked with two elite Cambridge colleges: King's and Trinity. This
was a distinctly selective subset of what was already a privileged minority of
the English intelligentsia of the 1930s.

There were two main varieties of British sympathizer with communism
in the 1930s. The first was the sort of Englishman, typically young and
upper middle class, who went to Spain during the Spanish Civil War of
1936–1939 to help save the Republic. Such men were progressives; they
saw themselves from the outset as part of the European Left family and were
familiar with the circumstances they were about to encounter. Most of them
returned disillusioned, and the best of them had something interesting to say
about their disillusionment, albeit after some hesitation. George Orwell—
who returned and immediately wrote up his memories of hope and lost illusion in *Homage to Catalonia*—did not hesitate.

The second group was those who threw in their lot with communism,
openly avowing their doctrinal allegiance. The young Eric Hobsbawm and
his future colleagues in the Communist Party Historians Group are perhaps
the best known English instance.

The young men of the Cambridge Five do not fit easily into either category. Their use-value to the Soviet Union lay precisely in the absence of any
outward sign of their political affiliation. From the outset, their identity was
covert; they were recruited as Soviet spies precisely because better known
left-wing intellectuals and students were self-evidently of no use in that
capacity.

Two of the Cambridge spies, Kim Philby and Guy Burgess, were—
despite their upper-class accents and wonderful education—English outsiders in England. Kim Philby inherited from his father, the orientalist and
dissenting empire-builder St. John Philby, an intense dislike of imperialism
and a well-hidden belief that Britain's imperial policies were ethically

indefensible and politically catastrophic. Many years later, when Philby was forced to escape from England and seek exile in Moscow (his cover about to be blown), he was clearly a man who had no doubts as to the integrity of his choices: if he was not altogether happy in the USSR, at least he understood perfectly well that this was the logical outcome of a lifelong choice.

Guy Burgess, according to his many acquaintances, was little more than a thug in gentleman's clothing. He was drunk much of the time; he was predatorily sexually active; and it is hard to take seriously the idea that his politics were the product of careful and rational thought. For just these reasons of course, he was the perfect spy—a veritable cliché, in the tradition of the Scarlet Pimpernel. But just why the British secret service (who recruited him from Cambridge) or their Soviet counterparts (who controlled him until his escape in the early '50s) should have thought that this was a man to be entrusted with sensitive and secret tasks remains a mystery.

The third of the five, the prominent art historian Anthony Blunt, may serve as perhaps the best illustration of the place these men held within the British establishment—and might have continued to hold had they not, more or less fortuitously, been unmasked. Blunt, after all, was the insider's insider: an aesthete and scholar doing the most conservative sort of curatorial, aesthetic art criticism. Here, we should not forget, was a man who ended up as the Curator of the Queen's paintings. And yet, during three long decades, he established and maintained an unwavering commitment to a political system—Stalinism—which represented at least in principle values, interests and goals transparently opposed to those he had publicly espoused throughout his career.

But even when Blunt was outed as a Soviet spy, in 1979, his standing in high society, and in the distinctive codes of that society in England, still protected him. After the Queen stripped him of his knighthood and Trinity deprived him of his honorary Fellowship, there was a move to expel him from the British Academy. A significant number of Fellows of the Academy threatened to resign were that to happen. These were not only men of the Left; there were in their number those who argued that one must distinguish between intellectual quality and political allegiance. Thus Blunt—a spy, a communist, a dissembler, a liar and a man who may have actively contributed to the exposure and death of British agents—was nonetheless deemed by some of his colleagues to be guilty of no crime serious enough to justify depriving him of the fellowship of the British Academy.

The Cambridge spies thus never incurred the stigma that attached to those found guilty of spying for Moscow in America. In the United States, spies were true outsiders: Jews, foreigners, "losers"—men and women with incomprehensible motives, unless it was the simple need for money. Such people—the Rosenbergs being the exemplary case—were severely punished: in the paranoid atmosphere of the 1950s, they were executed. I don't believe any British spy was ever thought of in those terms, much less treated so ruthlessly. If anything, their activities were romanticized in the popular mind; but above all, they were protected by their origins in the country's ruling class.

From the perspective of a foreign observer, those origins—and the betrayal implied by the crime—might be thought to have aroused greater outrage. But in practice they softened the blow. The Cambridge Five were fortunate, in a way, that they could not overcome their origins, no matter what choices they made about their politics and their lives. This is just further illustration of the spies' good fortune in being born English—at least in the twentieth century; by contrast with almost anywhere else in these decades, England was a safe country to betray or criticize. Intellectual engagement, even when carried to the point of espionage, could appear to carry far less risk than across the Channel or the Atlantic. After all, for most of the twentieth century it is hard to imagine someone in continental Europe approvingly citing E. M. Forster to the effect that one would rather betray one's country than one's friend.

While Maclean, Burgess, Philby and even Blunt paid dearly in purely personal terms for their commitments, most of the choices made by their fellow British intellectuals in those same years carried little if any cost. Eric Hobsbawm, who—perhaps unusually for a British scholar of his generation—was openly and officially communist throughout his career, only paid the relatively low price of being excluded from the Chair of Economic History in Cambridge. Forced to accept a (perfectly good) professorship at Birkbeck College, London, he had to await retirement before reaping the full rewards of a successful public intellectual life. As prices go, this would not seem particularly extortionate.

> *But surely it is not just about paying a price? The British elite is living in an entirely different world of opportunity and circumstance. Polish communists were murdered in 1937 and 1938, not by their own government, but by the Soviet leadership in the Moscow to which they had exiled themselves. Jews in Poland were killed in the early 1940s by Germans because they were Jews. Promising Polish intellectuals of Eric Hobsbawm's own generation were killed by both the Germans and the Soviets in 1939 and 1940 and by the Germans in the Warsaw Uprising in 1944. Had Hobsbawm found himself in Poland, he might readily have been killed in any one of these ways—and indeed in many others. Whereas in England, for all his prominent dissent and radical political affiliations, Hobsbawm becomes, if not the paramount then surely one of the most influential historians not just of his country but of the entire century.*

He paid no price for an allegiance which, in half of the world, would have ensured his exclusion not just from an academic career but from all forms of public life. In the other half of the world, his publicly affirmed commitment to communism might variably have been a benefit or a hindrance, but more likely both in short order. Whereas in England, his Party membership remains for most commentators little more than a passing curiosity. The same holds, to a lesser degree, for many of his contemporaries.

> *The world catches up with one. The Polish poet Alexander Wat wrote "Me from the one side, me from the other side of my pug iron*

stove"—a poem very similar in its way to T. S. Eliot's "The Waste
Land." Indeed, both works indirectly reveal a strikingly
comparable moment of development. Eliot would go on to religion,
while Wat moved, like so many Poles of his generation, to the left
and eventually Communism. But in both cases, we can see them
addressing and resolving what are essentially interior doubts. But
let us suppose, which is far from unimaginable (after all, Wat ends
up a sort of Christian), that they exchanged places. What becomes
clear is the terrifying element of contingency: from Germany
eastwards, youth and early adulthood present many more traps
and hooks with which to catch you out.

You don't need to go east: even France has the bloody meat hook of
Vichy, which catches a whole generation of French intellectuals. For that
matter, even in England you could play what were not yet risky games with
the promise of fascism in the 1930s. But these were just games. Fascism was
not remotely in a position to come to power in Great Britain. And so, just as
there were those on the left who toyed with a sympathetic engagement in
Republican Spain, on the far right we find a number of English poets and
journalists flirting with political friends from whom they could later disassociate without suffering long-term disapproval or social exclusion. Nazism
was a little different perhaps, although there was no shortage of English aristocrats and editorial writers ready as late as 1938 to defend Hitler as a bulwark against communism or disorder. But even though few cared about the
fate of Germany's Jews, aligning with a German dictatorship was still something of a stretch for an Englishman less than twenty years after the Battle of
the Somme. Italy was another matter, however, and support for Mussolini—
despite and perhaps in some measure because of his clownish behavior—
remained remarkably high.

If there was a common quality to fascist sympathy in England in the last
decade before World War II, it derived, I believe, from the modernist face
that fascism presented to foreign observers. In Italy above all, fascism was

not so much a doctrine as a symptomatic political style. It was youthful—thrusting, energetic, on the side of change and action and innovation. For a surprising number of its admirers, fascism in short was everything that they missed in the tired, nostalgic, gray world of Little England.

In this perspective, we can see that fascism was not at all the opposite of communism, as was popularly supposed on left and right alike in those years. It was, above all else, its contrast with bourgeois democracy which accounts for its appeal. When Oswald Mosley defected from the Labour government of 1929–1931, correctly charging his colleagues with a culpable inability to *act* in the face of unprecedented economic crisis, he formed a "New Party" which in due course metamorphosed into the British Union of Fascists. But note: so long as there was no fascist party of any consequence in English politics, expressing generalized sympathy for fascist "style" carried no stigma or risk. But once Mosley's Fascists, in 1936, began provoking civil violence and challenging the public authorities, that sympathy evaporated.

Was there really so little overlap between the occasional, voluntary fascist sympathies of intellectuals and the unthinking Tory view that National Socialism was a version of Germany that one could deal with?

These are issues of social, not political, distinction. The world of high Tory politics was not one into which most intellectuals were invited, nor would many of them have sought the association. Think of Tory grandees in remote country houses toasting Hitler's achievement in bringing order to Germany, admiring the Nuremburg rallies, or—more seriously—considering the case for an allegiance with the Nazi leader against the international communist threat. Such conversations did indeed take place among what Orwell would have called the stupider sort of British conservative. But intellectuals were rare in such circles and would probably have elicited scornful sneers even if they shared the views of their hosts. This, after all, is the world of

Unity Mitford: one of the Mitford girls into whose family Mosley himself had married. But the Mitfords, notwithstanding the successful literary career of two of the sisters (Nancy and Jessica), were resolutely upper class. Their interest in Hitler had little to do with his social programs, real or supposed.

It was empire that mattered most for such people. And it was their interest in preserving the British Empire which led them to suppose that a deal with Hitler authorizing the Germans to dominate the continent while leaving the British with a free hand overseas was both desirable and feasible. It was not by chance that after 1945, when Oswald Mosley could hardly revive his fascist organization in a country which prided itself on having just won an anti-fascist war, he decided instead to found a League of Empire Loyalists. The connecting thread was the belief that only empire—England's reliable white allies across the globe, together with her productive indigenous subjects in Africa and elsewhere—could protect Britain from the coming challenge of the rising world powers. Mosley, after all, was not alone in believing that London could not rely on America (already its chief economic competitor by the 1920s) and should not count on the French. Germany, in short, was the best bet. Germany might be the historical foe and her policies a touch distasteful to some, but neither consideration mattered very much.

This takes us back, in turn, to the pro-German school of imperialist thought that flourished in turn-of-the-century England, and is brilliantly dissected by Paul Kennedy in *The Rise of the Anglo-German Antagonism 1860–1914*. Before World War I there were those, Tories and Liberals alike, who reasoned that Britain's future lay in an alliance with Imperial Germany rather than with the then-emerging entente with France and Russia. If one bracketed their occasionally acerbic industrial competition (readily controlled by cartels and protection), Germany and Britain had essentially symmetrical and compatible interests. This perception remained widespread well into the 1930s; but because Germany was now Nazi, it took on a far more right-wing, anti-Semitic and, of course, anti-communist dimension. And therefore it has very little to do with the romantic modernist sympathy for fascism that occasionally surfaced in contemporary Cambridge or London.

> *This seems to suggest that Stalin's way of reasoning—that the capitalists can and will ally against the USSR—was not entirely baseless. For Stalin was right in some ways: Hitler was indeed planning to come after the Soviet Union and the bourgeois democracies were by no means averse to the prospect.*

> *The Molotov-Ribbentrop Pact of August 1939 the alliance between Hitler and Stalin, was shocking at the time. But it did buy time for the Soviet Union.*

It might have been even smarter had Stalin listened to his own spies and understood that the Germans were going to invade the Soviet Union in June 1941. But yes, certainly the Molotov-Ribbentrop Pact had the signal effect of confusing the West and blunting German aggression for a few months without obviously working to Soviet disadvantage. And we should not forget that, with a German invasion of Poland now looming, there was nothing that the western allies could do for Stalin even had they been disposed to offer him help. Here in the West we think of this as a moment of Anglo-French inadequacy when faced with the rape of Poland; but from Moscow's perspective the impotence of their western interlocutors was something that Soviet diplomacy also had to take into account.

> *The British and the French certainly don't do anything for Poland; but they do declare war on Germany—because Germany invades their Polish ally. And of course they have no Soviet ally at that point, Moscow's hand having already been revealed and played. The Soviets took advantage of the German attack to invade (eastern) Poland themselves and then strove for the ensuing*

twenty-two months to please Hitler in all possible ways. This left
Hitler free to invade Norway, the Low Countries and France, all of
which fell within a matter of weeks. Which, in turn, left
Churchill's Britain alone, facing the apparently invincible land
forces of Nazi Germany.

This brings me to a question I've been wanting to ask you from the
beginning—namely, was Winston Churchill an intellectual?

Churchill is in this as in so many other respects an unusual and interesting case. He comes from what is by British standards a major aristocratic family (the descendants of the Duke of Marlborough of Battle of Blenheim fame) but was himself the scion of a junior branch. His father, Lord Randolph Churchill, had been a significant player in late-Victorian politics; but he destroyed himself (through political miscalculation and syphilis), so his son inherited a polluted legacy. Moreover, despite being born in one of the great English palaces (Blenheim, near Oxford) and able to trace his roots further back than many British royals, Churchill was only half English—his mother was American.

Like most of his upper class peers, Winston Churchill attended a prominent public school (Harrow in his case)—and then failed. Like so many sons of lords and gentry, he joined the army—but instead of taking a commission in an elite Guards regiment, he opted to become a simple cavalry rifleman, joining up in time to take part in the last cavalry charge of the British army, at the Battle of Omdurman (Sudan) in 1898. Churchill's political career saw him switch on three different occasions between the Conservative and Liberal parties, in the course of which he rose to high cabinet rank—variously serving as Home Secretary, Chancellor of the Exchequer and Minister for the Navy, in which capacity he was responsible for the military catastrophe at Gallipoli (1915). In short, until 1940, his was the career of the over-talented outsider: too good to be ignored but too unconventional and "unreliable" to be appointed to the very highest office.

Unusually for a British politician, Churchill—whose financial situation was always precarious enough to require him to earn a living from his writings—commented with some distance upon his checkered career even as he was pursuing it. Either directly—as in *My Early Life*, or his memoirs of the First World War (which are not so much memoirs as an apologia for Churchill's own role at the time)—or in his properly journalistic writings on the Boer War (in which he took part and was briefly imprisoned and escaped), Churchill was both a participant in and a recorder of the events of his time. But then he also wrote copiously about the history of the British Empire and authored a biography of his colorful ancestor, the Duke of Marlborough. In short, Churchill contributed to history and literature while remaining actively engaged in public affairs—a combination far more familiar in France or even the U.S. than in England.

But this does not make him an intellectual. By English standards he was far too actively engaged at the very center of public policy making and public choices to be considered a dispassionate commentator; and by continental standards, of course, he was magnificently uninterested in conceptual reflection. His work consists of lengthy empirical narratives with occasional pauses to restate the story in a moral key, but little more. And yet: he was assuredly the most literary political figure in British history since William Gladstone. In any case, Churchill was unique for his time and has found no successor.

Anyone seeking "intellectuals in politics" in the image a Léon Blum in France or a Walther Rathenau in Germany will come up short if he confines his search to England. By this I do not mean that there were no intellectually gifted politicians here: but it is not their intellectual gifts for which they are best known. In a purely formal sense, Harold Wilson—the Labour Prime Minister from 1964–1970 and again from 1974–1976—was surely an intellectual. Born in 1916, he had been promoted to the rank of economics tutor at Oxford before the age of thirty and was very highly regarded in that capacity by his colleagues, before he entered politics and ended up—at the relatively young age of forty-seven—as head of the Labour Party.

In office, however, Wilson under-achieved and became the object of growing skepticism within the ranks of his own political family. By the end of his career he was widely regarded as louche, devious, dissembling, dishonest, cynical, detached and—worst of all—incompetent. To be sure, most of these attributes are compatible with membership in the intelligentsia, especially in a country where intellectuals are characteristically dismissed as "too clever by half." All the same, Wilson managed to fall between two stools: failing as a politician and disappointing his intellectual peers.

Another intellectual in English politics, but of a very different kind, was Herbert Henry Asquith: the Liberal Prime Minister from 1908 until 1916, when he was toppled by his Liberal colleague David Lloyd George and the opposition Conservatives in the middle of the First World War. Asquith was a genuine thinker, scholarly and self-reflective—a classic nineteenth-century liberal in the English sense of the word, increasingly adrift in a twentieth century setting that made little sense to him and to which he was temperamentally ill-suited. Like Wilson, but with more excuses, he too was perceived over time to have failed politically—though his early reforms and innovations paved the way for the later welfare state.

Perhaps the real difficulty facing anyone seeking intellectuals at the highest political levels in England is that the intellectual agenda which drove ideologically-configured political movements in continental Europe was quite absent in London.

What about Benjamin Disraeli?

For an earlier period, Disraeli would surely be the *locus classicus*. But it would be hard to say that Disraeli was ever pursuing an intellectual agenda, or that his purposes were fully realized in his political undertakings. He had unusually sharp political instincts, both about what was possible and what was necessary: about how much change was needed if you wished to keep the important things as they were. In this respect Disraeli is the living embodiment of the Edmund Burke–Thomas Macaulay version of English history: a story in which the country serially and successfully undertakes minor adjustments in order to avoid major transformations across the centuries.

But of course, it all depends what you mean by "minor" and "major." Disraeli was responsible for the 1867 Second Reform Act which added a million voters to the election rolls. Even if we assume that this too was a calculated release of the political safety valve—a move meant to head off popular demands for more radical reform—it still bespeaks a political intelligence beyond the norm. Disraeli, the first conservative politician to grasp the possibilities of mass electoral support and appreciate that democracy need not undermine the core powers of a ruling elite, was also unusual among his mid-Victorian contemporaries in appreciating at an early stage how much Britain would need to change if it were to remain a world power.

Disraeli had the sense that for the English to understand themselves, their own greatness and their own mission, he had to dress it up for them. That was true of Churchill as well.

Once again, understanding comes more easily to outsiders. Disraeli, remember, was born Jewish. Like Churchill—not quite so much an outsider but unquestionably a maverick—he was a gifted observer not only of his own country but his own party and his social class. One should not make too many claims for either man—Churchill in particular was deaf and blind to the inevitability of imperial decline—but each in his way had a fine appreciation for the peculiarities of the country he led. In our own times, such outsiders have been thin on the ground; I don't think anyone else meets that qualification—except, of course, Margaret Thatcher.

Mrs. Thatcher was by any definition an outsider in a party (the Conservatives) of insiders. To begin with, she was a woman. She was from the provincial lower-middle class—her father ran a grocer's store in remote Grantham. And although she did win a place at Oxford, she was quite distinctive in her choice of discipline: female chemists were rare indeed. She was to go on to build a successful career in the more socially retrograde of the two main political parties, taking over from a generation of influential men who had risen to power in the decades following the war.

While I would not go so far as to say that Mrs. Thatcher had a coherent ideological agenda, she most certainly harbored dogmatic prejudices to which radical policies could be appended according to convenience and opportunity. Although anything but an intellectual herself, Margaret Thatcher was unusually attracted to intellectual men who could assist her in justifying and describing her own instincts—so long as they were themselves outsiders and not tarred with the brush of convention. Unlike the more moderate conservatives whose policies and ambitions she so devastatingly thwarted, Mrs. Thatcher was quite unprejudiced against Jews, showing something of a predilection for them in her choice of private advisors. Finally, and once again in contrast to her conservative predecessors, she was rather sympathetic to the writings of economists—but only and egregiously those from one particular school: Hayek and the Austrians.

There is one other way to be an outsider in England, and that is to be ostentatiously religious, or Catholic. T. S. Eliot punctuates the lives of so many of the people we've discussed.

In the sixteenth century, in the course of the English Reformation and Henry VIII's seizure of Catholic lands and buildings, England's Roman Catholics were thrust into the outer darkness. And yet, the country boasts an unbroken heritage of extraordinarily influential and well-placed Catholic public figures: dukes, lords and gentry who were known to be of the Catholic persuasion but were nevertheless permitted a certain space and privilege on the understanding that they did not abuse these and made no claims upon the established (Anglican) church or the public realm. At least until the 1820s and the Catholic Emancipation Acts, English Catholics had to tread carefully: there was a reserved arena within which they could practice their faith and teach or write. But they were never fully integrated or at ease in the intellectual and political affairs of the nation.

This story is more complicated than it sounds. Anglicanism is not Protestantism. The Church of England was and is a weird animal: at its most conservative, it is far more ornate and tradition-bound than its Episcopalian brethren here in the U.S. In essence, High Anglicanism was Catholicism without the Pope (and without the Latin, until the Catholics themselves abandoned it). On the other hand, at its low end, the Anglican Church—as embodied in village communities, particularly in certain parts of eastern England where Catholicism was weakest—can resemble (except in its liturgy, long since formalized under episcopal authority) Scandinavian Protestantism: under-adorned, its authority vested in a single, often rather gaunt and morally and sartorially restrained pastor—the kind who figures so prominently in much English literature of the late nineteenth and early twentieth centuries, Protestant in all but name.

What unites this weird religion is its long-established identification with power. From that little church in a Norfolk village through the High Anglican cathedrals of Liverpool or York, this is the "Church of England." Historically, the link between church and state in England has been unusually intimate, the ruling elite overwhelmingly drawn from Anglican families and the church itself umbilically attached to the political establishment—not least via its great bishops, all of whom sit in the House of Lords and have in past times exercised real clout. The bishops and archbishops were typically born of a small network of families, reproducing across the years a class of ecclesiastical administrators who might just as easily have been army officers, imperial governors, royal ministers and so on. The establishment identity associated with Anglicanism is thus of far greater significance than its rather nebulous theological markers. This was above all an *English* church; its Christianity could at times appear almost secondary.

Eliot was to the 1930s what Matthew Arnold had been to the late Victorians: the voice of a certain moral nervousness in the face of modernity, passed through a literary and increasingly religious sensibility. We should not, however, neglect Eliot's Cambridge nemesis, the literary critic F. R. Leavis: liked and disliked in equal measure according to taste and sensibility.

Allowing for the many differences, one might compare his local standing to that of Lionel Trilling across the ocean—an influential interpreter and controller of literary taste, mixing high aesthetic judgment with occasional political intervention.

You can see the resemblance to the Bloomsbury circle in London: the very English idea that aesthetic preferences are foundational for political and (especially) moral views. To be sure, this was an indulgence that only people who had lived most of their lives in Bloomsbury or Cambridge could afford. There is something of this in Eliot too though his notion of aesthetic choices was so much broader than theirs and his moral engagement more all-embracing and, of course, constrained by an increasingly religious sensibility.

What we see at work, I believe, was a variety of approaches to the problem of restoring order and predictability to moral or aesthetic judgment. One of the concerns that would characterize the 1930s in England—and would echo down through the 1950s—was a fear of drowning in "relativism," whether intellectual or political. Like Sartre, strange as the comparison may sound, Eliot (and Leavis, so influential upon the generation of my teachers) spoke for the view that one must make choices, that not caring was no longer an option and that normative criteria for judgment needed to be identified, though it was not always clear whence they should be retrieved.

The emerging sense, in a variety of aesthetic and literary keys, that you needed to say what is right, what is wrong and why things are thus, was an important feature of the English age of commitment, in literature and politics alike. At times this sensibility edges into faith, an aspect of those years which we tend to underplay in secular retrospect.

3.

FAMILIAL SOCIALISM: POLITICAL MARXIST

My paternal grandfather, Enoch Yudt, was born in Warsaw, today the capital of Poland, then a westerly metropolis of the Russian Empire. Like so many young Jews of that time and place, Enoch was a socialist. His sympathies lay with the *Bund*, the first large socialist party in the Russian Empire. It was a Jewish party, operating in Yiddish, the native language of most east European Jews, but stood for socialist revolution in all of the Russian Empire, from Europe to the Pacific. His son, my father Joe Judt, left school at fourteen to become an odd-jobs man, first in Dublin then in London. He too was a socialist. As a boy he had belonged to *Hashomer Hatzair*, the socialist-Zionist youth movement committed to bringing young Jews to Palestine in order to build socialism there. This was a very different concept from the socialism of the *Bund*, which was quite insistent that Jews should change the social order where they were, rather than emigrate to exotic lands.

At some point before the Second World War, when my father was in his late teens, he moved on to the Socialist Party of Great Britain, a tiny Marxist splinter party based in London that drew heavily on Jewish autodidacts such as himself. By now he had more or less abandoned the Zionism of his youth, although he would experience moments of reversion. I was born in 1948, the year Israel was established and Czechoslovakia went communist, completing the Eastern Bloc under Soviet domination. I grew up in the world of the Cold War, taking for granted that the east European countries where my family came from were now and forever communist, their regimes sustained by the Soviet Union. Jewish politics and life were no longer attached to those places, but debates about Marxism certainly were.

My father and I would watch A. J. P. Taylor giving his hour-long, unscripted, brilliantly-presented television lectures on European history, while my father offered *Marxisant* criticisms from the armchair. For my thirteenth birthday my father bought me the three volumes of Isaac Deutscher's biography of Leon Trotsky, probably on the grounds that it was time for me to learn to distinguish the good guys from the bad (Stalin of course being the main villain in the story). Trotsky was an important figure for the socialist Left in those years. After serving as Lenin's closest collaborator in the Russian Revolution, he had been outsmarted by Stalin in the struggle for the succession that followed Lenin's death.

Deutscher's very sympathetic biography of Trotsky, which my father also read, helped sustain the legend of a Communism that might have been. People like my father were disposed to think well of Trotsky in large measure because they saw Lenin as misguided rather than malevolent: for them, the rot began with Stalin. It was not perhaps without pertinence that many of Trotsky's supporters and allies had been Jews. These biographical volumes were the first heavyweight books I was ever given. Much later, I reciprocated by offering my father a collection of Deutscher's works which included the famous essay "The Non-Jewish Jew." I am not sure that he was entirely pleased.

Deutscher's subject matter was already familiar to me. I think I began to read Marx at around that age; my father owned an abbreviated edition of *Capital* published by the Socialist Party of Great Britain. I also read *Wage-*

Labor and Capital; *Value, Price, and Profit*; Engels on *Socialism: Utopian and Scientific*; *The Communist Manifesto*; and *Anti-Dühring*, which I didn't understand at all. I suppose I was reading Marx through my teen years, with appropriately limited comprehension, about five years ahead of my contemporaries. I read Eric Hobsbawm's *Age of Revolution* when I was about fifteen, not long after it was first published in 1962. My father of course encouraged me to read George Orwell, the great English critic of totalitarianism, whose essays and novels I devoured in those years. I also read Arthur Koestler's *Darkness at Noon,* and his essay on communist disillusion in *The God That Failed.* These were the core texts of a dissenting left-wing education in the postwar decades and I was the lucky neophyte beneficiary.

It was always understood, at home, that Soviet communism was not Marxism, and that the Soviet communists, from Stalin onwards in any case, were thus not proper Marxists. My father used to regale me with his memories of anti-fascist demonstrations in the late 1930s in the East End of London. Communist organizers, he explained, would send people out to find and fight the fascists, before heading off to the café to await the outcome. Communists in this way of thinking were people who let the workers go out to get killed in their name and then reap the benefits afterwards. As a result, and quite unjustly, I learned to think of communist organizers as cynical and cowardly. This would have been a familiar view among members of the Socialist Party of Great Britain in the 1940s, where my father had most of his political acquaintances. By the 1960s however, my father and many of his SPGB contemporaries had retreated into a kind of disabused Marxist vernacular, which could explain anything and everything while demonstrating how everyone else had compromised and was selling out. So my teenage enthusiasm for the Labour Party, when it at last won the general election in 1964, received a cold shower at home: you weren't to expect anything from *that* lot.

My mother had the kind of attitude to my father's politics and ideas that, *toutes proportions gardées*, Heda Margolius Kovály showed to her husband's illusions in *Under a Cruel Star*, her incomparable memoir of life in communist Czechoslovakia: men are deluded, they tell themselves stories and believe in abstractions, whereas we women can see straight. But then Kovály's marriage to the Czech Jewish communist Rudolf Margolius was perhaps a closer one than that of my parents. Even after he was show-tried and sentenced to death in 1952, Rudolf remembered during his last visit with his wife to tell her that she looked beautiful.

By 1968, the year of Marxism's last chance in European politics, I was an undergraduate student at Cambridge. Unlike some of my friends, I was not on the front lines, nor did I play a leadership role. If I was angry, in those years, it was about the Vietnam War, a conventional if strongly-felt opinion at the time. I took part in the big Vietnam demonstrations of the late sixties; I remember very well in particular the famous Grosvenor Square march and the unconvincing assault on the American Embassy. I also took part in meetings and rallies in Cambridge and London. But this was England, and what that means can be described thus.

I was at a demonstration in Cambridge against Denis Healey, who was the governing Labour Party's Defence Secretary at a time when Labour was at least in principle supporting Lyndon Johnson's war. Healey was in his car leaving Cambridge after a lecture, driving south along Trumpington Street. A lot of students, myself included, were running alongside, jumping up and down, and screaming; a friend of mine, Peter Kellner, even leaped onto the car and began banging on the roof. The car got away, of course, and there we were, stuck at the wrong end of Trumpington Street with college dinner time fast approaching. So we started to run back to the city center. I found myself running alongside one of the policemen who had been assigned to control the demonstration. As we were trotting along, he turned to me and inquired, "So how was the demonstration, Sir?" And I, finding nothing bizarre or absurd in his inquiry, turned and responded, "I think it went quite well, don't you?" And then we continued on our way. This was no way to make a revolution.

I did go to Paris in spring 1968, and was swept away like everyone else. However, my residual socialist-Marxist formation made me instinctively suspicious of the notion, popular in France, that students might now be a—*the*—the revolutionary class. So whereas I was very impressed by the Renault strikes and other occupations of that year, I could never quite get enthused about Dany Cohn-Bendit and "Sous le pavé, la plage."

This distinction between leftist politics and mere student activism was first made explicit to me that autumn by the historian Eric Hobsbawm. In 1968, I was the secretary of the King's College Historical Society, as Eric had been many years before. Hobsbawm was in many important respects a true and loyal Kingsman: the College, where he had been a student in the 1930s and a fellow through the mid-1950s, meant as much to him in certain areas of his life as did the Communist Party with which he is more famously associated. He came to King's and delivered a subtle political sermon, implicitly dismissing the revolutionary youth of that year and inverting Marx's famous Eleventh Thesis on Feuerbach: sometimes the point really is not so much to change the world as to understand it.

This struck a chord: it had always been the analytical Karl Marx, the political commentator rather than the revolutionary prognosticator, who had most appealed to me. If you asked me which one essay by Marx I would recommend to a student, both in order to appreciate Marx's talents and grasp the central message, I think it would be *The Eighteenth Brumaire*, followed closely perhaps by *The Class Struggles* and *The Civil War in France*. Marx was a polemical commentator of genius, whatever the shortcomings of his broader theoretical speculations. For this reason, I was largely unmoved by the debates of the 1960s between advocates of the "young" and the "old" Marx, the philosopher of alienation and the theorist of political economy. For me, Marx was always and above all an observer of political events and social reality.

Let's start with some earlier political Marxists, the theorists and party men and women of the turn of the nineteenth and twentieth centuries. These were people who read Marx and each other and who simultaneously harbored authentic hopes of coming to power by way of revolution, general strike or perhaps even (though this was

then controversial) elections. This was the period of the Second
International, from 1889 to 1917, roughly the time between
Marx's death (in 1883) and Lenin's revolution. These were people
who were part of the establishment intellectually. They were often
university educated and spoke the philosophical language of their
time; they were in general rather confident about politics, not only
in the simple sense that they believed that time was on their side,
but also in that they thought that they could understand the order
of things. And also they were angry, and were articulate about their
anger—which distinguishes them from, let's say, intellectuals of our
day, who tend either to be angry or articulate but rarely both.

There is a distinct political generation, and a distinct profile of political parties. Think of the appearance of the Social Democratic Federation under Henry Hyndman in London, the rise of the Social Democrats in Germany under Wilhelm Liebknecht and August Bebel and Karl Kautsky and Eduard Bernstein, and the supremacy of Jean Jaurès in the French party, not to mention the Italians, the Dutch, the Belgians, the Poles, and of course the Russians.

Where did they come from? This was the first truly post-religious generation. If you went back a generation you'd be in the middle of the Darwin debates, or the Christian-socialist debates, or the religious revival debates of the late Romantic years. A number of these people talk about their emergence as political or thinking beings as having been bathed in the clear afterglow of what Nietzsche would have called the death of God. It's not just that they don't believe; the question of faith is no longer the most important thing for them. Whether they are post-liberated Jews or anti-clerical French Catholics or non-practicing Social Democratic Protestants from Northern Europe, they are clear of the older, purely moral terms in which social injustice had been critiqued. It seems to me you couldn't otherwise explain the obsessive materialism of Georgii Plekhanov and the Russians or of Jaurès and the French Left if you don't see this cohort as a generation who sought, with great energy, to think of society as a set of *secular* problems.

If there was a transcendental consideration in politics, it was not the meaning of society, but rather its purposes. This was a subtle but crucial shift. We can see it clearly if we take a detour into English liberalism. The liberal break from faith began obviously in the Enlightenment, where faith as a constituent part of the framework for thinking about human purposes simply evaporates. But there's a second stage, which is very important in England (and France): the collapse of actual religious belief in the third quarter of the nineteenth century. The new liberals, born into that milieu, recognized that theirs was a world without faith, an ungrounded world. And so they tried to ground it in new philosophical ways of thinking. Nietzsche touches on an aspect of this when he writes that men need realist grounds for moral action, and yet they can't have them because they cannot agree on what those grounds would be. They have no basis for those grounds—God being dead—and yet without them they have no grounds for action at all.

Thus Keynes, in *My Early Beliefs*, writes about his enthusiasm for G. E. Moore, the Cambridge philosopher. Moore, it seems fair to say, is what Nietzsche would have looked like had he been born in England. There's no God, there's radical non-necessity in all ethical matters, and yet we have to come up with rules to obey, even if they are only for the elite. So this elite speaks to itself about the rules of its own behavior and then the reasons that it can give the world at large for following them. In England this produced a selective adaptation of utilitarian ethics after John Stuart Mill: *we* will have Kantian ethical imperatives, but the rest of humanity will make do with utilitarian grounds for following them, because that will be our gift to the world.

That is what Second International Marxism looks like. It is a set of self-ascribed, neo-Kantian rules and norms about what is wrong and what should be, but with a scientific penumbra for the purpose of explaining—to themselves and others—how to get from here to there with the confidence that History is on your side. Strictly speaking one cannot extract from Marx's account of capitalism a reason why socialism should (in a moral sense) happen. Lenin understood this, recognizing that socialist "ethics" were a hangover from religious authority and a substitute for it. Today of course such ethics are most of what remains of social-democracy, but in the days of the Second International they posed a threat to socialism's hard historical realism.

Marxism held a distinctive attraction, not only for that first generation of educated, intellectual critics, but right up to the 1960s. Marxism, we tend to forget, is a marvelously compelling account of how history works, and why it works. It is a comforting promise to anyone to learn that History is on your side, that progress is in your direction. This claim distinguished Marxism in all its forms from other contemporary radical products at the time. Anarchists had no real theory of how the system worked; reformists had no story to tell about radical transformation; liberals had no account for the anger that one should feel at the present state of affairs.

You must be right about religion, and I wonder if you'd agree that it plays out in two distinct and opposing ways.

One is secular ethics: the Kantian revival of the late nineteenth century in the German-speaking lands as a substitute for religion, articulated best in the Second International by the Austro-Marxists in Vienna in the 1890s and 1900s, which the Italian Marxist Antonio Gramsci was smart enough to see needed to be institutionally organized. Hence Gramsci's idea of hegemony: in effect, the party intellectuals have to self-consciously reproduce the church hierarchy, thereby institutionalizing the social reproduction of ethics.

But then there's also the eschatology: the idea of final salvation, the return of man to his own nature, all of these incredibly motivating ideas for which one can make sacrifices in the secular world—the priority of sacrifice is Lenin's idea, essentially. And it seems to me that each of these two concepts are satisfying substitutes for religion, but that they take you to very different places.

That's right. And they arise in varying strength in different places. So the eschatological line of reasoning is very unappealing to Scandinavian Protestants, for example. It's not enough to say, as one does, that there was no reason for communism to do well in Scandinavia because social democracy had already bitten deep into the dominant peasant-worker constituency in places like Sweden. That is true, but it's not a sufficient explanation. In Scandinavia there was never going to be—except briefly in Norway among an angry fringe of neglected fishermen—a constituency for all-or-nothing, throw-it-all-over, once-and-for-all politics.

Nor was there going to be a subliminal drive for neo-religious organization. The organizational form—the Gramscian notion of hegemony, the idea that the party must substitute for organized religion, complete with hierarchy, elite, a liturgy and a catechism—goes some way to explaining why organized communism in the Leninist model does so much better in Catholic or Orthodox countries than in Protestant ones. Communism would always do better in Italy and France (and briefly in Spain) than social democracy.

The usual argument about the Catholic countries is that there was no substantial labor force capable of evolving the trade union as a form of organization within which a mass left party could take shape. But this is not quite true. There was a very large number of blue-collar workers in France, who were at various points quite well organized. It's just that they were not organized *politically*. The political organization of the working class in the Paris Red Belt, for example, was unquestionably an achievement of the communists; until then, the *syndicats* (trade unions) carried very little clout in large measure because of the absence of any organic link to any political party. They were quite suspicious of socialism precisely because of its organizational ambitions.

The evidence *a contrario* comes from the English case. There you have an advanced, skilled labor movement fully formed by 1870; from the 1880s onwards—i.e., at about the same time as social democracy was taking shape—an additional and increasingly significant unskilled labor force emerged in the larger cities: turbulent, disadvantaged and easily mobilized. The outcome was a rapidly expanding trade union movement, more or less legal from the early 1880s, whose political activities were channeled into a Labour Representation Committee in 1900 and became a full-scale Labour Party six years later, dominated and financed by its union masters for the rest of the century. But—in spite, or perhaps because of, the disproportionately Methodist and dissenting origins of the Labour leaders of those years—both the religious eschatology and the ecclesiastical organization that character-ized continental radicalism were altogether absent.

Isn't part of the secret of Marxism that it was surprisingly compatible with native national traditions of radical politics?

Marxism was the deep structure of European radical thought. More than he realized, Marx himself synthesized many early nineteenth-century trends in social criticism and economic theory: he was, for example, both an exemplary French political pamphleteer and a minor commentator on clas-sical British economics. And thus, this German student of Hegelian meta-physics bequeathed to the European Left the only version of its own heritage compatible with local traditions of radical anger and offering a story that could transcend them.

In England, for example: the moral economy of the eighteenth-century radical artisan or disinherited farmer fed directly into Marxism by insist-ing upon a narrative centered on capitalism's destructive creativity and the human wreckage left in its wake. Here, as in Marxism itself, we encounter the story of a lost world that we might yet regain. Of course, the older (and mor-alized) versions—in the pen of William Cobbett for example—emphasize *destruction*, above all the corrosion of human relations; Marx, on the other hand, turns that very destruction to advantage through his vision of a higher form of human experience that can emerge from the detritus of capitalism.

In this respect at least, Marx's eschatology is itself but an add-on to the profound sense of loss and disruption that early industrialization brought about. And thus, unbeknownst to himself, Marx furnished a template within which people could represent and recognize the story that they had been telling for some time. This is one source of Marxism's appeal. A faulty account of the workings of capitalism, together with a guarantee of future outcomes—few of which transpired—would not in itself have been able to capture the imagination of intellectuals, workers, political opportunists and social activists across four different continents over more than a century if its sentimental roots had not already been present.

> *It's the magic of Hegel, though, isn't it, Tony? Because what Marx*
> *is combining, in what you say, is an essentially conservative*
> *view, a spiritual view of the past, with the dialectical argument*
> *that what is bad for us is actually good for us. Think of Engels*
> *writing about the family, for example, but also Marx's idea about*
> *species-nature before it is corrupted by property: here you have*
> *descriptions of human integrity and harmony in the prehistorical*
> *or nonhistorical past that give pause even today thanks to their*
> *sheer intensity. Through Hegelian dialectics, nostalgia is combined*
> *with the capacity not merely to accept but to welcome whatever is*
> *destroying the beauty of the past. You can embrace the city, and you*
> *can embrace the factory: both represent creative destruction.*
> *Capitalism may seem to oppress us, and it may seem to alienate us,*
> *and it certainly pauperizes us, but nevertheless it has its own*
> *beauty and is an objective achievement, which we will later be able*
> *to exploit as we return our own nature to ourselves.*

Remember, this gives the Marxist a distinct advantage in dialectical confrontations. To liberals and progressives who assert that all is for the best, Marx offers a powerful narrative of suffering and loss, deterioration and destruction. Of conservatives, who would agree with this and augment the assertion by insisting upon the superiority of the past, Marx was of course contemptuous: these changes, however unappealing in the medium term, are the necessary and in any case unavoidable price we pay for a better future. They are what they are, but they are worth it.

> *The appeal of Marxism also connects both with Christianity and with Darwinism: both of them, in different ways, overtaken by philosophical and political sentiment by the last years of the nineteenth century. I think we are moving towards agreeing that socialists left them behind only to reinvent them in various ways. Think of Christianity and the meaning ascribed to Christ's suffering: its purpose is vouchsafed to us on this imperfect earth only to the extent that salvation awaits in the hereafter. As for Darwin's popularizers (and his vulgarizers, including Friedrich Engels): evolution, they insisted, was not merely compatible with a vision of political change but insisted upon it—species arise, they compete. Life—like nature—is quite bloody, red in tooth and claw, but the extinction of species (no less than classes) makes moral as well as scientific sense. It leads to better species and thus at the end of the day we are where we are, and things turn out for the best.*

By the early twentieth century, the Engelsian version was by far the more influential. Engels outlived Marx by thirteen years: long enough to implant his own readings into the received version of popular Marxist texts. He wrote more clearly than his friend. And he had the good fortune to be writing just after popular scientific thought had entered the political and educational mainstream thanks to Herbert Spencer and others. For example, Engels's "Socialism: Utopian and Scientific" is intelligible to any educated fourteen-year-old. But that of course is the problem. Engels's bowdlerization of nineteenth-century evolutionary theory reduced Darwin to a cautionary tale of everyday life. Marxism was now an accessible story of everything: no longer a political narrative, an economic analysis or even a social critique, but little short of a theory of the universe.

In its original forms, the neo-religiosity of Marx entailed a telos, an endpoint from which the whole story took its sense: it knew where it was going. In Engels's hands, it is constricted into a simple ontology: life and history come whence they come and go where they must, but if they have a discernable meaning it is certainly not derived from their future prospects. In this respect, and notwithstanding his many virtues, Engels resembled Herbert Spencer: mechanistic, over-ambitious in his claims, all-embracing in his vision, welding together from ill-assorted materials a story that could be applied to anything from the history of clocks to the physiology of fingers. This all-purpose account proved magnificently serviceable: it was at the same time accessible to all and could justify the exclusive interpretive authority of a clerical elite. Lenin's distinctive party model would be unthinkable without it. But for just this reason we have Engels to blame for the absurdities of dialectical materialism.

> *Let's return to your point that Marxism has more resonance in*
> *Catholic countries than Protestant countries because of certain*
> *kinds of ritual practices which have to do with how one uses*
> *language and in what settings. Can one make that kind of*
> *argument for Judaism and its engagement with radical politics?*

That Marxism is a secular religion seems self-evident. But just *which* religion is it tracking? That is not always so clear. It comprises much of traditional Christian eschatology: the fall of man, the Messiah, his suffering and humanity's vicarious redemption, the salvation, the rise and so on. Judaism is there too, but less in substance than style. In Marx and in some of the more interesting later Marxists (Rosa Luxemburg, perhaps, or Léon Blum)—and without question in the interminable German Socialist debates conducted in the pages of *Die Neue Zeit*—we can readily discern a variety of *pilpul*, the playful dialectical self-indulgence at the heart of rabbinical judgments and traditional Jewish moralizing and storytelling.

Think, if you will, of the sheer cleverness of the categories: the way in which Marxist interpretations can invert and slide athwart one another such that what is turns out not to be, and what was returns in a new guise. Destruction is creative, while preservation becomes destructive. The great shall be small, and present truths are doomed to perish as past illusions. When I mention these rather obvious aspects of Marx's intentions and inheritance, to people who have themselves studied the man and even written about him, they frequently grow uncomfortable. Not infrequently, they are Jewish and are rendered ill-at-ease by the placing of emphasis upon Marx's own Jewish background, as though one had alluded to family matters.

I'm reminded of the scene in Jorge Semprún's memoirs, *Quel beau dimanche*. After his family was expelled from Spain, he, at the age of twenty, was swept into the French Resistance and subsequently arrested as a communist. Sent to Buchenwald, he was taken under the wing of an old German communist—which doubtless explains his survival. At one point Semprún asks the older man to explain "dialectics" to him. And the answer comes back: "C'est l'art et la manière de toujours retomber sur ses pattes, mon vieux"—the art and the technique of always landing on your feet. And so it is with rabbinical rhetorics: the art and the technique—above all the art—of landing on your feet in a solid position of authority and conviction. To be a revolutionary Marxist was to make a virtue of your rootlessness, not least the absence of religious roots, while clinging—even if only half knowingly—to a style of reasoning which would have been very familiar to every Hebrew school student.

People forget that Jewish socialists were earlier and better organized than others in the Russian Empire. The Bund actually predates and for some time overshadowed attempts to create a Russian party. Indeed, to define his own position Lenin had to separate his followers from the Bund—a more important split than the better-known one between the Bolsheviks and the Mensheviks.

How do you see Lenin operating in this generation, in this milieu, in the Second International?

The Russians were a rather uncomfortable presence in the Second International, which was a collection of Marxist parties generally better integrated into national political systems than Russian radicals could possibly be within the tsarist autocracy. Questions of participation in bourgeois governments, the dominant issue in the International on the eve of the First World War, were of no interest to the subjects of an autocratic empire.

The Russian Marxists were themselves deeply divided between the materialist, German-style social democratic majority—exemplified by the older Plekhanov—and a radical activist minority led by the younger Lenin. This is, when you think about it, a conventional and familiar division among opponents of all authoritarian societies: between those who are willing to credit the good faith of an authoritarian ruler's marginal reforms, and those for whom such reforms are the greatest danger of all—they weaken and divide the forces seeking more radical change.

Drawing from Marxism, Lenin reinterpreted, revised and thus revived the native Russian tradition of revolution. In the previous generation revolutionary Slavophiles had indulged the pleasing thought that there was a distinct Russian story and a distinctively Russian trajectory to any radical action in that country. Some of them endorsed terrorism as a way to preserve the distinctive virtues of Russian society while undermining the autocracy. Though Lenin was impatient with the long-standing Russian heritage of activism, revolution by the act, nihilism, assassination etc., he insisted upon preserving the accompanying emphasis on voluntaristic action. But his voluntarism was girded by a Marxist vision of coming revolutions.

But Lenin was no less dismissive of the Russian social democrats who shared his distaste for pointless violence. In the Russian tradition, the opponents of the Slavophiles were the Westernizers, who essentially believed that Russia's problem was its backwardness. Russia had no distinct virtues; the goal of Russians should be to move the country onto the path of development already laid down by more westerly European countries. The Westernizers also took up Marxism, inferring from Marx and the political evolutionists that whatever had happened and would happen in the

West came first and in a purer form. Capitalism, the labor movement and the socialist revolution would all be experienced in the advanced countries in the first instance; in their Russian form they might come slower and later but would be worth waiting for—an attitude which aroused in Lenin paroxysms of rhetorical contempt. Thus the Bolshevik leader managed to combine a Western analysis with traditional Russian radicalism.

This used to be thought evidence of sheer theoretical brilliance, but I am not so sure. Lenin was a superb tactician and not much more, but in the Second International you could not be important unless you were of theoretical standing and thus Lenin presented himself and was advertised by his admirers as a Marxist dialectician of genius.

I wonder if Lenin's success doesn't also have to do with a certain audacity about the future. Lenin treated Marx as a determinist, a scientist of history. The more intelligent Marxists of the age—Gramsci, Antonio Labriola, Stanisław Brzozowski and György Lukács—refused to follow suit (though Lukács later changed his mind). But in this respect Lenin's was the dominant reading, following Engels.

Then Lenin decided that "scientists of history" are allowed not just to observe the experiment but to intervene in it, to nudge things along. After all, if we know what the results are in advance, why not get there more quickly, especially if the results are so very much to be desired. But then, believing in the grand idea gives you confidence about the present meaning of otherwise small, trivial and unglamorous facts.

This in turn told against the Kantian forms of Marxism, still widespread in those years: attempts to furnish Marxism with its own, self-sufficient ethics. For Lenin, ethics are retroactively instrumental. Little lies, small deceptions, insignificant betrayals and passing dissimulations will all make sense in the light of later

> *results and will be rendered morally acceptable by them. And what*
> *is true for small things ends up applying to big ones too.*

You don't even have to be confident about the future. The question is whether in principle you agree to allow the account to be rendered in the name of the future, or whether you believe that accounts should be closed at the end of each day.

A further distinction of consequence concerns those making future-dependent calculations on their own behalf or behalf of others, and those making such calculations and feeling at liberty to impose them on others. It is one thing to say that I am willing to suffer now for an unknowable but possibly better future. It is quite another to authorize the suffering of others in the name of that same unverifiable hypothesis. *This*, in my view, is the intellectual sin of the century: passing judgment on the fate of others in the name of their future as you see it, a future in which you may have no investment, but concerning which you claim exclusive and perfect information.

> *There are at least two ways of reasoning from the present to the*
> *future. One is to start from an image of the future and then*
> *working one's way back to the present, and then saying that one*
> *knows what the stages must be. Another is to start with the present*
> *and then to say, wouldn't it be just a bit better if the near future*
> *were something like the present but improved in a certain definable*
> *respect. And that seems to allow a distinction between policy*
> *planning and communist revolution.*

I agree that this distinction is significant. But you are slipping on a slight historical impediment: *both* of these ways of thinking about public policy have their roots in a single Enlightenment project.

Let us take the case of a classic nineteenth-century liberal like David Lloyd George. His innovative taxation projects, like the national insurance policies he introduced in the liberal governments of 1906 to 1911, entail a certain set of uninterrogated assumptions: certain sorts of present actions may reasonably be expected to generate desirable outcomes, even at the expense of short-term cost or political unpopularity. Thus even Lloyd George finds himself, as any coherent reformer must, implicitly claiming that his present actions are and only can be justified by future benefits that men would be foolish to oppose.

In this sense, there is no deep epistemological chasm separating socialism (or at least social democracy) from liberalism. Both, however, are quite distinct from a public policy based obsessively upon mathematically calculated planning devices. The latter only justify themselves to the extent that they can claim perfect or near-perfect knowledge of future outcomes (not to mention present information). Since neither present nor future information—whether about economics or anything else—is ever vouchsafed us in perfect form, planning is inherently delusory, and the more all-embracing the plan, the more delusory its claims (much the same can be, but rarely is, said of the notion of perfect or efficient markets).

But whereas liberalism or social democracy do not rise or fall upon the success of their claims on the future, communism does. Which is why I believe that the collapse of social democracy as a model, as an idea, as a grand narrative, in the wake of communism's disappearance, is unjust as well as unfortunate. It is also bad news for liberals, since whatever can be said against social democratic ways of conceiving of public affairs can also be charged against liberals.

Let me take a stab at epistemologically separating liberalism from Marxism. Liberalism starts with optimistic assumptions about human nature, but in practice it's easy to slide down a slope, where one learns that one should be a bit more pessimistic, which requires a bit more intervention, a bit more condescension, a bit more elitism, and so on. And that is, in fact, the history of liberalism, at least to the new liberalism of the early twentieth century with its acceptance of state intervention.

Whereas liberalism assumes an optimism about human
nature that erodes a bit with experience, Marxism, thanks to its
Hegelian heritage, assumes at least one non-contingent fact: our
alienation. The Marxist view goes something like this: our nature
is rather bad, but it could be rather good. The source of both the
condition and the possibility are private property, a contingent
variable. In short, change is truly at our disposal, and in a
striking form: with revolution comes an end not merely to the
regime of property but also and thereby to injustice, loneliness
and the badly lived lives. Because such a future is at our
disposal, nature itself becomes fungible—or rather, our present
unsatisfactory condition becomes unnatural. *In the light of such*
a vision, almost any radical step and authoritarian attitude
become imaginable and even desirable—a conclusion a liberal
simply cannot entertain.

Look, this epistemological and moral chasm does not separate liberals from Marxists so much as it divides Marxists among themselves. Thus, if we examine the past 130 years or so, we see that the most important line was the one separating Marxists who were attracted to the most extreme version of this story (especially in their youth) but who ultimately did not accept its implications—and thus, in the end, its premises—and those for whom it remained credible to the end, consequences and all. The notion that everything is or else it isn't—that everything is either one thing or another but cannot be both at the same time, that if something (e.g., torture) is bad then it cannot be dialectically rendered good by virtue of its results: this is and always was an un-Marxist thought and was duly castigated, as you know, as "Revisionism." Rightly so, because such epistemological empiricism has its roots in liberal political thought and represents—indeed always represented—a clean break with the religious style of reasoning which lies at the core of Marxism's appeal.

All the same, for much of the past century many social democrats who would have been horrified to think of themselves as anything other than Marxist—much less as "liberal"—were unable to make the ultimate move into retroactive necessitarianism. In most cases, they had the good fortune to avoid the choice. In Scandinavia, accession to power was open to social democrats without any need to overthrow or repress existing authorities. In Germany, those who were not willing to compromise with constitutional or moral constraints took themselves out of the social democratic consensus.

In France, the question was irrelevant thanks to the compromises imposed by republican politics and in England it was redundant thanks to the marginality of the radical left. Paradoxically, in all these countries, self-styled Marxists could continue to tell themselves stories: they could persist in the belief that the Marxist historical narrative informed their actions, without facing the implications of taking that claim seriously.

But in other places—of which Russia was the first and exemplary instance—access to power was indeed open to Marxists precisely because of their uncompromising claims upon history and other people. And so, following the Bolshevik Revolution of 1917, there was a sharp and enduring schism between those who would not digest the human consequences of their own theories, and those for whom these same consequences were nasty in just the way they had thought they would be, and all the more convincing for that reason: it's really hard; we've really got to make difficult choices; we have no choice but to do bad things; this is a revolution; if we are in the omelette-making business, this is not the moment to coddle the eggs. In other words, this is a break with the past and with our enemies, justified and explained by an all-embracing logic of human transformation. Marxists for whom all of this suggested mere repression were (not altogether unreasonably) accused of failing to grasp the implications of their own doctrine and condemned to the dustbin of History.

The thing that I find attractive about Karl Kautsky, the man who—until 1917—had been the intellectual authority of socialist

Europe, is that when the Russian Revolution breaks out he does not
simply stop thinking and swallow the consequences. Instead, like
other less prominent Marxist intellectuals, he subjects Lenin's
actions to the grid of a habitual and long-established Marxist
analysis. In contrast to certain other socialist leaders, he cannot
merely decide to believe that the Bolshevik Revolution was Marxist
because Lenin said so.

That's right. Karl Kautsky and Eduard Bernstein—who until 1917 had been at odds over the divisive squabbles concerning revisionism that had characterized prewar German socialist debates—could neither of them digest the implications of the Russian actions for critical Marxist thought (it is perhaps worth mentioning here that each in his way had been closer to Engels, and thus to conventional Marxism in earlier years, than anyone else).

Rosa Luxemburg, who had been critical of Kautsky and Bernstein alike for their quietist response to her radical urgency, was a different case. She was at least as conscious as them of the shortcomings of Leninism—indeed her critique of the Bolsheviks was perhaps the most intellectually rigorous of all—but unlike her German colleagues, she continued to insist upon the possibility and necessity of a radical break with the past: but on very different terms from those laid down by Lenin.

Faith in the possibility of such a break seems to be central, even as
late as 1917, especially as late as 1917.

By analogy with a medieval or early modern Christian religious
view of the world, what really matters is your salvation. If I am a
believer I should care more about your mortal soul than I should
care about your preferences, I should try to save you. Even if that
means torturing you, even if that means, in the end, killing you; if
I could save your soul, I would have done not only the right thing
but also that which it is self-evident that I should do.

That's a style of reasoning from which liberalism really does separate itself. That is, it takes people's purposes as emerging from them individually and as being empirically discernable to others and binding upon them. It was Hegelianism that introduced into Marx's thought the discernability of the deeper purpose and meaning of things, and thence into the Leninist understanding (such as it was) of the Marxist heritage.

In this way, the ultimate purposes of history—attained and understood in the light of the Revolution—became homologous with the immortal soul: to be saved at any price. This, then, was about more than just faith or belief in a trivial sense. For decades, it ascribed to "revolution" a mystery and meaning that could and did justify all sacrifices—especially those of others and the bloodier the better.

In order to understand why so many people attached themselves and their lives to Leninism and to the Soviet Union after the revolution of 1917, you have to think of community and historical setting as well as faith. The communist mirage is much more all-embracing than mere social democracy—democracy with the welfare state attached. Its vaulting ambitions appealed to people who thought in terms of holistic accounts of history and who generalized to the point of abstraction the relationship between social goals and individual commitment. No one ever talked of the god of social democracy failing for them. But the god of communism failing is a much larger story—and it is, of course, precisely about the loss of faith.

Yes, it's as though after the Russian Revolution of 1917 the Bolsheviks monopolized the mysticism. Why did faith come so easily to the fellow travelers, to those who identified with the Soviet Union during its bloodiest moments?

The story of the Soviet Union for those who had faith in it, whether as communists or as progressive fellow travelers, was actually not related to what they saw. To ask why people who went there did not see the truth is to miss the point. The majority of people who understood what was taking place in the Soviet Union did not need to go there to see it. Whereas those who went to the Soviet Union as true believers usually came back in the same condition (André Gide was a famous and rare exception).

In any event, the kind of truth that a believer was seeking was not testable by reference to contemporary evidence but only to future outcomes. It was always about believing in a future omelet that would justify an infinite number of broken eggs in the present. If you *ceased* to believe, then you were not simply abandoning a piece of social data which you had apparently misread hitherto; you were abandoning a story that could alone justify any data one wished so long as the future payoff was guaranteed.

Communism also offered an intense feeling of community with fellow believers. In the first volume of his memoirs, the French poet Claude Roy recalls his youthful fascism. The book is called *Moi*. But the second volume, which deals with his communist years, is significantly titled *Nous*. That is symptomatic. Communist thinkers felt part of a community of like-feeling intellectuals, which gave them the sense that not only were they doing the right thing, but also that they were moving in the direction of history. "We" were doing it, not just "me." This overcame the idea of the lonely crowd notion and placed the individual communist at the center, not only of a historical project, but of a collective process.

And it's interesting how often the memoirs of the disillusioned are cast in terms of the *loss* of community, as well as the loss of faith. The hard thing was not opening your eyes to what Stalin was doing, but breaking with all the other people who had believed it along with you. And so this combination of faith and the very considerable attractions of shared allegiance gave communism something that no other political movement could boast.

Of course, different groups of thinkers were drawn to communism for different reasons. One generation, born around 1905, people like Arthur Koestler, was attracted to Leninism in its earliest years and disillusioned at the latest by Stalin's show trials in 1936 or the Molotov-Ribbentrop Pact in 1939. That generation is thus quite different from those who were seduced by the image of the victorious Red Army in the Second World War, by the resistance heroism of communist parties (real and imagined) and by the sense that if America was the alternative, and America stood for capitalism in its crassest incarnation, then Communism was an easy choice.

That later generation tended to encounter disillusionment in 1956, in the form of the Soviet invasion of Hungary. Whereas for the earlier generation of communists it was the failure of social democracy and the apparently inexorable choice between fascism and communism which mattered most, by the 1940s and 1950s, the choices looked quite different—even though Stalin tried hard to present the Cold War as an essentially similar set of options. And so, fellow travelers—sympathetic to communism but not quite committed to joining it—matter more in the later story than in the interwar one, when the salient issue was whether and when people ceased to be communists and became . . . ex-communists.

> *The moment when one becomes a member of the communist party, or one declares one's association with communism is very important biographically. There's a kind of double temporal trap: from that moment forward, the revolution recedes before you, like a rainbow. You want to keep chasing it. Meanwhile receding behind you is that moment in your youth where you made that choice, and with it, probably made lots of good friends, or found new sorts of lovers. And I think people found it very hard to cut themselves off, from those people, from that moment.*

Again, think of Eric Hobsbawm's memoirs. There is this sense that all of his life, and his otherwise inexplicable allegiances, can be linked to the last year of the Weimar Republic in Germany. In 1932, he was living in Berlin as a fifteen-year-old, watching German democracy crumble, joining the Communist Party, and clearly feeling that this was the great turning point in the century and that he was making a choice at the moment of choice. That choice not only shaped the rest of his life but gave reason and meaning to everything that came before. Many of those who made that same choice but then rejected it in later years were then at a loss to explain exactly what now gave their life a meaning—other than the commitment to writing and speaking against the thing that once did.

If you think about former believers such as Ignazio Silone, or Whittaker Chambers, or Manès Sperber, you see two kinds of emotional undertone: the attempt to express the loss of faith, and the attempt to rationalize the faith that once was. The loss of faith, of course, is not nearly as attractive as faith: so while it may be rational to step away, you lose more than you gain. An interesting example of rationalization is Annie Kriegel, the French historian who was first a Stalinist and then later an anti-communist. Her memoirs are called *Ce que j'ai cru comprendre* (What I Thought I Understood). Sidney Hook's memoirs, *Out of Step*, are also a series of attempts to explain why "I thought I understood things clearly then." François Furet's *Le passé d'une illusion* is the same thing, under the guise of a history of the twentieth century. This is a way of asserting that "my" previous choices were not so much a matter of faith as a matter of reasonable responses to a certain situation. It is a way, therefore, of being proud, both of the choice to be a communist as well as the choice to cease to be.

> *There's a beautiful example of the hyper-rationalization in Furet, where he tells us that in 1947, he read Koestler's* Darkness at Noon. *Far from being convinced by Koestler's account of the terror in the Soviet Union that he should not become a communist, the young Furet was impressed by the rationality of both the interrogator and the interrogated during the Stalinist show trials.*

Recall, though, that Koestler had not freed himself from the charms of the dialectic when he wrote the novel. What Koestler wanted to show was why so many people had been seduced by these ways of thinking. But part of the reason the novel works so well is because he himself is still a little bit seduced.

> *Which is why* Darkness at Noon *is a good account from within, of why people were attracted to communism. But it's not a good account of what the Great Terror was really like, it says nothing about the hundreds of thousands of workers and peasants who were shot in 1937 and 1938.*

In Koestler's account—and he shares this with Hobsbawm—the good guys and the bad guys are all communists. In the first place, all of the victims—certainly all of the victims who matter—are communists. Moreover, the "perpetrators" are Stalinists who abuse "good" communism for their own ends and then exploit the law or their power to condemn fellow communists with whom they don't agree or whom they wish to remove. As you note, this is not the most important aspect of Soviet history in those years; and of course it does no justice to the Terror. But for intellectuals, it was what counted.

> *What really mattered to intellectuals was a milieu: people whom you knew—or people who were like the people you knew—and the things that happened to them. Beyond this milieu were the collectivized peasants who lost their land and starved by the millions in the early 1930s and then were shot in the hundreds of thousands later in the decade.*

There's a lovely essay by Koestler in *The Trail of the Dinosaur* called, "The Little Flirts of Saint-Germain-des-Prés." He writes about French fellow travelers and communists as peeping toms, peering through a hole in the wall at history, while not having to experience it themselves. The victims of communism could comfortably be re-described (and often were) as the victims not of men but of History. Communism thus passed as Hegel's spirit doing the work of history, in countries where history had failed to do the work for itself. From such a distance one can make arguments about History's costs and benefits: but the costs are borne by someone else and the benefits can be anything you wish to imagine.

In one sense this is rather like the debates over the Industrial Revolution that we studied in King's College when I was an undergraduate: it may have had terrible human outcomes in the short run, but it was both necessary and beneficial. The transformation was necessary because without industrialization there would not have been generated the wealth needed to overcome Malthusian impediments in agrarian societies; and it was beneficial because in the long run everyone's standard of living rose.

The argument thus resembles the case proposed by communism's Western apologists (on those occasions when they acknowledged the scale of its crimes). The difference of course is that no one was sitting in London in 1833, planning the Industrial Revolution and deciding that—whatever its costs—they were worth imposing on others for the sake of the long run benefits.

This point of view is summed up in Bertolt Brecht's obnoxious poem, admired by so many people: "Even the hatred of squalor/ Makes the brow grow stern. Even anger against injustice/ Makes the voice grow harsh. Alas, we/ Who wished to lay the foundations of kindness/ Could not ourselves be kind." In order, in short, to justify present crimes we must keep our eyes firmly focused upon future gains. But we do well to bear in mind that in such accounts, the costs are always assigned to others, and usually to another time and place.

This seems to me an exercise in applied political romanticism.
We see it in similar cases elsewhere in the twentieth century. In a
world where many people—intellectuals above all—no longer
believe in the afterlife, death has to acquire an alternative
significance. There must be a reason for it; it must be advancing
history: God is dead, long live death.

All of this would have been much harder to imagine in the absence of the First World War and the cult of death and violence to which it gave rise.

What communist intellectuals and their fascist counterparts had in common in the years after 1917 was a profound attraction to mortal struggle and its beneficial social or aesthetic outcomes. Fascist intellectuals in particular made death at once the justification and the attraction of war and civil violence: out of such mayhem was to be born a better man and a better world.

Before we set about congratulating ourselves on having said "goodbye to all that," let's remember that this romantic sensibility is by no means behind us. I well recall the response of Condoleezza Rice, then U.S. Secretary of State under President George W. Bush, to the Second Lebanese War in 2006. Commenting on the Israeli invasion of southern Lebanon and the scale of civilian suffering to which it gave rise, she confidently asserted that these were "the birth pangs of a new Middle East." And I remember thinking at the time, I have heard this before. You know what I mean: once again, other people's ordeals are being justified as History's way of delivering a new world, and thereby assigning meaning to events that would be otherwise unforgivable and inexplicable. If a conservative American Secretary of State can resort to such cant in the twenty-first century, why should European intellectuals not have invoked similar justifications half a century before?

Let's come back, then, to Eric Hobsbawm for a minute. How can it be that someone who made that kind of mistake, and has never corrected it, has become in the fullness of time one of the most important interpreters of the century? And his case is not unique.

The answer to that, I believe, is rather revealing. We have never quite lost that sense that—as Hobsbawm himself would probably still insist—you cannot fully appreciate the shape of the twentieth century if you did not once share its illusions, and the communist illusion in particular. At this point, the historian of twentieth-century intellectual life enters essentially unresolvable territory. The kinds of choices that people made in the 1930s (and their reasons for making them) are intelligible to us. This is true even if we cannot ourselves imagine having made that choice, and even though we know perfectly well that twenty years later many of those same people will regret their choice or reinterpret it in a favorable light: youthful mistake, the weight of circumstances or whatever.

> *Having been a communist, one has sympathetic understanding,*
> *one knows what it was like, one was engaged with what seemed to*
> *be the main issues of the time and one has that raw material from*
> *which to work. That gives one an advantage as a historian*
> *because sympathetic understanding is something that*
> *presumably we all want. However, if the claim is that there are*
> *intellectual advantages of having been a Stalinist, it seems to*
> *follow from this that one would also, from a purely methodological*
> *perspective, wish to have been an ex-Nazi too.*

The choice made by prominent Germans in 1933 to welcome the Nazis—and to accept their welcome of you, their appointment of you to high places at the price of your complicity and silence: this is *not* intelligible to us today, except as an act of human cowardice. And therefore it remains problematic in retrospect and we are altogether reluctant to allow "youthful mistakes" or "the weight of circumstances" to be invoked as mitigating circumstances. We are, in short, quite unforgiving of one kind of past political peccadillo, but tolerant and even sympathetic to another. This may seem inconsistent and even incoherent, but there is a certain logic to it.

I see little benefit to our understanding of twentieth-century history from inserting ourselves into the mind of those who formulated or propagated Nazi policies (one reason why I do not share the contemporary adulation of Jonathan Littell's *Les Bienveillantes*). I simply cannot think of a single Nazi intellectual whose reasoning holds up as an interesting historical account of twentieth-century thought.

Conversely, I can think of a number of reasons for reading carefully—if not sympathetically—the distasteful writings of certain Romanian and Italian fascist intellectuals. I don't mean that fascism in its non-German form was somehow more tolerable, more digestible to us because in the end it was not about genocide, the wholesale destruction of peoples etc. I mean that other fascisms operated in a recognizable framework of nationalist *ressentiment* or geographical injustice that was not only intelligible, but which had and still has some broader applicability if we wish to make sense of the world around us.

However, most of what German intellectuals in the Nazi era were saying—when they spoke as Nazis or Nazi sympathizers—applied uniquely to the German case. Indeed, Nazism—like the romantic and post-romantic national traditions on which it drew—was parasitic upon a set of claims about what it was that made Germans unique. Many of the Romanian—or Italian or Spanish—fascist intellectuals believed themselves, for much of the time, to be espousing universal truths and categories. Even at their most narcissistically patriotic, French fascist intellectuals like Robert Brasillach or Drieu la Rochelle fondly imagined themselves to be of relevance and interest well beyond the borders of France. In this sense at least, they are comparable to their communist counterparts: they too were proposing an account of modernity and its discontents. We have, accordingly, something to learn from them.

When the Italian liberal patriot Giuseppe Mazzini wrote about nationalism in the nineteenth century, he was confident that it could and should be a universal proposition in the ways you are suggesting: if national self-determination was good for Italy, then there was no reason in principle why it should not be good for everyone. There can be lots of liberal nations. And so fascism in the 1920s and '30s can be understood as a distorted postwar heir to such thinking: in principle a fascist of one nation can empathize with the ambitions of his fellow fascists in other lands. But a National Socialist can wish no such thing: Nazism is about Germany and cannot be a model for others since both its form and content are specifically German.

And yet I wonder whether, precisely because of what you say, National Socialism was not universal after all. Worship of a fantasy of one's own race is an extreme case, the extreme case. But surely, we all have this capacity to yield to the fallacy of our own uniqueness? Isn't the tendency to make exceptions for oneself the universal human flaw?

Perhaps. You are making a more abstract point which concerns not the thinkers themselves but what we might learn from the general nature of the fallacies to which they or rather their millions of victims fell prey. I would repeat that we can and must maintain a distinction between the Nazis and those intellectuals who, in their own eyes, preserved and insisted upon their own universal qualities—the characteristically Enlightenment idea that they were part of an international conversation: whether it be politics, or the origins of human society or the workings of capitalism or the meaning of progress and so forth. We can say with confidence that communist—or, with certain qualifications, fascist—intellectuals were the heirs to such conversations. We simply cannot say this about Nazis.

4.

KING'S AND KIBBUTZIM:
CAMBRIDGE ZIONIST

In 1963, my father suggested instead that I might like to go to Israel, where he and my mother had visited for the first time not long before. My parents found a Jewish youth organization, Dror, that was associated with a kibbutz movement and organized summer trips to Israel for young English Jews. I was charmed by the Israeli recruiters who ran the movement in London: Zvi and Maya Dubinsky, who represented Hakibbutz Hame'uhad, a long-established left-wing kibbutz movement. Zvi, the official proselytizer, was a charismatic committed Zionist in his late twenties; his wife Maya, born in Paris (and whose aunt, as it later transpired, was married to my second cousin) was beautiful and cosmopolitan. I went to Israel with them that summer and was completely swept away.

So began my romance with the kibbutz. Israel had attractive girls and friendly, straightforward Jewish boys untroubled by their Jewishness or surrounding hostility. Here was a place where the surroundings, without being particularly familiar, were all the same not quite different or alien. But as I threw myself into Zionism and its ideological penumbra, I think that even then I unconsciously held something of myself back. On the more ideological kibbutzim in those days, newcomers from the diaspora were assigned Hebrew names. The Hebrew name was either the biblical equivalent of a visitor's European name, or else bore some relation to it, and was part of the not-so-subtle process of extracting young Jews from their European heritage and inserting them into their Middle Eastern future. There being no biblical equivalent for "Tony," my newfound kibbutz friends took the "n" and the "t," inverted them, and tried calling me "Nathan." I rejected this out of hand; people just called me Tony.

I worked for seven weeks on Kibbutz Hakuk, in the Galilee. I understood later that in addition to being primed for immigration, I was cheap temporary labor: it made good economic sense for the kibbutz to send charming representatives to England at considerable expense, if they returned with young people willing to work on the farm. This, of course, was precisely what my sponsors were seeking. Hakibbutz Hame'uhad was the kibbutz movement of Achdut Ha'avodah, one of the main left-of-center political parties in Israel in those days. For the party, the kibbutz movement represented financial, social, political and symbolic capital, and we new recruits were its future. But if this was exploitation, no one objected. I certainly loved it: picking bananas, enjoying rude good health, exploring the country by truck, visiting Jerusalem with girls.

The essence of Labor Zionism lay in the promise of Jewish Work: the idea that young Jews from the diaspora would be rescued from their effete, assimilated lives and transported to remote collective settlements in rural Palestine—there to create (and, as the ideology had it, re-create) a living Jewish peasantry, neither exploited nor exploiting. I saw Israel through a rose-tinted lens: a uniquely left-of-center land, where everyone I knew was affiliated with a kibbutz and where I could project onto the whole Jewish population a peculiarly Jewish social democratic idealism. I never met an Arab: left-wing kibbutz movements avoided employing Arab labor. As I see now, this served less to burnish their egalitarian credentials than to isolate them from the inconvenient facts of Middle Eastern life. I'm sure I did not appreciate all this at the time—though I do recall wondering why I never saw an Arab in the course of my lengthy kibbutz stays, despite living near the most densely populated Arab communities of the country.

I was engaged, I was one of Milan Kundera's "dancers": I joined in the circles, I learned the language in both senses: literally and politically. I was one of them—or, more precisely, one of *us*. And therefore I can say, with some conviction, that I share with Kundera or Pavel Kohout the special knowledge vouchsafed to insiders of what it is like to be within the circle: looking smugly and disdainfully out on the unbelievers, the ignorant, the uninformed and the unenlightened.

I returned to England a committed socialist Zionist, and at the age of fifteen both parts of that identification were central to my faith. Zionism for me was without question an adolescent revolt, but not I think against any particular paternal or social norm or authority. I certainly was not embracing a form of politics that was alien to my parents: quite the contrary. Nor was I in revolt against the culture, clothing, music or politics of England—at least no more than anyone else at the time and perhaps somewhat less than many others. What I revolted against was my *Englishness*, or rather against the hitherto un-interrogated ambiguity of my childhood: being at once altogether English and at the same time unmistakably the child of east European Jews. In Israel in 1963 I resolved the ambiguity and became Tony Judt, Zionist.

My mother was horrified. She thought Zionism was just a showy form of Jewishness; and in her mind ostentatious Jewishness was both tasteless and imprudent. But she was also smart enough to see that Zionism could get in the way of my studies, which indeed it did. She continued to press the case for academic achievement before all else, whilst I was rather of the persuasion that it might be more fun to run a banana plantation on the Sea of Galilee than to study for A-levels (the British national leaving exams that qualify students for university admission).

In particular, my mother could see that I was very drawn to the charismatic couple who had first introduced me to Israel. It is certainly true that I was very attracted to Maya, who was not so many years my senior. I would not go as far as to say that she was the reason I devoted the next four years of my life to Zionism, but she was surely at the center of the story. Maya represented something, as my mother saw, that might seduce me away from my other self, the solitary, intellectual, self-referential child of my earlier years. For just this reason, my father was initially enthusiastic—until he too began to observe the same danger signals. Both of my parents then started to press hard against my desire to drop out of school and run off to a kibbutz.

We came to an informal arrangement: I could leave for Israel, but first I had to take and pass my A-levels. If I accepted these terms, it was because I was not that much of a rebel. In any case, I never did take most of my A-levels—but nor did I quit school. Instead, a year early and at the urging of my schoolmasters, I sat the entrance exam for Cambridge University. The regulations of the day stipulated that if you passed this exam at a high-enough level and were accepted by one of the colleges, you had attained the minimum requirements for admission to the University.

In the months leading up to the Cambridge exam, in the fall of 1965, I was energetically dating a girl from the Zionist youth movement, at the distinct expense of my exam preparation. Returning home one night at around two in the morning, I was horrified to find my father in the dining room, waiting for me. I was subjected to a lecture on the un-wisdom, to put it politely, of favoring female company over homework. I don't think I later resented the dressing down; perhaps even then I appreciated just what it was my father was doing for me. I unceremoniously dumped the poor girl, studied night and day, and performed better in that examination than in any test I have taken, before or since.

In those days, Cambridge colleges would send a telegram—a real telegram—to notify you if you won an open award. And so one evening in North London, at the home of some Zionist friends—the chief appeal of this particular household was that there were two very attractive girls of my own age—I got a phone message from my parents, saying there was a telegram for me. Naturally they had opened it and read that I had been awarded an Exhibition to King's College Cambridge. They asked me what this meant, and I explained that it was the offer of a scholarship and a place. You must come home, they insisted, we want to congratulate you. When I got home, all I could hear was bickering coming from somewhere upstairs. My parents, as it turned out, were engaged in an intense debate as to which side of the family had furnished the genetic material from which I had drawn in my success . . .

The following week, I sent a letter to the senior tutor at King's College, Cambridge, asking if he would permit me to quit my A-level preparation—in short, to drop out of high school. In a remarkably generous and comprehending response, the senior tutor replied that yes, because you took the French and German papers in your entrance exam, and performed to a level above that of the A-levels, you have met the qualifications as far as we are concerned, and you may do as you wish.

With intense relief I put six years of high school behind me and spent the spring and summer of 1966 in Israel on Kibbutz Machanayim. I chose Machanayim for no better reason than that the kibbutz organization instructed me to do so. Once there, I labored in the orange groves—easier work than in the lakeside banana plantations of Hakuk: the smell of citrus is much to be preferred to the presence of water snakes.

Machanayim was part of the same kibbutz movement as Hakuk, though its members took a somewhat harder line on day-to-day ideological issues (e.g., the distribution of electrical devices, clothing coupons, etc.). It was a bigger and better-organized community than Hakuk, but far less friendly and by no means receptive to dissenting opinion. I spent quite a few months there, but found the atmosphere increasingly stifling and inhospitable, redolent of a collective farm.

When my kibbutz colleagues learned that I had been accepted into Cambridge University and planned to attend, they were appalled. The whole culture of "aliyah"—"going up" (to Israel)—presumed the severing of links and opportunities back in the diaspora. The leaders of the youth movement in those days knew perfectly well that once a teenager in England or France was permitted to stay there through university, he or she was probably lost to Israel forever. The official position, accordingly, was that university-bound students should forego their places in Europe; commit themselves to the kibbutz for some years as orange pickers, tractor drivers or banana sorters; and then, circumstances permitting, present themselves to the community as candidates for higher education—on the understanding that the kibbutz would collectively determine what if any course of studies they should pursue, with the emphasis upon their future usefulness to the collective.

I went to university. As I can now see, I came to Cambridge in the fall of 1966 as a member of a rather distinctive generation. To be sure, it would be hard to write a book about England like Jean-François Sirinelli's *Génération intellectuelle*, a study of the cohort that graduated from the École Normale Supérieure in the late 1920s: Merleau-Ponty, Sartre, Aron, de Beauvoir and others who would dominate French intellectual and political life for much of the ensuing half century. Even if Oxford, Cambridge and the London School of Economics were grouped together (which they should not be), their graduates would still be too large in number and too varied in their affinities to constitute a coherent intellectual generation. And yet, all the same, there is something very striking about the generation that passed through British universities between the early 1960s and the beginning of the 1970s.

This was the generation of young people who benefited from the 1944 Education Act and subsequent reforms, which made British secondary education both free and open to anyone able to benefit from it. Those reforms established a system of elite, selective state secondary schools which were pedagogically old-fashioned, often modeling themselves upon the ancient public schools (which in England of course means private schools), but open to talent from all classes. In addition, there were also a smaller number of similarly elitist, meritocratic Direct Grant schools, technically private but subsidized by local authorities or the central government, such that the benefit for students was comparable.

The boys and girls from the lower or middle classes who attended these schools were those who had performed well in the national exam that was set at the age of eleven, and were thus offered an academic secondary education (those who failed the exam were all too often doomed to mediocre "technical" schools and usually dropped out at the minimum school leaving age, then fifteen). The most-talented or best-prepared students from the grammar or Direct Grant schools were then duly filtered through the fine mesh of the Oxford and Cambridge entrance exams.

In the course of the later 1960s the Labour Party abolished these selection procedures, establishing comprehensive education, as it was called, along the model of the American secondary education system. The result of this well-intentioned reform was all too predictable: by the mid-1970s, any parent who was in a position to buy their child out of the state system did so. And thus Britain proceeded backwards, from a recently established social and intellectual meritocracy to a regressive and socially selective system of secondary education whereby the wealthy could once again buy an education all but unavailable to the poor. British higher education has been over-compensating ever since: desperately trying to find ways to assess the children from the public sector and cream off the best of them, in the face of schools that all too often cannot provide them with the necessary background preparation for university.

The result is that Great Britain experienced a kind of *génération meritocratique*, as the French might have put it, which began with the first products of the Education Act and ended with comprehensivisation. Coming as I did right in the middle of this generation, I am very conscious of this process. I can confirm that in the Cambridge of my day—for the first time—there were a substantial number of students whose parents had not attended university; or, as in my own case and that of a number of my friends, whose parents had not even completed secondary education. This made my Cambridge a very different sort of place from the Cambridge of previous generations, where students were typically the sons and grandsons of former students.

It was a distinctive feature of this meritocratic and upwardly mobile academic generation that an unusual proportion of us were interested in making a career in the academic or academic-related worlds. This, after all, was the route through which we had been promoted and achieved success; it was what interested us and it was how we saw ourselves in relation to the backgrounds and communities from which we had emerged. Thus a disproportionate number of my peers would graduate and enter academic life, the upper end of school teaching (often teaching in very good secondary schools of the sort from which they had themselves graduated), publishing, the higher reaches of journalism and government service.

Academic life in those days held out prospects that it no longer does for most people: it was rewarding and it was exciting. Academics themselves of course were not necessarily adventurous people—and in the nature of the liberal professions they did not attract a large number of risk takers. But that was not the point. Knowledge, ideas, debate, teaching and policy making in those days were not just highly respectable and reasonably well-paid avenues to a career; they were also and above all what smart and interesting people *wanted* to do.

King's College, Cambridge, despite its long-established liberal and unconventional reputation, was unabashedly elitist. Everyone I met in my first year there had done very well in the entrance exam and most of them were extremely smart, although their interests varied widely. I became close friends with Martyn Poliakoff, who is now a Fellow of the Royal Society and Professor of Inorganic Chemistry at Nottingham University in England. While the rest of us were variously taken up with sex, politics and pop music, Martyn did not appear particularly interested in any of these. His father was a Russian scientist and businessman; his grandfather had played a major role in the construction of the railways in the Russian Empire—Martyn himself had been encouraged to learn Russian, a language he still speaks. He married a mathematician from Newnham College (one of the three women's colleges of the day) and he is rare among my friends of the time in having stayed married to the same person.

Another friend, John Bentley, was the first member of his family to attend university; on the face of it this was about all we had in common. John came from a working-class family in Leeds, in the north of England, and his chief apparent interest in life, other than women, beer and his pipe (in ascending order), was walking the moors. And yet, when I think of England today with any affection, it is John's world that comes to mind, not my own. John read English and became a schoolmaster in the north of England, in Middlesborough, teaching English literature for four decades: I have no idea whether this was what he always wanted. He and I have maintained a light-hearted, often amusing, sometimes scabrous, rather close and affectionate relationship now enhanced by the magic of e-mail.

In our own way, my Cambridge generation was of course very sensitive to the nuances of background. In the United States, you could ask someone which high school they attended and for the most part you would learn very little about them. The response would leave open a variety of social and cultural background possibilities, except of course at the social extremes. It has been my observation that, for the most part, American university students know remarkably little about the secondary school experience and setting of their fellows. But in England, once you knew the school that someone had attended, you knew almost everything necessary to set them in a very specific and detailed background.

I recall the first evening we all got together, a shy bunch of late teenage boys newly installed in Cambridge residencies. Instinctively and predictably, the first thing we asked each other was which school we had attended. I remember asking Mervyn King, now the Governor of the Bank of England, which secondary school he went to. Unsurprisingly, for our cohort, he too came from a lower-middle-class family and had attended a grammar school for the talented children of the local community. The contrast with our Cambridge teachers leapt to the eye: I was taught, I think, exclusively by men who attended Winchester, Haileybury or other elite fee-paying public schools.

We were thus the very epicenter of a great sociological shift and yet we did not, I think, feel like outsiders. King's was the college of John Maynard Keynes and E. M. Forster, and so utterly self-consciously unconventional that no one except a homophobic reactionary could possibly have felt truly ill at ease there. I felt and behaved, I think, as though this were *my* Cambridge, and not the Cambridge of some alien elite that I had been mistakenly permitted to enter. And I believe that the same inclusive sentiment was felt by the old guard of King's, with perhaps a handful of exceptions. To be sure there was another Cambridge operating in parallel, the preserve of a social and economic minority, of whose goings on we knew little and about which we could not have cared less. In any case, we had the better-looking girls.

In Cambridge that fall of 1966 I spent a lot of time going back and forth to London, mostly in order to attend meetings of Dror. I was dating a particularly attractive girl, Jacquie Philips, who was in the Zionist youth movement and whom I had met in 1965. She was my link to London, at a time when most of my contemporaries and friends were forming links within Cambridge. Though Jacquie was involved—like me and to some extent through me—with Zionism, she was not herself a very political person. She had, I think, been drawn to the movement for the usual reason—because she wanted to spend the summer in Israel—and had then remained because it was a pleasant social community and because she and I had become involved. In any case, our connection to Zionism and to each other was to land us once again in Israel.

In the spring of 1967, just before the Six-Day War, I played an active part in organizing support for Israel during the prelude to the conflict. Zionist organizations, kibbutzim and factories in Israel had issued a plea for volunteers to come and work there, replacing reservists who had been called up in anticipation of battle. From Cambridge I helped set up a national organization to find and send volunteers. Then I myself went to Israel, accompanied by Jacquie and another friend, Morris Cohen, boarding the last plane to leave for Israel before Lod airport closed to incoming flights. Once again I had to seek permission from King's to leave my studies prematurely (albeit in this case by just a few weeks, with my first year exams already behind me) and once again this permission was generously granted.

When we arrived, there was a bus waiting to take that particular plane-load of volunteers to Machanayim. But I had no intention of returning there and informed the bus driver that the three of us at least were destined to be dropped off at Hakuk. Dissembling, I claimed that this was the settlement to which we had been assigned. Israel was then under total blackout, in anticipation of war, and I had to give directions to the driver in the dark. When we arrived, Maya Dubinsky happened by good fortune to be in the dining hall: this was fortuitous, since we were not expected and had shown up without any warning.

Maya, whom I had not seen for two years, was not perhaps in the best state to receive us. She was in the middle of an affair—by no means her first— and the kibbutz, far from girding its loins for battle, was uncomfortably divided between Maya's friends and the supporters of her lover's jilted wife. Romantically chasing memories and adventure, I had walked into nothing so much as a banal village sex scandal.

But there we were. During the course of the war and the immediate aftermath I worked once again on a banana plantation by the Sea of Galilee. But a few weeks later the victorious Israeli army issued a call for volunteers to join the army as auxiliaries and help with postwar tasks. I was nineteen, and this was irresistible. So I volunteered with a friend, Lee Isaacs: together we made our way to the Golan Heights and were attached to a unit there.

We were supposed to be driving captured Syrian army trucks back into Israel, but I was quickly and somewhat disappointingly assigned to translation work instead. By this point I spoke Hebrew with reasonable competence, and I had fluent French. The place was awash in English and French-speaking volunteers who had arrived in Israel from all over the world with little or no command of the language. I thus became for a short while a three-way interpreter between young Israeli officers and the French and English-speaking auxiliaries assigned to their units.

As a consequence, I saw more of the Israeli army than I might have done had I merely driven trucks down to the valley, and it was quite an eye-opener. For the first time I came to appreciate that Israel was not a social-democratic paradise of peace-loving, farm-dwelling Jews who just happened to be Israelis but were otherwise like me. This was a very different culture and people from the one I had learned to see, or had insisted upon imagining to myself. The junior officers I met were drawn from the cities and towns rather than the kibbutzim, and thanks to them I came to appreciate something that should have been obvious to me long before: that the dream of rural socialism was just that. The center of gravity of the Jewish state would be and must be in its cities. In short, I realized that I did not live and had never lived in the real Israel.

Instead, I had been indoctrinated into an anachronism, had lived an anachronism, and I now saw the depth of my delusion. For the first time I met Israelis who were chauvinistic in every meaning of the word: anti-Arab in a sense bordering upon racism; quite undisturbed at the prospect of killing Arabs wherever possible; frequently regretting that they had not been allowed to fight their way through to Damascus and beat down the Arabs for good and all; full of scorn for what they called the "heirs of the Holocaust," Jews who lived outside of Israel and who did not understand or appreciate the new Jews, the native-born Israelis.

This was not the fantasy world of socialist Israel that so many Europeans loved (and love) to imagine—a wishful projection of all the positive qualities of Jewish Central Europe with none of the drawbacks. This was a Middle Eastern country that despised its neighbors and was about to open a catastrophic, generation-long rift with them by seizing and occupying their land. By the end of that summer I left Israel feeling claustrophobic and depressed. I did not go back until two years later, in 1969. But when I did, I found that I intensely disliked almost everything I saw. I was now regarded by my former kibbutz colleagues and friends as an outsider and a pariah.

Thirty years later I returned to the subject of Israel, publishing a series of essays critical of Israeli practices in the West Bank and America's uncritical support of them. In the autumn of 2003, in what became a notorious essay published in *The New York Review of Books*, I argued that a one-state solution, however implausible and for most of the protagonists undesirable, was now the most realistic prospect for the Middle East. This assertion, driven as much by despair as expectation, aroused a firestorm of resentment and misunderstanding. I do feel as a Jew that one has a responsibility to criticize Israel vigorously and rigorously, in ways that non-Jews cannot—for fear of spurious but effective accusations of anti-Semitism.

My own experience as a Zionist allowed me to identify the same fanaticism and myopic, exclusivist tunnel vision in others—most notably the community of American cheerleaders for Israel. Indeed, I now saw (and see) the Israel problem as increasingly a dilemma for *Americans*. All of my writings on the Middle East have been explicitly or implicitly addressed to the problem of American policy in the region and the pernicious role played by diaspora organizations here in the U.S. in stirring and exacerbating the conflict. Thus I have found myself engaged willy-nilly in an intra-American debate, one in which Israelis themselves play only a peripheral role. In this debate I have the luxury not only of being a Jew, and thus oblivious to moral blackmail from censorious fellow-Jews; I am also a Jew who has lived in Israel and been a committed Zionist—indeed, a Jew who even volunteered to help the Israeli army at the time of the Six-Day War: an occasionally serviceable asset in the face of self-righteous criticism.

When I discussed a one-state solution, I was deliberately trying to pry open a suppressed debate. On the one hand, I was casting a stone into the placid pool of yea-saying, uncritical assent that characterizes the self-defined Jewish "leadership" here in the U.S. But the other audience for my writings was and is non-Jewish Americans actively interested in the Middle East, or even just concerned over U.S. policy there—men and women who feel silenced by the charge of anti-Semitism whenever they raise their voice: whether on the excesses of the Israel lobby, the illegality of the occupation, the impropriety of Israeli "Holocaust" blackmail (if you don't want another Auschwitz, don't criticize us) and the scandals of war in Lebanon or Gaza.

It was people like this, across the country, who would invite me to come and speak: to church groups, to ladies' organizations, to schools and the like. Normal Americans with an above-average awareness of the outside world, these were readers of *The New York Times*, viewers of PBS, school teachers, all of them in search of a guide for the perplexed. And here, unusually, was someone willing to come and speak openly without any discernable partisan agenda or ethnic identification.

I was not, am not, and do not come across as anti-Israeli. I understand just how much there is amiss in the Arab world and don't feel in the least inhibited in talking about it. I have Israeli friends and Arab friends. I am a Jew who is not at all reluctant to discuss the troubling consequences of our contemporary obsession with Holocaust commemoration. For all my uncompromising style, I am not a natural polemicist and above all I am no party man. And so I would open a conversation with high school children, with church goers or reading groups, and would be told at the conclusion how grateful they were for the rare opportunity of an open discussion on these freighted subjects.

> *The tension between Jewish assimilation (in your case Cambridge*
> *and the academic career) and Jewish engagement (in your case the*
> *Israeli years) is there from the beginning of modern Jewish politics.*
> *In fact you could see Theodor Herzl's original Zionism of the late*
> *nineteenth century as an attempt by a rather assimilated Jew to*
> *export a better form of European life to the Middle East—in the*
> *form of a Jewish national state in Palestine.*

There were different Europes, different kinds of European Jews, different Zionisms. In strictly intellectual terms, we can speak thus of Jews in Germany or Austria or France who—like Herzl—had grown up in the disenchanted world of late nineteenth-century Europe and for whom Zionism was in part, at least, an extension of their cosmopolitan European existence. But that simply does not apply to the Jews—the overwhelming majority, at least among Ashkenazim—who lived further east: in the Pale of Settlement and Russia proper. And of course, these were the Jews who were to matter most in the coming decades. Theirs was still a religious world—an enchanted world, for all its troubles—and therefore rebellion and separation for them took an altogether more dramatic turn.

But then we can also see a difference, one that we have already
discussed, between a central European Jewish experience of
disappointed assimilation, and a more east European Jewish
experience of separation and temptation to revolution. That's
present in Zionism, too especially; in the Russian version of Labor
Zionism that you experienced. The idea that one can recreate an
ideal rural community is not just a Zionist idea, it's rather and in
fact above all a Russian socialist idea.

One of the great confusions in the history of Zionism, as perceived in retrospect, is the failure to see the huge tension between the Zionist thinkers and other radicals who emerged from the Russian Empire and those whose roots lay in central or Western Europe. This tension goes beyond the question of what sort of a country they were setting out to invent; it speaks to very different attitudes towards their critics and opponents.

Radicals in the Russian Empire, Jewish or otherwise, could rarely see the point of compromise. From the point of view of the early Russian (or Polish) Zionists, marinated in the uncompromising narrative of a tragic past, History was only and always a narrative of conflict—and a narrative in which the winner takes all. Conversely, the central Europeans could at least imagine a liberal view of History again as the story of progress in which everyone can find a place, and where progress itself assures space and autonomy for all. This unmistakably Viennese way of thinking was from the outset dismissed by clear-headed Russian radicals like Vladimir Jabotinsky as mere flannel. What the Jews were seeking in Palestine, he used to say, was not progress but a state. When you build a state you make a revolution. And in a revolution there can only ever be winners and losers. This time around we Jews are going to be the winners.

Despite my early indoctrination in a more moderate and socialist variant of Zionism, I came over time to appreciate the rigor and clear-headed realism of Jabotinsky's criticisms. In any case, it was the Russian tradition, in the case of Jabotinsky's Revisionist Zionism a tradition of *reactionary* revolution, that was to prevail. Today, it is the heirs of Jabotinsky's Revisionist Zionists who govern and dominate Israel, not the rather uncomfortable blend of left-Russian utopianism with central European liberalism that governed the country for its first three decades.

In revealing respects, Israel today resembles the small nationalist states that emerged in Eastern Europe after the end of the Russian Empire. Had Israel—like Romania or Poland or Czechoslovakia—been established in 1918 rather than 1948, it would have closely tracked the small, vulnerable, resentful, irredentist, insecure, ethnically exclusivist states to which World War I had given birth. But Israel did not come into being until after the Second World War. As a consequence, it stands out for its slightly paranoid national political culture and has become unhealthily dependent upon the Holocaust—its moral crutch and weapon of choice with which to fend off all criticism.

The radical separation of the Jews from Europe—first the mass murder and then the relocation of Jewish history from Eastern Europe to Israel—put them at a distance from the newly-emerging secular ethics of post-Christian Europe. We can hardly fail to note that Europe today is not merely post-Christian—its traditional faith and practices largely abandoned—but also post-Jewish in a more dramatic sense.

Today's Europe the Jews have served in the role of something like a collective messiah: for a long time they were a considerable irritant—they caused a lot of trouble, they introduced a lot of troublesome revolutionary or liberal ideas. But when they died— were exterminated en masse—they taught Europeans a universal lesson which, after three or four decades of uncomfortable contemplation, Europeans have begun to make their own. For Europeans, the fact that the Jews are no longer with us—that we killed them, leaving the remnant to flee—has become the most important lesson bequeathed us by the past.

But this incorporation of Jews into the meaning of European history was only possible precisely because they were gone. On the scale of what once was, there really are not many Jews in Europe, and very few who would contest their role in Europe's new mnemonic ethics. Nor, come to that, are there many Jews left to make a significant contribution to European intellectual or cultural life, at least not in the way they used to before 1938. In fact, such Jews as there are in Europe today constitute a contradiction: if the message that the Jewish people have left behind required their destruction and expulsion, their presence only tends to confuse matters.

This leads to a positive—but only conditionally positive— European attitude towards Israel. The meaning of the State of Israel for Europeans is bound up with the Holocaust: it points to a lost messiah from whose legacy we have at least been able to draw a new, secular morality. But the actually existing Jews in Israel disrupt this narrative. They cause trouble. It would be better—so goes this thinking—if they did not cause so much trouble and allow us Europeans to interpret them in peace—hence the focus upon Israel's misdemeanors among European commentators. Here, as you may see, I am defending Israel.

Very well: in your Christian version of Jewish history, Jews—Christlike—can only truly win when (or rather, after) they lose. If they appear to be victorious, to be gaining their ends (at someone else's expense) there is a problem. But this otherwise elegant European appropriation of someone else's story for quite other purposes raises complications. The first of these, as you rightly note, is that Israel is there.

This is rather as though—allow me to offend you—Jesus Christ had been reincarnated as a rather venal but otherwise talented version of his former self: installed in a Jerusalem café, saying much the same things as he always used to and making his erstwhile persecutors feel guilty for crucifying him—even as they resent him deeply for reminding them of it. But think what that would mean. It would suggest that within short order—a mere generation or two—the uncomfortable recollection of Jesus' suffering would be altogether effaced by the irritation aroused by his endless invocation of it.

And thus you would end up with a story looking like this. The Jews—Jesus-like—become the martyred evidence of our own imperfections. But all we can see in them is their *own* imperfection, their obsessive insistence upon living off our shortcomings to their own advantage. I believe we are even today seeing this sentiment emerge. In the years to come, Israel is going to devalue, undermine and ultimately destroy the meaning and serviceability of the Holocaust, reducing it to what many people already say it is: Israel's excuse for bad behavior.

We used to hear this line of argument from the lunatic or fascist fringes. But today it has already entered and become a commonplace in the counter-cultural intellectual mainstream. Go to Turkey, for example, or Amsterdam or even London (though not yet America): in any serious discussion of the Middle East or Israel, someone is going to ask you—in perfect good faith—whether the time has not come to distinguish between Israel and the Holocaust, since the latter should not be allowed to serve as a Get Out of Jail Free card for a rogue state.

I don't see why the idea of Jesus coming back and hanging out as the annoying café intellectual should offend a Christian! That's not so far from what he was the first time around. Surely the whole point about Him is that He is in fact human; if He wants to wash the feet of prostitutes, I think He's meant to. So I fear you have failed to offend—Jesus in a Jerusalem café is a nice image.

Seriously, though: something is going on here between America and Europe with regard to the Holocaust. Although each side claims to treat it as the source of a moral universal ("thou shalt not . . ."), in the most important recent practical instance, the Iraq War, the lessons applied were strikingly different. The Holocaust is quite easily seen as an argument both for war and for peace. It seems as though from a European point of view, the message of the Second World War and the Holocaust goes something like this: avoid illegal, aggressive wars justified by lies—these will bring out the worst in you, and you may do dreadful things. To be sure, you won't do the most dreadful thing of all but you may go further down that road than you imagine.

By way of contrast, the American response might run thus: Munich taught us that if you don't stand up to aggression, then dreadful things will happen to innocent people. And Munich—appeasement, or a blind eye turned to the crimes of others—applies in whatever scenario is current. We must therefore do all we can to prevent a recurrence of a situation resembling that of Europe on the eve of the Second World War.

In this account, the Iraq war speaks directly to the suffering of the Jews because the innocent bystanders likely to be swept into the vortex are the Israelis. Saddam Hussein, as we were frequently reminded, was an enemy of the Israelis; meanwhile, the Israeli government supported and confirmed the narrative by actively encouraging—against its own interests, in my own view—the invasion of Iraq for its own reasons.

Very well, then: how should we adjudicate between the two positions? It is possible to do so, but not if we confine ourselves to abstractions. What is at issue is an interpretation not of ethics but of history. If Munich is not an appropriate analogy—and I believe it is not—this is because there are too many local circumstances and variables for the past and present to be tidily laid across one another. But if I wish to make this case I have to begin with those circumstances and variables. In short, I have to begin with the facts.

This is simply not an argument that lends itself to resolution by the juxtaposition of competing ethical stories.

Ever since Ben-Gurion, Israeli policy has quite explicitly insisted upon the assertion that Israel—and with it, the whole of world Jewry—remains vulnerable to a re-run of the Holocaust. The irony, of course, is that Israel itself constitutes one very strong piece of evidence to the contrary. But if we accept, as we surely should, that neither Jews nor Israelis face imminent extermination then we are forced to recognize that what is happening is the political leveraging of guilt and the exploitation of ignorance. As a state, Israel—in my view irresponsibly—exploits the fears of its own citizens. At the same time it exploits the fears, memories and responsibilities of other states. But in so doing, it risks over the course of time consuming the very moral capital that enabled it to exercise such exploitation in the first instance.

To my knowledge, no one in the Israeli political class—and certainly no one in the Israeli military or policy-making elite—has ever expressed any private doubt as to Israel's survival: certainly not since 1967 and, in most cases, not before then either. The fear that Israel could be "destroyed," "wiped off the face of the earth," "driven into the sea" or in any other way exposed to something remotely resembling a re-run of the past, is not a genuine fear. It is a politically calculated rhetorical strategy. Perhaps that is fair enough: one can see the use value to a small state in a turbulent region of asserting at every occasion its vulnerability, helplessness and need for foreign sympathy and support. But that does not explain why outsiders take the bait. The short answer, of course, is that it has very little to do with the realities of the contemporary Middle East and everything to do with the Holocaust.

It has a lot to do, I think, with the sentiment of guilt widespread in a community that you have not explicitly named: American Jews who don't make aliyah.

A Zionist, we used to say, is a Jew who pays another Jew to live in Israel. America is full of Zionists. American Jews have a very unusual identity problem: they are a substantial, well-established, prominent and influential "ethnic" minority in a country where ethnic minorities have a distinctive and—in most cases—affirmative place in the national mosaic. But Jews, uniquely, are an ethnic minority which cannot exactly describe itself thus. We speak of Italian-Americans, Hispanic-Americans, Native Americans and so forth. These terms have acquired distinctly positive connotations for the people they describe.

But whoever spoke of "Jewish-Americans" would be immediately suspected of prejudice; certainly American Jews themselves would not use the term. And yet they are, of course, Jews and they are American. So what is it that distinguishes them? Surely not their religion, with which most have long since lost touch. With the exception of an atypical minority, American Jews are unfamiliar with traditional Jewish cultural practices. They don't have a distinctive private or inherited language—most American Jews are quite ignorant of Yiddish and Hebrew. Unlike Polish-Americans or Irish-Americans, they have no fond recollections of "the old country." So what is it that binds them together? The answer, in very simple terms, is Auschwitz and Israel.

Auschwitz stands for the past: the memory of the suffering of other Jews in other places at other times. Israel represents the present: Jewish achievement in the form of an aggressive, self-confident military state—the anti-Auschwitz. With the Jewish state, America's Jews can establish an identification tag and positive association without actually having to move there, pay taxes there or in any other way switch national allegiances.

There seems to me something pathological about this transference of contemporary self-description onto people quite unlike oneself in other times and other places. It surely cannot be healthy for American Jews to identify so fondly with Jewish victims in the past, to the point of believing—as many surely do—that the best reason to keep Israel in business is the likelihood that another Holocaust is just around the corner. Does being Jewish really require you to anticipate a re-run of 1938 wherever you look? If so, then I suppose it really does make sense to offer unconditional support for a state which itself claims to expect something along those lines. But it hardly constitutes a normal way of life.

Well, if we're going to talk about American Jews, I think there are two other factors at work. I would accentuate one of your observations and suggest that those American Jews who have the most effectively articulated views on America's Middle East policies are not identifying with Israel as such. Rather, they have cast their lot with Likud—or perhaps those elements in Likud which make them feel most guilty. The Israeli Right, in other words, makes its American audience feel bad—and they, in turn, authorize it to behave badly.

But there is more. American Jews, I believe, have something in common with blacks—a shared quality which is not always evident to outsiders: Jews, like blacks, know who they are. American Jews can readily identify fellow American Jews. Israelis cannot. In my entire life only one American Jew has ever asked if I am Jewish, and that was in a confusing setting, on a bridge in Prague. Israelis ask me all the time.

When Israelis come to the U.S., it's only a slight exaggeration to say that they look around and they don't have a clue who is Jewish and who is a Baptist from Kansas. American Jews, by contrast, live their life constantly identifying these distinctions—distinctions of which other Americans may be altogether unaware. After all, non-Jewish Americans usually cannot tell a Jew from anyone else and shy away from drawing the distinction.

This is not just good manners: most Americans really cannot see who is and who is not Jewish. I think that in general if you asked people in America, is Paul Wolfowitz a Jew, they would . . . no,

Tony, I'm telling you, these are my people. They would stop and think about it, and they would say, you know, now that you mention it, maybe he's a Jew.

Well, if you are right—and I shall have to take your word for it—that's very interesting.

Whereas an American Jew looks at Paul Wolfowitz and says, yes, that's one of ours—and oh my goodness what is this mess he is getting us into? What consequence is this going to have for us Jews, this crazy war in Iraq (or, as it might be, this wonderful war in Iraq)?

This places Jews in America in a peculiar position. They know who they are, but the society around them does not—or at least much less than American Jews often think. Moreover, the society around them does not really care very much—again, certainly less than American Jews think. Are most Americans troubled by the knowledge that Steven Spielberg is Jewish? I don't believe so. I don't even think that they care much that Hollywood itself is overwhelmingly Jewish. Jewish achievement or prominence simply doesn't have much resonance in this country, one way or the other.

It is as though we had preserved one half of traditional Ashkenazic patterns of separation—knowing who your own people are—but have quite lost the other half, because we lack the tradition of a Christian peasantry instinctively and suspiciously aware of the Jews in their midst. The United States is simply too large and too diverse—and Jewish settlement too geographically concentrated—for this kind of awareness and recognition to be sustained.

Perhaps. But surely you should incorporate into your account the striking success of the anti-racist legislation, the multicultural politics and the political correctness of the past forty years. In a variety of ways, Americans have had it brought home to them that one should not obsess—one may not obsess—over whether someone is black, or Jewish, or whatever it might be. Eventually, reinforced by law and practice, indifference becomes systemic. If you tell people often enough that identifying others by their color or religion or culture is bad behavior—and there is no countervailing pressure in the form of racist parties, institutionalized prejudice, mass fear or any other form of demagogic mobilization—then eventually people do the right thing from habit.

There has never been any comparable legislative or cultural pressure towards assimilation and ethnic indifference anywhere else in the world except for France. And the French case, as you know, was driven by a very different set of considerations and circumstances. Even so, some of the effects were comparable. Allowing for the fact that there is the odd prominent personality with an unmistakably (foreign) Jewish name like Finkielkraut, it is quite commonplace for French audiences, listeners and readers to be unaware that an intellectual or public commentator is Jewish—and to be indifferent to such information.

To take perhaps the best-known contemporary case, I have never heard Bernard-Henri Lévy—who could hardly be mistaken for anything other than Jewish, if only thanks to his name—described as a Jew, even by those who hold him in contempt. It seems to be understood that whatever your qualities or shortcomings as a public figure in France, these can be quite adequately catalogued, whether favorably or otherwise, without resort to an ethnic tag. Note, though, that this was most assuredly not the case before 1945.

An interesting question arises, it seems to me, apropos your suggestion that Jews in America have a strictly subjective sense of their separate identity and that this is not shared by outside observers. If it really is true that only Jews can identify one another, then the United States must be a standing challenge to the very premises of Zionism. After all, if you can come to a country in which—in the fullness of time—people will not be aware that you are Jewish unless you wish them to be, then we have realized one of the great ambitions of the assimilationists. In which case, why do we need Israel?

So it is a curious paradox that in one of the few countries where assimilation has really worked, we find Jews almost uniquely obsessed with precisely those circumstances in which assimilation has either failed or been outright rejected: mass extermination and the Jewish state. Why, in America of all places, would Jews be so taken up with such matters?

Now I should remind you that my Zionist teachers have an answer to such paradoxes: even if the gentiles like you and treat you as one of their own, you will not like yourself. Indeed, you will like yourself even less for just that reason. And you will seek other ways in which to assert your distinctive Jewishness. But the price of assimilation is that the Jewishness you assert will be perverse and unhealthy.

Sometimes I think the Zionists have a point.

There's something else that matters here, I think, which has to do not just with a general trajectory of assimilation, but with America and its geographical and political distance from Eastern Europe and the Middle East. The two experiences which matter most—the Holocaust, Israel—are not even events in the history of American Jews, certainly not in any direct way for most people.

Indeed so. Because most American Jews can trace their ancestors' arrival in this country to a time well before either the Holocaust or the birth of the state of Israel.

But see now, I'm mounting a defense here of the American Jewish preoccupations with Auschwitz and Israel. Look at it from an American Jewish point of view: there you were, stumbling along, assimilating into American life; it's sometimes comic, sometimes hard, but the transition had more or less worked itself out . . . and then you are hit from the outside.

Think of American Jews during the Second World War and the difficulties they had in responding to the Holocaust. Hitler declares that Jews started the war and that his enemies are fighting on behalf of the international Jewish conspiracy, placing American Jews in an awkward situation. And there was far more anti-Semitism in the United States in the 1930s and 1940s than there is today.

Many American Jews reasoned that if they treated the murder of Jews as a casus belli, *they would be falling into Hitler's trap. Accordingly, many opted for silence and inaction—while resenting Hitler for placing them in such a predicament. In those years, anyone who wished the United States to go to war was prudently advised to maintain a certain discretion regarding the very evil which we, today, treat as the central event of that war.*

I appreciate that. And I agree that the history of American Jews is in many respects the story of a belated response—often delayed by a generation or more—to events in Europe or the Middle East. Consciousness of the Jewish catastrophe—and its aftermath in the creation of the State of Israel—came well after the fact. The generation of the 1950s would much rather have continued to look the other way—something I can confirm from the different but comparable British experience. Israel in those years was like a distant relative: someone of whom one spoke fondly and to whom one sent a birthday card regularly, but were he to visit you and overstay his welcome, it would be embarrassing and ultimately an irritant.

Above all, very few of the Jews of my acquaintance in those years would have wished to go and visit that relative, much less live with him. And if this was true in England, how much more so in the U.S. Americans, rather like Israelis in this respect, valued success, achievement, promotion, individualism, the overcoming of impediments to self-advancement and a dismissive unconcern with the past. The Holocaust, accordingly, was not an altogether untroubling story, particularly with regard to the widespread view that Jews had gone "like lambs to the slaughter."

I would go further. I don't think the Holocaust fitted at all comfortably into American Jewish sensibilities—much less American public life as a whole—until the national narrative itself had learned to accommodate and even idealize stories of suffering and victimhood. The English were always comfortable with Dunkirks—embarrassing failures recast as heroic successes. But Americans were historically unsympathetic to failure until quite recently and preferred either to deny it or find some positive moral dimension.

Accordingly, there was a long period during which American Jews continued to resort, by habit and preference, to an older narrative: a tale of escape from the old land—un-regretted—and arrival in a new home where past identities counted for little. Irving Berlin was a Russian Jew. But rather than think, talk or write about his Russian Jewishness, he excelled at writing American tunes, with catchy upbeat narrative verse, for musical self-celebration: something he did much better than most native-born Americans. Berlin was idolized. But who in those decades celebrated Isaac Bashevis Singer? All of this would change, but not I think before the 1980s.

Aren't there some intermediate stages, and some other reasons why American Jews hesitated to identify themselves with the Holocaust? Think of the Cold War and what that entailed. The West Germans were arguably the most important American ally on the European continent from the early 1950s, a hard reality which required their hasty rehabilitation. And Adenauer, the Christian Democratic Chancellor, quite deliberately proposed exchanging West German support and allegiance for American agreement not to talk about the unpleasant recent past.

Meanwhile, in West Germany—and not only there—there was that bizarre reversal of allegiances whereby the Left went from

admiring plucky little social democratic Israel to disliking Zionist
imperialism, while the Right abandoned anti-Semitism and
learned to love our strong little allies in the Jewish state.

The international perception of Israel has a history of its own. When
the country was born, Stalin was the midwife. The view from the left,
communist and non-communist alike, was that for ideological and genea-
logical reasons a state comprising east European Jews from socialist backgrounds must surely be a sympathetic partner. But Stalin quickly realized,
quicker than most as it happens, that Israel's natural trajectory would be to
form an allegiance with protectors in the West, particularly given the growing importance of the Middle East and the Mediterranean for Western security and Western economic interests. The rest of the left was slow to grasp
this point: throughout the '50s and well into the '60s, Israel was still associated with and admired by the mainstream political and intellectual left.
Indeed, the country was governed throughout its first three decades by a
political elite exclusively composed of self-styled social democrats of one
kind or another.

It was not so much the Six-Day War of 1967, but rather the period
between that War and the Yom Kippur War of 1973, that the international
Left abandoned Israel. This, I believe, had more to do with Israel's treatment
of the Arabs than with its domestic policies, which hardly changed in those
years.

It is true that the Six-Day War brought many Jewish Americans
around to Israel, though its impact was less than in Europe, I
think. But the contemporary understanding of the Holocaust has
something to do with the idea that one should use violence to defend
human rights in extreme cases. The Holocaust becomes a more
comfortable association when it is identified not only with
victimhood but with human rights—and thus with military
intervention on behalf of those rights.

*Thus when one recalls how Americans justified intervention in the
Balkan wars of the 1990s, it is clear that everyone involved was
invoking the Holocaust as a template: the worst human rights
violation of all time, the thing that must "never happen again."
The generation in political authority by then had been taught to
think thus, and it was arguments along these lines which were
ultimately invoked to justify U.S. intervention against Serbia.*

*Such arguments could resonate effectively with respect to events
happening in Europe. Curiously, the universalization of the
Holocaust actually made best sense in its point of origin—it made
sense in Europe above all, because older Europeans instinctively
grasped the reasoning and intuitively agreed with the conclusions.*

*But this same reasoning has, I believe, a very different resonance
when applied to the world at large—or when applied by
Americans, as it so often is, to Israel and the Middle East. Here the
risk is that the universal quality of the lesson to be drawn from
Auschwitz then comes to apply to Israel, which in turn is
transformed from a country to a universal metaphor: never again
will a place like Israel suffer an event like the Holocaust. But seen
from anywhere outside America—in the Middle East itself, for
example—this extension of a moral analogy into the local political
arena seems a little peculiar.*

The farther away you get from the shores of the United States, the more
Israel's behavior looks like simply political exploitation of a victim narrative.
Eventually, of course, you get so far away that you arrive in countries and
continents—east Asia, Africa—where the Holocaust itself is an unfamiliar
abstraction. At this point, all that people can see is the bizarre spectacle of a
small, unimportant country in a dangerous region leveraging the most pow-

erful country in the world to its own advantage, but to the detriment of the interests of its protector.

Accordingly, there are three dimensions to· this peculiar situation. There is the uncritical American engagement, mediated through an unsophisticated universalization of the meaning of a European genocide. Then there is the European response: wait a minute, even though we readily concede that the Holocaust was everything you say it was, this constitutes misappropriation. Finally, there is the rest of the world: what, they ask, is this western story that you are imposing upon us with grotesquely distorting geopolitical consequences?

> *Let's return to America, to the source. I'm going to mount a defense now of American Jews and their worldview, which would go something like this: Coming from England, Tony, you don't have the deep, confusing religiosity of the gentile to contend with. It simply isn't there. To be sure, people belong to the Church of England; it's a respected and socially useful institution, marking the calendar and giving widows something to do. But it could hardly be said to be a fount of fervent religiosity.*

> *Whereas here in the United States, once you step away from a handful of neighborhoods on the east and west coasts, you encounter the Christians—real Christians. They celebrate Christmas, and some of them really mean it. Easter too with all of its threatening bloody resonances. And then, as you go farther afield into the countryside—which admittedly is something not so many American Jews willingly do—you encounter ever stranger forms of fervent, exotic Christian belief.*

> *And that—although I think the comparison is very imprecise, this is my sense—makes American Jews at some reflexive level think*

about Russia, or Poland or Ukraine or Romania: there too were
people who had different rituals and who actually believed in them,
who might be not just different but truly threatening. I think it is
this fear, usually of course unarticulated, that stands behind the
inchoate anxiety around the prospect of another Holocaust and
which accounts for the desire to maintain Israel as a future refuge.
This seems to me unreasonable and profoundly mistaken, but not
at all beyond comprehension.

Now, another response to this—a minority response, the
neoconservative response—has been engagement. I have in mind
the alliance between American Zionists who believe that Israel
should exist as a homeland for other Jews and American Christian
fundamentalists who believe that Israel should exist as a gathering
point for Jews before their fiery extermination in the coming
apocalypse. On the one hand, you have Jews who know little about
Israel; on the other hand, Christians who know little about Jews.
But they have overlapping visions and overlapping reasons for
wanting Jews to go to Israel and indeed for wanting wars in the
Middle East. I can't help but think that, in retrospect, this will
seem one of the stranger alliances in the political history of Jews: it
makes the Revisionist Zionist cooperation with Poland in the
1930s seem downright prosaic.

Let's look at this more broadly. Just as you are arguing that America
looks a little bit different thanks to the strange, intense religiosity of the surrounding non-Jewish world, America is also different in the intense, aggressive, civic egalitarianism that the Constitution imposes and that is repeatedly
drummed into people as part of what it means to be American. As you noted,
I grew up in a country where Christianity in its rather watered-down, Anglican form was the default condition of life, right up to and including the
established institutions of the state—indeed, above all, the established insti-

tutions of the state. I am much better informed in the matter of the New Testament, Psalms, hymns, catechisms and rituals of the Christian church than any American Jew I know who has not professionally studied them. Unlike Americans, I lack this visceral insistence in my own self upon the distinction between religion and civic or national identity. And so America is different in that way, too: it is different at both extremes. Would you agree?

Very much so. But there is something in this difference too which makes American Jews more different from you than perhaps you realize. Identifying intensely with the state in the church-state division allows a level of ignorance that was and is unimaginable in Europe. American Jews, for example, have trouble making the distinction between different kinds of Christian religiosity. By which I not only mean the various confusing Protestant denominations, but the core differences between fundamentalists and non-fundamentalists; practicing Catholics and non-practicing Catholics; or even Catholics and Protestants.

These conflations arise from an astonishing cultural ignorance, a breathtaking unfamiliarity with the New Testament. This is something which distinguishes American Jews from English Jews much more than one might have expected at first glance—because you might suppose that, if only out of self-defense, American Jews would take an afternoon and familiarize themselves with these mysterious and, after all, rather brief addenda to the Bible.

This, I think, is why the Christian world that spreads out into the Great Plains and across the Rocky Mountains is far more alien and perhaps more threatening than you would suppose. Whereas in England, it seems to me, Christianity has broader and more familiar cultural references. When you, for example, speak of the King James Bible, you are not merely alluding to one among a

number of versions of the Holy Book. You are talking about a
cultural text, as universal and familiar as Shakespeare. That
is a perspective shared by few American Jews.

In England, religiosity at its minimal but therefore most easily assimilated textual or mnemonic level was still universal in my childhood. I don't know any English Jews who would be profoundly uneasy were they to get on a train and—finding themselves in deepest Lincolnshire—step down at Lincoln Station and walk into Lincoln Cathedral, or for that matter the local parish church. The odds are that they would find it quite a comfortable and even familiar experience, especially if they were born before 1960. Whereas I assume that someone from the Upper West Side deposited by chance in northwest Texas, in a Baptist church, might well be uncomfortable for all manner of reasons.

Did you ever have the sense that someone was trying to read you
out of the American Jewish community?

In his comments in *The New Republic* apropos my notorious *New York Review* essay, Leon Wieseltier famously observed that I was clearly a Jew who had spent too long at dinner parties in New York, listening to people criticize Israel, and was embarrassed by the association and seeking to distance myself from it. This seemed to me a curious misreading: I have always *hated* dinner parties and would go a long way to avoid them! I still do, though, of course, today I no longer have to think up reasons to decline invitations.

Moreover, hearing Israel criticized would never arouse in me embarrassment as a Jew—on the one hand, I don't identify with the country; on the other, I suffer no confusion or insecurity over my Jewishness. So that seems an odd way to blackball me from the right-thinking American Jewish community, to which I never in any case belonged. It might have been a more effective charge to suggest that I was so troubled by Israel's behavior *because*

I was Jewish. However, as you have already pointed out to me, I don't much mind being expelled from communities: perhaps I rather even enjoy it. Such exclusion offers the opportunity once again to see oneself as the outsider, and for me this has always been a safe, even a comfortable position in which to find myself.

Well, parachuting into downtown Manhattan and then defining yourself in opposition to mainstream American Jewry is certainly a program for success in making yourself an outsider!

The risks were never great. Let us suppose that I had been drummed out not from a community which, like Groucho Marx, I never particularly wanted to join in the first place, but instead from a place and a society which constituted the source of my income and my professional standing. That would have been a different story. So I respond with genuine discomfort when people say: oh, you're such a hero for taking unpopular stances.

To be sure, no one objects to being admired or respected for writing well or for saying something true or interesting. But the fact is that it took very little courage to publish a controversial piece about Israel in *The New York Review of Books* while holding a tenured chair at a major university. If I took any risks at all, these were highly localized—I probably lost a few New York friends; decidedly contingent—I suppose I foreclosed publication possibilities in one or two journals.

So I certainly don't regard myself as brave. I just see myself—if I want to indulge a little immodesty—as rather more honest and outspoken than some other people I know.

5.

PARIS, CALIFORNIA: FRENCH INTELLECTUAL

At Cambridge, and then in Paris, socialism was not just a political objective but my area of scholarly study. In some respects this did not change until well into early middle-age. When I first went up to Cambridge as an undergraduate in 1966, it was the thirtieth anniversary of the Popular Front, the French left-wing coalition that had briefly held power in France, with the socialist Léon Blum as prime minister. At the time, this anniversary prompted an outpouring of books describing and assessing the failure of the Popular Front. Many of those who engaged this subject did so with the explicit goal of teaching lessons that would ensure success the next time around: a transformative alliance of left-wing parties still seemed both possible and desirable to many.

I was not myself primarily interested in the immediate political issues implied in these debates. From the perspective of my particular upbringing, revolutionary communism had been a disaster from the start, and I saw little point in reassessing its present prospects. On the other hand, I went up to

Cambridge in the middle of Harold Wilson's cynical, depleted, apologetic and increasingly unsuccessful Labour administration. There seemed little to be expected from that quarter. So my interest in the prospects for social democracy led me abroad, to Paris, which suggests that it was politics which brought me into French studies rather than the other way around.

Although this may appear odd in retrospect, given my own politics and given the turbulence there, I needed Paris to become a proper student of history. I was awarded the annual Cambridge fellowship for a post-graduate place at the École Normale Supérieure, an ideal perch from which to study and observe French intellectual and political life. Once settled there, in 1970, I became a true student—more than I had ever really been in Cambridge—and made serious headway on my doctoral thesis about French socialism in the 1920s.

I started to seek out academic guidance. In Cambridge, you were not exactly taught: you just read books and talked about them. There was considerable variety among my teachers there: old-fashioned, liberal English empiricist historians; methodologically sensitive intellectual historians; and there were still a few economic historians of the old interwar left-wing school. In Cambridge my doctoral supervisors, far from inducting me into historical methodologies, kept disappearing from under me. The supervisor to whom I had been assigned, David Thomson, died shortly after I met him for the first time. My second supervisor was a very sweet, elderly historian of Third Republic France, J. P. T. Bury, who served excellent sherry but knew little about my subject. I don't believe we met more than three times over the course of my doctoral work. Thus I was completely undirected for the first year of doctoral studies in Cambridge, 1969–1970.

Not only did I have to come up with the subject of my thesis, but I had to invent from whole cloth the *problématique*, the questions that it would make sense to ask and the criteria I should invoke when answering them: why did socialism fail to fulfill its own promises? Why did socialism in France fall short of the achievements of northern European social democracy? Why was there no uprising or revolution in France in 1919, despite expectations that there would be and radical upheaval elsewhere? Why was Soviet communism so much better able in those years to inherit the mantle of the French Revolution than the locally-grown socialism of republican France? Deep in the background were the implicit questions about the triumph of the far right in the 1930s. Was the rise of fascism and National Socialism simply to be understood as a failure of the left? That was how I thought about it at the time; only much later did these specters of questions take on life for me.

I read everything I could get my hands on. I worked out as best I could what the sources must be for such a subject and where to find them; I then set about reading them. The one thing I could usefully do in England, before moving to Paris and getting access to French archives, was to read the French press of the post–World War I era. And so I went down to London for the Lent term of 1970, moved in with Jacquie Phillips's mother and worked my way through the French collection in the British Museum newspaper collection at Colindale, reading my way into a closer familiarity with 1920s France. In the nature of things, this *séjour* brought me closer still to the Phillips family, and Jacquie and I got married the following year. We had a large and fairly traditional Jewish wedding, under a chuppah, complete with the breaking of a glass.

Taking up my fellowship at the École Normale Supérieure, I was on my way to another sort of engagement: with France, French history and French intellectuals. Thanks to my Cambridge preparation, I knew exactly with whom I needed to speak in Paris, made my own contacts there and pretty much supervised myself (although I had been formally assigned a French academic advisor—Professor René Rémond—we did not much care for one another, and by mutual agreement we only ever met once).

I was suddenly at the epicenter of the intellectual establishment of republican France, past and present. I was well aware that I was studying in the very building where Émile Durkheim and Léon Blum had studied at the end of the nineteenth century, or Jean-Paul Sartre and Raymond Aron thirty years later. I was blissfully content, surrounded by intelligent, like-minded students in a campus-like setting in the 5th arrondissement which combined residential comfort with a uniquely accommodating library from which one could actually borrow books (almost unknown in Paris then and since).

For good and ill, I began to think and talk like a *normalien*. This was partly a matter of form: taking stances and adopting a style, scholarly and other; but it was also a process of osmotic adaptation. The École was brimming with absurdly overeducated young Frenchmen, with swollen egos and shrunken chests: many of them are now distinguished professors and senior diplomats across the world. It was an intense, hothouse atmosphere very different from Cambridge, and I learned a way of reasoning and of thinking that has remained with me. My colleagues and contemporaries argued with admirable rigor and depth, though sometimes they were less open to evidence and example of the sort provided by worldly experience. I acquired the virtues of this style but doubtless also its vices.

Looking back, I owe much of my identification with French intellectual life to my encounter with Annie Kriegel, the great historian of French communism. I made contact with her in Paris quite simply because she had written *the* book on my subject, her two-volume magnum opus: *Aux origines du communisme français*. Her insistence on understanding communism historically—the movement rather than the abstraction—exercised a great influence upon me. And she was a dramatically charismatic person. Annie, in turn, was amazed to find an Englishman who spoke decent French, and who was interested in socialism, rather than the then-fashionable communism.

Socialism in those years seemed dead as a historical topic. The French Socialist Party had done poorly in the parliamentary elections of 1968 and had then collapsed in 1971 after a weak showing in the recent presidential elections. To be sure, it was duly reconstructed by the opportunistic François Mitterrand, but as a soulless electoral machine under a new name and shorn of its old spirit. In the early 1970s the only left-wing party with long-term prospects appeared to be the communists. In the presidential election of 1969 they had taken fully 21 percent of the vote, far outstripping all other parties of the left.

Communism, then, appeared to occupy the central place in the past, present and future of the French Left. In France as in Italy, not to speak of lands farther east, it could and did present itself as the victor of history: socialism seemed to have lost everywhere but in the far north of Europe. But I was not interested in winners. Annie understood this and saw it as a laudable quality in a serious historian. And so it was thanks to her and her friends—not least the great Raymond Aron—that I found my way into the history of France.

Annie Kriegel was a tough, complicated woman. Misleadingly diminutive— she stood four-foot-eleven—Annie had joined the French Resistance at the age of sixteen (her contemporary Maurice Agulhon, later the author of *La République au village*, recalled her keeping a sub-machine gun on the wall of her dorm room long after the liberation). She became a doctrinaire Stalinist in the early 1950s, the organizational secretary and de facto political commissar of the communist student movement in Paris. Like so many others in her generation, she fell away from this youthful political allegiance in the aftermath of the Hungarian Revolution and its repression by the Soviets in 1956. She then became in due course the acknowledged expert on the subject of her own past affiliations.

By the time I met her, Annie was applying to Israel and Zionism the same unquestioning commitment and fervor that she had once reserved for the USSR. Curiously, or perhaps not, it thus came about that I found myself closely drawn to a woman whose communist past and Zionist present were almost equally antipathetic to me. And yet Annie Kriegel was one of my two great intellectual influences in the early 1970s (George Lichtheim was the other). It says a lot about Annie that although I dissented from her own conclusions in my doctoral dissertation, she agreed enthusiastically to preface the latter when it was published in France as my first book (*La Reconstruction du Parti Socialiste, 1921–26*).

Indeed, I cited Annie in that work only to disagree with her; as a general rule I avoided discussion of the secondary literature on my subject altogether. I was quite determined not to write just another conventional

English- or American-style historical monograph which engages all the interpretations and then tentatively adds some minor revision of its own. I wanted instead to see what I could achieve on my own account.

If this sounds a touch self-important for a young scholar in his twenties, my excuse must be not only that I simply did not know about much of the secondary literature, but also that I had never been *taught* to engage it. In historiographical matters, I was largely self-educated. Despite my degree in History from Cambridge, I was something—perhaps too much—of an autodidact. More than I could have understood at the time, I had thus placed myself in a long and occasionally distinguished tradition of historians who owed much—too much—of their education to their own undirected reading.

In Paris in those same years I also got to know Boris Souvarine, one of the founders of French communism, but perhaps best known as the author of the first (and still one of the best) accounts of Stalin and Stalinism. It was from Souvarine that I learned—or perhaps had confirmed—something that I have tried to convey in a number of my books: the deep Marxist faith that undergirded the politics of the old European Left, independently of where they stood on the spectrum of radical politics. Souvarine told me a funny story that illustrates this point rather nicely.

Charles Rappoport was another figure from that founding communist generation, and he and Souvarine were talking sometime in the early twenties about Jean Longuet, one of the leaders of the French Socialist Party in the era of World War I. Longuet was a natural compromiser, always seeking a middle way between Lenin and the mainstream European socialists and much resented for his maneuverings by his radical colleagues. He was also Marx's grandson. Thus Rappoport turned to Souvarine and remarked, "You see, the thing about Longuet was that *il voulait contenter tout le monde et son grand-père*": he wanted to please everyone and his grandfather, a witty allusion to "*Il voulait contenter tout le monde et son père*," the punch line of *Le Meunier, Son Fils et L'Âne*, one of La Fontaine's best-known fables. This perfectly captured Longuet and his kind, desperately seeking to square their

Marxist loyalties with whatever situation they found themselves in. But the whole story with all of its references captures something else essential about intellectuals of the Left: the shared references that arose not only from a common political aim but from a great deal of reading.

By choosing to study in my dissertation the years 1921–1926, I kept a certain distance from the 1930s and the issue of the Popular Front. But all the same, I was already drawn to the tragic figure of Léon Blum, who was at the center of Socialist Party politics as I described them in the 1920s, and would of course go on to serve as prime minister of France in the next decade. At the time I would not have thought of writing biographically-inflected history; but Blum was already central to my account, because he embodied something beyond political socialism: a sustained attempt to bring nineteenth-century ideals to bear upon twentieth-century mass politics.

Although I did not and do not enjoy conducting interviews, I interviewed Léon Blum's son and his daughter-in-law, Robert and Renée-Robert Blum. I was trying, however clumsily, to find my way inside the mental world of the generation of European intellectuals born between 1870 and 1910. Blum himself was born in 1872: shortly after Rosa Luxemburg, three years before Luigi Einaudi, seven years before William Beveridge, and ten years before Clement Attlee and John Maynard Keynes. What Blum shares with all of these is the distinctive late nineteenth-century mix of cultural self-confidence informed by a duty to engage in public improvement.

In taking an interest in the period before 1939, but confining my attention to the left-wing heirs of liberal Europe, I was unquestionably sidestepping certain crucial questions about political and above all intellectual life in those decades. What was missing in interwar thought of the left and center was any appreciation of the possibility of *evil* as a constraining, much less a dominating, element in public affairs. Deliberate political criminality, of the kind that was undertaken by the Nazis, was simply incomprehensible on its own terms to most contemporary observers and critics, whether right or left.

The fact that the Stalinist famines and terror of the 1930s were not understood by most western commentators illustrates the point. The First World War had certainly buried many of the progressive illusions of earlier decades; but it had not yet substituted for them the very impossibility of poetry. Indeed, there were those for whom the 1930s were by no means Auden's "low, dishonest decade."

Richard Cobb, the Oxford historian, who was born in 1917, recalled the Paris of the Popular Front as a happy place, full of hope and optimism. For Cobb and many others the thirties were a time of huge energies, just waiting to be mobilized. By no means everyone was overwhelmed by the sense of doom or the end of an era. The Popular Front itself (in France as in Spain) was a remarkable coalition of socialists, communists and radicals. The reforms that it brought to France, including paid vacations, a shorter work week, recognition of union rights and more, went well beyond what Blum's allies had anticipated. The communists, especially, under instructions from Moscow to support a left-wing bourgeois government in France against the emerging threat of Nazi Germany, had no interest in frightening the middle class, much less in promoting revolution.

Yet to those on the right, a revolution seemed indeed to be taking place. The brilliant reactionary critic Robert Brasillach, writing in *Je suis partout*, was quite convinced that he was living through a re-run of the French Revolution. But this was, Brasillach thought, a revolution whose consequences would outdo those of its French and Russian forebears, because it might actually succeed without even doing violence to its own principles. Worse still, it was led by Léon Blum, a Jewish intellectual.

What interested me in Blum as a Jew was precisely that: the hatred he aroused. We find it hard today even to imagine the degree of overt, unapologetic prejudice and dislike that someone like Blum could inspire in those years, primarily and simply on account of his Jewish origin. On the other hand Blum himself was often deaf to the scale and implications of public anti-Semitism and its invocation against him. There was, of course, a certain ambivalence in Blum's own identity: unashamedly and totally French, he was no less overtly and proudly Jewish. In later years he combined great sympathy for the newborn Jewish state in the Middle East with near indifference to the Zionist message itself. These ostensibly incompatible identifications and enthusiasms were perhaps not so far from my own at various times, which may explain my long-standing interest in the man.

At the time, though, I was keeping Jewish issues far away from my academic concerns. Despite my recent and animated engagement with Israel, I would not in those years, in the early 1970s, have thought to make of Blum's Jewishness a subject of study. Jewish political engagement had absorbed all my adolescent attentions. But once I dropped it, it was as though I no longer saw, much less engaged with, Jewish issues in my professional life. In retrospect, I can see that I had finished my "Jewish decade" and was wholly engaged upon preparing myself for its French successor.

What obsessed me in the course of the 1970s were institutions, political parties and social theories: all of which I tended to regard, without ever explicitly saying so, as the product of social conditions. In the Cambridge of the day and in their different ways, Quentin Skinner and John Dunn were teaching the history of ideas with privileged reference to the cultural, epistemological and textual contextualization of intellectual production. I give them full credit for my interest in thinking seriously about what it means to interrogate ideas initially developed and expounded in another time or place. But context for me remained social, or at most high political, rather than religious, cultural or hermeneutic.

In Paris I did what an academic should do: I wrote a dissertation, found a publisher for it and sought out new fields. But in other respects I did not know quite what I was doing and where I was heading. I had no clear sense of how to become a scholarly historian or what it would mean, although I was fitted for little else. In the end I was able to square my various interests and affinities with an academic career, but only as the result of good fortune and the generous help of others.

Completing my PhD, I was at first unable to find a fellowship or secure an academic position, and had become resigned to taking a post in a prestigious boys' school in South London. Thanks to John Dunn, my friend and mentor at King's, I held off accepting the position just long enough to learn that I had been offered a Research Fellowship at King's.

If I was able to get my foot in the door at Cambridge, this was largely thanks to George Lichtheim, the great historian of Marxism and socialism, a benefactor whom I never met. I had read all of his important books between 1968 and 1973, and was doubtless in great debt to his perspective: that of a sympathetic but relentlessly critical observer of the Marxism of the late nineteenth and early twentieth centuries. Both Lichtheim and Annie Kriegel apparently wrote very strong letters of support for me, based in both cases upon their reading of my doctoral dissertation. I owe them everything—and cannot think of two people to whom I would rather be indebted.

But Lichtheim and Kriegel represented a minority taste, and both were outsiders—at least to English academia. Richard Cobb, the leading English-speaking French historian of the day and an influential figure in my field, never really regarded me as a historian. For Cobb, I was a disciplinary interloper with all the worst instincts of a French intellectual: writing politics under the guise of historical scholarship.

Thanks to his veto, I was unsuccessful in every other Oxbridge fellowship and post for which I applied in those years. My dissertation failed to find a British publisher. Although it secured me the King's Fellowship it was only ever published in French: I was offered a book contract by the *Presses de la Fondation Nationale des Sciences Politiques*, who must have received an unusually strong recommendation before committing themselves to a first book by an unknown Englishman—probably from Annie Kriegel.

The fact that I never tried again to find an English-language publisher probably suggests something else: I really *was* an intellectual rather than an academic, and utterly naïve when it came to career calculations or strategic planning. It simply never occurred to me that publishing my first book in French was a foolish move if I wished to make it in the American or British historical profession. Cobb was not entirely wrong: there had been something of a category error. I was on the career path of an English historian, but thought of myself as a dissenting French intellectual and acted accordingly.

In the early 1970s, it was still possible to teach history in England and yet be completely detached from the North American academic community. The Atlantic was much wider in those days. However, a couple of years after I won the fellowship at King's, chance and the briefest of human contacts offered me an opportunity to go to California. I happened to dine at King's one evening with F. Roy Willis, a former undergraduate Kingsman who now taught at the University of California at Davis and had written an early history of European unification, *France, Germany and the New Europe*. Nine months after our brief encounter, he called me up in Cambridge and asked if I would like to come for a year to Davis.

In proper American fashion, Willis named an annual salary. I hesitated: it was so much more than I was getting in Cambridge that I wondered if I'd misheard him. He in turn misunderstood my hesitation and increased the offer: my first and one of my more successful forays into negotiation! Jacquie and I flew into Boston the following summer, and after a short stay with a friend in Cambridge, Massachusetts, we purchased a huge old Buick and made our way across the country.

That year in Davis, 1975–1976, was my first exposure to the United States. It was a wonderful experience. Nothing hung on it. I taught broad courses in European history for the first time, and realized that I could not do in California what almost everyone did back in Cambridge, which was read out my lectures. Instead, I learned to extemporize and became a competent college teacher.

My American students approached learning very differently from their British peers. In California I was teaching young people who did not actually know very much but who were not ashamed to admit it and were keen to learn. In England, few people past the age of sixteen ever admit to ignorance, certainly not in Cambridge. This makes for a more confident conversational style, but it also means that the typical English student often goes for years without reading certain foundational texts because no one ever questions his or her familiarity with them.

Upon our return to England in 1976, Jacquie and I began to drift apart; in December 1976 we separated, divorcing two years later. The reasons for this breakup are not hard to seek. California had broadened my horizons; and although I had declined the offer of a permanent position in Davis, returning to Cambridge proved disappointing and ultimately unsatisfying. Before we left for the States, Jacquie and I had been living in a tiny two-bedroom apartment; when we returned from California the time had obviously come to buy something larger. But the act of purchasing property, as so often, concentrates the mind. Until then, as it seems to me in retrospect, I had just proceeded along the monorail laid out for me in graduate school; now I was no longer so sure that I wanted my life to take this shape. I could not quite accept that this was all there was to it: one career, one university, one house, one wife.

After Jacquie and I separated, I went off to live in France for a while to research my second book, *Socialism in Provence*. Most of the first half of 1977 was spent in lower Provence, in the department of the Var where my sources were located—and where Nicholas Kaldor, the Cambridge economist and King's fellow, had offered me the use of his home in La Garde-Freinet, a small town about twelve kilometers north of Saint-Tropez. It was a lovely old eighteenth-century Provençal town house in a street of empty, shuttered houses—sun-baked on one side, shadows and grass and hills on the other. I was happy to be single again, for the first time since the age of eighteen: living alone, with just a purpose and the handful of possessions that I needed in order to work and live: a car, a suitcase full of clothes, just about enough money and a house that was mine until the summer.

Life in La Garde-Freinet had old-established routine. Before the tourists arrived in the summer, the region was still very much old Provence, complete with a few surviving geriatrics who spoke the traditional dialect. The daily movements of sheep and shepherds, the ancient patterns of the rural economy and the street life of the hill village remained reminiscent of the nineteenth century. My subject—the economic and social sources of rural socialism in Provence—surrounded me still. I was *bien dans ma peau* in every way.

Each morning I would get up, stumble out of my door into the venerable convertible Citroën DS 19 that I had bought upon returning from the U.S.; start it by rolling down the hill (the starter motor was shot) and—since the road ran downhill all the way from there to the coast—would give the car a daily charge, enough to get me back home. I would park in Sainte-Maxime, buy myself a baguette, some cheese, some fruit, a bottle of mineral water and the local newspapers, and sit on the beach for three hours, intermittently swimming and reading; then it was back to the car and up the mountain to a shower, a nap, and then many hours of work on the book, deep into the night.

I spent afternoons in village libraries, municipal archives, the departmental archives in nearby Draguignan and the urban archives of the coastal city of Toulon. I've since researched other books, but never on the same intensive scale nor with the same local familiarity. The experience confirmed me in the view that no historian should undertake a source-based work of primary research unless he is assured of close access on a long-term basis to the archival materials. Long-distance research based on occasional flying visits is at best frustrating, and usually insufficient to its purpose.

I was now in my late twenties and breaking up with my first wife, to my parents' disappointment. Of course, I would divorce again, my sister Deborah would divorce twice, and in the end even my parents themselves got divorced; but mine was the first divorce in our immediate family. Although I later learned that divorce and multiple marriages, with various permutations and blendings, were quite common in the history of my family, my parents and I were assimilated enough into 1950s England to think of divorce as something unusual and to be avoided.

Aside from my emerging inability to find the right wife, however, it seemed to my parents that mine was a life well lived, if somewhat opaque to them. It was not obvious (to them) that I was in any recognizable sense "working," the more so as my employer appeared to have no objection to my disappearing to the South of France for six months. My mother, who (like all in her generation) had been deeply influenced by the unemployment of the 1930s, was afraid that Cambridge would take away my job if I stayed away too long. With time, they came to understand academic life, research and tenure—although I am not sure that either of my parents fully grasped what exactly I was up to before the publication and success of *Postwar*.

In 1977, as I thought and wrote about French rural laborers and the nineteenth-century French working class, I suppose that I was still defending and even practicing a certain sort of Marxism—at least as historical approach—while keeping my distance from it politically and only half acknowledging its impact upon my work. My first book too had been about Marxists, but it was not at all social history as then conceived, dealing as it did mainly with political parties and activists.

I had nothing against what I thought of as classical social history. Quite the contrary: more than anything in those years, I was motivated by the example of Maurice Agulhon and his *La République au village*. Agulhon had revealed and illustrated the sources of political radicalism that formed in the French countryside during the course of the first half of the nineteenth century; in particular, he described the widespread hopes for a certain rural socialism, dashed in 1851 by the coup of Louis Napoleon Bonaparte.

Influenced by Agulhon and other historians of the rural French south, I set out to write a grassroots social history of my own: a regional study of late-nineteenth-century Provence, even though at some level this sort of nuts-and-bolts historical writing was not my natural forte nor did it correspond to my intellectual instincts. I buried myself in those Var archives. Many years earlier, an old teacher of mine in Cambridge, Christopher Morris, had advised me (somewhat sententiously) that a historian should know the price of pigs in the annual market. Well, after a few years' research, I knew the price of pigs (and much else) in the annual markets of the Var for every year from 1870 to 1914. I too (this research seemed to announce) can do proper social history. And I did. And after that I never did it again.

I was genuinely perplexed by social historical writing of the 1970s. Economics, politics and even society itself were slipping out of focus and indeed out of the field altogether. I was irritated by the use of selective social and cultural data to displace conventional contextual or political explanations of major events: thus the French Revolution might be reduced to a gender revolt, or even an adolescent expression of intergenerational discontent. What had once been taken as self-evidently the most important features of major events in the past were replaced by those aspects which had hitherto been altogether peripheral.

I studied modern history because it had seemed self-evidently a path to intellectual engagement and civic investment. But how do you engage intellectually as a citizen, much less appeal to your fellow citizens, when what you are doing is so obviously preoccupied with social marginalia of interest only to your fellow scholars? Many of my colleagues appeared to be taking part in a sort of half-conscious academic *charivari*: a free-spirited reversal of roles in which second-rate social historians had been offered the freedom to come out and dominate the field, disparaging and overthrowing the major scholars whose publications and concerns had governed the profession for decades past.

I was thus at odds with the major trends in my own discipline: these were tending towards modernization theory, on the one hand, and—with a little delay—towards "cultural studies" on the other. What I found particularly galling, I suppose, was the claim of many of these new approaches to social history to extend or enrich a Marxism which they largely misunderstood.

Modernization theory, in those years, benefited from its respectable antecedents in 1950s writing on industrial society: notably by Ralf Dahrendorf and Raymond Aron. In its crasser forms, however, it proposed a narrative of progress with a clear and un-interrogated end point: industrial society and its political doppelganger—democracy. This all seemed to me a rather blatant and unsubtle teleology, offering a vision of certainty about past processes and future outcomes that I found alien as a historian—and even, odd as it may sound, as a Marxist historian. As for cultural studies, I found them depressingly superficial: driven by the need to separate social data and experience from any economic roots or influences, the better to distinguish their claims from the discredited Marxism on which they otherwise drew shamelessly.

In the political and academic debates of earlier decades, Marxism had always been treated in the final analysis as a historical model powered by the engine of proletarian interest and action. But for just this reason, as the blue collar proletariat diminished in numbers and relevance throughout advanced societies, Marxism appeared vulnerable to the implausibility of its premises.

What happens, after all, when the proletariat ceases to function as an engine of history? At the hands of practitioners of cultural and social studies in the 1970s the machine could still be made to work: you merely replaced "workers" with "women"; or students, or peasants, or blacks, or—eventually—gays, or indeed whichever group had sound reason to be dissatisfied with the present disposition of power and authority.

If this all struck me as jejune and callow, I owed my irritation to the distinctive course of my own education. By the 1970s I was caught in something of a time warp. I understood and in large measure shared the world view of the Eric Hobsbawms and the E. P. Thompsons more than the preoccupations of my own academic generation. These were men who were formed by the problems of the 1920s and the 1930s, the problems that I had chosen for my own in my dissertation.

American contemporaries in particular seemed to me to be moving on a little too fast, before even acquiring a full understanding of what it was they were losing. I, on the other hand, having completed a PhD at the age of twenty-four, was already a faculty member at a time when my peers were just getting to know their graduate supervisors, and were being encouraged to look for new areas of interest and new methods. Navigating alone, I lacked generational bearings. So it is perhaps not surprising that I reacted more than once against the proclivities of my own generation.

I made some bad choices in those years. Not long after returning to Cambridge from Provence in 1977, I got involved with Patricia Hilden, a graduate student from Davis who had come to work with me. Because of her influence, I made an exception for women's history in my critique of the new social history, even though I was really quite ignorant of the subject and what little I knew had not impressed me. But Patricia was a very aggressive and self-confident feminist, sharp and unforgiving: a curiously seductive mix. So, with shameless inconsistency, I indulged women's history even as I remained unforgiving in my dismissal of all other kinds of hyphenated or identity studies.

Our relationship was misconceived from the outset, and not only because it forced me onto intellectually dishonest territory. For the next several years I traveled back and forth from England to America; largely following Patricia, who seemed never to be satisfied where she was. In the spring of 1978, I applied for and was offered two junior jobs in the United States, at Harvard and the University of California at Berkeley. I chose Berkeley ostensibly because Harvard seemed too much like the Cambridge I was leaving. This, at least, was the reason I gave myself. But the main consideration was that Patricia wanted to return to California. I too liked the idea of going back there, although my intellectual interests were already moving away from the social-historical focus that had aroused Berkeley's interest in me.

I was thus stuck teaching social history at Berkeley from 1978 to 1980: rather against the grain of my own preferences. One semester I offered a course on the history of socialism and communism in Europe. Over two hundred students turned up, so what began as a seminar became a large lecture course. When I reached Leon Trotsky and the tragedy of the Russian Revolution, the source of my popularity became clear. Ever since the 1920s there have been Marxists (Leninists really) who saw Trotsky as the path not taken, the history that somehow went off course, the king across the water. In northern California in the late 1970s, as it turned out, they were still around. A group of young people came up to me after my Trotsky lecture and said, in effect: "Tony, we're really enjoying your course, and we wondered if you could come speak to the Fourth International Group in San Francisco about Trotsky's mistakes—and how to avoid them next time."

Here, in a distant land, was a reflection of my father's youthful preoccupations, and perhaps my own: what had gone wrong with the revolutionary Left? Was its failure not maybe partly responsible for the horrible violence of the 1930s and 1940s in Europe? For these students, as indeed for my father and some of his friends, such questions still invited answers that were personal in nature: the solution to the dilemma of Leninism was Trotsky, not Stalin. I had never seen matters quite that way myself, and was long distant from any sort of revolutionary Marxism. But I recognized a familiar sensibility, a familiar yearning. I realized that what I was really teaching was a sort of historically-inflected vocational course on how to practice far left politics. Berkeley had its charms.

But Patricia had insisted that we live in Davis rather than in Berkeley. And so we settled there, which meant that I had to commute to Berkeley: a hundred kilometers each way on the university bus. That same summer (1979) we were married in Davis. But the following semester, I did at least get to move to Berkeley—Patricia, ever dissatisfied with her present location, had by that time returned to a post-doctoral position in England.

In the course of my second year in California, it became perfectly clear to me that I was out of place. Berkeley felt a long way from Europe, and further still from my interests. In the American system departments and universities award promotion and "tenure" to promising junior faculty, holding out the prospect of permanent future employment as a professor. Securing tenure for oneself (or denying it to others) is thus the dominant obsession of university life, since anyone thus promoted thereby achieves rank, prosperity, autonomy and security: no mean reward.

My own tenure case at Berkeley proceeded under the shadow cast by a long article I published in 1979 criticizing popular trends in social history, under the title "A Clown in Regal Purple." Various colleagues in the history department pompously advised me that, on account of this notorious essay, they would have to vote against me. As one of them explained it to me, this was not because of the essay's controversial content, but rather because it had "named names." In particular, William Sewell, one of those whom I had listed as a perpetrator of the more misguided sort of social history, was a Berkeley graduate. For a young assistant professor like myself to dismiss the work of his colleagues' students was *lèse-institution*, and unforgivable. Lacking both institutional loyalty and prudential instincts, I of course had never understood the extent of my offense. Thanks to that essay, the tenure vote in my department was split, albeit with a positive majority. Whatever my long-term prospects, the atmosphere felt poisoned.

And so I decided to return home to England if I could. A job opened up in the Politics Faculty at Oxford, a university lectureship carrying a fellowship at St. Anne's College. I applied and was offered the post. I returned to England unambiguously happy. I was to miss my California days—cruising down the coast on Highway One in a convertible Mustang, swapping political notes with the Trotskyists etc. And I missed my students. But I have never regretted leaving Berkeley.

Here, right in the middle, I'd like to break the narrative.

> *Both in private and in professional life you are a rebel on the Left,*
> *but not a rebel against the Left. Even your Zionism is socialist, and*
> *you rebel against Israel when you discover that not everyone's is. As a*
> *scholar you are taking up very traditional subjects for a Marxist*
> *historian, and your dissatisfaction in the 1970s has something to do*
> *with the abandonment by left-wing colleagues of Marxist*
> *categories—which creep in to the end of your article "A Clown in*
> *Regal Purple." There you speak of a total collapse of social history,*
> *amounting to a "loss of faith in history." But I think you're making,*
> *at that stage of your life and career, a last attempt to convince*
> *yourself that everything can be made to fit within Marxist categories.*

> *But only so much of the history of the twentieth century can be*
> *understood within the categories of Marxism, or indeed within the*

larger framework of enlightenment and its variations, of which Marxism is one. And given what you said in our earlier discussion about the fascists I think you agree. So let's discuss the far right before we return to the Left or its failings. Let's insert the intellectual life of the far Right, and talk about the fascists.

We've already spoken and we'll speak again about the emotive and intellectual appeal of Marxism and Leninism. After all, the Popular Front is a form of anti-fascism. And yet logically before anti-fascism must come fascism: Mussolini's rise to power in 1922, the seemingly similar rise to power of Hitler in 1933, the growing influence of the Romanian fascists in the 1930s—for that matter the weaker but still important current of fascist thought in France and Britain.

So let me begin by asking you about the subject that you didn't choose to write about in your dissertation. Why do we so readily neglect the fascist intellectuals of the 1920s and 1930s?

When we spoke of the Marxists we could begin with concepts. The fascists don't really have concepts. They have attitudes. They have distinctive responses to war, depression and backwardness. But they don't start out with a set of ideas that they then apply to the world.

I wonder if another reason why we have trouble remembering the fascists is that insofar as they had arguments, they were usually arguments against something: liberalism, democracy, Marxism.

Until the late 1930s (or even the early 1940s during the wartime occupations), when they start becoming involved in policies of real consequence, like anti-Semitic legislation, fascist intellectuals don't stand out clearly from much other political discussion in the interwar years. It is hard to separate the Frenchmen Pierre Drieu la Rochelle and Robert Brasillach, who were palpably fascist, from the editorials of the right-of-center mainstream French press on important subjects such as the Spanish Civil War, the Popular Front, the League of Nations, Mussolini, America.

Criticisms of social democracy or of liberalism or attitudes towards Marxism or Bolshevism are also very difficult to separate. That's largely true even in Germany before 1933, where much the same set of attitudes on foreign policy runs from, say, the liberal Gustav Stresemann through the Nazis. And in Romania, of course, the people we would now identify as fascist intellectuals—Mircea Eliade, Emil Cioran—were not just mainstream, they were the dominant intelligentsia.

What might be the intellectual virtues of fascist intellectuals?

Let's take the case of Robert Brasillach. He was seen by contemporaries as one of the sophisticated voices of the far right. And he's typical in being young; he comes of age in the 1930s. He wrote very well—as did quite a few of the fascist intellectuals. They were often witty and more sardonic than left-wing intellectuals, who tended to be heavy-handedly serious. There's an aesthetic sensibility, which allows for a sympathetic and cultivated response to modern arts. Brasillach, for example, was a cinema critic—and a very good one. If you read his work now, and if you're fair, you see that his criticisms of the left-wing films of the 1930s, precisely the ones most admired now, are quite biting.

In contrast to the postwar generation of dominant left-wing intellectuals—the Sartre generation, which is the immediately succeeding generation of dominant intellectuals—the fascist intellectuals of the 1930s, tended to be less prone to asserting views about everything. They're not all-purpose intellectuals; they tend to focus on certain areas and be known for that. They tend to be quite proud of being cultural critics, or foreign policy experts, or whatever it might be, and don't wander aimlessly across the whole range of public policy. Some of them are admired, if reluctantly, by a much wider range of people than if they'd simply been thought of as all-purpose fascist intellectuals. So Brasillach has a lot of admirers for his film criticism, and some of his other cultural essays, even though he's publishing them in a right-wing rag like *Je suis partout*. This specialization made, I think, fascist intellectuals much better placed to defend themselves against the charge of being mere wordsmiths.

Finally, in the case of someone like Brasillach, there was a sort of cultivated individualism which, of course, goes well on the right and tends to be uncomfortable on the left. Right-wing intellectuals look like the dandified cultural critics of, say, the 1830s and 1840s; they are a more recognizable and sympathetic social type than the ideological intellectual of the later generations on the left. Someone like Brasillach doesn't in any very active or consistent way identify with a political party. Now, part of the irony, of course, is that there aren't political parties of any significance on the far right with which he can identify in France. But it's true in other places, too. Most right-wing intellectuals—Jünger, Cioran, Brasillach—were not party men. All of these are strengths in an intellectual world.

Where did the fascist intellectuals come from? Can we speak of a purely intellectual genealogy of the fascists?

The mainstream genetic story is that fascism arose from the uncertainties of the pre–World War I generation when confronted by the war and the immediate postwar period. What you then have is a warped and distinctively new kind of nationalism transfigured by the energy and violence of the First World War into a political movement of a new kind, a mass movement, potentially, of the right. Zeev Sternhell, by contrast, emphasizes that the pre–World War I attitudes towards democracy, or decadence, together with the experience of the war and the failure of the Left in the war, turn a whole generation towards fascism. In this account, the real origins of fascism, and above all, its economic policies and its critique of democracy are on the *left*.

You don't have to choose between these stories. It's not difficult to find individuals who followed both trajectories. And it may also be that both of them are a little bit anachronistic. If you could stop the clock in 1913, the year before the outbreak of the First World War, and inquire after the political stance and likely future affiliations of the younger generation, you would see that the divide between the Left and the Right isn't quite the point. Most of the movements deliberately defined themselves as neither left nor right. They refused to be defined within the French revolutionary lexicon which had for so long provided the parameters for modern political geography.

Rather, they saw the debates within liberal society as themselves the problem rather than as containing a solution. Think of the Italian futurists in their manifestoes and their artistic endeavors of the decade before World War I. In France there was a survey, *"Les jeunes gens d'aujourd'hui,"* (The Young People of Today), which became a sort of manifesto of the young right, although its authors didn't claim to set out that way. What young people had in common is a belief that only they can seize the century. We would like to be free, they asserted: we want to release the deep energies of the nation. In 1913 you wouldn't have known whether this sentiment was left or right: it would quite plausibly have served as a left-wing modernist manifesto—there has to be change, there will be radical departures, we must go with the present and not be confined by the past. But at the same time, these expressions of frustrated youthful impulses sound classically *right* in tone: national will, national purpose, national energy. The nineteenth century was the bourgeois century. The twentieth century would be the century of change, coming upon us so fast that only the young and uncommitted could hope to seize the day and go with it. Speed was of the essence: the airplane and the automobile had just been invented.

In Germany, everyone from vegetarian groups to bicycle clubs to hiking clubs to nature societies found themselves—with exceptions—leaning toward the nationalist right. Conversely, the very same sort of people in England—wearing remarkably similar clothes and taking similarly-motivated exercise—inclined towards the left: talking about William Morris wallpaper, lifting the working people to a higher cultural level, spreading knowledge about contraception and diet for the greater good of the masses etc.

> *After 1913, there is the First World War itself, and then the*
> *application of the principle of national self-determination, and the*
> *Bolshevik Revolution. I wonder if we can't separate out some of*
> *these factors in the emergence of fascism by time and place.*

What is surprising even in retrospect is that the violence of the First World War did not have the effect we would suppose today. It was precisely the bloody, deadly aspect of war which was so celebrated by those for whom it was the defining moment of their youth. When you read Ernst Jünger, or Drieu la Rochelle, or the angry responses to Erich Maria Remarque, you find that the retrospective celebration of togetherness in conflict gave the war a very special glow for many members of the Front Generation. Veterans were divided between those who harbored a lifelong *nostalgie de la boue* and those who were forever alienated from all forms of nationalist politics and militarism. The latter may have been in the absolute majority, especially in France and Britain; but they were decidedly not in the majority among intellectuals.

The Bolshevik Revolution took place in late 1917, so before the war's end. This means that even before the postwar period really began there was already the looming threat of a second disturbance: a European revolution facilitated and justified by the disruption of the war and the injustice (real or perceived) of the peace settlements. If you go country by country, starting with Italy, you see that without the threat of a communist revolution there would have been far less space for fascists to offer themselves as a guarantee of traditional order. Indeed fascism, at least in Italy, was uncertain as to whether it was radical or conservative. It fell to the right in large measure because of the success of its right wing in presenting fascism as the appropriate response to the threat of communism. Absent the specter of left-wing revolution, the left fascists might well have dominated. Instead, Mussolini had to purge them, as did Hitler ten years later.

Conversely, the relative weakness of the revolutionary Left in postwar Britain, France or Belgium restricted the credibility of right-wing efforts to exploit the communist bogey over the coming decade. In Britain, even Winston Churchill was ridiculed for his obsession with the Red Threat and the Bolsheviks.

Many of the fascists admired Lenin, admired his revolution,
admired the Soviet state, and saw one-party rule as a model.

Ironically, the Bolshevik Revolution and the creation of the Soviet Union posed far trickier problems for the Left than they did for the Right. In the early postwar years, very little was known in Western Europe about Lenin and his revolution. Accordingly, there was a lot of self-serving abstract recasting of Russian developments in accordance with local preferences: this was a syndicalist revolution, an anarchist revolution, a Marxist socialism adapted to Russian circumstance, a temporary dictatorship and so on. The Left had to worry that this revolution in a backward, agrarian country did not conform to Marx's predictions, and might therefore generate warped and even tyrannical outcomes. Whereas for the fascists, those aspects of Leninism which most troubled conventional Marxists—the emphasis on voluntarism and Lenin's hubristic willingness to accelerate history—were what they found most pleasing. The Soviet state was violent, decisive and firmly led from above: in those early years it was everything that future fascists longed for and found lacking in the political culture of their own societies. It confirmed for them that a party can make a revolution, seize a state and govern by force if necessary.

In those early years the Russian Revolution also generated effective
and even beautiful propaganda. As time went on, moreover, the
Bolsheviks had a distinctive knack for exploiting public places.

I would go further. The public face of fascism and communism was often strikingly similar. Mussolini's plans for Rome, for example, look frighteningly like Moscow University. If you knew nothing of the history of Nicolai Ceauşescu's House of the People, how would you determine whether it was fascist or communist architecture? There was also a shared (and superficially paradoxical) conservatism of taste in the higher arts, after the initial enthusiasm of the revolutionary years. In music, in painting, in literature, theater and dance, communists and fascists were extraordinarily wary of innovation or imagination. By the 1930s aesthetic radicals were as unwelcome in Moscow as they were in Rome or Berlin.

I'm struck that for the Romanian fascists, singing in public was very important. And I wonder if fascism doesn't depend—here comes a kind of Marxist argument about fascism—on a certain level of technological development, where people can be moved easily but information less so? After all, a chorus is a means of communication that makes sense before radio, which was scant in the interwar Romanian countryside.

We're at exactly the point when societies of Europe are entering the age of the masses. People can read newspapers. They work in very large agglomerations and are exposed to shared experiences—in school, in the military, traveling by train. So you have self-conscious communities on a grand scale, but for the most part nothing resembling genuinely democratic societies. Accordingly, countries like Italy or Romania were peculiarly vulnerable to movements and organizations that combined non-democratic form with popular content.

I think that this is one of the reasons why so few people understood them; certainly, their critics did not. Marxists could not find any "class logic" in fascist parties: therefore, they dismissed them as mere superstructural representatives of the old ruling class, invented and instrumentalized for the purpose of mobilizing support against the threat from the Left—a necessary but far from sufficient account of the appeal and function of Fascism.

It therefore makes sense that in the aftermath of World War II, with the establishment of stable democracies in much of Western and parts of Central Europe, fascism lost its purchase. In later decades, with the coming of television (and *a fortiori* the internet), the masses disaggregate into ever-smaller units. Consequently, for all its demagogic and populist appeal, traditional fascism has been handicapped: the one thing that fascists do supremely well—transforming angry minorities into large groups, and large groups into crowds—is now extraordinarily difficult to accomplish.

Yes. The thing which fascists did well was de-fragmentation in a transient way and on a national level. I think probably now no one can do that, at least not in the same way.

The prospects for fascism today depend upon a country being trapped in some combination of mass society and fragile, fragmented political institutions. As of today, I can think of nowhere in the West where these conditions obtain in a sufficiently acute form.

However, it does not in the least follow that fascist-style demands—or individuals of a fascist disposition—have gone for good. We have seen them only recently in Poland and in France; we can observe them doing quite well in Belgium, Holland and Hungary. But today's proto-fascists are handicapped: in the first place, they cannot openly avow their natural political allegiance. Secondly, their support remains confined to individual cities, or single interest projects: the expulsion of immigrants, for example, or the imposition of "citizenship tests." And finally, would-be fascists today confront a changed international environment. Their instinctive propensity to think in exclusively national terms sits ill with the contemporary emphasis on trans-state institutions and inter-state cooperation.

Perhaps the fascists were the last to believe that power was beautiful.

That power was *beautiful,* yes. Communists of course believed to the end that power is *good:* invocations of power, properly surrounded by the right doctrinal packaging, could still be presented without apology. But the unapologetic presentation of power as beauty? Yes, that was uniquely fascist. But I wonder whether you are correct for the non-European world. Think of China, after all, the most obvious case in point.

I fear that China is an excellent case in point.

Returning, though, to Europe: fascism and National Socialism are often explained as the outcome of unjust peace settlements after the First World War. Though the Americans introduced the principle of national self-determination, in practice borders were drawn in large measure as in the past: to punish defeated enemies and reward allies.

But in fact it almost doesn't seem to matter whether states got, so to speak, too much or too little territory as a result of the First World War. The Romanians, to take an obvious case, got too much—and they were a central showpiece of fascism in interwar Europe. So the argument that it's a matter of dissatisfaction with peace settlements is hard to make.

The Italians were certainly among the victors. Yes, there were things that they wanted and did not get; but they were on the winning side, like the Romanians. And fascism comes to power notwithstanding. So perhaps we need a deeper explanation, one which would account for the dissatisfaction of fascists regardless of how much territory their countries got in the name of national self-determination.

With territory, and indeed precisely with more territory, the problem is all the greater. Fascists always resented the presence of minorities in their midst: living evidence that the national state, however physically extensive, is not quite how they wanted it. A cancerous presence—of Hungarians, Ukrainians, Jews—is spoiling the poet's image of Romania, or the patriot's image of Poland, or whatever it might be.

Such sentiments can coincide perfectly well with the feeling that for all its recent expansion, the nation is still too small in some other sense: in the eyes of other nations, or when compared with other civilizations. And so even the most self-regardingly aesthetic and sophisticated and cosmopolitan fascists—Romanians being a nice case in point—frequently descend to the crudest, most resentful nationalism. Why, they ask, do people not appreciate how important we are? Why do people not understand that Romania (or Poland, or Italy) is the cultural center of Europe? So the distinction between the unhappy countries and the happy countries becomes very hard to make. Even the countries that got everything they wanted didn't get what they wanted in some larger sense; they didn't become the country they had thought that the war would make them—but which, deep in themselves, they always knew they could never be.

> *The idea that creating a state will be the end of history or realize*
> *the aspirations of the masses turns out very quickly not to be true,*
> *as in Poland or the Baltics. The variant is that you have a small*
> *state already but you believe that all you need is more territory, as*
> *in Romania—that also turns out very quickly not to be true.*

It is just this conundrum that allows fascists to recast the problem in their own terms. The issue, they would argue in the 1920s, is not the absence of a state (no longer a problem for most European nations after 1919); instead, it is the presence of the wrong kind of state. The state—bourgeois, liberal, cosmopolitan—is too weak. It has been modeled upon ill-advised imitations of western precedents. It has been obliged by force to accept and compromise with the presence of the wrong kind of people, and is thus ethnically polluted, and so forth.

But for fascists in the early interwar years, the gnawing awareness of national weakness was often driven by economic reality. Most of the small countries of central and southern Europe (whether victorious or defeated) were materially devastated: either as a result of the war or by virtue of the territorial rearrangements that followed. In particular, trade collapsed. The old empires, whatever their shortcomings, were large zones of free trade; the new nation-states were anything but.

Fascism here thrived on a distinctive weakness of the contemporary democratic Left: social democrats had no economic policy. Social democrats most certainly had social policies and general ideas about how they would pay for them. And of course they had theories—even economic theories—as to why capitalism was dysfunctional. But they had little idea about how to manage dysfunctional capitalist economies now that they found themselves in a position of responsibility.

Thus the utter silence of the democratic Left in the 1920s and through the Great Depression left fascists with a free hand, at liberty to propose radical economic measures with little competition. Indeed, many of the most interesting converts to neo-fascism in those years were young, highly-educated and promising left-wing professionals like Henri de Man, John Strachey, Oswald Mosley and Marcel Déat, all of whom abandoned socialism in disgust at its failure to respond imaginatively to the economic catastrophe.

> *The fascists were able to have their way in early experiments*
> *with the welfare state precisely because they were unencumbered*
> *by the Marxist disagreements about reform versus revolution,*
> *unconcerned by orthodoxies of any kind. And so they were free to*
> *say: perhaps we should plan, the Soviets do it, it seems to work;*
> *or, perhaps we should steal from the Jews and redistribute, that*
> *seems practical.*

To do them justice, there was also a more sophisticated consideration: why don't we instrumentalize the state to plan and impose economic policies, rather than go through the tedious mechanisms of parliamentary politics. In the future, let us simply pronounce the policy, rather than seek support for it. This version of the argument appeared most frequently in the writings of former left-wingers disillusioned with "bourgeois democracy," or else in the projects devised by impatient young men never previously involved in politics. Why, they asked, must we model public policy on individual behavior? A man ought not to borrow more than he can repay, but no such restriction applies to a state.

And this, of course, is where fascism comes in: the idea that the state is free to do what it wants. Print money, if that's what's needed; reassign expenditure and workers where needed; invest public funds in infrastructure projects even if they don't pay off for decades; it doesn't matter. These ideas were not fascist per se: indeed, in sophisticated forms, they would soon be associated with the writings of Keynes. But in the 1930s, only fascists were interested in adopting them.

In Germany Hjalmar Schacht could easily—if one forgets his acquiescence in Nazi anti-Semitism—be thought of as an adaptor of Keynesian theory and New Deal practice. Partly for these reasons, fascism really was not only respectable but—until 1942—the institutional umbrella for quite a lot of innovative economic thinking. It was uninhibited about the use of the state, bypassing political impediments to radical policy innovation, and happy to transcend conventional restrictions on public expenditure. Note, however, the consequent taste for foreign conquests as the easiest way to make up the deficit.

> *That's an important difference; Keynes is making proposals for equilibrium within national economies, whereas Schacht and his successors relied on plundering others.*

> *That said, I wonder if we might not be too hastily cutting off the fascists from real continuities in European thought. The idea that one's nation is not the people living in the country but rather those who speak a language, or associate with a tradition, or worship in a*

certain church, derives quite directly from the Romantics and can be
seen in nineteenth-century nationalism very readily as well. I mean,
the intonations of the latter appear naïve and somehow harmless to
us when read today, but nevertheless, there does seem to be a
continuity that you could chart between Fichte and Herder on the one
hand and fascists a century later on the other.

These continuities can always be unearthed. You begin with Byron, for example, celebrating Greece and its virtues as the fount of all good, everywhere. And you end with the Romanian poet Mihai Eminescu—clearly *not* someone who believes that all the world would benefit from the generous embrace of Romanian cultural identity, but rather that the whole of Romania would benefit from the exclusion of non-Romanians from the territory that defines the place in which Romanians exclusively should reside. In other words, with the rise of nationalism, the Romantic notion shrinks and inverts over time. And what began as a celebration of universal identity becomes little more than a defense of place.

This is even true of France. Take Victor Hugo for example. His romantic concept of "Frenchness"—even in his anti-Napoleonic mid-century tract, *Les Châtiments*—celebrated qualities of France that all persons of good faith might share. France in this account is a distillation of human virtues and human possibilities. However, by the time you reach interwar writers on the subject of France, their country has become not a universal model but rather the victim of history: of Germany, of Britain, of its own mistakes and so on. Invocations of France in this key are little more than neo-Romantic recollections of a misplaced glory in urgent need of recovery. The map of France (corresponding for these purposes to comparable maps of Romania, Poland, Germany etc.) becomes a sort of right-wing talisman: a god-given perfection in space and time, the best and only possible France.

Communists tended to worship what they saw as the non-
contingent: that which had to be, that which was coming for

everyone, that which was inevitable and therefore desirable.
Whereas the fascists believed in history too but they loved the
voluntarist, the contingent, the random. After all, your language is
random, your ethnicity is random, your mother tongue and your
fatherland are random. And you have to will yourself to love them
in that way. Which may explain the style and the dandyism as well.

I see the appeal of your generalization; but even in the embrace of the contingent the fascists were far from consistent. It is terribly easy to make the mistake of talking about some abstraction called "fascist intellectual positions." Fascism varied from country to country, and from person to person. The dandified intellectuals of the world of someone like Brasillach are very different in their indulgence of the particular from violence-hardened nationalist intellectuals such as Ernst Jünger, or from the fascist policy intellectuals. You know, someone like Drieu la Rochelle didn't know one end of an economic argument from another. Whereas Marcel Déat, the socialist-turned-fascist, was a very talented *normalien*, with a solid grasp of Keynesian economics. So unlike communist intellectuals, they are not bound together by anything remotely as firm as an allegiance to a project or even an event. They are like fascism itself: much clearer in style and in enemies than in content.

Communists accept violence as the objective requirement of the
unfolding of history. Fascists seem to like violence as the method of
imposing their own subjectivity on others. The dandies can be quite
violent. I mean the Romanians.

The space between cultural conversation and rhetorical murder is a very thin one. I'm not talking about Codreanu and the semi-religious nuts of the student movements, who shade into real Romanian fascism. I'm talking about people who would have been absolutely *salonfähig* and respectable in any university common room in the world—and, indeed, later on, were: Mircea Eliade, to name but one.

They were perfectly able to talk about expelling the Jews, or slaughtering the Hungarians, or the need to use violence to cleanse the polluted body of Romania of all its malignant minorities. They regarded the borders, the Romanian borders, as an outerskin to be protected from violation. This is a language of anger, even though the people themselves don't seem to be individually particularly angry. It's as though they are permeated by an extreme rhetoric, even when they wish to say something not obviously or necessarily extreme.

This was observed, but not always commented upon, by people who encountered them. In his journal of Bucharest in the 1930s and early 1940s Mihail Sebastian writes of conversations with Mircea Eliade and Nae Ionescu. They go to cafés in downtown Bucharest, and they are having what looks like a sort of Parisian-style coffee and conversation about architecture, or painting, or whatever. And suddenly, as Sebastian records in his diary, Eliade will come out with some utterly vicious comment about Jews. What's interesting is that it doesn't occur to him that this might be an odd thing to say to Sebastian, who is a Jew. And it doesn't fully occur to Sebastian himself until later. It is as though being vicious about minorities was so natural a part of conversation that it would have taken a great effort of self-awareness, as it seems, to imagine the offense that might be being given, or that a breach might be opened.

> *Sebastian is unusual, I think, because although he seems unperplexed by it, he nevertheless does note it. And that's where I think his Jewishness comes through, that he bothers to write it down. I think that for Sebastian this is precisely politics drifting away from culture. Because anti-Semitic comments seem odd, to say the least, once you know that Jews are being burned in Bukovina. What makes those diaries so fascinating is that Sebastian does not really know what happens in World War II; he is killed in an accident in 1945 and never learns about the Holocaust as we understand it. He is writing about Romania and a particularly Romanian descent.*

That is a small instance of the larger problem for people like us: how should we find our way back into that world of fascist conversation? And we need to be careful with the labels. By any measure, the Iron Guard and Corneliu Codreanu are much more directly fascist in what they do, and how they organize, how they mobilize, their politics, their propaganda, etc. The intellectuals don't get down on the street and cut people's throats and hang them up on butcher's hooks and so on. On the other hand, Codreanu is operating in a slightly different key, and to call him fascist—while it captures something about what he *does*—fails to identify precisely what it is he is saying.

> *Codreanu's organization was known as the Iron Guard, but it was actually called the Legion of the Archangel Michael—Codreanu had a vision of the Archangel Michael in his prison cell. I think the principles of the thing were: to love God, to love each other, to fulfill our mission etc. One wouldn't deduce such objectives from a textbook definition of fascism.*

And they would look very strange to some of the cynically non-religious, irreligious, anti-religious fascists farther west.

> *Earlier, with respect to Marxism and liberalism, you spoke of the first generation to grow up in a world without religion, in which faith was not the issue. That might be the case individually for liberals or for Marxists, but sociologically, it matters a great deal which God everyone else doesn't believe in, or might still come to believe in. And so the Romanian case is of course Christian Orthodoxy, and that seems to matter.*

> *It must inform the particular version of their cult of death. The Romanian fascists really had a fixation with individual death— and not just the death of the person you were killing, but the death*

that you awaited yourself, as a resurrection. This does seem to be a
perversion of Christianity and not something else.

This brings us to the Catholic countries which are governed from
the right in the 1930s—Spain, Portugal, Austria, Italy. France
joins the list during the war.

In Catholic countries, unlike Orthodox countries, the Church has a
secure and more or less autonomous institutional base. And there are particular loyalties and institutional traditions within each Catholic country. In
France the overwhelming majority of the population is nominally Catholic
and in half the country, grosso modo, actively Catholic. The Catholic Church
is in a historically determined oppositional position: it has been excluded
from power, functionally and legally—and yet it remains hugely influential
for most of the twentieth century. It did not attach itself to parties of the far-
right; it was firmly attached to conventional parties of the right of center.
That is one of the reasons why fascism did not come to power in France,
except later and by external fiat, during the Second World War.

The other reason, of course, is that the French party which sociologi-
cally comes closest to looking like a fascist party—with a resentful and frightened lower middle class, fearful of left-wing revolution and resentful of
wealth and power, is the Radical Party. It was, for contingently French reasons, attached to the left: in its anti-clericalism and in its association with the
French Revolution as the basis for the legislation that its supporters favored.
This is perhaps one of the reasons, by the way, why French fascist intellectuals did not have an obvious party allegiance of any collective significance.

You could look at Belgium or Holland and say that the Catholic parties
there are the dominant organizational form in which right-wing politics gets
expressed. The Vatican itself was dominated from 1938 till 1958 by a far-
right organizational structure and hierarchy, so that the overlap of Catholic
authority and conservative politics was very comfortable in those years.

Meanwhile, the Conservative Party in England did nothing without working closely with the Anglican hierarchy. That is one of the reasons why it was such a successful umbrella party, thereby minimizing the opportunities for a separate fascist movement. Occasional bursts of extremism could break out within this conservative, church-bound party and be defused as culturally reactionary politics of an old kind.

In 1933 Hitler comes to power, and it becomes clear by, say, 1936 at the latest, that Nazi Germany is going to be the powerful right-wing state in Europe. How do all these fascists in their own domestic contexts come to terms with this?

They usually reemphasize their association with *Italian* fascism. Fascism in Italy, which has no overtly racist connotations, and—for most European countries—no particularly threatening associations, becomes the sort of respectable international incarnation of the politics that they would like to see practiced at home. This happened in England, where Oswald Mosley greatly admired Mussolini. Many on the French right traveled to Italy, read Italian and professed a familiarity with Italian life. Italy even played a certain role in protecting Austria from Nazi Germany, between 1933 and 1936.

But it was still perfectly possible in those years to express admiration for Hitler, and a lot of people did. Mosley's wife and his sister-in-law both went to Germany, met Hitler, and reported all kinds of admiring things about his strength, determination, originality. There were some French visits to Germany, although fewer; French fascists were mostly formed in the nationalist mold originally, and nationalism in France in those days was by definition anti-German, as well as anti-English.

The Romanians showed very little interest in Germany, at least until the war. They perceived themselves as extensions of Latinate culture, and were much taken up with the Spanish Civil War, which they saw as the great cultural choice of the 1930s. All in all, most Romanian fascists were slightly reluctant to associate with Hitler: less because Hitler represented any specific distasteful policy, more because he was German. Many of them had been shaped by an anti-German mood arising from World War I during which the Germans had decisively defeated the Romanians (though at war's end Romania, as an ally of the Entente, was regarded as a victor). Romania gained a tremendous amount of territory at the end of the war, especially from Hungary, but that was thanks to its alliance with France and Britain. Since Hitler was out to destroy the postwar order created by those peace settlements, Romanians had reason for restraint. Once Hitler demonstrated that he could dictate borders in Europe, from 1938 forward, Romanians had no choice but to deal with him. Indeed, once Hitler arranged for some Romanian territory to be returned to Hungary, they had no choice.

Sometimes, although this was exceptional, the German character of German National Socialism was an attraction. Consider Léon Degrelle, the fascist leader in Belgium. Degrelle, even though he was a French speaker, represented a kind of Belgian revisionism, more widespread in the Flemish areas. The revisionists correctly saw Germany as more sympathetic than the French, or Dutch, or English neighbors, who were committed to the status quo. They were particularly concerned about minor territorial revisions and Flemish language rights, all of which the Germans cleverly give them in 1940, once they occupied Belgium. But the outstanding case of pro-German fascism was in Norway with Quisling's party. These Norwegians saw themselves as extensions of *Deutschtum*, as part of the great Nordic space in which they could hope for a role in Nazi ambitions. But until the war they were of little significance.

Yet German National Socialism also had a certain European appeal. The Germans had a story that the Italians did not: of Europe, a post-democratic, strong Europe, dominated by Germany, but in which other countries, Western countries, would benefit as well. Many intellectuals in the West were drawn to this—and some deeply believed in it. The European idea, as we tend to forget, was then a right-wing idea. It was a counter to Bolshevism, obviously, but also to Americanization, to the coming of industrial America with its "materialist values" and its heartless and ostensibly Jewish-dominated finance capitalism. The new, economically-planned Europe would be strong—indeed, it could only be strong if it transcended irrelevant national boundaries.

All of this was very appealing to the younger, more economically-oriented fascist intellectuals, many of whom would end up administering occupied countries. So after 1940, after the fall of Poland and Norway and especially France, the German model took on, briefly, a certain glow.

Against that has to be set the problem of the Jews. It was then, during the war, that the race issue became unavoidable—and many intellectual fascists, especially in France and England, could not get past that. It was one thing to pronounce endlessly on the charms of cultural anti-Semitism; quite another to line up behind the mass murderer of whole nations.

Hitler's rise to power also brings about, after a delay of a year or so, a complete reorientation of Soviet foreign policy, as expressed by the Communist International. The Soviets take up the banner of anti-fascism. No longer were communists to combat everyone to their right, including first and foremost the social democrats. As of 1934 they were to form electoral alliances with socialist parties and win elections in the name of a Popular Front. So anti-fascism allows Soviet communism to present itself as an attractive universal cause, uniting all foes of fascism. But this universalism, given the circumstances of the time, was largely realized in France. The French Communist Party becomes much more important than it had any right to be. The German KPD no longer exists . . .

. . . and most other European communist parties were irrelevant. The only game in town was the French Communist Party (PCF). By 1934, Stalin realized that it was all he had left as a usable lever within any of the remaining Western democracies. The PCF suddenly went from being a rather small, though noisy participant in French left-wing politics to being an important instrument of international affairs.

The PCF was a peculiar animal. It was rooted in a long and strong national left-wing tradition, operating in the only country that had both an open democratic political system and a strong revolutionary left. It began large, in 1920. Everywhere in Europe the Bolshevik Revolution forced socialists to choose between communism and social democracy, and in most places the social democrats did better. Not so in France. There the communists remained larger till the mid-twenties.

Then, steadily, thanks to Moscow-imposed tactics, internal splits and their inability to present a rational case for voting for them, they shrunk. By the 1928 elections the PCF parliamentary group was small, and following the elections of 1932, microscopic. Stalin himself was rather shaken at the collapse of communism as a force in French political life. By then all that was left was communist domination of labor unions and municipalities in the Paris "red belt." But this was a lot: in a country where the capital city is everything and where there was no television but much radio and many newspapers, the omnipresence of communists in strikes, disputes and on the street, in all the radical suburbs of Paris, gave the party far greater visibility than its numbers justified.

Fortunately for Stalin the PCF was also strikingly malleable. Maurice Thorez—an obedient stooge—was put in charge in 1930, and the Communist Party went from utter marginality to international prominence in just a few years. With Stalin's switch to the Popular Front strategy, communists were no longer forced to claim that the real threat to workers on the left was the "social fascist" socialist party.

On the contrary, it was now possible to form an alliance with Léon Blum's socialists, to protect the Republic against fascism. This may have been a largely rhetorical device for protecting the Soviet Union against Nazism, but it was a very comfortable one. Longtime domestic left-wing preferences for an alliance against the Right sat neatly with the new communist foreign policy preference that bourgeois republics should ally with the Soviet Union against the international Right. The communists, of course, never joined the government that grew out of the unified front in the elections of spring 1936, but they were regarded by the Right, not altogether wrongly, as the strongest and most dangerous constituent party within the Popular Front coalition.

> *Stalin's interpretation of Soviet state interest had changed in such a way that it now appeared consonant with French state interests. And so all of a sudden, rather than Thorez having to say at every occasion that he was really looking forward to giving up Alsace and Lorraine to the Germans, as the previous line dictated, Germany could become the great enemy—a much more convenient position to take.*

It goes further than this. The countries that had somehow let France down by refusing to form a common front against the rising threat of Germany became countries which were now letting the Soviet Union down by failing to guarantee free passage for the Red Army in the event of war. Poland had signed a non-aggression declaration with Germany in January 1934, and everyone knew that Poland would never willingly allow the passage of Soviet troops. So French and Soviet interests seemed somehow intermeshed, and it suited a large number of French people to believe this. The Popular Front was also a reminder of the Franco-Russian alliance of the 1890s through the First World War, which was the last time France was strong in international affairs.

There was also a distinctive French attitude to the Soviet Union, in which thinking about Moscow is always somehow the same thing as thinking about Paris. The question of Stalinism was seen in France primarily as a historical conundrum: is the Russian Revolution the legitimate heir to the French? If so, should it not be defended against all foreign threats? The shadow of the French Revolution thus kept getting in the way, making it hard to see clearly what was happening in Moscow. So the show trials, which began in 1936, were seen by many French intellectuals, by no means all of them communists, as Robespierrian terror rather than totalitarian mass murder.

> *The Popular Front allows a certain conflation between communism and democracy. Because Hitler is getting rid of the*

*remainder of German democracy at the same time: he bans the
German Communist Party in the first half of 1933. A year later
the USSR encourages communists to work within democracies. And
then there's the nice coincidence that the French Communist Party
continues to function in a system which is democratic.*

The French Communist Party had been around, remember, for a dozen years by then. So it was still possible for a lot of people who wanted to believe well of it to treat it as "one of us" when it came to traditional left-wing alliances. And indeed, many communists themselves were not unhappy to find themselves back in the family.

*And it's a rather loud and dramatic family reunion: not just the
formation of the Popular Front government in June 1936, but all
the gestures that went before it, with the communists starting to
sing La Marseillaise and the public meetings in Paris . . .*

. . . of socialists and communists coming together in big demonstrations symbolically at the Place de la Nation, and the Bastille, and the Place de la République and so on, in ways which would surprise anyone who was familiar with the previous ten years of head-bashing encounters in left-wing suburbs. There was a strong desire to recover this lost left unity, now intersecting with the growing fear of Nazism.

In 1936, for the first time, all three left-wing parties, with some exceptions at the local level, agreed not to stand against each other in the second round of elections—in other words, to ensure that there was a left bloc which won. And in most cases, that meant it was the socialist, the middle candidate between the Radicals and the communists, who was the acceptable compromise. And therefore, to everyone's amazement, Blum's socialists emerged as the largest single party in France for the first time—and, numerically at least, the dominant party in the Popular Front coalition. Everyone, including most socialists, had expected that the Radicals would dominate.

Blum was perfectly well aware of who the communists were: he had been their chief target for many years. But he was profoundly desirous of left-wing solidarity, mutual cooperation and an end to the bitter intra-left schism. Blum was just the man to serve as not just a figurehead, but a spokesman for this unity.

What is it exactly about Blum which allowed him to fulfill this role, so well from one point of view, but also so hatefully from another?

Blum was a Jewish theater critic from an Alsatian background, with a high-pitched speaking voice. He was more intellectual than most intellectuals and never compromised sartorially: pince-nez, spats, the whole bit. He was hugely popular with peasant crowds in the South where he represented Jean Jaurès's old constituency and equally at home with miners and railway workers.

On a personal level, it turns out that Blum was, in an unusual sort of way, charismatic. He was so obviously honest, so manifestly meant what he said, so clearly wasn't trying to be anything other than he was, that he was actually quite appealing and accepted on his own terms. His style—which to us would seem rather romantic and a bit elegantly over-polished for political use, especially on the left—was actually regarded as evidence that the Left had a leader of class. And of course one deeply hated by communists, on the one hand, and the French right on the other.

Blum was also the only person who understood what his party, the Socialist Party, had to do to remain a political force in France. If socialists abandoned Marxism and tried to become a sort of social democratic party on the northern European model, they would simply blend into the existing Radical party, with whose social base they had much in common. On the other hand, socialists could not compete with the communists as a revolutionary, anti-system party. And so Blum walked a narrow path between pretending to lead a revolutionary party committed to the overthrow of capitalism, while functioning in practice as the nearest thing France had to a social democratic party.

The communist strategy was based on the assumption that the radicals would win and form a benign left-of-center government which would frighten no one and therefore be a solid leader of the Republic, but which could be pushed towards a pro-Soviet foreign policy. Instead they got a socialist government, led by a man who was at least rhetorically committed to transforming France's administration, its institutional structure and its social policies. The communist leadership was not at all interested in radical change in France, let alone revolution. It was interested in a France that would serve the interests of the Soviet Union.

Blum had problems. He was handicapped by the fragility of his coalition. The Radicals wanted almost no policy innovations at all, and the communists only wanted changes in foreign policy. They did not want to create domestic difficulties that could weaken the government. Their mission was to keep a left-wing government in power and direct its foreign policy toward Soviet interests. The socialists were thus left alone, demanding, and pushing through parliament, limitations on work hours, colonial reforms, recognition of unions in factories, paid vacations and so on.

Blum knew little about economics. He was largely uninformed about notions of deficit financing, public investment and so on. Accordingly, he did little, with the result that he was resented on all sides. The Right saw him as excessively adventurous; the Left were disappointed by his unimaginative response. He was overwhelmed.

All the while, Blum also had trouble finding allies abroad. Spain too had a Popular Front government, but under threat from a military coup. Blum, for all his personal sympathy, did little to help. He was concerned to the point of paranoia about losing British support, which accounts for his reluctance to provide aid to the Spanish Republic.

Paris was a special place for the Left, and not just for the French left. It became a kind of capital of European communism in the

*second half of the 1930s, at a time when Soviet policy back in the
Soviet Union was especially destructive and bloody. Would you
agree with the proposition that because German and other left-
wing political refugees could live safely in anti-fascist Paris, their
own loyalty to Stalin could continue?*

*Hitler's victory and the subsequent crushing of the German
Communist Party, the KPD, was a terrible blow to their own
communist faith, to their own attitude of deference towards
Stalin. But in Paris such people had a nicer variant of left-wing
politics with which to comfort themselves. Communism seemed
permitted by the softer line of the Popular Front, and seemed
possible because of the arrival of an actual Popular Front
government in France.*

It did not seem implausible in those years to fear that the final battle
would be between communism and fascism, with democracy squeezed in
the middle: you had better know which side you were going to choose. Even
in England, Orwell could not publish his memoir of the Spanish Civil War,
Homage to Catalonia, with a mainstream left-leaning publisher: the *bien-
pensant* Left did not wish to be associated with attacks on communism. But
Paris also had a direct effect on the communists as well. Think of Arthur
Koestler, who in his memoirs concedes that he had abandoned Stalinism but
could not openly acknowledge his apostasy because of the need to maintain
anti-fascist unity. The logic of anti-fascism was binary: he who is not with us
is against us. This made it much harder to criticize Stalin, since this could
seem to help Hitler.

*Koestler is coming from Kharkiv, from Soviet Ukraine, where he
had spent time. He's seen forced collectivization and famine. He's
one of the very few intellectuals of the group that we've been talking
about who actually sees with his own eyes the worst of the Soviet*

project. And then he arrives in a Paris where, as you say, it was impolite to talk about such things.

Koestler broke the silence—and I think this is very important—over the Spanish Civil War, not over the Soviet Union. Paris was the place to talk, but Spain was the place to go. Orwell and Koestler both went to Spain, as did many of the best thinkers of the Left.

In 1931 the monarchy in Spain had been overthrown and a republic declared. Spain had had a sort of soft version of Mussolini from 1923 until then. No one had taken much notice. Whatever admiration there was for Mussolini-type figures was confined to the *Duce* himself and the Spanish leader Primo de Rivera was hardly known. But once the Republic emerged, the political configurations in Spain—still of no great concern to most foreigners—became rather more salient. On one side, the Church and the army saw themselves as incarnating eternal Spain; on the other side were Andalusian anarchists, Catalan autonomists and syndicalists, Basque nationalists, Asturian miners: all of whose radical political and economic demands dovetailed with demands for local autonomy and long-standing resentment of Madrid. At first none of that meant much to outsiders. But this began to change in 1934 when the Asturian miners rebelled and were suppressed, and what now looked like a familiar, worker-based, class confrontation became international news. These events coincided exactly with a clerical-authoritarian coup in Austria and came just a year after Hitler's rise to power in Germany.

But why did Spain become so very important in 1936? Part of the answer is that for most observers, the country was following a now-familiar pattern: that of a democratic republic under threat from fascist—or, at any rate, anti-democratic—forces. In Spain's case, the anti-democratic forces in question were palpably reactionary: the army, the landowners and the Church. Landowners especially—and legitimately, from their point of view—felt threatened by the policies of the victorious Popular Front coalition: progressive taxation of middle-sized farms and much talk of the collectivization of land. This was very appealing to the new government's supporters in the south, especially, but less so to the small property owners of the center and the west. Thus the left bore some responsibility for pushing potential middle-of-the-road electors to the right in those years. But obviously the central fact about Spain in 1936 was the military coup, mounted against a democratically-elected government. In historical terms, this was a fairly conventional Spanish coup, in which the army, as so often, claimed to speak and act for the nation against a political class that was betraying its interests. But this time, the civil war between the army and the politicians absorbed into itself a series of internal conflicts and local civil wars, each one of them exacerbated by association with the national schism.

And so there was the European civil war: taking shape in Parisian discussion, in Soviet doctrine, in Hitler's and Mussolini's speeches. All these appeared to be reflected in the Spanish lens. Throughout Europe, it thus suited the Left and Right alike to assert that within the Spanish conflict, communism was playing a major role: whereas, in fact, the communist presence only began to matter once Stalin declared his support for the republicans in October 1936. The rest of the Left was internally divided, and even on Orwell's sympathetic account, politically incompetent and militarily marginal.

Thus the conflict in Spain became a European intellectual, political and military conflict largely because of foreign redescription of it: communism against fascism, workers against capitalists, rather than Catalonia against Madrid, or the landless workers of the south against the land-owning, rural middle class of the west, or strongly Catholic regions against largely anticlerical regions. The Spanish communists claimed a central role, when actually they were initially peripheral; the local socialists and the republican center could not outbid them—the more so because with the passage of time, they desperately needed all available support.

The price that the non-communist defenders of the Republic paid for Soviet assistance was increased communist influence in areas they now controlled. Meanwhile, within republican-dominated regions, there were districts that were now virtually autonomous, run by communists, socialists or anarchists. There was thus a sort of revolution going on within the revolution: sometimes truly radical, sometimes just a case of communists seizing local control to suppress left-wing competition.

> *If you were an intellectual in exile, France chose you. Paris was*
> *simply there. But Spain was an active choice. Why did so many*
> *people go to Spain to fight?*

Going to Spain to fight for the republic had a huge appeal. It was a way to be anti-fascist, involved in a society facing very simple choices, in an appealing setting. There were some volunteers for the right, including some Romanians, but overwhelmingly, volunteers came for the left, as the underdog against the forces of reaction. But you were also finally—remember, we're now a generation away from World War I—able to go out and do something about the growing threat to democracy, to republics, to progress, to the world of the Enlightenment and so on. It could be described in very intellectual ways and was the romantic place to go and die.

> *So returning to Arthur Koestler—for his own sake and also as an*
> *example. Why is it Spain, do you think, that prompts him finally*
> *to reject the Soviet model and to cease to follow the communist line?*

Koestler was on death row for a while—but in a fascist prison, so it is not self-evident why the experience should have focused his mind on what was happening in Moscow. I think it was because he was away from Paris, in part. Separated from the hothouse community of progressive intellectuals, away from the setting in which there were many good reasons not so much to pretend, but to keep silent about your doubts.

For Koestler was now in Spain, and Spain was about action; it was no longer about mythology, or unity, or anything else. I think it was easier for him to tell the truth to himself when he did not have to encounter the next morning fellow ex-communists who had opted to remain silent and were loathe to say what they really thought.

Once that threshold is crossed, the rest comes amazingly quickly.
You invoke Darkness at Noon, *his book about the Stalinist show*
trials, which is written—

by 1940. The three books which are relevant to this aspect of Koestler's story—*Spanish Testament, Scum of the Earth* and *Darkness at Noon*—were written at an astonishing pace, within two years. The first reflects on his Spanish experience, the second reflects upon the reality of Europe in 1940 and what had become of Koestler's world, and the third is the consequence of the first two: with that experience, and following the loss of so much else, Koestler could now write openly about the tragedy of communism.

Later Koestler writes of his disillusionment himself. But it strikes
me that Koestler's chapter in The God that Failed *is of a*
qualitatively different nature—

than all of the others—

—because Koestler tells in plausible and compelling detail his
reasons for joining the Communist Party.

I think that if there were an Orwell-Koestler derby, a contest
between the two of them for the most significant political
intellectual writing in English, you unlike most people would put
Koestler ahead of Orwell.

Orwell functions, it seems to me, in two ranges, the very high and the very low. The low is the English insight into the peculiarities of the English, the distinctive nuances of class and illusion in England. And it was this unmatched skill with the small sketch that served him so well in Spain in *Homage to Catalonia*, even though larger conclusions are being drawn.

At the other end, Orwell is of course the best novelist in English of totalitarianism—though he does not rise to the level of the Russian master-pieces. Here, he is operating in the highest of ranges, on the largest of issues: in *Animal Farm* and obviously in *1984*, the characteristic features of totali-tarianism are sketched in for the purpose of pointing large lessons in the price of faith and delusion and power in our time.

Koestler seems to me to operate in neither the small range nor the very large. It is precisely in the middle range where he excels. His interest lies not in depicting ideological models and their shortcomings, but rather in illus-trating attitudes of mind, and misperceptions of the world: he has rather less interest in the world that is being misperceived.

This makes him (much more than Orwell, who on these matters can be abruptly dismissive) unusually empathetic to the biggest story of the twenti-eth century: how so many smart people could have told themselves such stories with all the terrible consequences that ensued. This, Koestler does better than anyone. And it is precisely, of course, because he himself was one of them. Whereas Orwell—who was never deluded in this way—is an unequalled observer of such people but not particularly empathetic.

But for both of them the link back from Spain to the Soviet Union is quite extraordinary. There's this passage towards the end of Orwell's Homage to Catalonia, *in connection with the fracas in Barcelona, about the telephone exchange, where he writes that the consequences of this are not just in Barcelona, they're not just in Spain, the consequences of this will be felt in the entire world. Which, out of context seems absurd—*

Even bizarre.

—but he's exactly right. Because what he's got his finger on is part of the logic of the Great Terror in the Soviet Union. Stalin was indeed thinking about Spain and the Soviet Union as part of the same struggle. He was seeing these matters in exactly the same way as

Orwell, although of course with the opposite valuation. He was
concerned that what might happen in Spain must never be allowed to
happen in the Soviet Union. For him the struggle was all one. And
because for Stalin it was all one, that means that Orwell is correct . . .

. . . in seeing it as one. Those who did not believe Orwell in 1939 would be forced to backtrack in later years: from 1945 through the mid-fifties, a crucial element in all the Soviet Bloc trials of those years—whether in Poland, Czechoslovakia, Hungary, Bulgaria, Romania, East Germany—would be the actions of the accused during the Spanish Civil War. The point, driven home repeatedly, was that dissent, or even independent thought, was unacceptable to the communist hierarchy. The relative autonomy of individual communists in Spain—or, to a lesser extent, during the French Resistance—had to be retrospectively punished.

In that sense, communist strategy in Spain turns out to have been a dry run for the seizure of power in Eastern Europe after 1945. Obviously, this was very hard to appreciate at the time. Moscow, after all, was the only significant and effective backer of the Spanish republic. The Soviet Union was increasingly regarded as the only remaining bulwark against the rise of fascism in Central and Eastern Europe—and therefore Spain too. Everyone else, including Britain, was more than happy to compromise . . . so long as they were not affected themselves.

So let us pull back a little from the comforts of Paris and the
challenge of Spain. This was the moment of the Moscow show trials,
the height of the Terror. Through the 1930s, what was happening
in the Soviet Union in terms of scale and repressiveness was
incomparably worse than anything being done in Nazi Germany.
The Soviets were starving millions of people as Hitler came to
power; in the Great Terror of 1937 and 1938 they had a further
700,000 people shot. At most, the Nazi regime could be held
responsible for about ten thousand deaths before the war.

For a start, Nazi Germany was still in some respects a kind of *Rechtsstaat*, strange as that may sound. It had laws. They might not be attractive laws, but so long as you were not a Jew or a communist or a dissenter or handicapped or otherwise socially undesirable you would not have to fall foul of them. The Soviet Union too had laws: but *anyone* could fall foul of them just by being re-categorized into the class of enemies. So, from the perspective of the victim, the USSR was far more frightening—because less predictable—than Nazi Germany.

After all, we should recall that a very significant number of visitors from the democracies traveled to Nazi Germany and found no fault with it. Indeed, they were rather charmed by its successes. To be sure, there were deluded Western travelers to the Soviet Union too. But Nazi Germany did not have to put on a show. It was what it was, and many people quite liked it.

The Soviet Union, by contrast, was largely unknown and decidedly not how it described itself. But many people needed to believe in its self-definition as the homeland of revolution—including quite a few of its victims. Today, we do not know what to make of the many Western observers who accepted the show trials, minimized (or denied) the Ukrainian famines, or believed everything they were told about productivity and democracy and the great new Soviet Constitution of 1936.

But don't forget that people who knew everything there was to know often believed these things too. Take, for example, the memoirs of Evgeniia Ginzburg: there she is, swept into the Gulag, passing through all the worst prisons of Moscow, dispatched by train to Siberia. Not only does she encounter fellow victims, women who are still great believers—and who are convinced that there must be logic and justice behind their suffering; she herself remains committed to a certain communist ideal. The system, she insists, may have gone badly astray: but it could still be fixed. This capacity—this profound need—to believe well of the Soviet project was so firmly embedded by 1936 that even its victims did not lose faith.

But I think the other thing to remember if we are to make sense of the show trials, at least before 1940, was that even their critics in the West had no points of comparison. What was lacking was a historical example through which to grasp the significance of contemporary events. Paradoxically, the more liberal the observer, the more democratic his country, the harder it was to make sense of Stalin's behavior. Surely, a Western observer might comment, people just don't confess to terrible crimes unless there is some truth in the accusation?

After all, if you plead guilty in an English court or an American court, that is an end to the matter. So if the men whom Stalin was accusing were pleading guilty with such alacrity, who are we in England or America to express skepticism? It would be necessary to entertain *a priori* the hypothesis that they had all been tortured. But this in turn implied that the Soviet Union must be morally and politically corrupt, a system devoted not to social revolution but to the preservation of absolute power. Otherwise, why would it do such things? But to entertain such thoughts in 1936 took a degree of clarity and independence of mind that was quite rare.

It was indeed very rare that a European from beyond the USSR actually saw the worst of the Soviet crimes and then came back to Europe to talk about them. I mean, one thinks of Koestler's friend in Kharkiv, Alexander Weissberg, who—like Koestler—saw the famine in Ukraine. Then he was swept up in the arrests that preceded the Terror. Weissberg survived by a fluke: he was one of the prisoners exchanged between the Soviets and the Germans in 1940. As a result, he ended up in Poland, survived the Holocaust and wrote his own memoir about the Terror—a corrective to his friend Koestler's novel.

Well, it's like Margarete Buber-Neumann, who published her *Prisoner of Hitler and Stalin* in 1948.

Buber-Neumann and Weissberg were on the same NKVD transport out of the Soviet Union in 1940, straight into the arms of the Gestapo.

It is not just that a lot of people believed in the system even after they
were repressed in the Soviet Union. It is that in general, those who
were punished were quite sure that there had been some kind of
mistake. And if that is what you think, it can only be because you
hold the system itself to be fundamentally sound. You are a victim of
a judicial mistake, whereas your fellow prisoners are surely
criminals. You see your own case as exceptional, and that seems to
rescue the victims of the universal system.

Notice how different all this is from the condition of the inmates of Nazi camps: they know perfectly well that they have done nothing and have been incarcerated by a criminal regime. To be sure, this does not improve your chances of survival, and it certainly does nothing to lessen the suffering. But it does make it a lot easier to see straight and tell the truth.

Conversely, the experience of communism leaves its intellectual survivors peculiarly preoccupied with their own beliefs—more than they are with the crimes themselves: in retrospect, it is the delusory allegiance which accounts for their trauma, more than anything they have suffered at the hands of their jailors. The title of Annie Kriegel's memoir—*What I Thought I Understood*—nicely captures it. It is the sense of reiterated self-interrogation: did I misunderstand it? What is it that I understood? What did I see and what did I fail to see? In short, why did I not see straight?

Soviet terror was individualistic. And so there were the individuals
in the show trials who individually confessed to totally implausible
crimes, but they did it as individuals. But the arrests were also
individual for the most part, even during the mass actions. Of the
700,000 people shot in that period, in 1937 and 1938, most
were arrested in the middle of the night, individually. This left them
and their families in no position to understand what had happened.
And that terrifying grayness, that indefinite uncertainty, remains
part of the landscape of Soviet memory through to the present.

That, I think, is why when we think of Orwell as someone who was simply clear-eyed, we are missing half the picture. Like Koestler, Orwell had this capacity to imagine conspiracies and plots— absurd as they might seem—taking place behind the scenes and then treat them as real: thereby making them real for us.

I think that that's a crucial point. Those who got the twentieth century right, whether in anticipation—like Kafka—or as contemporary observers, had to be able to imagine a world for which there was no precedent. They had to suppose that this unprecedented and ostensibly absurd situation was actually the case—rather than supposing with everyone else that it was grotesquely unthinkable. To be able to think the twentieth century in this way was extraordinarily difficult for contemporaries. For the same reason, many people reassured themselves that the Holocaust could not be happening, simply because it made no sense. Not that it made no sense to the Jews: that was obvious. But it made no sense for the Germans either. Since they wanted to win their war, surely the Nazis would exploit the Jews, rather than kill them at great expense.

This application to human behavior of a perfectly reasonable moral and political calculus, self-evident to men raised in the nineteenth century, simply did not work in the twentieth.

6.

GENERATION OF
UNDERSTANDING: EAST
EUROPEAN LIBERAL

I came home from California to the land of Margaret Thatcher, who had
become Prime Minister in 1979 and would remain in office through 1990.
If in Berkeley I was still preoccupied with what I saw as the callow cultural
concerns of the post-Marxist scholarly Left, in England I was suddenly confronted with a revolution in political economy—coming from the right.

I had taken for granted certain achievements of the Left, or rather of
social democracy. In the 1980s in Thatcher's Britain I quickly saw how easily
past gains might be unraveled and undermined. The great achievements of
the social-democratic consensus of the mid-twentieth century—meritocratic
schooling, free higher education, subsidized public transportation, a workable national health service, state support for the arts and much else—could
all be undone. The logic of Thatcher's program was, on its own terms, impec-
cable: Britain, in post-imperial decline, could no longer sustain the level of
social expenditure of an earlier period. My resistance to this logic was not

only a matter of intuitions about the high social costs of such policy; it was also the result of a new kind of thinking about politics, which allowed me to see that any such guiding logic was probably a mistake.

My new position at Oxford was in Politics, which required of me both analytical and prescriptive thinking and afforded me the occasion to improve my skills in both; the more distanced perspective of the historian could be set aside, at least in part. For my teaching, I was now reading (often for the first time) contemporary writers like John Rawls, Robert Nozick and Ronald Dworkin—as well as the classics of liberal and conservative thought. For perhaps the first time, then, I was obliged to think in terms of competing genres of political explanation. No longer was I taken up above all with the inadequacies of Marxism; *all* political theories as it now seemed to me were by their very nature partial and incomplete accounts of the complexities of the human condition . . . and the better for it.

I was becoming a pluralist, in Isaiah Berlin's distinctive sense of the word. Indeed, I came to Berlin's writings in the course of those years, although I had read some of the better known essays earlier. (As for Berlin himself, I hardly knew him at Oxford: we only met on a couple of brief occasions. My allegiance was strictly intellectual.)

The Berlinian lesson most pertinent to daily political analysis and debate is the reminder that all political choices entail real and unavoidable costs. The issue is not whether or not there is a right and wrong decision to be taken, nor even whether you face a choice such that the "right" decision consists in avoiding the worst mistakes. *Any* decision—including any right decision—entails forgoing certain options: depriving yourself of the power to do certain things, some of which might well have been worth doing. In short, there are choices which we are right to make but which implicitly involve rejecting other choices whose virtues it would be a mistake to deny. In the real world of politics, as in most other arenas of life, all worthwhile decisions entail genuine gains and losses.

If there is no single good, then there is likely no single form of analysis that captures all the various forms of the good, and no single political logic that can master all of ethics. This was not a conclusion readily attainable through the categories or methods of contemporary continental political thought. In this tradition, the dominant concept was one of absolute benefits and foregoable costs: political argument in this key had a zero-sum quality. There were good and bad systems and objectives, right and wrong choices deriving from their no-less right or wrong premises. In this way of thinking, reinforced in the recent past by the experience of total war, politics really was described and treated as an all-or-nothing, win-lose, life-death game. Pluralism by definition was a category mistake, a deliberate deception or a tragic delusion.

It was also in those years that I read the best critique of Marxism ever published. At the time of the publication of *Main Currents of Marxism,* in 1979, I still knew little of Polish political or intellectual history, though I had heard of Leszek Kołakowski back in the 1960s when he was still the leading revisionist Marxist in Poland. He lost his chair, in the History of Philosophy at Warsaw University, in 1968 after the communist authorities accused him, reasonably enough, of being the spiritual leader of a generation of rebellious students. His departure from Poland constitutes as good a moment as any from which to date the end of Marxism as a serious intellectual force in continental Europe. Kołakowski eventually made his way to All Souls College, Oxford, where I met him for the first time shortly after the English translation of *Main Currents* first appeared. Those three volumes are a monument of humanistic scholarship. I was astonished by the sheer scale of the undertaking, and could not help being struck by the seriousness with which Kołakowski approached Marxism even as he set out to eviscerate its political credibility.

Kołakowski's perspective—that Marxism, especially in its heyday, merited intellectual attention but was bereft of political prospects or moral value—was to become my own. After reading Kołakowski, who saw Leninism as a plausible if not inevitable reading of Marx (and in any case the only politically successful one that we have), it became increasingly difficult for me to maintain the distinction, inculcated in me since childhood, between

Marxist thought and Soviet reality. I never knew Kołakowski well. Indeed, I was actually quite shy (all the more so after reading his masterwork) and would probably not have asked to meet him. But my then-wife, who was anything but shy, insisted on doing so and thus the three of us had lunch in Oxford sometime in the early eighties. After that I met Leszek on a number of occasions, most recently not long before his death. He remained for me an object of unstinting admiration and respect.

It was in those years that I met one of my closest friends in the decades to come. Richard Mitten was from a lower-middle-class family of German background in Missouri; he had attended Southeast Missouri State University and gone to work, as an enthusiastic Trotskyist, in the rail yards in Chicago. He then, by a series of happy chances, went on to study at Columbia and Cambridge. Rich never completed his Cambridge History Ph.D., perhaps because he unwisely undertook to study the Austro-Marxists in early-twentieth-century Vienna. This subject, important and fascinating though it was, required a sophisticated linguistic and intellectual training which Rich was indeed to acquire over the years, but largely by establishing himself in Vienna and making his life there. The relocation cut him off from his home university context—in much the same way that people in my generation used to get trapped in Paris: "going local" and becoming scholars or intellectuals truly embedded in the world of their studies, but for just this reason failing to complete the project that brought them there. Rich did, however, complete a doctorate at the University of Vienna itself, teaching there and at the Central European University in nearby Budapest. He now directs the International Studies program at Baruch College in the City University of New York.

My other close friend in England in those years was also American. David Travis, who like Rich was about five years my junior, had been an undergraduate in a seminar I taught at Davis back in 1975. In that time I was considerably younger than most American faculty, and David was rather older than most American undergraduates—he had worked for the California Department of Fish and Game—a circumstance which facilitated our friendship. With my encouragement David applied to Cambridge to undertake a PhD in Italian history, and thus he was living in England when I arrived in Oxford. Two years later, David was elected to a postdoctoral research fellowship in Oxford and we were able to enjoy feeling American and "un-English" together.

On one occasion—sated with college food—we went to the McDonald's in Oxford, where I ordered a quarter-pounder with cheese. The polite young woman behind the counter replied, "I'm sorry, we're out of cheese." How could McDonald's possibly be out of *cheese*? And yet, it was so—globalization still lay ahead. Another time we went to see *Brother from Another Planet*, the John Sayles film of 1984, in a frozen little cinema in east Oxford heated by an open electric fire in the aisle. The film concerns a black space alien fleeing arrest who lands in New York by accident and is taken to Harlem where the local population treat him as perfectly normal. There is a hilarious moment in the subway when he and a newfound friend get on the northbound A train. The friend (a New Yorker) says to him, "I can show you that I have magical powers, I can make white people vanish." As the train reaches 59th Street, from which point it runs express to 125th Street in the heart of black Harlem, the friend says, "when the doors open, I shall make all the white people disappear." The doors open and all the white people duly get out—to the alien's astonishment. David and I were rolling in the aisles; everyone else in the cinema remained blankly silent. My self-serving sense of cultural marginality was entertainingly confirmed.

Shortly after I arrived in Oxford, my wife Patricia—always in character—decided that she wanted to return to the U.S. She applied for an opening at Emory University in Atlanta, was offered the job and took it up in January 1981. In order to accompany her, I accepted a visiting professorship there the following year. I intensely disliked Atlanta: a gray zone of humidity, boredom, suburbia and isolation. Emory itself, perceived by its faculty as an oasis of culture and sophistication in the southern desert, seemed to me a sad and mediocre place: a view that I have not had occasion to revise, however unjust it may appear. A high point of my stay there was the visit of Eric Hobsbawm, who was attending a conference in Atlanta. We were probably both happy enough to enjoy one another's company for a few hours in the alienating surroundings of Atlanta's featureless downtown business district.

The most important and enduring consequence of my Atlanta sojourn was the visit of a Polish political sociologist (now historian), Jan Gross. Because I was in the Politics department in Oxford, I was assigned at Emory to the department of sociology, as a visiting professor of political sociology. The dean of the faculty, anxious to improve the rather dowdy quality of the department, took the opportunity to put me on a search committee to replace a retiring political sociologist. Most of the applicants under consideration were generic clones of the midwestern quantitative model in American sociology.

And then there was Gross. Jan was a political emigrant from Poland, forced into exile during the anti-Semitic campaign of 1968. He had completed a PhD at Yale where he held his first academic position. I remembered having read his book about German rule in wartime Poland, and immediately thought: *this* is the man. I managed to get him short-listed along with three respectable but interchangeable political sociologists. So Jan was invited to Atlanta and gave what must have seemed to his audience an almost entirely incomprehensible talk: Galicia this, Volhynia that, Belarus the other—drawing on material from what would become his classic study of the wartime Soviet annexation of eastern Poland, a topic of no interest to Emory's sociology department.

He and I had dinner, and we talked about Solidarity, the labor union in communist Poland that had just been suppressed by martial law in December 1981. Solidarity, a genuine mass movement that had succeeded in attracting intellectual support from right and left alike, had helped reintroduce Poland to the West. Jan, like many others of the Polish generation of

1968, was in touch with intellectuals back in Poland, and was actively engaged in interpreting Polish developments for western audiences. I found the man and the subject altogether fascinating; in the course of that evening I felt for the first time that my stay in Atlanta was not wasted: far from having landed on Planet Zurg, I was once again truly among people like me.

After the search committee duly recommended (over my minority dissent) that they should appoint one of the clones, I went behind the department's back to the dean: you can reproduce this mediocre sociology department if you wish, I advised him; or else you can bring in Jan Gross, a true European intellectual and major scholar, a man who understands sociology, but many other things as well, and who would transform the standing of your social studies division. The dean, who was no fool, promptly hired Jan. The sociology department never forgave me.

Jan's wife, Irena Grudzińska-Gross, was an established scholar (of comparative literature) in her own right, and they had two small children. Like Jan, she had been active in the student movement in Warsaw in 1968, and like Jan had left the country thereafter. In the course of his time at Emory Jan became firmly established as a major figure in east European studies and one of the most prominent historians of the region. Later he would move to New York University and thence to Princeton. The monograph that he went on to publish, on the Soviet annexation of eastern Poland, *Revolution from Abroad*, is a rare vertical monument on the blasted heath of Sovietology, a discipline whose subject was to self-destruct a few years later. In later years, Jan was to publish two controversial studies of the experience of Jews in wartime and postwar Poland: *Neighbors* and *Fear*. The former in particular became an instant classic, transforming the way the Holocaust, and Polish participation in it, are discussed in Poland.

Thanks in large measure to Jan and Irena, Eastern Europe and east Europeans began to offer me an alternative social life which in turn—and very appropriately for the region—became a renewed and redirected intellectual existence. Were it not for Jan and Irena, I would have been even more reluctant than I was to return to Atlanta in the fall of 1984 as a visiting professor. By that time Jan and Irena had settled there with their family, and I spent quite a lot of time at their home. I think Patricia hated it. Jan, Irena and I shared a common sense of isolation and *dépaysement*. We felt European in an environment which was not just American but southern American and thus doubly foreign: we smoked, we drank, we stayed up late, we talked ideas, we switched for emphasis or show into French and Italian, we discussed Solidarity, we swapped cultural insights and jokes. Patricia, who could not sustain such exchanges and who deeply resented her implicit exclusion, wanted nothing so much as to go home, read *Newsweek* in bed and chew pumpkin seeds.

In early 1985 Patricia and I separated. I was intensely relieved; but all the same the change in circumstances left me uncertain and depressed. Jan, with whom I stayed in close contact even after returning to Oxford, suggested that I divert myself by making new friends. In particular, he recommended that I make contact with some of his own Polish friends and contacts in Paris—a city to which the Polish exiles of 1968, like so many before them, had been instinctively drawn. I duly took their names: Wójciech Karpiński, Aleksander Smolar, and Barbara Toruńczyk, editor of *Zeszyty Literackie*, a leading Polish literary review.

At the end of the Oxford Hilary (spring) Term of 1985 I took a vacation in Europe, first visiting David Travis in Rome and then returning through Paris. Once there, I decided on a whim to look up Barbara Toruńczyk—known as Basia in the Polish diminutive. She invited me over to a catastrophic, messy flat where for six hours or so I watched her edit *Zeszyty*. Then she turned to me: "Now I'm going skiing in the Savoy Alps with some friends; do you want to come?" I had actually just arrived from Rome by train that morning, but I accepted nonetheless, heading south that same night on another train with a cohort of energetic, ski-intent Poles: broke but adventurous.

I had not skiied for years, and was in any case never much good. It was late in the season and the pistes were dangerous: the snow had melted in patches, forcing us to dodge grass and rocks. We could not use the skilift, and were obliged instead to hike up the mountainside around Briançon. Thus I worked hard, partly out of sheer terror and partly no doubt to impress Basia, with whom I was left alone once the others returned home.

Barbara Toruńczyk is an unusual and fascinating woman. Courageous and talented—she had been singled out by the police as an instigator of the Polish student rebellion and was now single-handedly editing the most impressive literary magazine in Eastern Europe—she brought me closer still to Poland. Like Jan, Basia was my close contemporary: I was becoming conscious of the spiritual bond that bound our generation together across the political divide.

My 1968, to be sure, had been very different than that of my Polish friends; my education now involved coming to understand those differences. Like most Western Europeans of my generation, I had been only vaguely aware of events happening beyond the Iron Curtain that year. I did go to Paris but I did not go to Poland, where students were being tear-gassed, beaten, arrested and expelled in numbers that would have been shocking in the West. I was only vaguely aware that the rulers of communist Poland had assured their citizens that the student movement there was organized and led by "Zionists"; and that they were issuing travel documents to Poles of Jewish origin, allowing them to leave but depriving them of any right to return.

I was also, I confess, embarrassed at my ignorance of Europe's east and very aware of just how different my 1960s had been from the experience of Jan, Basia and their peers. I had actually *been* a Zionist, an entertaining and largely cost-free indulgence, at exactly the moment when *their* government was accusing them (and thousands of other people) of "Zionism" in order to isolate them from the Polish mainstream and their fellow Poles. We had all experienced disillusion: I had been disabused of my Zionist dreams, they of what remained of their reformist Marxism. But whereas my illusions had cost me nothing more than time, my Polish contemporaries had paid a substantial price for theirs: on the streets, in prison and eventually in forced emigration.

I found myself in the course of those years slipping comfortably into another world, taking my place upon an alternative timeline: one that had probably always been there lurking implicitly below the surface, molded by a past of which I had only ever been half conscious. A past in which Eastern Europe ceased to be just a place; its history was now for me a direct and highly personal frame of reference.

After all, Jan, Irena, Basia and the others were not just my contemporaries; we could all, but for small twists of fate, have been born in the same place. My father's father, after all, came from Warsaw. Most of his acquaintances—the old men and women of my childhood—had come from thereabouts. My education was at once markedly different from that of my Polish peers and yet colored by frequent common references and shared staging points. Wherever my generation came to maturity, it had slipped the bonds of Marxist dogma at about the same time, albeit for different reasons and in different circumstances. To be sure, History had afforded those in the East a privileged perch; it was Leszek Kołakowski, important both to my Polish friends and to me, who famously observed that reforming socialism was like frying snowballs. In Western Europe, the message took a little longer to get across—a generation, let's say.

Basia Toruńczyk took great trouble to convey to me the importance of the lost world of Polish culture, literature and ideas: lost to the West, of course, but also lost to Poles themselves thanks to the destructive impact of Soviet hegemony. It clearly mattered a lot to her, and the frustrations attendant upon the use of a third language (French, which we spoke together) probably made the task even harder. But then we westerners were never truly expected to penetrate the mystique. Timothy Garton Ash once told me a story. His wife Danuta is Polish, his sons thus bilingual. On one occasion when the boys were small, he was explaining to the older one—then known as Alik and now rather as Alec—that he had to go to Michigan to give a lecture. "What are you going to talk about, Daddy?" the boy asked. "I'm going to tell them about Poland," Tim replied. There ensued a silence. Then little Alik switched instinctively from English into Polish, and said, "*oni nic nie zrozumieją*": they won't understand anything.

Timothy Garton Ash was the Englishman who *did* understand East-ern Europe. Although we both lived in Oxford, I only met him thanks to Basia. You absolutely must meet Garton Ash, she insisted: *on rozumie—il comprend:* he *understands.* Tim was very young then, still under thirty. He had already published his wonderful book about Solidarity and was seen by many as the one person in the English-speaking world who could pre-sent Poland with sympathy and indeed with understanding, without laps-ing into apologetics. The three of us met in my apartment for dinner. I felt an immediate and natural affinity with Tim (even before learning, many years later, that we grew up within a few streets of each other in southwest London).

Tim's book on *The Polish Revolution* is a serious work of political anal-ysis. But it is also a deeply engaged book, written by someone who makes no pretense of distance or cold objectivity. Poland was Tim's Spain, and his passages on Gdańsk bear comparison with Orwell's account of Barce-lona in the Spanish Civil War. In later years, after a decade of brilliant essays on east-central Europe, Tim would watch his subject disappear from under him in the best possible way. He had got it right and he was to play an active part in its dismantling. That first dinner we talked about Thatcher, about Oxford, about Eastern Europe; we teased Basia about the "understanding" thing; and we had a very pleasant evening indeed. I don't think I quite grasped it at the time, but "understanding" was becoming for me an increas-ingly central objective: harder, deeper and more enduring than merely "being right."

Meeting Tim further contributed to the making of a new milieu: it exposed my ignorance of the history of Europe's other half, but at the same time brought me closer to "home." Curiously, many of my contemporaries from Eastern Europe were from more exalted backgrounds than mine: in most cases they were the sons or daughters of the communist elite. Basia would describe them as the "banana youth"—a play on the French and Pol-ish idea of a "golden youth," a privileged adolescence, for the bright and the fortunate. For me, bananas recalled a socialist Zionist fantasy; for them, bananas were a sign of grace, since in communist Poland they were typically available only at special stores for the Party elite.

I was now an insider in a community of outsiders, a new and rather pleasing sensation. But even so, I maintained a certain distance. My particular path into Eastern Europe, despite my multiple Polish friendships, lay through Czechoslovakia. I had come to this at Oxford, but altogether fortuitously. In 1981, the prominent English left-wing historian and publicist E. P. Thompson had written a particularly foolish essay in the *New Statesman* criticizing an anonymous Czech intellectual for suggesting that things were worse in his country than in the West and that the propensity of the west European Left to condemn both sides equally (or even to blame their own governments for international tensions) was mistaken. I wrote a letter to the *New Statesman* saying how provincial I thought Thompson's response and how characteristically ignorant of reality east of the Iron Curtain.

In the course of a conversation shortly thereafter, Steven Lukes, the Oxford sociologist, asked if I would be interested in meeting some of his Czech friends and colleagues. And so it was that I found myself in London at the apartment of Jan Kavan. Jan, who had been one of the student activists of the Prague Spring of 1968, had escaped to Britain in 1969 (his mother was English). He was then at a low point—depressed, taking medications, convinced that neither he nor his homeland had much of a future. He had also just given a long and rather self-promoting interview to London Weekend Television about the underground smuggling of books into Czechoslovakia. In retrospect, Jan was terrified that in his enthusiasm he had given away confidential information that could prejudice his friends.

Since our meeting coincided with this dilemma, Jan Kavan—vastly overestimating the influence of an obscure Oxford don—begged me to use my standing to convince the television network not to run the program. And so, in almost complete ignorance of the subject, the program and the context, I introduced myself at London Weekend Television and pressed Kavan's case. The journalists there, sensing precisely the scandal that I was seeking to head off, became even more interested in running the program. I don't think anything terrible happened as a consequence, but there is no doubt that his performance added to Kavan's reputation as a somewhat unreliable character: following his country's liberation he would eventually become foreign minister, but only after quashing rumors that he had collaborated as an informer with the communist authorities.

Meanwhile, I returned to Oxford conscious of the slightly ridiculous nature of my intervention and the embarrassing extent of my ignorance. That same day I took myself to Blackwell's bookshop and bought *Teach Yourself Czech*; a few months later I enrolled in a university Czech language class. And I decided that in due course I would start teaching East European politics and contemporary history in the Oxford Politics faculty. There ensued a year of hard reading: conventional national histories, political science journals, primary materials—focused above all on Czechoslovakia, but broadly based in the whole central European region.

The first book that I read from cover to cover in Czech was Karel Čapek's conversations with Tomáš Masaryk, a marvelously open and honest series of exchanges between Czech writer and Czechoslovak president. But then everything that I read in those years seemed urgent, original and immediately relevant. The contrast with French history, drowning as it seemed to me in the 1980s in cultural theory and historical marginality, was invigorating. I don't think I had realized how truly bored I was with France after studying it for two decades: Eastern Europe offered me a fresh start.

My Polish friends were sometimes skeptical of this newfound Czech interest. The language in particular struck them as altogether unworthy of serious attention. Jan Gross offered me the example of a scene in *Othello*, where the eponymous tragic hero cries "Śmierć!" which is Polish for "death." In Czech, this comes out as a string of impacted consonants, "Smrt!" To my English ear, it sounded little different in Polish; but to Jan the distinction was crucial, marking off a small and provincial Slav region from a country and a language with a proud and resonant history. I think that I felt I could get a grip on Czech history and the Czech language much quicker than I would those of Poland, perhaps precisely for Jan's reason. But there was also something about the self-demeaning, self-mocking, ironic, eternally *depressed* quality of Czech literary and political culture which attracted me.

I would only begin to write about Eastern Europe when I was invited to do so, and this was not for a while. Daniel Chirot, the University of Washington scholar of Romania with whom I had previously exchanged thoughts on the sociology of backwardness, asked me to contribute a paper to a symposium in Washington at the Woodrow Wilson Center; the following year, in 1988, this became "The Dilemmas of Dissidence," published in a new journal: *East European Politics and Societies*. I surveyed the countries of communist Europe, seeking after the small openings that oppositionists had found for politics, noting the differences among the cases. Gorbachev had been in power in the Soviet Union since 1985 but in 1987 or 1988 there was little sign that the satellites were about to gain their freedom. So this was not a triumphant article, but a modest attempt at an empirical sociology of concrete groups about which, at the time, little was known.

More perhaps than I saw at the time, I was concerned with the connection between "living in truth" and actual politics. The piece began with a citation of Kafka's *The Trial*, where K. says that if we must accept that the law is grounded only in necessity, then lying becomes a universal principle. This was my first substantial contribution to east European scholarship, written just before the revolutions.

Eastern Europe had opened up for me a new subject and a new Europe; but it also coincided with a radical shift in perspective and, as it seems to me upon reflection, maturity. My Oxford years, 1980–1987, and the political philosophy which I read and taught there, seem to have prompted a certain modesty and reflection. I had reached the end of my particular road. My article "A Clown in Regal Purple," rather like *Socialism in Provence*, albeit in a very different key, represented the fruition of whatever early training I received: like my other writings of the 1970s and early 1980s, they demonstrated intellectual dexterity; a certain quick cleverness which in retrospect I associate with my years at Cambridge and Paris; but also a certain weakness for dialectical exhibitionism. Thus in seeking to demonstrate that social history was at a dead end, I had probably inadvertently illustrated the limits of my own approach in those years.

I had grown up, as it were, speaking French (and perhaps Marx). I knew my subject intimately: I was intensely familiar with France—geographically, historically, politically, culturally, linguistically. The result was rather like living with someone for too long: the very familiarity and intimacy that once made everything so easy can become sources of irritation and ultimately of disrespect. Czech, on the other hand, was a language and a world that I had begun to learn in my thirties. I was reading my way with frustrating slowness into a subject that I could never hope to master as I had mastered the French Left. The result was an appropriately humbling awareness of my limitations which did me no harm at all.

And yet, it was thanks to Oxford and to Eastern Europe that I would come back to French history, refreshed and even inspired: my last major work as a French intellectual, so to speak, would be *Past Imperfect*, a self-conscious reckoning with the philo-communism of the postwar French Left informed by the contacts and readings of my Oxford years. It was there that I had completed my third book, *Marxism and the French Left: Studies in Labor and Politics in France 1830–1982*. This book of hitherto unpublished essays constituted, as I now see, my own "goodbye to all that." At the time I thought of it quite differently: as a partial chronicle of the end of socialism, in its distinctive French form.

Like so much of my early work, *Marxism and the French Left* had more impact in France than in the English-speaking historical community. On this occasion I owe its resonance to François Furet, the historian and obituarist of the French Revolution, who generously wrote an introduction to the French translation which appeared in 1986. Furet's own *Penser la Révolution française,* first published in 1978, was an astonishing exercise and had influenced me hugely. In a remarkably compact series of essays, Furet had successfully and definitively historicized the national tradition of historical writing about the French Revolution, brilliantly illustrating at once how political the interpretations had been from the outset and the ways in which a two-hundred-year-old model of analysis and appropriation had run into the ground.

In 1986 I was due to take a sabbatical from Oxford. I had long since decided to spend the year in Stanford, where the Hoover Institution offered unequalled holdings in Eastern European history and European intellectual history more generally. For some time I had been planning a new departure, a book about French intellectuals and the communist mirage, drawing on my new readings in east European history in particular. I applied for and was offered a fellowship at the Stanford Humanities Center, and went there for the year 1986–1987. Since I had married Patricia Hilden in California, a move back had the additional benefit of facilitating the initiation and rapid completion of divorce proceedings there as well.

In California I became very close friends with Helen Solanum, the West European librarian at the Hoover Institution. Helen was a friend of Jan and Irena Gross, through whom we first met; as with them so with Helen, I found many common interests and overlapping perspectives. She was born in Poland on August 31, 1939, the day before the German invasion of her homeland that began the Second World War. Her family escaped eastwards, into the region invaded and occupied by the Soviet Union after September 17, 1939. Like tens of thousands of other Jews, Helen and her family were then deported in 1940 to Soviet Kazakhstan, in terrible conditions: her sister was to die there. After the war Helen's family initially returned to Poland, to Wałbrzych in Silesia. There she was instructed by her parents to forget Russian, just as in the Soviet Union she had been warned to forget the family's native Yiddish. She was now six years old, living in territory assigned to Poland after the German defeat, and from which Germans had been expelled.

And she was a Jew, living in a country from which more than ninety percent of her fellow Jews had been expunged. Having survived the war in Kazakhstan, Helen's family now faced prejudice, persecution and worse from the surrounding population. Prudently, they moved on. From Silesia, where the Polish government had initially planned to resettle Jews, they made for a German displaced persons camp: like so many of the survivors in those months, they felt safer in defeated Germany than in the liberated lands farther east. After unsuccessful efforts to secure admission to the United States, the family settled for France, where Helen was to live for ten years before permission to enter America was finally granted.

"Solanum" was not of course the family name. It derives from the Latin for "potato": her memories of Kazakhstan were dominated by death and potatoes, and so Helen elected association with them in an act of retrospective homage. She was a formidable linguist: in addition to her youthful Polish, Yiddish and Russian, she had acquired good Hebrew, near-native French and of course perfect English in addition to the Spanish and Portuguese she studied in college. Friendship with Helen afforded me privileged access to the closed collections in the tower of the Hoover Institution, an unmatched trove of obscure French publications and much else besides. The Hoover Institution has short, invaluable runs of journals, periodicals, provincial newspapers and other material that are almost impossible to find in France, much less outside.

In its original conception, *Past Imperfect* was to be a history of left-wing intellectual life in Paris in the years following the Second World War, coincident with the transition to communism in central and Eastern Europe. By the late 1980s, of course, it had become conventional in France to dismiss Jean-Paul Sartre and his fellow-traveling contemporaries as talented and influential to be sure, but foolishly soft on communism. But I was not interested in retrospective score-settling. What I had in mind was more ambitious. I had set out to write a case study of a national shortcoming: the striking incoherence, in politics and ethics alike, that marked French intellectual responses to the rise of totalitarianism.

Moreover, I always thought of this subject as comprehensible only in a broader context reaching from the disillusion of the Popular Front through the years of collaboration and resistance and into the depressing and divisive political climate of the postwar decade. It was a story that the French themselves had yet to confront. By the late 1980s French scholars were catching up with their American and British colleagues confronting Vichy and the myths of the Resistance and the troubled history of France's collaboration in the Final Solution. Indeed, the cult of self-interrogation over the "Vichy syndrome" was building to a peak. But very few serious historians were writing about the moral dilemmas of the Cold War years and the compromises these had entailed. Once again, my subject matter was not—or not yet—in the scholarly mainstream. I completed the book in 1991, as the Soviet Union collapsed.

Rereading *Past Imperfect*, I am struck by its central European perspective. The emphasis on civil society, for example, and my critique of intellectuals' propensity to place History and the state upon a pedestal, directly reflected my involvement with debates emerging from Central Europe in the late 1970s, dating in particular from the foundation of Charter 77.

This conception of public life, rooted in the idea of dissent *from* a state-centered polis, represented a direct challenge to the French conception of citizenship, with its emphasis upon the initiative and centrality of the republican state. As a consequence, many French critics read this aspect of *Past Imperfect* as a characteristically *English* attack on the French political tradition. In essence, they took me to be asking: why are the French not more like the English—more liberal, more decentralized. Why, in short, is Sartre not John Stuart Mill?

But this was to misread my purpose. What I was arguing, or trying to argue, was quite different. The book was an illustration and critique of a distinctively French way of conceiving of the place of the state—a conception by no means, of course, confined to France, though its roots lie in the French eighteenth century—which has on more than one occasion done great harm to the civic space. This was a critique which emanated naturally and organically from the experience of state-centered politics in Europe's eastern half; but as late as 1992 it was still substantially unfamiliar to many western readers, not to mention sensitive French critics.

It was a liberal critique, but the liberalism was perhaps not as recognizable as I might have wished. I was not concerned with the long-established case against economic planning, nor was I remotely sympathetic to the emerging consensus critical of the welfare state. Despite my close attention to a particular historical time and place, my argument was essentially conceptual and even ethical: the intellectual impropriety and political imprudence of assigning to any one institution, any monopolistic historical narrative, any single political party or person, the authority and resources to regulate and determine all the norms and forms of a well-ordered public life. The good society, like goodness itself, cannot be reduced to a single source; ethical pluralism is the necessary precondition for an open democracy.

I'd like to follow that thought, and see if we can't use it to unify the periods before and after the Second World War. The idea of the single, uniform good takes us back to our discussion of Popular Fronts, since the whole premise of prewar international politics was the reducibility of ethics to a unity, and the expression of that unity in a single system. On the left, the political instantiation of anti-fascism is the Popular Front, which reduces Europe to fascists and anti-fascists and which is designed ultimately to protect the homeland of revolution, the Soviet Union. And as you noted in connection with Spain, the way the Soviets set up governments in Eastern Europe in the first place was precisely on the Popular Front model.

Yes, the Popular Front has to be your starting point if you want to understand the politics of the late 1940s. In Eastern Europe you had communists in office, or as part of the ruling coalition, looking for a way to dominate certain key ministries though much less concerned in the beginning with the high offices of state. The appeal to the notion of a Popular Front, to a government of national unity, was a mask under which you could, for example, absorb the local socialist party. You split the unreconstructed, anti-communist socialists, whom you could not hope to attract, from the softer ones, who wanted left-wing unity or were vulnerable to communist pressure, or were just frightened.

You ended up with a large party of the left, consisting of communists and whatever element of the socialist party you've been able to put together; you then encouraged the local equivalent of the Popular Front's radicals, or the West's postwar Christian Democrats, into lining up with the progressive front—again, often separating them from their more far-sighted or recalcitrant members, usually a minority. And so you produced a large umbrella party, or front, or united coalition, which then was in a position to justify repressive measures against those parties it could not absorb. Arguably, that's what Spain was in miniature, particularly in Barcelona, in 1938. In France, Léon Blum in February 1948 wrote an editorial in the socialist newspaper *Le Populaire*, acknowledging that he'd been wrong to believe that it was possible for socialists to work with communists.

In a deeper way, there is a unity to that period from the mid-1930s to the mid-1950s which was obvious at the time and which is obscured now. It's a unity of sensibility; it's a unity of social and cultural context, in that so much changed from the mid-fifties onwards. The Second World War cannot really be framed within six years. It doesn't make any sense to start our understanding of the Second World War the day that Britain happens to declare war on Germany, or when Germany invades Poland, which is still arbitrary. For East Europeans it makes no sense to end the story in May 1945. Limiting the account to 1939–1945 applies only in countries which were largely unaffected by popular fronts, by occupation, by extermination, and by ideological or political reoccupation in later years. Which means it's a story which only makes sense for England.

The east European experience begins with the occupation, with the years of extermination, with the German-Soviet encounter. The French story makes no sense if you separate Vichy off from what came afterwards—because so much of what came afterwards was a function of remembering or mis-remembering Vichy. And Vichy makes no sense if you don't understand the de facto civil war that France was in from the Popular Front until the German attack. The whole story is side-shadowed by the Spanish Civil War, which ends in April 1939 but is in fact central to our understanding, not only of Soviet purposes, but of Western responses. And that story has to begin, like that of the French Popular Front, with the victory of the left in the elections of 1936. And, in a rather different key, faith in communism, illusions (willful or naïve) about Stalinism, in West and East alike, make no sense if you begin in 1945—or continue past 1956, when circumstances change quite sharply. So it would make sense to treat the years 1936–1956 as a single period of European history.

> *In the very special French case, one continuity over those two decades is that of regard for the achievements of the Soviet Union. Furet makes the argument that Sartre and the others are bound by the imaginary of the French Revolution and therefore tend to see the Bolshevik Revolution as an echo of the French Revolution. They also want to embrace that revolution within a French history, somehow, to make the universal French and the French universal. And I was wondering whether that isn't part of the kind of pathetic dilemma of the postwar French intellectuals, that they were still working at making the Soviet Union French.*

The projection of the Revolution abroad has a double significance. One, it's the emotional projection of France as the Middle Kingdom, the French model both in its desirability and in its natural primacy. In that sense, you know, it's easier to understand the French if you remember the Americans, this tendency we have to suppose that the rest of the world is just waiting to be like us. But the other part of it of course is the Marxist notion that revolutions have a structure, that there's a story about revolutions, it's part of a story about history, and the Revolution which takes place in Russia must be in some sense the local version—allowing for the difference in time and circumstance—of what took place in France. It's not their republican revolution, but at least it's their anti-feudal revolution. And *mutatis mutandis* more violent because Russia is much bigger and less civilized than France.

It also, it seems to me, allows for a kind of false realism: we know
that revolutions are bloody because we went through one, and
therefore, one thinks one is being tough and even appropriately
cynical when one in fact is ignorant and naïve.

Remember that after World War Two there was a significant increase in macho realism in French intellectual writing: particularly among women. It was Simone de Beauvoir who argued that the only good collaborator is a dead collaborator, and so forth. Sartre was talking about the occupation as having been sexual, with the Germans "penetrating" the French. That's the implicit tough guy stand of existentialism: you are made by the choices you make, but the choices you make are not open-ended: they're the ones history presents you with.

This was the French way of making Marx's point in *The Eighteenth Brumaire:* "Men make their own history, but they do not make it under circumstances chosen by themselves, but under circumstances directly encountered, given and transmitted from the past." Well, says the postwar existentialist, here we are, having to make our own history, but we didn't get to choose the circumstances. And the Russians didn't either. Our choice is either to abandon the Revolution or accept its shortcomings.

In your work, in Past Imperfect, *the collapse of the French republic*
in 1940 plays a major role, but it comes in from the sides, as
though we readers already have a sense of what Vichy must have
been and what the war must have been like for France. But that's
not actually in the book.

Vichy was a cataclysmic shock in a way I don't think I fully gauged back then. We Anglo-Americans don't have the beginnings of a sense, I think, of what it meant for that generation of the French to see not just the defeat but the end of the Republic. The country collapsed not just institutionally but morally, in every way. There wasn't a Republic left, just people running. There were old established Republican politicians scared witless at the thought not of a German victory but of a communist uprising that they thought was going to come out of it. Accordingly, they rushed into the arms of the Germans or Pétain or whoever would save them from that. There were warriors—Pétain, Weygand, all the others from World War I who were icons of interwar France—lining up to give the Germans everything they asked. All of this in just six weeks.

The end of the war was not much better. World War II for France is four years of occupation followed by a few months of liberation, mostly consisting of American bombing and shelling and an American takeover, so it seemed, of France. There was no time to digest the meaning of all this. The nation had been artificially recast between the wars as a Great Power. America had withdrawn into isolation; England into semi-isolation; Spain collapsed internally; Italy was under Mussolini; Germany fell into Nazism: France was the only significant democratic power left in Europe.

After 1945, that story fell apart. The French needed to reconstruct their community, make sense of their divisions and reassert their common values. Somehow they needed to find not just something to be proud of, but a story around which the country could unite. But this sentiment, closely tied to the mood of resistance and liberation, was quickly displaced by the appreciation that France's recovery depended on the restoration of Europe, something that could not be achieved without American protection and assistance. But this was the perspective of a small, well-informed administrative elite.

The intellectuals remained resolutely anti-European—or at best un-European. Most of them (Raymond Aron is the best-known exception) saw plans for European unification or integration as a capitalist plot, and they remained no less anti-American: the newfound hegemony of the U.S. they resented as little more than an imperial takeover—or, worse, German victory by other means. For such persons, France had had the additional misfortune to get caught on the wrong side of the Cold War.

That's why there was so much emphasis in France upon neutrality. Very few truly believed that France could be neutral in a war between the Soviet Union and the United States, or England. But there was a widely-shared sentiment that France *should* be, so far as possible, neutral in conflicts between the Great Powers simply because it had no interest in them. Britain was widely mistrusted: because of the wartime destruction of the French fleet by the Royal Navy and London's secret deals with Washington after the war— agreements that France kept discovering after the fact. So between a resentful awareness that France could no longer "go it alone," and the distrust of the country's new "friends," many intellectuals on left and right alike effectively invented a postwar world in their own image: a world conforming to their ideas and ideals but which bore little relationship to international reality.

France is a great power after the war, if only intellectually. Indeed, it seems that the self-contained, discursive character of leftist politics in France matters more as France itself matters less.

So if French peasants in the nineteenth century embrace a program which isn't really in their interests, but socialists get elected as a result, as in the France of your second book on Provence, it doesn't really matter so much. If Léon Blum has to muddle through his own Marxism in the 1930s and finds his hands tied, that may be something of a national disaster; if Blum is more confused than he should be when he finally gets into power, that's a European problem. But after the war, when France matters least *as a traditional power, then—at least I think this is your argument if one puts all the books together—discourse matters more because the French only matter in so far as people are listening to them or not listening to them.*

That's very well said and summarized. I think that there were many things coming together in the postwar years. Latin American interest in things French peaked in the forties and fifties. America, New York in particular, still appeared parochial, at least in intellectual affairs: there was nothing coming out of America comparable to the European scene. Most American intellectuals would have agreed in those years: they were still in thrall to the European civilization of their parents or grandparents. Remember too that a whole new generation of European intellectuals had only recently migrated to America thanks to communism and Nazism. In due course, they would remake and revitalize American intellectual life, displacing France and much of Europe along the way. But for the time being, Europe retained its intellectual centrality—and France was the only game in Europe. Moreover, French was still the only foreign language to which most outsiders had easy access, so French writings and thinkers were accessible. Once again, and for the last time, Paris became the capital of the century.

> *So there is a continuity of illusion. What about disillusion? If one runs this argument, on a European scale now, from 1936 through to 1956, what are the key moments when people are disillusioned with communism?*

The year 1936 had seen a re-illusioning with Marxism: the rebirth of faith in Marxism as a popular politics in countries that had seen no mass political action since the early 1920s. The Popular Front meant more than just electoral victories in Spain and France: it was also strikes, occupations, demonstrations—the rebirth of popular left-wing politics. For most left-wing observers, the civil war in Spain had the same effect. For every Koestler, or Orwell, or Georges Bernanos in France, there were dozens and dozens of left-leaning journalists who wrote with enthusiasm of the positive role the communists were playing defending the Spanish Republic during the Civil War.

Then came the Molotov-Ribbentrop Pact in August 1939—the alliance between Stalin and Hitler. This was disillusioning for soft supporters and for most older communists. Conversely, it doesn't appear to have damaged the faith of the harder, younger generation recruited in the 1930s. But people who had come to communism because they hated fascism, rather than because they believed in history and the Revolution, were profoundly shaken by the Pact.

Within two years, however, the very grounds for despairing of Stalin were now reasons for once again throwing in your lot with him. Hitler attacked the Soviet Union on June 22, 1941. At that point it became plausible to claim, in retrospect, that the Molotov-Ribbentrop Pact had been a brilliant tactical ploy. Stalin had no choice: Germany was strong, and the West was cynically maneuvering to leave Stalin and Hitler to destroy each other—why on earth would Stalin not protect himself, at least in the short run, until he was in a position to defend the homeland of revolution?

As for the outcome of the Second World War: it too appeared to confirm the farsighted wisdom of Stalin's brutal calculations. The Soviet Union's western allies and many of their citizens were all too willing to accept the Soviet account of events in return for Moscow's role in the defeat of Nazism. It wasn't just Soviet propaganda which presented the mass shooting of Polish prisoners at Katyn, for example, as a German rather than a Soviet war crime. Most Westerners found this version of events perfectly credible; and even if they harbored doubts, they preferred to keep these to themselves.

The big change came with the communist takeovers and the Cold War, which forced many intellectuals to do what they'd managed to avoid doing since the 1930s: distinguish between the interests of Western democracies and the interests of the Soviet Union. By the 1950s, it was very difficult to fudge the choice: how could you be a defender both of republican, democratic France and the Soviet Union of Josef Stalin—except at a level of historical abstraction that bore no relation to real politics?

You couldn't back the Communist Party in France or Italy after 1947 and still claim that you were a defender of liberal democracy. Because the Soviet Union itself did not believe that this was possible, progressives were forced to choose, however little they wished to do so. This fundamental issue informed everybody's choice, even if the moment of decision varied by country and circumstance. For some, the breaking point came with the palpably faked elections in Poland of January 1947; for others, it was the coup in Czechoslovakia in February 1948, the Berlin Blockade beginning that June and lasting almost a year, or the North Korean invasion of South Korea in June 1950.

For many of those who were still loyal communists when Stalin died in March 1953, the telling moment came with Khrushchev's "secret speech" of February 1956. Khrushchev tried to save the Leninist core by abandoning the Stalinist penumbra—a considerable embarrassment for men and women who had spent a lifetime justifying Stalin by reference to Lenin. As for the revolt in Hungary that followed shortly thereafter, I think this mattered more to communism's peripheral friends and supporters. It demonstrated that, rather than allow a country to emerge freely from under its authority, even the Soviet Union of Mr. Khrushchev would send in tanks and kill people to achieve its ends.

Meanwhile, the electorates of the West were becoming less ideological and less confrontational: their interests were now more parochial and above all economic. What this meant was that Marxism as a language of ever greater political and social confrontation became marginal to the political culture. It retreated first to the intelligentsia and thence to the academy, which is where it washed up by the 1970s.

It seems to me that anyone who by 1956 would have been disillusioned by the use of violence must not already have believed. Because an awful lot of the attraction to communism, at least among intellectuals, actually had to do (as Koestler put it about his young self) with a certain taste for violence. And Merleau-Ponty makes this explicit as well. And I tend to think that one of the things which is happening in 1956 as well is that Khrushchev's verdict on Stalin, that we will no longer endorse the same kinds of violence, makes Marxism and the USSR less interesting.

The violence is now disconnected from the ideas, or at least grand ideas. The Hungarian compromise that followed the uprising in Budapest in

1956 is telling, but more about politics than ideology or even economics. János Kádár reforms the economy somewhat, while denying that he is doing so, or that what he is doing in any way compromises the system. Hungarians are allowed to consume and are more or less left alone, provided that they do not actively work against the system. "You pretend to work, and we'll pretend to pay you." He who is not against us is with us. From the point of view of Moscow and its satellites and the West, the logic is similar: you pretend to believe, and we'll pretend to believe you.

The invasion of Hungary weakens intellectual faith in the Soviet Union, under the narrative that it had been presenting for the previous thirty years. Twelve years later, Soviet tanks are in Prague, putting down the reform movement that we recall as the Prague Spring. That is something more. The intervention in Czechoslovakia destroys faith in the Marxist narrative itself: not just in the Soviet Union nor merely in Leninism, but in Marxism and its account of the modern world.

Between Budapest in 1956 and Prague in 1968 is the great era of revisionism, in both Eastern and Western Europe. Revisionism gave rise to the illusion in the East that a certain amount of carefully negotiated space for dissent was possible and worth achieving. It opens up the illusion in the West that it is coherent to be a dissenting communist, whereas the category "ex-communist" was still frowned upon. In the East one final generation is drawn to Marxism: the generation of Leszek Kołakowski, who is the most interesting revisionist in the 1960s before becoming the most profound critic of Marxism in the 1970s. The younger generation in Western Europe, if it's attracted to radical politics, is attracted to a version of Marxism which doesn't even concern itself with the problems of the Soviet Union or Eastern Europe.

The Czech reformers of 1968 were among the last in the East to embody that kind of naïve, revisionist attitude towards politics itself. That we Czechs can be a model of Marxism, so much so that we could teach the West a thing or two—and also teach Moscow a thing or two.

In the West among the Left the Soviets go from being the point to being beside the point. Khrushchev begins it, Brezhnev ends it. His justification for the Warsaw Pact invasion of Czechoslovakia, the Brezhnev Doctrine of "fraternal assistance" is so obviously a cover for great power politics, and what he is crushing is obviously a movement of Marxists, of communists. It is violence, but it is no longer interesting: it is traditional rather than personal or ideological. The Brezhnev Doctrine is an alibi, not a theory. And meanwhile the USSR has rivals for the title of homeland of revolution.

Right. There were three ways that you remain a vociferous critic of the whole Soviet project and still be on the far left. The first and least significant was what Perry Anderson called Western Marxism: the obscure intellectuals of the German, or Italian, or French, or English Marxist left who had been defeated by official communism, but continued to proclaim themselves spokesmen for a certain kind of internally consistent, radical Marxism: Karl Korsch, György Lukács, Lucien Goldmann, most importantly and slightly differently Antonio Gramsci. But these were all people like Rosa Luxemburg, whose image was also resurrected in these years, and Trotsky himself: they had the salient virtue of being losers. Being on the winning side of History was the Soviet trump card from 1917 through 1956: thereafter, the losers began to look good. At least they had clean hands. The rediscovery of these individual dissenters—either official dissenters or subterranean dissenters, Karl Korsch being the most marginal, Gramsci the most important— became a way for academics and intellectuals to place themselves in a line of dissent from a respectable Marxism. But this newfound genealogy came at the price of detachment from the actual history of the twentieth century.

The second and slightly more important way in which it became possible to think of yourself as overtaking communism on the left was to identify with the young Marx. This meant sharing the renewed appreciation for and emphasis upon Marx the philosopher, Marx the Hegelian, Marx the theorist of alienation. Marx's writings up to early 1845, chiefly the "Economic and Philosophical Manuscripts" of 1844, now moved to the center of the canon.

Party ideologists like Louis Althusser took up the cudgels against this, insisting to the point of absurdity that there was an epistemological break in Marxism, that anything Karl Marx wrote before 1845 is not in fact "Marxist." But the advantage of rediscovering the young Marx was that he furnished you with a whole new vocabulary. Marxism becomes a more diffuse language: accessible to students and serviceable for new, substitute revolutionary categories—women, gays, students themselves and so on. Such persons could now be readily inserted into the narrative despite having no organic link to the blue-collar proletariat.

The third and most important factor, of course, was the Chinese Revolution and the rural revolutions then under way in Central America, Latin America, East and West Africa, Southeast Asia. It seemed that the center of gravity of history had moved away from the West and even the Soviet Union to unambiguously peasant societies. These revolutions coincide with the flowering of peasant studies and studies of rural revolution in Western Europe and the United States. Mao's peasant communism had a distinctive virtue: it could be invested with any meaning one chose. Moreover, Russia was European, whereas China was "the third world": a consideration of increasing importance to a younger generation for whom Europe and North America were a lost cause for the Left.

Well, it's a way that the Soviet Union fails by succeeding. Lenin's idea, or deviation, depending on your point of view, was that one could build up a replica of bourgeois, industrial society after the Revolution—

And then overthrow it—

from within and build socialism. And what happens instead is that by the time you build up the replica of capitalism, the original

has moved on to something which is much nicer. And you're stuck
with the replica, which increasingly seems unattractive and unable
to compete—either with the comforts of the West or the excitement
of the Third World.

The Soviet Union goes from being horrible to being boring, in the eyes
of its critics; and from being full of hope to lacking promise, in the eyes of its
supporters.

Think of Nikita Khrushchev himself. On the one hand, he goes to
America and gets in an argument with Nixon about who makes better fridges.
On the other hand, he comes back to Moscow and indulges himself in revolutionary enthusiasm about Cuba. So the Soviet Union comes off poorly
twice over: it's a poor copy of America, and it's desperate to see itself renewed
in Cuba.

Whereas Mao, and (after Mao) lesser Maos elsewhere, have no such dual
ambition. And the Cultural Revolution, which is really a sort of vicious replica
of aspects of Stalinism, was perceived by my contemporaries in Cambridge in
the late 1960s as a refreshing burst of energy and youthful determination
always to renew the Revolution, in contrast with the staid old men in Moscow.

China is another way that Lenin's success is his failure. Because
what Lenin and Trotsky were counting on was that if they had one
premature revolution in a backward country, the mature
revolutions would follow in the Western industrialized or
industrializing countries. And that's not what happens; what
happens instead is that the Leninist revolt becomes the thing in
itself. It becomes the model of revolution which can spread to other
agrarian countries, still less suited to revolution from a traditional
Marxist perspective.

Stalin's destruction of the Soviet intelligentsia was piecemeal. And
essentially retail. Mao murdered wholesale; Pol Pot was universal. What do

you do, faced with the risk that intellectuals, or urban dwellers, or the bourgeoisie (what's left of them) might form a discontented, critical opposition,
or even a dissenting oppositional potential, as yet unformed? You simply
abolish them. You annihilate them. By the time the logic of revolutionary
exterminism reaches Cambodia, communist ideological purposes have
merged with Nazi collective categories.

*We have been speaking as though the only story were the
disillusionments of the 1950s and 1960s. But there was a group of
intellectual critics of Marxism and the Soviet Union who were
either disillusioned with Marxism much earlier or who had in
some cases never held much truck with Marxism at all: the Cold
War liberals.*

The real Cold War at the intellectual and cultural level, and also at the
political level in many countries, was not fought between the Left and the
right but *within* the Left. The real political fault line fell between communists and fellow traveling sympathizers, on the one side, and social democrats, on the other side—with special cases as in Italy, where the socialists
were for a while on the side of the communists. Culturally, the fault line was
drawn by the inherited cultural politics of the 1930s.

Once you understand this, you can see who the Cold War liberals were.
They were people like Sidney Hook: a Jewish Marxist turned non-Marxist,
but specialist on Marx, who went to City College in New York. He was born
in 1902, from the Brooklyn immigrant Jewish left-wing community, attracted
to communism as an ideology. Hook found himself repelled by the rise of
Stalin and for a time sympathetic to Trotsky. Later he came to see Trotsky as
either deluded, or a variant of Leninism which was itself not significantly
superior to Stalinism. He became an aggressively socialist critic of
communism.

The "aggressively socialist" is crucial. There's nothing reactionary
about Sidney Hook. There's nothing politically right-wing about him,

though he was conservative in some of his cultural tastes—like many social-ists. Like Raymond Aron, he was on the opposite side of the barrier from the sixties students. He left New York University disgusted with the university's failure to stand up to the sit-ins and occupations—that was a very Cold War liberal kind of stance. But his politics were always left of center domestically and a direct inheritance from the nineteenth-century socialist tradition.

Raymond Aron, born three years after Hook, had a lot in common with him. The generation of Cold War liberals—born in many cases in the first decade of the twentieth century—were a little older than the run-of-the-mill progressives, whose defining experience was the Second World War rather than the 1930s. Aron, like Hook, was Jewish—although that mattered less in his generation of French intellectuals; and he received an elite education at the École Normale Supérieure, rather than a popular state college education. But like Hook, he became a great expert on Marxism—though unlike Hook he was never a Marxist. His own distaste for authoritarian rule was shaped rather by firsthand observation of Nazism during an extended stay in Germany.

After World War II, Aron took the view that for Europeans, the choice between America and the Soviet Union was a function not of which of the two you thought was a good place but which of the two you thought less bad. Aron is often misunderstood as some kind of right-wing conservative: he never was. Indeed, by any conventional standard, he was left of center. His contempt, however, was reserved not for the idiocies of the Right—for which he had no time at all—but for the foolishness of the fellow-traveling Left, including former friends like Jean-Paul Sartre and Simone de Beauvoir.

There were people like Hook or Aron in most countries in Europe: knowledgeable about Marxism and with few illusions about the United States. They had no trouble identifying what was wrong with America—racism, a history of slavery, capitalism in its rawest form—but this was no longer the issue. The choice you faced was two large imperial groupings: but it was only possible and, indeed, desirable to live under one of them.

Of course, there were variations. Some Cold War liberals were unhappy and embarrassed when faced with the more extreme forms of right-wing anti-communism. Others, like Hook or Arthur Koestler, were not embarrassed at all. You can't help people, as Koestler put it, being right for the wrong reasons. Cold War liberals never expressed anything other than disgust for McCarthyism in American politics; but they also insisted that there was a central truth that McCarthy and Nixon and others had identified. Communism really *was* the enemy: you had to make a choice, and you could not pretend there was a third way.

It was the Cold War liberals who dominated organizations like the Congress on Cultural Freedom, who published journals like *Encounter*, or *Preuves*, and so on, and who organized well-publicized counter-meetings against communist peace propaganda.

We know now the extent to which Cold War liberals were not only organizing themselves but being organized.

The journals and the congresses of those years were financed by the CIA, chiefly through the Ford Foundation. It may be that I'm insensitive to something here, but my view of the matter goes something like this: the culture wars of the 1950s were largely conducted on both sides by front organizations. In the circumstances of the time, who are we to say that the social democrats and liberals should have denied themselves financial resources to combat a huge Soviet propaganda machine?

The CIA was funding a propagandistic Marshall Plan. But remember who the CIA was in the early 1950s. It was not the FBI; and it was not yet the clunky, incompetent, servile CIA of the post-Reagan years. There were still many of the smart young people who had joined the CIA through the wartime OSS: they had a good deal of discretion in how they chose to work against Soviet subversion and propaganda.

Raymond Aron is very good on this in his memoirs. I mean, he says, we should have thought: where's this money coming from? We didn't. But if you had put us up against the wall, we'd probably have admitted that it was probably coming from some source that we'd rather not know about. Aron is right: these were not people with much governmental experience. Aron himself spent just six months in office at the Ministry of Information headed by André Malraux in 1945: his only experience of government. Koestler never ran anything. Hook was a professor of philosophy.

In intellectual terms, is there a distinct Cold War liberalism?

It's best to think of the Cold War liberals as the heirs to American Progressivism and the New Deal. That's their *formation*, in the French sense of the word, that's how they were molded, that's what shaped them intellectually. They saw the welfare state and the social cohesion it could generate as a way to avoid the extremist politics of the 1930s. That is what fueled and informed their anti-communism: the latter was also driven by a background many of them shared in anti-fascist activities before 1939. The anti-fascist organizations, the fronts, the movements, the journals, the meetings, the speeches of the thirties have their counterpart in the anti-communist liberalism of the fifties.

Before 1939, progressives and liberals were on the defensive. The notion of a defensible middle ground was squeezed between the arguments and appeals of fascism and communism. As Mark Mazower writes in *Dark Continent*, if you stopped the clock in 1941 it would have been hard to argue that history was self-evidently on the side of democracy. But the 1950s were different.

The optimism of the Cold War liberals was born of victory in World War II and the unexpectedly successful resolution of the immediate postwar crisis. Communism made no further advances in Europe after 1948, or 1949 at the latest with East Germany, and meanwhile the Americans had shown themselves able and willing to support liberal economics and democratic institutions in the rest of Europe. The Cold War liberals believed that history was on their side: liberalism was not only a possible and defensible way of life, but it would triumph over its adversaries. It needed to be defended not because it was inherently vulnerable, but because it had lost the habit of aggressively asserting its virtues.

> *Earlier you quoted Koestler about the inevitability of people being right for the wrong reasons. That quotation has a second part, which is to the effect that shying away from such people comes from a lack of self-confidence. If there was an event which then did undermine the confidence of some of the Cold War liberals, and I'm thinking in particular of Aron, it was the European student revolts of 1968.*

In Aron's case, it's also the Six-Day War of 1967. He was profoundly disturbed by Charles de Gaulle's publicly expressed distaste for Israel and Jews; and—like many secular Jews of his generation—found himself wondering whether his Jewish identity and his relationship to Israel should not play a more important part in his sense of politics and collective purpose than he had allowed it to do until then.

The year 1968 is crucial because a new generation was emerging for whom all the old lessons seemed irrelevant. Precisely because the liberals had won, their children had no grasp of what had been at stake in the first place. Aron in France, Hook in America, the political theorist Jürgen Habermas in Germany all took a very similar view: the crucial asset of Western liberalism was not its intellectual appeal but its institutional structures.

What made the West a better place, in short, were its forms of government, law, deliberation, regulation and education. Taken together, over time, these formed an implicit pact between society and the state. The former would concede to the state a certain level of intervention, constrained by law and habit; the state, in turn, would allow society a large measure of autonomy bounded by respect for the institutions of the state.

It seemed to many in 1968 that this implicit contract was under strain. For Aron or Habermas, the enemy, as in the 1930s, was those who sought to break it: to reveal, in the contemporary vernacular, the truth beneath the falsehood and the illusions of liberalism. There were, we should recall, grounds for some of these assertions. In France, thanks to Gaullism's monopoly of power and office, politics appeared "blocked." In Germany, the Social Democratic Party lost a generation to the so-called extraparliamentary left, who argued that the party had discredited itself by cohabiting with a coalition government led by a Christian Democratic chancellor who had once belonged to the Nazi party.

By the 1970s the Cold War liberals are aging, and the U.S.–Soviet confrontation has lost some of its ideological sharpness.

Something else was changing, less visibly but at the foundations. The Cold War liberals suffered from the end of the intellectual and political monopoly that had been exercised by the New Deal reformers and their European counterparts from the 1930s to the 1960s. The western world from Roosevelt to Lyndon Johnson and even to Richard Nixon was dominated by progressive domestic politics and "big government." In Western Europe, Social Democratic–Christian Democratic compromises, welfare states and the de-ideologization of public life were commonplace.

But this consensus began to fracture. In 1971, the U.S. ceased to back its dollars with gold reserves, thereby breaking the Bretton Woods international monetary system. Then came the oil price inflation and the associated economic recessions of that grim decade. Most Cold War liberals had never really thought about Keynesianism: as the basis of economic policy, it was just a given. They certainly didn't think about the larger purposes of good government: that too went without saying. So when these and other assumptions were called into question by a new generation of conservative policy intellectuals, the liberals could offer little in response.

So where is liberalism going to come from in the 1970s?

From elsewhere. From people for whom liberalism remained a goal as yet unachieved. People for whom the logic of a liberal state stood sharply opposed to that of their own rulers. Intellectuals for whom liberalism had never been an un-interrogated default condition of politics, but rather a radical objective to be sought at considerable personal risk. By the 1970s the most interesting liberal thought was in Eastern Europe.

Despite their differences, Adam Michnik in Poland, or Václav Havel in Czechoslovakia, or the Hungarian liberals of their generation, all had something in common: lifelong experience with communism. In Eastern Europe, in Warsaw and Prague in any event, 1968 was thus not a revolt against the liberalism of the fathers, much less a protest about the mirage of political freedom. It was a revolt instead against the Stalinism of the sixties generation's parents—a revolt often conducted under the guise and in the name of a reformed or a restored Marxism.

But the dream of Marxist "revisionism" was to fall beneath the police batons in Warsaw and the tanks in Prague. So what the liberals of east-central Europe had in common was a certain negative starting point: there is nothing to be gained from negotiating with authoritarian regimes. The one thing you truly wish to achieve is, by definition, something the regime cannot concede. Any negotiation conducted under such circumstances must always be an exercise in bad faith on both sides, its outcome pre-ordained. Either there must follow a confrontation in which the would-be reformers are defeated— or else their more malleable representatives will be absorbed into the regime and their energy dissipated.

From these straightforward observations, the new generation of east European thinkers reached an original conclusion concerning the metaphysics of authoritarian politics. In the circumstances of a regime that cannot be overthrown—but with which one cannot effectively negotiate—there remained a third option: to act, but to act "as if."

The politics of "as if" could take two forms. In some places it was possible to behave as though the regime was open to negotiation, taking seriously the hypocrisy of its laws and—if nothing else—revealing the emperor's nakedness. Elsewhere, particularly in states like Czechoslovakia where even the illusion of political compromise had been destroyed—the strategy consisted of acting at an individual level as if you were free: leading, or trying to lead, a life grounded in non-political notions of ethics and virtue.

Such an approach required, of course, acceptance of exclusion from politics as the regime (and many outsiders) might define it. Whether you describe this, in Havel's words, as "the power of the powerless," or as "anti-politics" (György Konrád), it was something of which Western liberals had no experience and for which they lacked a language. In effect, the dissidents of communist Europe were arguing for the recreation and re-imagining of society at purely rhetorical and individual levels—beyond the reach of a state which had set out quite deliberately to eviscerate or incorporate society as we understand it.

What the dissidents were doing was forging a new *conversation*. Perhaps this is the easiest way to grasp their purposes, which were quite deliberately deaf to the regime and to its response to them. You simply behaved as though you were treating the law, the language of communism, the constitution of the separate states and the international agreements they had signed as though they were operational and could be trusted.

The most important of these agreements here was the so-called "third basket" of the Helsinki Final Act of 1975, by which the Soviet Union and all of its satellite states committed themselves to observe basic human rights. The regimes of course did not expect to have to take this seriously, which is the only reason they appended their signatures. But from Moscow to Prague critics seized upon the opportunity to focus the attention of the regime on its own legal obligations.

In this sense, if no other, there was some correspondence to what Western radicals thought they were doing in 1968: obliging the authorities to divulge through their behavior the truth of their system. And thereby, with luck, educate fellow citizens as well as foreign observers about the contradictions and lies of communism.

It is part of a larger history of human rights. The "third basket" of Helsinki is grasped, as you say, by Czechs and Ukrainians and

*Poles and Russians and pretty much everyone in the Soviet bloc—a
handful here, a hundred there, to be sure. But it was also picked up
by groups in the West—Amnesty International, Human Rights
Watch—who are doing, in a way, the same thing. That is, they're
taking these human rights commitments literally. And then
"human rights" as a term—but also as a policy—came to
prominence under Jimmy Carter and was applied under Ronald
Reagan as well. One can point to inconsistencies, but it is an
example, I think, of a new form of liberalism which is coming
partly out of Eastern Europe.*

This was indeed a reborn language of liberalism—and not just of liberalism but also of the Left. We instinctively and rightly think of organizations
like Human Rights Watch or Amnesty International as left-leaning organizations, and so they are. The Left could no longer talk the way it had in the
past—bound institutionally or emotionally to the language of Marxism. It
needed a whole new language.

But we must not get carried away. However much we may admire Charter
77 in Czechoslovakia and the courage of its various signatories, the fact is that
only 243 people signed it in the first place, and no more than about a thousand
more over the course of the next decade. The truth is that in Czechoslovakia in
particular, the retreat from politics—the privatization of opinion—had come a
very long way since the crushing of the Prague Spring. "Normalization"—the
purging of thousands of men and women from any public or visible function
or job—was a success. Czechs and Slovaks abandoned public life, retreating
into material consumption and *pro forma* political conformism.

Poland of course was a different story, or on a different timeline. Intellectuals and former student radicals had managed during the 1970s to build
contacts with a genuine working-class movement, especially in the ship-
building cities along the Baltic Coast. After several false starts workers and
intellectuals actually cooperated during the great strikes of 1980: "Solidarity" became a mass movement with ten million members.

But Solidarity too was defeated—at least initially—by the imposition of martial law in December 1981. And even in Poland I recall Adam Michnik being very pessimistic of the prospects of anything coming of all this. Solidarity was underground and the regime was about to start yet another cycle of borrowing money from abroad to pay for consumer goods: as late as 1987 it did not seem as though there was anything to stop this miserable routine from lasting indefinitely.

It is striking that east European intellectuals came to these matters from individual and historical experiences which had very little to do with the classic understanding of a bourgeois life or of a liberal education.

Quite so. Havel, to take the most obvious case, is not a political thinker in the conventional, Western sense. To the extent that he reflects any established tradition, he is in the continental heritage of phenomenological and neo-Heideggerian thought: a well-developed current in his native Czechoslovakia. In a way, however, Havel's apparent lack of intellectual roots worked in his favor. Had he been perceived as just another central European thinker adapting German metaphysics to communist politics, he might have been both much less attractive and much less comprehensible to Western readers. On the other hand, it was the distinctive phenomenological juxtaposition of "authenticity" and "inauthenticity" that furnished him with his most powerful image: that of the greengrocer who places the sign "Workers of the World Unite!" in his window.

It is the image of a lonely man. But the deeper point is that everyone under socialism is alone: but their actions, however isolated, are not without meaning. If just one greengrocer took down just one sign and acted on his own moral initiative, it would make a difference to him and to everyone who came into his shop. This argument is not merely applicable to communism. But for local readers, it could be read that way and this made it immediately accessible.

Havel was thus comprehensible to his Czech audience and his foreign audiences at the same time. Much the same was true, for rather different reasons, of the other famous literary dissident from Czechoslovakia, the novelist Milan Kundera. I have Czech friends who are profoundly resentful of Kundera's Western popularity; why, they ask, do other Czech authors (often more favored by their home audience) pass unread beyond the border? But Kundera was very stylistically familiar to French readers for example, his playful experiments very much in a Parisian key, and he was readily adaptable to French intellectual and literary life.

> *The genius of Kundera's idea of Central Europe is that it enriches*
> *Western Europe by Czech women and pastries and an expanse of*
> *historical references and good writing. He gave the West Bohemia,*
> *in both senses of the word.*

The emphasis upon Central Europe that emerged in the 1970s was remarkably limited in practical scope: it was the image of Habsburgia reduced to its urban core. Seen thus, with all the emphasis placed upon the cosmopolitan and intellectual heritage of the Europe of Vienna, Budapest and Prague, Central Europe is conveniently relieved of its problematic history and internal conflicts. It is also shorn of its most alien elements: religion, peasants, the wilderness of the European East.

This mythological Central Europe of Western imaginings also and crucially excludes Poland—or most of it. The country has long posed slightly uncomfortable dilemmas for Western observers, even as it insists upon its own centrality in their culture. Since the 1960s, above all, central Europe in the Western imaginary has been conflated with "Jewish Europe": the fin-de-siècle Mitteleuropa of Stefan Zweig, nostalgic and sympathetic. But Poland doesn't fit this story. Poland is not a place where Jews live, in Western imagery today: it is a place where Jews die. Meanwhile, the Poles' own losses seem to shrivel into insignificance compared not just with Jewish suffering but with the tragic destruction of the sophisticated world of Habsburg Austria: victim, by its own account as well as ours, of the serial brutality of Germans and Russians alike.

> *It's interesting that this Central Europe, as you don't quite say, is Jewish, although of course Kundera is not. I think that this Central Europe idea of the 1970s is permitted by the evolution of the Holocaust narrative. The Holocaust emerges as a concept in the 1960s along with the Civil Rights movement in the United States. It has to do with a certain idea of regaining the city. What is urban and cosmopolitan is not only nostalgic, but also progressive.*

> *What gets lost in Kundera's Central Europe is not just the peasants, the Slavs, the Christians, the ugly reality, the non-Habsburgian world, but also really serious currents of thought. Havel's roots are in phenomenology. This is terribly awkward because if there is any strand of philosophy which has been poisoned in its reception by the Holocaust, it's precisely phenomenology. And Havel gets that in under the radar screen. This is something I've come to understand from Marci Shore, who's working on the phenomenologists now.*

Just as Holocaust awareness was becoming much more the central motor of engagement with the recent European past in the West, it meant, for parallel reasons, reducing Central European and particularly German-speaking thought to those aspects of its history which were related, dysfunctionally, to the possibility of the Holocaust. Thus other aspects of Central European history and thought—notably those of enduring interest or with positive local consequences—become harder to acknowledge.

Speaking of phenomenologists, think of Karol Wojtyła. The Western difficulty in registering the Polish pope in all his dimensions is very striking. His Catholic qualities are reduced to the national cult of the Virgin Mary. His critics focused on the uncompromising universalism of his ethical stand, treating him therefore as nothing more than a representative of a reactionary east European tradition. This made it seem both unnecessary and somehow too generous to look seriously at his intellectual legacy, or the intellectual legacy on which he drew.

I think the problem is this: Central Europe has such enormously problematic history in the twentieth century that its more subtle intellectual and social and cultural currents are virtually invisible to outsiders. In any case, this is, as Larry Wolff pointed out long ago, a part of the world which is serially rewritten in Western minds according to a preexisting script.

Let me mention another Pole, someone who probably had more influence on the history of the world than any Polish intellectual except, perhaps, the pope: Jerzy Giedroyc, the editor of Kultura, *the most important journal for Poles during the communist era.*

Giedroyc was perhaps the most important Cold War liberal, although he never wrote anything much and almost no one outside of Poland has heard of him. He managed to create an entirely parallel Polish and also east European intellectual life from one house in Maisons-Laffitte, just outside Paris. He designed the eastern policy, or rather the grand strategy, that saw Poland through the difficult years of the 1990s, after the collapse of the Soviet Union. But he did all of this without anyone in France—where he lived and worked— really noticing his work of the 1950s through the 1980s.

There's a very funny moment in Jerzy Giedroyc's conversations with Barbara Toruńczyk in 1981, where she's asking him if the West has had any influence on him, and he says categorically no. And then, whether he has tried to influence France. And he says,

something like: my dear lady, there's no sense in that, all you're
going to get out of the West is tears and money.

It's a more complicated story than that. Czesław Miłosz talks about unrequited love, tears that should flow on more than one face. Eastern Europe doesn't just want sympathy and support; it wants to be *understood*. And it wants to be understood for itself, rather than for the Western purposes to which it can be applied. And *my* experience of engaging with Central Europeans of all kinds, at every political and generational level, from the sixties through the nineties, was always defined by *their* sense of not being understood.

I think that no reasonably sensitive Western observer encountering Central Europeans in the twentieth century could avoid that experience of unrequited love. We are distinctive, one is told; and our distinctions and our distinctiveness are lost to you. And we spend our time alternating between trying to explain this to you and throwing up our hands in despair that you couldn't possibly get it.

I wonder if that couldn't be seen as a deep failure of communism.
Communism was supposed to embody, exemplify and spread a kind
of universal, therefore universally comprehensible, culture. But in
Eastern Europe it creates these inward-looking and, in their
culture, rather ethnically centered places. And that's why
Kundera's image of a cosmopolitan Central Europe is essentially
anti-communist. Even the intellectuals later on are going to know
the major European languages much more poorly than they would
have in the supposedly barbaric interwar period. So much of the
banal problem of understanding even prominent writers such as
Havel or a Miłosz is that somebody has to translate their work.

The break between generations seems to me crucial. The Central Europe of Nicholas Kaldor, a Hungarian economist whom I knew in Cambridge, was still a German-speaking Central Europe. No one translated anything because everyone spoke German to each other and could and did publish in German. But the next generation was writing in Hungarian. The only foreign language that they learned obligatorily was Russian, which was useless twice over: because they did not want to use it and because they therefore never learned it properly. And so, everything had to be retranslated to reach the West.

You see this with Adam Michnik, that rare European of truly historical significance who cannot function in English. His work and words have to be translated out of French (an unusual strategy these days), and with the consequence that he is less audible to Americans than he would have been to, say, an English or French audience thirty years ago. I would go further: those intellectuals from Eastern Europe who do flourish in Western cultures and languages are increasingly unrepresentative. The kind of Bulgarian who ended up in Cold War Paris—Tzvetan Todorov, for example, or Julia Kristeva—swims easily enough in French intellectual life. But they furnish us with a very distorting and distorted image of the culture from which they emerged.

But then, of course, one can reverse the thought and remember that translation of these difficult languages very often involved personal, risky, sometimes very difficult choices and outlays of money in places where it was scarce. When Miłosz decides to leave Poland in 1951, he basically hides out in Maisons-Laffitte, near Paris, where Kultura *has its house and its little press. He lives there for a year. And Giedroyc takes a decision that he's going to publish* The Captive Mind, *which can then be translated. But it can only be translated because Miłosz chooses to leave and because Giedroyc chooses to look after him.*

But what I find interesting is the politics of it, because Giedroyc doesn't believe the argument of Captive Mind *for a minute. He doesn't think that Miłosz is right to use these complicated literary metaphors, Ketman and Murti-Bing, to explain the appeals of communism in power to intellectuals in need. He*

thinks that in Poland it is only and always about money and
cowardice. Nevertheless, he sees that it would be politically good to
publish Miłosz: it would furnish Polish writers with an alibi for
their intellectual crimes under Stalinism.

It's a useful untruth.

That is exactly how Giedroyc describes it. It also provides a kind of
alibi for Western Marxists, communists, people recovering from
communism as well, because it's so easy to understand one's own
attraction to Marxism in terms of Ketman, yielding outwardly
while believing yourself to be resisting inwardly, or of Murti-Bing,
enjoying the end of doubt by accepting the one truth.

When I've taught *The Captive Mind*, the undergraduate response is enormously enthusiastic. Students want to know who Miłosz's friends A through D are, and so on, but they are also and above all swept away by the arguments and by the prose. But I've also taught the book in graduate seminars. There I've had a somewhat different response: surely this is marginal and atypical? This is an intellectual telling of other intellectuals in a world of high moral choices and ethical compromises that says nothing to the larger set of pressures and choices that Poles faced in those years.

And it's very hard to say who's right among your students. I mean,
one is struck in contemporary Eastern Europe, Poland for
example, that there is a generation of young, right-wing men and
women who don't actually remember communism and who have no
sympathy whatsoever for not only the idea, but for any of the
motives that might have drawn people towards the Party. And they
tend to be enthusiasts of lustration, the compulsory review of the
past of people who now hold influential positions. But, of course, I
tend to think that this is the gracelessness of late birth. Precisely

because they're the most ambitious ones, and they want to clear the
older generations away, they would have been the same people who
under communism would have collaborated.

There are two kinds of conformism. One is banal conformism, arising from self-interest or lack of insight: the conformism of communism in its last years. The other kind of conformism is that of Kundera's dancers, the believers of the 1940s and 1950s. You know, the circle of people seeing only each other's faces, turning their backs to the world while they believe they are seeing everything.

Clever writers like Pavel Kohout or Kundera himself are swept up into faith and belief and a larger collective narrative, in which their own and other people's autonomy is of secondary consideration. And that's the more dangerous conformism: if only because it is far less able to grasp the potential scale of its own crimes. The oddity, of course, is that from an external point of view—the perspective of the observer from the outside—the subtle conformism of the circle-dancing intellectual is much more attractive than the selfish choices of the pusillanimous subject.

That's the remarkable feature of Kundera, his honesty as a novelist
on that issue of the attraction of Stalinism. He portrays as
seductive the behavior which today we find unappealing and which
he himself looks back on with distaste.

The revelation in 2008 that Kundera was reportedly spying for the
police as a young man (in communist Czechoslovakia in 1951)
strikes me as a complete misunderstanding. If he was a believing
communist—and he was—then it was indeed his ethical duty to
report his suspicions to the police, and there's no reason for us to be
shocked by this.

What we're revealing in our surprise is merely our own
misunderstanding. Half a century on, we have simplified the

picture to the point where every opponent of communism must have been a nice liberal all his life. But Kundera was not a nice liberal. He was a believing Stalinist: that, after all, is the point of his novels. We need to extend our empathy if we are to make sense of that time and place and understand how communism appealed precisely to people like Kundera.

It's the same point that Marci Shore makes in one of her essays when she quotes Kohout's enthusiastic paean to Klement Gottwald as he stood bareheaded in Old Town Square in 1948. This was the communist who was president of Czechoslovakia, the man who was going to lead us forward into the wonderful new world. And this is the same Pavel Kohout who will go on to be a hero of sixties-era literary and cultural dissidence. It's the same man. But you can't read the latter back into the former.

There are some interesting points of overlap between the Cold War liberals and the east European dissidents. For the Cold War liberals, as we look back at them, it is something of a problem that they had nothing to say about economics. For East Europeans to be silent of the subject was an asset: it increased their acceptability in the West.

Central European intellectuals had given up on economics—to the extent that they ever really cared. Economics had come to seem like political thinking and therefore corrupt. Economic reform was only possible when and where it was totally disconnected from any explicit ideological justification. Some writers, Havel among them, saw macroeconomics as repressive in and of itself.

So they avoid the subject—at just the moment when Margaret Thatcher is making her revolution in Britain, and as Friedrich Hayek was coming back into Western favor, with his assertion that

intervention in the economy is always and everywhere the
beginnings of totalitarianism.

This is the end of the history of reform communism. If you go back and read the Czech economist Ota Šik, for example, or the Hungarian economist János Kornai, you will see that as late as the 1960s they were still trying to save the essence of a socialist economy by injecting aspects of the market into a single-party command economy. But I don't think that their illusions started to sound silly because the West was no longer Keynesian. I think that Šik and Kornai and others began to realize that what they were proposing was palpably unworkable.

The nearest thing to a workable version of reformed communist economics was either Yugoslavia or Hungary. But Yugoslavia—the Yugoslavia of "workers' control" and "self-management"—was a myth and I think some of the better economists could already see that. The myth rested upon the idealization of local production and a distant echo of the notion of factory-based collectives and local syndicalist autonomy.

As for the Hungarian system, it worked. But it worked precisely and only because of its fifth wheel: the private sector. The latter was allowed to exist on good Kádárist principles (you pretend to be X and we'll pretend to believe you). So long as the private sector of the Hungarian economy did not press its existence too insistently upon the authorities, then it was allowed to perform the role unofficially assigned it. But no one could with a straight face call this socialist economics.

I don't believe that even when disillusion set in, all reform communists became free-market ideologues. In fact, hardly any of them did. Even the Poles, who swung rapidly in the 1980s, in the illegal Solidarity years, towards the notion of budgets, currencies, reforms and real macroeconomic criteria, did not necessarily metamorphose into Hayekians. For the most part it was historically illiterate economists of a younger generation who went in that direction. One Hayekian of an older generation, the egregious Václav Klaus, is now president of the Czech Republic.

*But it strikes me that in that pre-1989 world, even though
the dissidents we're talking about were not free-market
economists, and the ones we've been talking about in general
haven't been economists at all, there was something in their
conclusions which could make the free market charming.
When you live in a planned economy, a little bit of the market
here and there sparkles, enlivens and recalls something lighter.
It seems to resemble civil society, that thing which is neither the
individual nor the state.*

The free-market grocer has much more interesting things in his window than Havel's grocer.

*It's more than that. Think about Leopold Tyrmand's diary of
Stalinistic Poland in 1954, and the person who cleans his shoes
or launders his ties. These are attractive figures: double holdovers
since they're probably Jewish, and of course Tyrmand himself
is Jewish and never says so, but they're also holdovers from
prewar capitalism, charming survivors from a vanished
world who exemplify a bourgeois ethic of cleanliness and
fashion.*

And then Miłosz in the last chapter of The Captive Mind *writes
about the people who find a way to steal a couple of shirts and sell
them—and that's of course not charming in actual capitalism,
right, try shoplifting in New York, or for that matter in Warsaw
today; but in that communist setting it seems like individualism.
And even Havel, in "Power of the Powerless," with the idea that if
you're a brewer, what you should really do is brew good beer. Which
if not exactly a capitalist ethic is an ethic that seems like it could be
squared with capitalism.*

This point of view captures and illustrates an illusion that was once widespread in the West as well: the purest form, the morally purest form of capitalism is basically artisanal production., i.e., that the important quality of a brewer is that he makes good beer. Whereas of course in capitalism, the important quality of a brewer is that he sells lots of bottles of beer.

The uncharming qualities of capitalism are its middle ground. At the small end, it's the fellow who is free to make good beer or sell a couple of shirts or ignore the state's productivity guidelines and just be his own man; and at the top end, it's the pure theory of Smith, or, in its more Lockean form, of freedom as the highest aspiration of ethically self-concious human endeavor. The middle ground is rather less appealing: it is what capitalism must be to survive. There has never been a purely "Smithian" market; and we know from copious experience that well-intentioned artisans do not normally survive the competition. If the skilled bakers of France survive today, it is thanks to subsidy. To put it no finer, the state recycles the profits of capitalism in its less appealing forms to sustain the more aesthetically appealing marginal entrepreneurs.

That doesn't seem to me to be at all reprehensible. But it does rather detract from the charms of the system at the level of high theory. For a while in Eastern Europe the attractions of moral firmness and the refusal to compromise were extended quite self-consciously from political dissidents to economic laws: there were to be no compromises over capitalism, which was to be taken over root and branch. I suspect that this level of ideological rigidity is less common today, except in the more doctrinaire circles of Václav Klaus and Leszek Balcerowicz and a few other true believers.

The argument for privatization, as it was building in the 1970s and 1980s, and the argument for trickle-down economics in the United States, borrowed from the human rights rhetoric. The right to free enterprise, went the argument, is one more right, which is important and pure in the same way that these other rights that we care about are important and pure. And it seems that there was a

kind of mutual ennoblement going on there, where the market was
being presented not just as a certain kind of economic system, but
also as an instance of a kind of freedom which these poor dissidents
over there, in the Soviet Union and Eastern Europe, represent.

The link is Hayek. Remember, Hayek's argument for the unrestricted market was never primarily about economics. It was a political case drawing on his interwar experience of Austrian authoritarianism and the impossibility of distinguishing between varieties of freedom. From a Hayekian perspective, you cannot preserve right A by sacrificing or compromising right B, however much you gain by so doing. Sooner or later you will lose both rights.

This view of things fed comfortably back into the circumstances of communist Central Europe: a standing reminder that the loss of political rights must follow in short order from the compromise of economic freedom. And this in turn conveniently buttressed the Reagan-Thatcher view: that the right to make any amount of money unhindered by the state is part of an unbroken continuum with the right to free speech.

It is perhaps worth reminding ourselves that this is not what Adam Smith thought. And it was certainly not the view of most neoclassical economists either. It would simply never have occured to them to suppose a necessary and permanent relationship between the forms of economic life and all other aspects of human existence. They treated economics as benefitting from internal laws as well as the logic of human self-interest; but the notion that economics alone could supply the purposes of human existence on earth would have struck them as peculiarly thin gruel.

The twentieth-century defense of the free market had very particularly Central European (Austrian) origins, tied to the interwar crisis and Hayek's distinctive interpretation of it. This interpretation and its implications have been fed back to Central Europe, in exaggerated and distilled form, via Chicago and Washington. For this peculiar trajectory, of course, the communists must take indirect but primary responsibility.

For that particular metamorphosis to take place, the market had to
become more than just a constraint on the state, it had to become a
source of rights, or even a source of ethics. The market ceases to be
something which has its own boundaries, allowing for private life
because of private property at the individual level, or defending
civil society against the state. In the Hayekian argument or its
implicit east European doppelgänger, the market expands its remit
and embraces the public and the private simultaneously. Far from
laying the conditions for a moral life, it is the moral life and
nothing else is required.

If Eastern Europe had been set adrift by a Gorbachev in the mid- or late 1970s, there would have been huge debates about the implications of this. The Left would have had to completely rethink the grand narrative of Marxism. But it seems to me likely that back then there might have emerged a competing narrative into which a version of the market could fit: a revolution within the categories of radical politics, to be sure, but still recognizably taking its distance from conservative or classical liberal starting points.

By the last decade of the twentieth century however, opposition in Eastern Europe was frequently and plausibly presented not just as a revolution within politics but also against them. This transformation gave the smarter neo-liberals their opening: a way to ditch the dissidents while stealing their clothes. If politics as usual has been replaced by "anti-politics," then we live in a post-political world. And in a post-political world, shorn of ethical meaning or historical narrative, what remains? Certainly not society. All that is left, as Margaret Thatcher famously insisted, are "families and individuals." And their self-interest, economically defined.

7.

UNITIES AND FRAGMENTS: EUROPEAN HISTORIAN

I left Oxford in 1987 and took up a job in New York. Within two years, I found myself caught up in the marvelous turmoil of the revolutions of 1989. I was sitting in a Viennese taxi in December of that year and had just learnt by radio of the fall of Ceauşescu in Romania, the last and most violent drama in the sequence that brought about the fall of communism in the region. What would this mean for our picture of postwar Europe, with its inbuilt assumption that the east European communist regimes were here to stay? And what, in turn, would the transformation of Europe's eastern half entail for Western Europe and its newfound European Community?

I remember thinking quite explicitly that someone would have to write a new book about this. The old story was unraveling fast, although the shape that we would give it in the future would not emerge for some time to come. Having decided in short order that this was a book that I might like to write, I sat down and started to read for it—a process that took an unanticipated decade. But by the time the Soviet Union came to an end in December 1991, I was quite sure that my decision was the right one.

In 1992, five years after arriving at New York University, I became the chair of the History Department. In this capacity it would have been imprudent in the extreme to invite seduction by graduate students in my department, much less seduce them myself. But that, happily, is exactly what happened. In the NYU History Department in the early 1990s, I was perhaps the only eligible male (unmarried, straight, under seventy). Jennifer Homans had been trained as a ballet dancer at New York's School of American Ballet and had danced professionally in San Francisco and Seattle before retiring as a result of injury and perhaps diminished motivation. She had then studied French at Columbia University and gone on to win a graduate fellowship at NYU where she started work in American history.

Growing dissatisfied with this subject—increasingly reduced to hyphenated identity histories, which had replaced the no less soporific but more pedagogically serviceable micro-political monographs of an earlier generation—Jennifer met Jerrold Seigel, the prominent intellectual historian who had joined NYU from Princeton a few years earlier, and grew seriously interested in European history. Meanwhile, however, she had maintained an active engagement in the world of dance, working for the National Dance Institute founded by Jacques d'Amboise, and this interest had taken her to Prague where she interviewed dancers and became fascinated by Eastern Europe.

Inquiring of her fellow graduate students who, if anyone, taught Eastern European topics at NYU, Jenny was given my name, and came to my office to ask if I would be teaching that fall. I had no intention of doing so, and as head of department did not need to; but I decided on the spur of the moment that more than anything else I had been awaiting the opportunity to conduct an independent study on east European history. Moreover, my busy schedule required us—at my suggestion—to conduct a lengthy tutorial at a restaurant on Fifth Avenue, by which time my rapidly-changing agenda had become clear to me if not yet to my "student." In any event, we maintained the fiction of scholarly distance, publicly and privately denying the mutual attraction, for fully three months until Thanksgiving 1992.

I was with Jenny in France that December when I first became a *public* person. We had left at semester's end for Paris, where I met for the first time her parents, whom I liked immediately. We rented a car and drove through Alsace, Switzerland and Austria, reaching Vienna in time for Christmas. Thence we motored on to Italy, stopping in Venice long enough for me to propose marriage. And so we were happily driving back to Paris when I stopped somewhere in Burgundy to telephone Nicole Dombrowski, a student who was house-sitting for me. "Well," she said, "have you seen this week's papers and the reviews of *Past Imperfect*?"

I, who had been otherwise engaged, replied that I had no idea what she was talking about. But it transpired that my new book was being conspicuously discussed on the front page of *The New York Times Book Review*, as well as in *The Washington Post*, *The New York Review of Books* and *The New Yorker*—more or less simultaneously. Not one of these journals had ever before reviewed anything I had written, much less with such prominence. And so I became, almost overnight, rather well known. Within a year I was writing for *The New York Review* and other public forums. This in turn accelerated my move into political writing and serious journalism—at a disconcerting velocity.

One consequence of writing for a broader public was a growing disposition to write about people and places that I admired, and not just those whom it gave me pleasure to excoriate. In short, and notably in the essays that I would later gather into *Reappraisals*, I was learning to praise as well as condemn. This was probably a natural function of maturity, but it was also stimulated by a critical prod from a French colleague, sometime between the appearance of *Past Imperfect* and the writing of *The Burden of Responsibility*. Irritated by my remarks about his countrymen, he asked me whether I truly thought that all French intellectuals were like that. What about the good guys? But of course, I replied: Camus, Aron, Mauriac in his own way and others besides. In that case, he responded, why don't you write about *them*?

The thought germinated for a while, encouraged by a timely intervention from Robert Silvers, who requested a review of Camus's *The First Man* for *The New York Review of Books*. Here was an opportunity. Who are the twentieth-century figures I would wish to recall and commemorate? What is it that binds them together in their attraction for me? I started to write (mostly) nice things about Hannah Arendt. Then followed a cascade of extended essays on twentieth-century thinkers, prominent and obscure: Koestler, Kołakowski, Primo Levi, Manès Sperber, Karol Wojtyła and so on. I have no doubt that my work improved as a consequence. It is actually much harder to write well about someone you admire: dismissing Althusser, ridiculing Martin Amis, diminishing Lucien Goldmann—child's work. But while it is easy enough to assert that Camus was a great writer, Kołakowski a brilliant philosopher, Primo Levi our greatest Holocaust memoirist and so on, if you wish to explain precisely why these men matter so much, and what influence they have exerted, then you have to think a little harder.

The other prod to praise came from François Furet, the historian of the French revolution who had written the preface to the French edition of *Marxism and the French Left*. As chair of the Committee on Social Thought at the University of Chicago, he invited me in 1993 to deliver the Bradley Lectures. Devoted to three Frenchmen—Léon Blum, Albert Camus and Raymond Aron—these lectures, duly expanded, became *The Burden of Responsibility*. A small book, *Burden* nonetheless probably comes nearer than any of my other writings to capturing who I am and what I do, in the form of close accounts of people I most admire. Only after completing it could I turn my mind fully to *Postwar*.

I had made a start in mid-decade whilst living in Central Europe. From December 1994 to March 1996 Jennifer and I stayed in Vienna as guests of the Institute for Human Sciences (IWM). Then as always I found Vienna dusty and boring in the summer, freezing and boring in the winter: and therefore a quite wonderful place. Today, this medium-sized Central European city—for one brief early-twentieth-century moment the intellectual and cultural cradle of modernity—is just another capital of a little EU member state, heavily over-invested in memories of empire. In my experience, you could shape any sort of life that you wished: social life was possible, but so was splendid isolation.

For just these reasons, many people find the Austrian capital depressing. But I rather liked Vienna's dowdy, half-empty sense of a lost past, the feeling that everything interesting lay behind it. Krzysztof Michalski's Institute was perfectly adapted to my needs. In contrast to most such establishments, one was at liberty to maintain complete privacy, without having to make effortful contributions to the collective "intellectual agenda." I also appreciated the absence of people in my own field, which meant that I did not have to talk shop. I could work for hours, I could read a lot, I could walk aimlessly. The nights were silent.

I believe that I had a rather good relationship with Michalski, based upon a certain shared taste for gloomy irony. He may too have seen in me a fellow spirit. For all his success in raising funds and support and connections for his self-made institution, Michalski was and remains something of an outsider—just as he had been in his native Poland where, despite being of their generation, he was never truly one of "them": the gilded children of the communist aristocracy. The IWM was not a great center of intellectual production—in my experience, most of the people there never wrote very much, or if they did, their best writing lay behind them. But I don't think this mattered. What Michalski was superb at forging was a medium for intellectual *distribution*. His Institute was an ideal place in which to meet smart people, an attribute not to be underestimated.

While in Vienna I drafted a sketch for the last part of *Postwar*, entitled *Grand Illusion: An Essay on Europe*. It was based on a set of rather skeptical lectures that I gave in Bologna in 1995; the core thesis—that the EU risked being de-stabilized by a mixture of excess ambition and political myopia— remains credible. Shortly thereafter, I read *Europe: A History*. Published in 1996, it was the work of Norman Davies, the prolific historian and apologist of Poland. Thoroughly preoccupied in planning my own history, I was preternaturally sensitive to the ways in which Davies's version was very much *not* the sort of book I wanted to write. In particular, his magnum opus suffered from a certain nudge-nudge, wink-wink quality, in which the author intrudes imprudently into the historical narrative.

But then perhaps I too indulged myself a little in the review that I subsequently wrote for *The New Republic*. I found Davies's *Europe* deeply insensitive on the subject of the Holocaust, his iconoclastic revisionism a touch blunt. I also felt quite strongly that what amounted to a polemic about the neglected importance of Eastern Europe should not be allowed to masquerade as an objective history of the continent at large. And then there were the factual mistakes . . . Davies responded with a letter to *The New Republic* which made clear that what most galled him in the review was my dismissal of him as a slightly absurd figure, frustrated at his exclusion from Oxford and tilting childishly at the ivy-clad dons for their ignorance of his beloved Poland (I compared his attitude to Mr. Toad's famous couplet from the *Wind in the Willows*: "The Clever Men at Oxford Know all that there is to be knowed, But they none of them know one half as much as intelligent Mr. Toad.").

Some years later, Davies wrote me a note, slightly barbed but genuinely friendly, praising my criticisms of Israel—in 2002, I think. He followed up with a further message of support the following year, on the occasion of a furor aroused by my *New York Review* essay on the One-State Solution. I replied graciously enough, remarking how curious it often is, the way one finds oneself agreeing with someone for one's own reasons—slightly barbed, no doubt, but not offensive and not intended to be. And then, to my utter surprise, Davies contributed to *The Guardian* a generous and insightful review of *Postwar*; I acknowledged this and wrote to appreciate his "gentlemanly" gesture. Perhaps the nicest thing that Davies said about *Postwar*—and certainly the highest compliment from his perspective—was something to the effect that Judt was "especially good on Czechoslovakia."

In 1995, I was offered the Nef Chair of Social Thought at Chicago; after agonizing for a while, I turned it down. Looking back, I now realize that I was beginning to see myself in a different light: not just as a historian, nor even as a "public intellectual," but rather as someone who might apply his skills and energies to a new task. I was drawn to the idea of forging an institutional forum to encourage the sort of work I admired and to bring together the sorts of people I found interesting and whom I wanted to support. This, as it seemed to me then, was more readily achieved in Manhattan than in Chicago, much less in the rarified atmosphere of Hyde Park.

New York, after all, was special. Until I moved there I had spent my entire adult life in Cambridge, Berkeley and Oxford: each, in its way, an isolated ivory tower. But here in New York the universities—NYU, Columbia, CUNY Graduate Center—could not pretend to separate themselves from the city. Even Columbia, gloriously isolated upon its little hill on the Upper West Side of Manhattan, could hardly deny that the reason most of its faculty and students were drawn there (rather than to its competitors in Princeton, New Haven or Cambridge, Mass.) was precisely its location in what was still, if perhaps anachronistically, thought of as the world's most cosmopolitan city.

From an academic point of view, New York resembles the continental European model rather than the Anglo-American template. The most important conversations in town are not those conducted among academics behind college walls, but the broader intellectual and cultural debate exchanged across the city and taking in journalists, independent writers, artists and visitors as well as the local professoriate. Thus, at least in principle, universities are culturally and intellectually integrated into the wider conversation. In this sense at least, by staying in New York I could also remain European.

I returned from Chicago to New York with a practical proposition for my own university. I would happily stay, if they would agree to help me establish an institute: a home for the ideas and projects I had been hatching over the course of the past decade. NYU proved remarkably accommodating to this proposal, including my insistence that there be no interference then or ever in the programs we pursued or the people we invited. The university has been true to its word and thanks to its help I have been able to build the Remarque Institute.

I don't believe that I would have stayed here in New York if I could not have had this Institute; I certainly felt no particular warmth for the history department, then and now on its absurd trajectory of political correctness and historical "relevance." But nor do I believe that there are many other institutions in the world which would have proven so supportive. NYU, like King's College Cambridge in an earlier decade, facilitated for me a crucial career move and I am truly grateful.

When I founded the Remarque Institute I was just forty-seven: still the youngest person at almost every professional meeting I attended. At conferences of historians, in think tanks and research institutes and on scholarly boards, I was surrounded by elderly, established seniors. At the Council on Foreign Relations and other august institutions, I would take part in panel discussions on foreign policy with men I had been watching on television for three decades. More than anything else, I wanted a forum where I could hear, meet, encourage and promote younger talent.

Furthermore, I had it in mind to do something that is still not very well done in most universities, whether in the U.S. or overseas. I was interested in identifying young people whose work did *not* slot neatly into particular "schools," who were *not* natural fits in established post-doctoral programs but who were just plain smart. I wanted to offer such people resources, contacts, opportunities and ultimately promotion by giving them an opportunity to meet one another, to pursue their own work on their own terms without social or pedagogical obligation, and above all to exchange views across conventional disciplinary, or national, or generational boundaries.

What I wanted to create did not even have a name. Above all, I was setting out to facilitate an international *conversation*: providing it with an institutional infrastructure and practical resources, but otherwise emphasizing the opportunity offered young people rather than the formal structure within which they would take advantage of it.

Over time, the Remarque Institute has acquired a reputation and renown far exceeding our size or scope. It has mounted workshops, symposia, conferences; we have an annual Seminar in Kandersteg, Switzerland, for promising young historians; the Remarque Forum brings together some of the more interesting young people in North America and Europe, reaching into academia, journalism, the arts, the business world, public service and government to promote a truly informal international conversation; we run regular seminars in New York, Paris and Florence characterized by the relaxed setting of the presentations, the open-ended quality of their discussions, and above all by the abundance of young participants.

We have been able to help extraordinarily promising young people decide upon their scholarly or professional paths: by practicing a different sort of academic and intellectual exchange, I hope that we have encouraged emerging scholars to renew and sustain their enthusiasm for a profession that can all too often seem dowdy, musty and unworldly.

We have certainly been rather successful in bringing senior and junior academics together and in opening up conversation athwart professional generations. The refreshing quality of many of the encounters at the Institute—characterized by a lack of constraint and the absence of conventional politesse towards the mediocre and the fashionable—has proven enduring and, I hope, seductive. In any case, we appear to be serving some worthy purpose.

I'd like for us to be a bit more explicit about what it means to become and be a historian who is not mediocre and is not serving fashion. Building an institution around a historian is the reverse of the way things are usually done. We tend to think that institutions build historians, and then we try to figure out just how that has influenced the work, and ask in what way, if any, historians really can be scholarly. And a lot of us, not you in particular, but a lot of us have spent time going back and showing how previous historians were prisoner in one way or another to one of these schemes, whether they knew it or not. Now that we're all aware of that, what is history for? How can it be done respectably?

Obviously there was the grand narrative approach, which had either a liberal or a socialist form. The liberal form was best captured—pejoratively—by Herbert Butterfield's notion of the "Whig interpretation of history": that things improve—the point of history may not be for things to get better, but as a matter of fact they do. I remember that it was always the case in a certain genre of French economic history, to take a parochial example, that the implicit question was why on earth French economic history failed to track its English counterpart. Why, in other words, was industrialization delayed? Or why were markets underdeveloped? Why did agricultural sectors survive so long? All of which was just to ask why French history had not followed the English example more closely. Issues like the peculiarities of German history, the idea of a *Sonderweg* or special path, imply similar assumptions and debates. So there was that liberal perspective, Anglo-American at its core but perfectly peripherally functional when applied to, as it were, backward societies.

The socialist story was adapted from the liberal history of progress. It differed in the presumption that the history of human development would be blocked at a certain point—the mature stage of capitalism—unless it moved forward purposefully and consciously towards a pre-established objective: socialism.

There was another perspective, which we on the Left tended to think of as either under-interrogated or else consciously reactionary: that history is a moral story. In that case, history ceases to be a narrative of transition and transformation. Its moral purpose and message never alter: it is only the examples that change with time. In this key, history can be a horror story endlessly recycled by participants ignorant of the consequences of their own behavior. Or else (and as well) history becomes a *conte moral*, illustrating ethical or religious messages and purposes: "history is philosophy teaching by example," to use the famous line. A fable with footnotes.

Today we don't really feel comfortable with any of that. It's hard to talk about the story of progress. I don't mean that we cannot see progress everywhere we look if we choose to look for it, but we can also see so much regress that it's hard to say that progress is the default condition of the human story.

The only area in which there has been a naïve return to that way of thinking is in the crasser versions of economic thought of the last thirty years: economic growth and free markets as not merely the necessary condition for human improvement but the best account of it. As for public ethics, Kant notwithstanding, we still lack a consensual basis which is not religious in origin.

The consequence of the impossibility of both the Whig and the moralizing approaches is that historians don't know what they're doing anymore. Whether that's a bad thing is a different question. If you asked my colleagues: what is the purpose of history, or what is the nature of history, or what is history about, you would get a pretty blank stare. The difference between good historians and bad historians is that the good ones can manage without an answer to such questions, and the bad ones cannot.

But even if they had answers, they'd still be bad historians—they would simply have a framework within which they could operate. Instead of which they have little templates—race, class, ethnicity, gender and so on—or else a residually neo-Marxist account of exploitation. But I see no common methodological framework for the profession.

What about the ethics of history as something that you do?

That's professional ethics—Durkheim plus Weber rather than Butterfield minus Marx—as it were.

In the first place, you cannot invent or exploit the past for present purposes. This is less obvious than it might seem. Many historians today do indeed regard history as an exercise in applied political polemic. The point is to reveal something about the past that conventional narratives have camouflaged: to correct some misreading of the past, usually in order to engage as *parti pris* in the present. When this is undertaken with crass shamelessness, I find it depressing. It so obviously betrays the purpose of history, which is to understand the past.

That said, I'm very conscious of the fact that I have perhaps indulged in such an exercise myself. *Past Imperfect* was an attempt to correct not only a significant misreading of the recent past but also—albeit secondarily—to identify comparable missteps in the present. So I am ill-placed to insist that historians should never write about the past with no concern for contemporary implications.

The fine line, it seems to me, goes thus: there has to be a plausibility in your story. A history book—assuming its facts are correct—stands or falls by the conviction with which it tells its story. If it rings true, to an intelligent, informed reader, then it is a good history book. If it rings false, then it's not good history, even if it's well written by a great historian on the basis of sound scholarship.

The best-known example of the latter was A. J. P. Taylor's *Origins of the Second World War*. It is a beautifully written tract, the work of a consummate diplomatic historian: an expert in the relevant documents, a competent linguist and highly intelligent. At first sight, all of the constituent parts of a good history book were present. So what was missing? The answer is hard to pin down. Perhaps the issue is one of *taste*. To claim—as Taylor did—that Hitler was not responsible for World War II is absurdly counterintuitive. However subtly expressed, the argument is so implausible as to be poor history.

But the question then arises: who is to assess the plausibility? In this case, I would be satisfied by my own response, given my expertise. But I could not begin to judge the plausibility of an account, say, of the rise of medieval cities—assuming it to be the work of a competent, accredited scholar. That is why history is of necessity a collective scholarly undertaking which rests on mutual trust and respect. Only the well-informed insider can judge whether a work of history is good.

I readily concede that what I have just described is a seat-of-the-pants exercise. After sitting on innumerable committees considering candidates for appointment or promotion, there must have been dozens of occasions when I said: this work is not very good—only for someone to respond "How do you know?" Many of my colleagues would rather hedge their bets and defend a weak candidate with the claim that her argument is "original," or her work "unconventional." To which I would respond: "Indeed. But it rings false. It's not a plausible account of its story; it doesn't feel like a work of good history." My younger colleagues find this a completely mystifying proposition: for them, it's good history if they agree with it.

> *Historians don't historicize themselves very well. This means that they tend to be intrigued by arguments which either confirm what they think anyway or in some provocative way dismantle what a lot of other people think. Both are equally bad: provocation is just another form of conventionality. But it's hard for historians of a given generation, milieu or clique to stop thinking about their own presuppositions and judge something according to a kind of sense of reality, which is what I would call what you're talking about.*

I think that historians today, except the very best of them, suffer from a sort of double insecurity. First, the discipline is not very clear where it sits in the world of scholarly categories. Is it a humanity? Is it a social science? In American universities the dean of the humanities is sometimes responsible for history, but sometimes it is the concern of the dean of social science. When I became dean of humanities at NYU, I insisted that history be included in my remit—to which the dean of social sciences (an anthropologist) responded: it's all yours.

Historians used to rather like the idea of being included among the social sciences—and of course they sought access to the funding that such a categorization would bring. In the 1960s and 1970s, the humanities often lacked clout in the institutional structures and decision-making processes of American universities. The social sciences—sociology, anthropology, political science, economics to a lesser extent, linguistics, psychology—regarded themselves (and were often seen by others) as scientific, in the same sense that one might use for physics. Meanwhile, the humanities—slipping into the cesspit of Theory—were coming to regard history as culpably lacking in self-reflective meta-categories and disgustingly empirical in what passed for its methodology.

This sense of inferiority goes a long way to account for the fascination of today's historians with theory, with models, with "frameworks." These tools, such as they are, offer the reassuring illusion of intellectual structure: a discipline with rules and procedures. When people ask what you do, you can confidently reply that you work in "subaltern studies," or in "the new Cultural History," or whatever it might be—much as a chemist might describe himself as specializing in Inorganic Chemistry or Biochemistry.

But this only leads us back to the problem that you have identified: these labels are utterly present-minded. And the "critical" approach of historians often amounts to little more then applying, or declining to apply, a certain label to one's colleagues. The process is embarrassingly solipsistic: to label someone else is to label oneself.

But whereas others can be dismissed as consciously or inadvertently biased, one's own work is always scrupulously free of contamination—hence the great pains taken to demonstrate that the writer's own commitments are self-aware, self-critical and so on. And so you get these broken-backed monographs: beginning and ending with large, theoretical claims about the deconstructive purpose of the research. But the chapters in the middle are actually quite empirical—as any good history must be—with the occasional deconstructive clause thrown in to cast doubt on the very evidence that the author has unearthed. Books like this are unappealing to read and—a related point—they lack intellectual self-confidence.

You can't write general history that way. In the 1960s, Quentin Skinner wrote a series of brilliant articles recasting the methodology of the history of ideas. He showed how incoherent it was to write intellectual history if you neglected to set the ideas in their context. Words and thoughts had distinctive meaning for, e.g., seventeenth-century readers and writers; we may not extract them from this setting if we wish to understand what they meant at the time.

When you read Skinner's essays, it is tempting to conclude that a coherent narrative history of ideas is simply impossible. The very act of rendering the material comprehensible for present-day readers must do violence to its meaning and thus undermine the project. Yet, ten years on, Skinner published *The Foundations of Modern Political Thought*: a beautifully constructed, two-volume narrative history of European political thought from late medieval times to early modernity. In order to succeed—and succeed it does—the book studiously sets aside its author's own meticulous methodological historicism. And so it probably has to be.

> *It seems that what history has going for it, and one of the reasons that it survives, even as literary criticism falls into crisis and political science becomes unintelligible, is precisely that its readers agree that it should be well written.*

A badly written history book is a bad history book. Sadly, even good historians are often clumsy stylists and their books languish unread.

You know, when I used to visit friends, I would often find on their bookshelves a familiar mixture: classical fiction, some modern fiction, travel books, the odd biography—and at least one popular work of history. The latter, usually something favorably reviewed in *The New York Times* or *The New Yorker*, would be the mainstay of conversation. Typically, it was the work of an academic who had succeeded in writing a general book. But such authors were and remain uncommon: the market for history books is enormous, but most professional historians are simply unable to satisfy it.

> *I feel, Tony, as though there's an ethical aspect to this, as well. And I don't know how to put it except in a way which is going to sound dreadfully eighteenth-century and metaphysical, but—*

What's wrong with the eighteenth century? Best poetry, best philosophers, best buildings ...

—that we owe something to the language. That not only should we write well because that means that people buy our books and not only should we write well because that is what history is, but also because there aren't that many crafts anymore that have a responsibility to the language. Whatever sort of responsible craftsmanship remains, we're right in the middle of it.

The obvious contrast would be the novelist. Ever since the rise of the "new" novel in France in the fifties and sixties, novels have been colonized by non-standard forms of language. This is hardly new: remember *Tristram Shandy*, not to mention *Finnegans Wake*. But historians cannot follow suit. A non-standard history book—written with no regard to sequence or syntax—would be simply incomprehensible. We are forced to be conservative.

If you took the literature of early eighteenth-century England or France, and compared it to the fiction of today, you would find that style, syntax, structure and even orthography have all changed quite dramatically. Try to get a child to read *Robinson Crusoe* in the original—the story is wonderful, but the prose is truly rebarbative. Conversely, if you compare an eighteenth-century history book to a well-written twenty-first-century history book, you will find remarkably little change. Gibbon's *Decline and Fall of the Roman Empire* is perfectly accessible to a modern historian—or even a modern schoolboy: the structure of the argument, the layout of the evidence and the relationship between evidence and argument will be instantly familiar. All that has changed is that Gibbon permits himself a shameless moralizing tone, not to mention intrusive argumentative asides—precisely the kind of thing that critics held against me in *Past Imperfect*.

To be sure, history writing wandered somewhat further afield in the first half of the nineteenth century: the romantic exaggerations and frills of a Macaulay, a Carlyle or a Michelet are altogether alien to our ear. But fashions reverted and later nineteenth-century historians, albeit somewhat prolix, are perfectly accessible today. I suppose it is true too that even the romantics have their contemporary heirs: the bombastic, syntactically incontinent quality of their writing is effortlessly and serially reproduced by Simon Schama in our own time. And why not? It's a style for which I do not care; but many people love it and it has a classical pedigree.

Speaking of Gibbon and the fall of empires, I wanted to ask you about the relationship between historical knowledge and a sense for contemporary politics. One argument for knowing history is that you can avoid certain mistakes.

As it happens, I don't think neglecting the past is our greatest risk; the characteristic mistake of the present is to cite it in ignorance. Condoleezza Rice, who holds a PhD in political science and was the provost of Stanford University, invoked the American occupation of postwar Germany to justify the Iraq War. How much historical illiteracy can you identify in that one analogy? Given that we are bound to exploit the past in order to justify present public behavior, the case for actually knowing history is unanswerable. A better-informed citizenry is less likely to be bamboozled into abusive exploitations of the past for present errors.

It's terribly important for an open society to be familiar with its past. It was a common feature of the closed societies of the twentieth century, whether of Left or Right, that they manipulated history. Rigging the past is the oldest form of knowledge control: if you have power over the interpretation of what went before (or can simply lie about it), the present and the future are at your disposal. So it is simple democratic prudence to ensure that the citizenry are historically informed.

Here, I worry about "progressive" history teaching. In our childhood, certainly in mine and I imagine in yours, history was a bunch of information. You learned it in an organized, serial way—usually along a chronological timeline. The purpose of this exercise was to provide children with a mental map—stretching back across time—of the world they inhabited. Those who insisted that this approach was uncritical were not wrong. But it has proven a grave error to replace data-laden history with the intuition that the past was a set of lies and prejudices in need of correction: prejudices in favor of white people and men, lies about capitalism or colonialism or whatever it might be.

You cannot teach children American history by saying: it is widely believed that the Civil War was about the abolition of slavery, but *ha!*—I can assure you that it was really about something else altogether. For the poor little things in the front row are turning to one another and asking: "Wait a minute, what's she talking about? What is the Civil War? When did it happen? Who won?"

These supposedly critical approaches, intended—let us be generous— to help children and students form their own judgments, are self-defeating. They sow confusion rather than insight, and confusion is the enemy of knowledge. Before anyone—whether child or graduate student—can engage the past, they have to know what happened, in what order and with what outcome. Instead, we have raised two generations of citizens completely bereft of common references. As a result, they can contribute little to the governance of their society. The task of the historian, if you wish to think of it this way, is to supply the dimension of knowledge and narrative without which we cannot be a civic whole. If we have a civic responsibility as historians, this is it.

The trick seems to be both coherent and critical at the same time. Somehow, traditional renderings are easier to make cohere and criticism tends toward fragmentation.

My young assistant, whom you just met (Casey Selwyn), took an undergraduate course at NYU that was supposed to be an introduction to Russian history. It was taught by exposing the students to debates about crucial aspects of Russian history. When she looked at the readings that she bought, there was not a single narrative history. The course presumed that NYU undergraduates—nineteen-year-old Americans with little more than high school history behind them—had somewhere picked up the narrative line of

Russian history from Peter the Great to Gorbachev. The instructor lazily, and more than a little presumptuously, saw it as his task merely to help them interrogate the story. According to Casey, the course was a catastrophe: students cannot interrogate what they don't know.

Historians have a responsibility to explain. Those of us who have chosen to study contemporary history have a further responsibility: we have an obligation towards contemporary debates, in a way that is of course inapplicable to, say, the historian of early antiquity. And that probably has something to do with the reasons why he is a historian of late antiquity, and we do the twentieth century.

Jan Gross and I were once sitting on the steps of the library at Columbia University. He was working on *Neighbors*, his book about the murder of the Jews of Jedwabne in summer 1941 by their Polish neighbors. Turning to me, he mused: in another life I would certainly have done Renaissance art history—much nicer material. I replied that while this was obviously true, it seemed to me not altogether accidental that he had chosen otherwise. And, like the rest of us, having made it he was bound to feel under a certain civic responsibility to engage the debates entailed in his work.

> *I think there's an ethical question inscribed there which looks backward. And it's something like this. Is history about, as Aristotle said, what Alcibiades did and suffered? Or do sources from the past merely provide raw material which we turn to political or intellectual ends?*

> *I think that a lot of apparently critical history is actually authoritarian. That is, if you're going to master a population, you have to master its past. But if the population has already been educated—or induced—to believe that the past is nothing but a political plaything, then the question of whether the play-master is their professor or their president becomes secondary. If everyone's a critic, everyone seems free; but in fact everyone is in thrall to*

whoever best manipulates, with no possibility of resort to fact or
truth as self-defense. If everyone's a critic, everyone's a slave.

History's fundamental ethical responsibility is reminding people
that things actually happened, deeds and suffering were real,
people lived thusly and their lives ended in such and not other
ways. And whether those people were in Alabama in the 1950s or
Poland in the 1940s, the underlying moral reality of those
experiences is of the same quality as our experiences, or is at least
intelligible to us, and therefore real in some irreducible way.

I would break that thought into two parts. The first is simply this: the job of the historian is to make clear that a certain event happened. We do this as effectively as we can, for the purpose of conveying what it was like for something to have happened to those people when it did, where it did and with what consequences.

This rather obvious job description is actually quite crucial. The cultural and political current flows in the other direction: to efface past events—or exploit them for unrelated purposes. It's our job to get it right: again and again and again. The task is Sisyphean: the distortions keep changing and so the emphasis in the corrective is constantly in flux. But many historians do not see it this way, and feel no responsibility of this kind. In my view, they are not real historians. A scholar of the past who is not interested in the first instance in getting the story right may be many virtuous things but a historian is not among them.

However, we have a second responsibility. We are not merely historians but also and always citizens, with a responsibility to bring our skills to bear upon the common interest. Obviously, we must write history as we see it, however unappealing it is to contemporary taste. And our revelations and interpretations are as open to abuse as our subject matter. Recall that Jan Gross's *Neighbors* was reviewed in *Commentary* and elsewhere as further evidence that Poles are timeless anti-Semites and that everything "we" had always thought about the bastards was right. There was nothing Jan could do about such abusive appropriations of his work; but of course he has a responsibility—a historian's responsibility—to respond. We are never free of that.

Accordingly, we must operate in two registers simultaneously. The only loosely comparable analogies are the disciplines of biology and moral philosophy, repeatedly constrained to engage and respond to misinterpretations of their claims and arguments. But history is more accessible than the first and more open to political abuse than the second. Indeed, we are perhaps the most exposed discipline in these ways. Maybe this is why most of our colleagues write books for their friends and the library shelf. It's safer that way.

> *I tend to think that good historians have a kind of negative*
> *intuition. That is, they can tell when things are likely not to be*
> *true. They may not know when things are true, and they may not*
> *know facts—God knows, very few of us know very many facts at*
> *this point. But I think they tend to have a certain intuition about*
> *which things* ne passent pas ensemble, *which things are likely not*
> *to go together.*

That's what I mean by plausibility. A good history book is a book where you feel the historian's intuition at work. And it doesn't matter whether you yourself don't know the material.

> *Let me ask a related question—but from the bottom up. One of*
> *the claims that was made in various forms from, let's say,*
> *1988 to 2003 was that history is over. You know: from harmless*
> *cocktail party Fukuyama-Hegelianism to the toxic Texas*
> *variant in fashion after September 11, 2001. Either it's*
> *goodbye to all that and so much the better now that we are all*
> *bourgeois liberals playing free-market croquet together; or else we*
> *croquet-playing people have never seen anything like this,*
> *everything is new, there are no precedents and therefore no*

rules—and so we can choose whose heads we will beat in with our croquet mallets. Iraq had nothing to do with 9/11? It doesn't matter; the old rules of cause and effect are defunct, we can invade anyway.

But if we took that to be so, and raised our children as though history were indeed "over," would democracy be possible? Would a civil society be possible?

No, I deeply believe it would not. The necessary condition of a truly democratic or civil society—what Popper dubbed the "open society"—is a sustained collective awareness of the ways in which things are ever changing, and yet total change is always illusory. As for Fukuyama, he did nothing more than adapt the communist story for his own purposes. Instead of communism itself providing the end and objective towards which history moves, the fall of communism was assigned that role. The job of the historian is to take such tidy nonsense and make a mess of it.

Thus each time some fool declares that a Saddam Hussein is Hitler reincarnate, it is our job to enter the fray and complicate such simple rubbish. An accurate mess is far truer to life than elegant untruths. But in discrediting political mis-statements, we remain obligated to put something in their place: a narrative line, a coherent explanation, a comprehensible story. After all, if we are not clear in our own mind just what was and was not the case in the past, how can we offer ourselves to the world as a credible source of dispassionate authority?

So there's a balance, and I won't say that it's easy to strike. If you only want to make messes—if you see the task of the historian as blurring all lines—you become irrelevant. If we make history chaotic for our students or readers, we lose any claim upon the civic conversation.

I'm now going to mess with your analogy of the historian as messmaker and cleaner.

*I wonder if we aren't a bit more like the guy who comes in
and moves your furniture. That is to say, the room is not
empty; the past is not empty, there's stuff in it. And you can
deny that, but then you bump into the furniture all the time and
hurt yourself. The furniture is there whether you accept it or not.
You can deny the reality of slavery in the U.S. or you can deny the
horror of it—*

But you'll keep bumping into angry black people.

*And I wonder if the historian's job is to deny that claim to total
freedom of movement, which actually hurts ourselves and others,
and which opens the way to political unfreedom. There are some
things—barriers—that we all should know about. Like the
furniture in the room.*

I disagree. You and I are not the people who put the furniture in the
room—we are just the folks who label it. Our job is to say to someone: this is
a large couch with a wooden frame—it is not a plastic table. If you think that
it's a plastic table, not only will you be making a category error, and not only
will you hurt yourself every time you bump into it, you will use it in the
wrong ways. You will live badly in this room, but you don't have to live quite
this badly in this room.

That is to say, I profoundly believe that the historian is not here to
rewrite the past. When we re-label the past, we do it not because we have a
new idea of how to think about the category "furniture"; we do it because we
think we have come to an improved appreciation of what kind of furniture
we are dealing with. A piece of furniture marked "large oak table" may not
always have been labeled thus. There must have been times when it seemed
to people to be something else: the oak, for example, may have been so obviously part of it because everything was made of oak that no one would speak
of it. But right now, the oak counts more because—e.g.—it's an unusual

material. So what we are dealing with is a large *oak* table, and it's our job to bring out the emphasis.

> *I think you're right, it's labeling furniture. Or maybe it's more like*
> *making paths by leaving traces. You know, something like how in*
> *European parks, the paths are signaled. Someone has gone through,*
> *and they've put a red cross or a green circle that's filled in on every*
> *fiftieth tree. If you're following the green-circle path, you follow those*
> *trees, and so on. The trees are there whether you like it or not, but the*
> *paths are created: there might be other paths—or no paths at all. But*
> *without some path you can't see the forest. Someone has to be there to*
> *mark the way.*

I like that, so long as it's understood that we mark the way, but we cannot constrain people to take it.

> *There are lots and lots of paths, real and potential, marked and*
> *unmarked, through this forest. The past is full of stuff. But if you*
> *don't have a path through it, you stare at the ground, you search*
> *for footing, you can't appreciate the trees.*

I'm enough of a pedagogue to say we should think of it thus. The first thing is to teach people about trees. People shouldn't wander into forests, even ones with marked paths, if they do not know what a tree is. Then you teach them that lots of trees together constitute a forest. Then you teach them that one way to think about the forest—but there are others—is as a place capable of containing paths.

Next, you point out what you (the historian) take to be the best path through the forest, while acknowledging that there are other paths, though in your view less satisfactory. Only then are you free, as it might be, to "theorize" about paths: whether they are human creations, whether they distort the "natural" shape of the forest and so forth. My fear is that more and more of our young colleagues, bored by mere tree description, derive greatest satisfaction from teaching the etiology of paths.

> *So here is an irony which you seem to want to address. The twentieth century is full of tragic events which one ought to remember and remembrance is a sort of cult in Europe and, to a lesser extent, in the U.S. But at the same time we seem unable really to remember anything much.*

Nature doesn't mind paths, but nature abhors a vacuum. And we have taken to remembering events in a vacuum. Accordingly, we invoke them in isolation: "never again," Munich, Hitler, Stalin and so forth. But how can anyone make sense of such invocations and labels? In American and European high schools today, it is not uncommon for students to graduate having taken just one course in World History: typically this will be either the Holocaust, World War II, totalitarianism or some comparably excerpted horror from mid-twentieth-century Europe. However well-taught, however sensitively sourced and discussed, such a course emerges from nowhere and, inevitably, leads nowhere. What possible pedagogical purpose can it serve?

> *How valuable is the history of the Holocaust for the development of civic awareness of Americans?*

The vast majority of the non-specialist educated American public has been taught that the events of World War II in general and the Holocaust in particular are unique, *sui generis*. They have been encouraged to see that past as a single catastrophic moment, a historical and ethical reference against which the rest of human experience is implicitly compared and found wanting.

This matters because the Holocaust has become the moral measure of every political action we undertake: whether it concerns our foreign policy in the Middle East, our attitudes towards genocide or ethnic cleansing or our propensity to engage or retreat from the world. You will recall the tragic-comic image of Clinton-Hamlet in the White House, agonizing over whether or not to intervene in the Balkans, with Auschwitz dangling before him as the historical referent. American public policy on crucial areas of national interest is hostage to a single, isolated instance of human history— often of marginal relevance, always selectively invoked. You asked me what was the downside of this emphasis on the Holocaust? That is the downside.

But now let me play devil's advocate. Suppose that rather than having just this piece of historical education, Americans had none whatsoever— never studied or read anything about the past, much less the recent European past. They would be shorn of morally serviceable references to past crimes and would have no historically-exploitable names or moments to which they could allude in the course of policy debates on which they could call to move public opinion.

There is some advantage to being able to invoke Hitler—or Auschwitz or Munich. At least the present would thereby call on the past rather than ignore it. As things now stand, we do this in a half-baked and increasingly self-defeating way; but at least we do it. The point is not to abandon such exercises; the point is to engage in them in more historically-sensitive and informed ways.

A curious related problem is the Americanization of the Holocaust, the belief that the Americans went to fight in Europe because the Germans were killing the Jews—when in fact that had nothing to do with it.

Indeed. Both Churchill and Roosevelt had good grounds for keeping the Jewish issue under wraps. Given contemporary anti-Semitism in both countries, any suggestion that "we" were fighting the Germans to save the Jews might very well have been counterproductive.

Exactly. It makes the whole thing look altogether different when you appreciate that—not so long ago—the United States was a country where it would have been difficult to mobilize people to fight against the Holocaust.

Right—and this is not something people like to think about themselves. Neither Britain nor America did much for the doomed Jews of Europe; the U.S.A. did not even enter the war until December 1941, by which time the extermination process was well under way.

Nearly a million Jews were dead by the time the Japanese bombed Pearl Harbor. Five million were dead by the time of the Normandy landing. The Americans and the British knew about the Holocaust. It wasn't just that they had intelligence reports from the Poles almost immediately after the first use of gas chambers. The British had decoded radio transmissions about the shooting campaigns in the east and decoded telegrams with the numbers of Jews gassed at Treblinka.

We might want to recall such numbers: an excellent exercise in civic education and national self-knowledge. At times such numbers tell a tale—a tale we prefer to forget.

A few years ago I reviewed Ernest May's history of the fall of France. In the course of that essay, I enumerated the scale of French losses in the course of the six weeks of fighting that followed the German invasion of May 1940. About 112,000 French soldiers (not to speak of civilians) were killed: a figure that exceeds American deaths in Vietnam and Korea together—and a rate of killing far greater than anything the U.S. has ever experienced. I received a pile of correspondence from otherwise well-meaning readers who assured me that I must have gotten the figures wrong. Surely, they wrote, the French don't fight and die like that? Recall that this was in 2001, shortly before the paroxysmic patriotic obscenities that followed 9/11 ("freedom fries" etc.). Americans have trouble with the idea that they are not the world's most heroic warriors or that their soldiers have not fought harder and died braver than everyone else's.

Something comparable happened when I published, also in *The New York Review*, a comment to the effect that France has had six Jewish prime ministers, while here in the U.S. of A. we were still awaiting our first successful Jewish vice-presidential candidate: this was when the execrable Joseph Lieberman had just been nominated to Al Gore's presidential ticket and the country was awash in self-congratulation at its ethnic sensitivity and openness. On this occasion I was positively deluged in mail—not all of it abusive—from readers who assured me that France was and always would be profoundly anti-Semitic, in contrast to our own tolerant heritage.

On these and other occasions I have often thought that what America needs more than anything is a critical education in its own history. That France has a contemptible record of official anti-Semitism is well-known. French anti-Semitism was above all cultural—and under the auspices of the Vichy regime, of course, that cultural prejudice shaded into active participation in genocide. But *politically*, French Jews have long been free to rise high in the service of the state: and of course they had access to higher education while Harvard, Columbia and other places were still imposing rigid quotas on Jews and other minorities.

> *I think,* toutes proportions gardées, *we've now reached our Léon Blum moment with Obama.*

> *But returning to history and its purposes. Are history and memory kindred? Are they allies? Are they enemies?*

They are step-siblings—and thus they hate one another while sharing just enough in common to be inseparable. Moreover, they are constrained to squabble over a heritage they can neither abandon nor divide.

Memory is younger and more attractive, much more disposed to seduce and be seduced—and therefore she makes many more friends. History is the older sibling: somewhat gaunt, plain and serious, disposed to retreat rather than engage in idle chit-chat. And therefore she is a political wallflower—a book left on the shelf.

Now, there have been many who—with the best of intentions—have blurred and confused these siblings. I think, for example, of those Jewish scholars who invoke the long-standing Jewish emphasis upon memory: *zak-hor*. They stress that the past of a stateless people is always in danger of being recorded by others for their own purposes and that it is thus incumbent upon Jews to remember. That's fine and I find myself in some sympathy.

But at this point, the duty to remember the past gets confused with the past itself: the Jewish past becomes conflated with those bits of it which are serviceable for collective memory. And then, notwithstanding the first-rate work of generations of Jewish historians, the selective memory of the Jewish past (of suffering, of exile, of victimhood) merges with the remembered narrative of the community and becomes history itself. You would be astonished at how many educated Jews of my acquaintance believe myths about their "national story" in ways that they would never countenance if offered comparable myths about America or England or France.

These myths have now locked themselves into official records as the openly espoused justifications for the State of Israel. This is not a uniquely Jewish shortcoming: the little country of Armenia, or the modern Balkan states of Greece, Serbia and Croatia to name but four, all came into being on the basis of comparable mythological narratives. The sensitivities involved here are such that getting the actual history right becomes almost impossible.

But I profoundly believe in the difference between history and memory; to allow memory to replace history is dangerous. Whereas history of necessity takes the form of a record, endlessly rewritten and re-tested against old and new evidence, memory is keyed to public, non-scholarly purposes: a theme park, a memorial, a museum, a building, a television program, an event, a day, a flag. Such mnemonic manifestations of the past are of necessity partial, brief, selective; those who arrange them are constrained sooner or later to tell partial truths or even outright lies—sometimes with the best of intentions, sometimes not. In either event, they cannot substitute for history.

Thus, the exhibition at the Holocaust Memorial Museum in Washington does not record or serve history. It is selectively appropriated memory, applied to a laudable public purpose. We may approve in the abstract, but we should not delude ourselves as to the outcome. Without history, memory is open to abuse. But if history comes first, then memory has a template and guide against which it can work and be assessed. People who have studied twentieth-century history can visit the Holocaust Museum; they can think about what they are being shown, assess it in a broader context and bring to it a critical intelligence. At this point, the Museum serves a useful purpose, juxtaposing the memories it records with the history in the mind of its audience. But viewers who knew only what they were being shown would be (and most are) at a disadvantage: cut off from the past, they are being spoon-fed a version that they are in no position to assess.

One way to mark the difference between history and memory is to notice that there is no verb for history. You know, if someone says "I'm making history," they mean something very special and usually ludicrous. To "historicize" is a technical term, conventionally restricted to scholarly exchange. By contrast, "I remember" and "I recall" are perfectly conventional things to say.

This points to a real difference: memory exists in the first person. If there isn't a person, there isn't a memory. Whereas history exists above all in the second or third person. I can talk about your history, but I can only talk about your memory in a very limited and usually offensive or absurd sense. And I can talk about their history, but I can't really talk about their memory, unless I know them extraordinarily well for some reason. I can talk about the

history of eighteenth-century Polish aristocrats—but it would be
absurd for me to talk about their memory.

Because memory is in the first person, it can be constantly revised,
and it becomes more personal with time. Whereas history, at least
in principle, takes the other direction: as it is revised, it becomes
ever-more open to the perspective of third parties and thereby
potentially universal. A historian can start with concerns which
are immediate and personal—they perhaps have to be—and then
work away from them. Sublimating his starting perspective, he
comes up with something altogether different.

I would dissent partially in one respect. Public memory is an incarnated, collective first-person plural: "we remember . . ." The result is calcified summaries of collective memory; and once the remembering persons are gone, these summaries substitute for memory and become history.

Think of the difference between the Mémorial in Caen, which is now the official museum of France's twentieth-century wars with Germany, and the Historial in Péronne, which was established by an international committee of professional historians, including your Yale colleague Jay Winter. Both are French national sites, but the difference between them is revealing.

The Historial is pedagogical. It offers a conventional, linear narrative presentation of its subject—and thus, in today's progressive environment, a rather radical and I think effective approach to the teaching of public history. The Mémorial, on the other hand, is all feeling. There is almost no pedagogy, except the overall memory message that the visitor is expected to take away with him. The Mémorial indulges in tricks and ploys and technology to help the visitor recall what he thinks he already knows about the Second World War. If you did not already bring some memory to bear on your experience, the Mémorial would be meaningless. It provides the ambience, but the visitor is responsible for the history. This contrast between the Historial and the Mémorial seems to me precisely the contrast we need to preserve and

accentuate. If we really must have Mémorials, then people should at least be
encouraged to visit the Historials first.

> *Do you see a way in practice to a sort of history which is
> constructive in the building of civic communities? It's easy for us to
> dislike the great nineteenth-century national historians who had
> that mission, Michelet and Ranke and Hrushevs'kyi. They were
> modified Whigs; history was going in a certain direction, towards
> national greatness, or unification, or liberation. We can dismiss
> their teleology and we do. And it's likewise easy for us to scorn
> politicized history with its narcissism and methodological
> shortcomings and dismiss memory as a dysfunctional and
> dangerous substitute for history. But how would one actually go
> about institutionalizing history such that it builds a sense of
> community, without falling prey to any of these fallacies?*

My first wife was an elementary school teacher. Many decades ago, she
invited me once to teach the French Revolution to her class of nine-year-
olds. After giving the matter a little thought—I had no comparable experience of grade school teaching—I brought a little guillotine into the classroom
and we began the session by chopping off the head of Marie Antoinette.
After that, I found that the narrative history of the French Revolution went
down quite well, with the help of a few visual aids.

So from teaching third graders to teaching graduate students in Berkeley, NYU, Oxford and elsewhere, experience has taught me this: it is universally true that young people who don't yet know history prefer it to be taught
in the most conventional and straightforward way. How else are they to
understand it? If you teach it back to front, starting with its deeper meanings
and interpretive squabbles, they will never get it. I don't mean you should
teach it in a boring way, merely in a conventional one.

Having said that, I recognize that there is a competing concern. In order
to teach history in a conventional way, you need a reasonably agreed set of

references as to what the conventional history you're going to teach actually *is*. Many societies, and not just our own, have become far less confident in the last thirty years about interpreting their past. It is not only Americans who no longer know how to tell a coherent national story without feeling embarrassed or resentful. The same is true in Holland, or France, or Spain.

Pretty much every European country today is in turmoil over how to teach its past and what use to make of it. In the worst cases—Britain comes to mind—conventional national accounts have been abandoned altogether, and children are taught a confusing series of competing partial narratives, each one attached to a moral or ethnic perspective.

A decade or so ago, I was at Yale to attend a lecture by Marc Trachtenberg. A group of Yale graduate students who were in the audience offered to take me out for dinner afterwards. They were strikingly anxious, paranoid even, at what they saw to be their poor job prospects. Because Yale was regarded (then as now) as a rather conservative history department, Yale-trained diplomatic historians were being turned away even as post-everything cultural historians from lesser institutions were finding easy employment.

I remember saying to them: for heaven's sake, hang tough. It is an altogether good thing that we have at least one first-rate institution training young historians in real scholarly techniques: how to interpret diplomatic archives and other sources, learning exotic languages and feeling no cause to apologize for the traditional high-political subject matter on which they are working. Sooner or later, I assured my listeners, the pendulum will swing; and then it will be to your advantage to have been thoroughly trained in the traditional rigors of a traditional sub-discipline.

I still believe that. History as a self-confident narrative discipline will return: indeed, from the point of view of the reading public, it never left. It is extraordinarily difficult to imagine any society doing quite without a coherent and agreed narrative of its past. So it is our responsibility to produce that narrative, justify it and then teach it.

All such national stories will have unavoidable shortcomings. There will be blind spots. Any narrative that is sufficiently general to be true for everyone is bound to shortchange a minority, perhaps many minorities. It was always so. You know, the English history I was taught in school had no Jews in it; we might as well have been invisible.

It was only later that I learned, to my amazement, that "we" Jews had been expelled from England by Edward I and that by the time of Cromwell there was a complicated Jewish history with implications right down to our own time. It is not that I actively surmised that Jews were not there, simply that somehow no one mentioned it and I gave the matter no thought. Today, of course, such a "silence" would be regarded as reprehensible, bordering on prejudice and perhaps something worse. Someone—presuming to speak on behalf of all Jews—would insist upon the insertion of a Jewish "quotient," or perhaps even an obligatory "counter-narrative" to offset the story of English progress. Maybe it has already been done? But this cannot be the way forward.

> *When you were writing* Postwar, *how were you thinking about these things? Did you think that your book might become the conventional account of postwar European history? Did you think that the book is taking apart national histories into their various pieces? Did you think about unities and fragments?*

I certainly thought long and hard about how to design the book.

On the other hand, I don't think I spent much time thinking about your questions when I was writing it, and I am not sure that it would have done me much good to do so. What I *was* striving for was a way to break down conventional East-West categories; to reassert, but without overdoing it, other fault lines; to deal with small countries without making it look as though I was deliberately overcompensating; to use examples that were deliberately not the conventional ones to make a point, but without looking as though I was trying to be clever.

I can say hand on heart, Tim, that it was only after I had finished the book that I looked back on it and saw that it was not too bad—and indeed that it actually addressed some of the issues you have raised. Only then did I think: well, this might indeed become the way to think about postwar Europe, at least for a while. At the time of writing, I did not have such thoughts: they would have been inappropriate.

I think if I had a purpose, it was to do two things. In the first place, I wanted to nudge the prism a little. I was trying to get the reader to think of something other than "the rise of the EU" when she thought about these decades. I wanted my readers to think of them as a "social democratic moment," rather than "the '60s." I was hoping to encourage readers to think of Eastern Europe not as some alien communist suburb of Russia but rather as part of a single European story—albeit one with very different and complicated subplots.

My second, lesser ambition was to write a history that successfully incorporated culture and the arts rather than expelling them to a footnote or an appendix. Films above all, but also novels and plays and songs, float in and out of the narrative as illustrations or examples. This is unusual for a general history, and I am quite proud of it. But once again, it wasn't until the end that I thought of these ambitions as somehow constituting a different and distinctive history.

Maybe I am just not sufficiently ambitious—or commercially alert?—to come to such objectives at the outset. But in truth, I believe that great over-arching goals, whether methodological or interpretive, are often the enemy of good writing. I was probably too frightened at the scale of what I had undertaken to insert such goals into the project from the outset. And if I had, it would probably not have worked.

8.

AGE OF RESPONSIBILITY: AMERICAN MORALIST

In the 1990s I steadily expanded my range of public writing: moving out from French history to political philosophy, social theory, east European politics and history, and thence into foreign policy issues, both European and American. I would never have had the intellectual or social self-confidence to propose those subjects myself. It was Robert Silvers, the editor of *The New York Review of Books*, who taught me in spite of myself that I really could do this sort of writing; that I could think and comment upon subjects far removed from my formal scholarly concerns. Silvers offered me the occasion to write about things that I would have thought beyond me. I shall be eternally grateful to him for this opportunity.

I was operating in two different registers; and I was overworking. While writing for *The New York Review* and other journals on a regular and even frequent basis, I was also writing *Postwar* and other books, in addition to starting a family and pursuing a busy teaching and administrative schedule.

It took considerable intellectual effort, planning and time, to keep all these apart. But at least I avoided the mundane routines characteristic of the established historian: conferences, professional associations, professional publications. Here, at least, I benefited from being—as old Richard Cobb had always insisted—not quite a historian; and thus not in the least disposed to waste time building a career path among historians alone.

Much of what I was writing was a sort of evaluative intellectual history, the essays that would be collected in *Reappraisals*. The twentieth century is the century of the intellectuals, with all of the accompanying treasons and accomodations and compromises. The problem is that we live today in an age when the illusions, disillusions, and hatreds take front and center. So it requires a conscious effort to both identify and save the core of what was good about intellectual life in the twentieth century.

Within twenty years, it will be quite hard for anyone to remember exactly what all that was about. Above all, perhaps, there was the question of truth—or, rather, the two kinds of truth. Can someone who has accepted a larger political truth, or narrative truth, redeem himself as an intellectual or as a human being by staying close to smaller truths, or to truthfulness itself? That was a question put to the twentieth century by me, but perhaps also a question put to myself by me. I was trying to answer that question at the same time as I began to write as a political intellectual myself.

I would defend what are for most American historians two contradictory methodological propositions. Firstly, that the historian must write about things in their context. Contextualizing is part of the explanation, and therefore separating oneself off from the subject matter in order to contextualize is what distinguishes history from alternative, equally legitimate ways of explaining human behavior: anthropology, political science or whatever it might be. Contextualizing in this case requires time as the relevant variable. But my second contention is this: no scholar, historian or anyone else is—merely by being a scholar—ethically excused from their own circumstances. We are also participants in our own time and place and cannot retreat from it. And these two contexts need to be methodologically separated; yet at the same time, they are inextricably bound.

The New York Review helped me to become someone who wrote publicly about public intellectuals; but it was New York City which made me a public intellectual. Although I had no plans to move on and made no attempt to find employment elsewhere, I don't believe I ever intended to stay in New York forever. But thanks to September 11, 2001, I would become increasingly and polemically engaged in American public affairs.

I think it is fair to say that it seemed to me increasingly urgent to plunge into an American conversation: to demand that we discuss uncomfortable matters openly and without constraint at a time of self-censorship and conformity. Intellectuals with access to the media and job security in a university carry a distinctive responsibility in politically troubled times. I was in a position in those years to speak out with very little risk to my professional situation. This appeared to me almost the definition of civic responsibility, at least in my own local case: a trifle sententious, perhaps, but that was how I felt. And thus, curiously enough, I found a way to become American.

What sort of American did I want to be? The French have a word for some of their greatest writers, from Montaigne to Camus: they call them *moralistes*, a term both more embracing than its English equivalent and quite lacking the implied pejorative nuance. French *moralistes*, whether actively engaged in fiction writing or practicing philosophy or history, are far more likely than their Anglo-American counterparts to inform their work with explicit ethical engagement (in this respect, at least, Isaiah Berlin too was a *moraliste*).

Without aspiring beyond my station, I think that I too was engaged in something along these lines: my historical studies, no less than my journalistic publications, were driven by an explicit set of contemporary concerns and civic commitments. I too was a *moraliste:* but an American one.

Let's begin with the Dreyfus Affair, with the entrance of the
intellectual into modern politics, on a question of what you call

*smaller truth: whether or not a man betrayed his country. A French
army officer of Jewish origins was falsely accused of treason, and
defended by a coalition of French intellectuals. This moment,
January 1898 in Paris when the novelist Émile Zola published his
famous letter "J'accuse," is seen as the beginning of the history of
the political intellectual. But it strikes me that this moment cannot
be seen only in historical terms, that from the beginning an ethical
element is built in to our sense of what an intellectual is.*

Bernard Williams posits a distinction between truth and truthfulness.
The Dreyfusards were trying to tell the truth, which is truthfulness, rather
than acknowledging higher truths, as their opponents wanted them to. By
"higher truths," they meant that France comes first, or that the army must
not be insulted, or that the collective purpose trumps individual interests.
This distinction is what lies behind Zola's letter: the point is simply to tell it
as it is, rather than to find out what the higher truth is and then adhere to it.
You tell whatever you know in the form in which you know it.

Now: that's not what intellectuals end up doing in the twentieth century; very often, they end up doing exactly the opposite. In some ways, the
model for the twentieth century intellectual was as much the anti-Dreyfusard
as the Dreyfusard. Someone like the novelist Maurice Barrès was not interested in the facts of the Dreyfus case. He was interested in the *meaning* of the
Dreyfus case. And I'm not sure that we have always fully understood the
nature of the origins of twentieth-century intellectual exchange. This was a
split in the personality which stays with us throughout the century.

*At around the same time, in imperial central Europe, Tomáš
Masaryk is revealing ostensibly medieval Czech epic poems to be
forgeries and defending Jews from the blood libel. Despite the
obvious differences, here too you have an intellectual defending the
little truths against what seem to be the demands of the big
national story.*

Absolutely. It struck me forcibly that in my education, except as part of twentieth-century diplomatic history, I'd never heard of Masaryk in this context until well into my forties. And yet it was so patently a similar European moment. Someone who is utterly devoted to what he regards as the true interests of his future country finds himself completely at odds with those for whom getting the national story straight has absolute priority. And that's of course exactly what binds Masaryk and Zola together. And it's what gives Western and Eastern European liberals their common starting point in the twentieth century—a shared reference that they were not to rediscover until the 1970s.

If one actually reads Zola's famous article "J'accuse," it's ill-formed, overlong and contains lots of references that one cannot possibly understand; there's nothing compelling about the text aside from the big headline. And I wonder if that doesn't have something to do with the problems that we have for the next century or so—namely, that truthfulness is ugly and complicated, whereas higher truth appears to be pure and beautiful.

In these years, the people who are moved to get involved in public debates about abstractions of good and bad, truth and falsehood, are still journalists, playwrights, popular professors with a public following and so on. In later decades it will be philosophers, later still come sociologists and so on. Within each professional milieu, there will be a style of reasoning which will exclude or encourage certain forms of truth and falsehood.

In the early decades of the century, most intellectuals were literary types of one kind or another. Their rhetorical habits retained many traces of nineteenth-century speech, which to a twenty-first-century ear can sound redundant and overblown. Such men and women saw themselves occupying a public function midway between the soothsayer and the investigative journalist. Twenty years later, all has changed. The intellectuals whom Julien Benda attacks in the 1920s, in his *Trahison des Clercs*, for abstraction and

excessively theoretical reasoning, saw nothing of a betrayal in their stance—
for them abstraction *was* truth.

Whereas this would have seemed mere nonsense to a journalist like
Zola. Truth was facts. Masaryk, despite his philosophical formation, saw
things in the same way. Back in 1898, few would have argued that authenticity and abstract reason could ever trump direct engagement with truth and
falsehood. Intellectual engagement was about revealing something to be
false. A generation later, intellectual engagement consisted of proclaiming
abstract truths.

*That's a subject we've discussed earlier: the immanence of moral
values in history—located in the future and dictating the present,
per Leninism or Stalinism; or else located in the will of a Leader,
per fascism or National Socialism.*

*The reaction of many intellectuals to this sort of politics was to
reject ethics as such, or for the existentialists to regard it as
something that must be asserted into a necessary emptiness.*

*And then there is this moment in the late 1940s where Camus very
earnestly says: but what if we were all simply wrong? What if
Nietzsche and Hegel have misled us, and there really are moral
values? What if we ought all along to have been talking about
them?*

You have to imagine Maurice Merleau-Ponty, Simone de Beauvoir and
Jean-Paul Sartre—all of whom were present when Camus said that—rolling
their eyes at his philosophical innocence. Arthur Koestler was also present,
though we cannot be so sure how he responded.

But let's say Camus is right. Then what are those moral values? That is,
if the calling of an intellectual is to do more than seek truthfulness as against
falsehood and as distinct from higher truth, what else should he or she be

doing? If intellectuals no longer stand for any larger truth, or should avoid the sort of posture which suggests they do, then where exactly are they standing? What is the view from nowhere, to use Thomas Nagel's phrase?

I think that in one form or another, this is the challenge facing any serious intellectual today: how to be a consistent universalist. It is not just a simple matter of saying: I believe in rights, freedoms or this or that norm. Because if you believe in people's freedom to choose, but you also believe that you know better than others what is good for them, then you face a potential contradiction. How can one as a consistent universalist impose one culture or one set of preferences on another—but how can one decline to do so if one takes one's own values seriously? And even if we allow that this problem could be resolved, how can we be sure that we have avoided other contradictions in a necessarily complex political world? Ethical universalists like Václav Havel or André Glucksmann or Michael Ignatieff, all of whom favored the 2003 Iraq War on general principles, found themselves facing contradictory practical consequences for which their tidy abstract absolutes had not prepared them.

> *The idea of preemptive war fails the first Kantian test, which is to act as though what you were doing creates a rule. I wonder if there's any way to get to the universal, at least for secular intellectuals, which doesn't start with another Kantian premise: that the ethical resides in the individual human being. One thing that the Iraq War had in common with a number of other adventures is that it was portrayed in a kind of stylized, abstract way using general concepts such as liberation. Which allowed us to overlook things that we really ought to know: that war is awful, it kills people, individuals are now going to kill and die.*

The attraction of the notion that the ethical resides in the individual is that it reduces it to a decision-making process or a set of evaluations of interest, or whatever it might be, that cannot be collectivized and therefore imposed.

But it can lead to another problem, the magnifying upwards of ethical categories from individuals to collectives. We think that we understand quite clearly what we mean when we say that liberty is a universal human value, that the rights to freedom of speech, freedom of movement, freedom of choice inhere in individual people. But I think, ever since the nineteenth century, we have moved rather too easily from one man's freedom to speak of collective freedoms, as though these were the same kind of things.

But once you start talking about liberating a people, or bringing liberty as an abstraction, very different things begin to happen. One of the problems with Western political thought since the Enlightenment has been this movement back and forth between Kantian ethical evaluations and abstract political categories.

There clearly is a problem with the analogy between individuals and collectivities which arises most gaudily in the case of the nation. The liberal idea of the nation was very much the liberal idea of the individual—that nations existed, they had a kind of destiny, they had a right to liberty and that was why national self-determination seems so unproblematic to right-thinking liberals.

But couldn't you just say that that's a category error?

You could defend the notion of the nation as collective individual by saying that the individual is a constructed entity, too: coming into being over time, acquiring memories, prejudices and so on. After all, what matters about a nation is not the truth or falsehood of its claims about the past but rather the collective desire and choice to believe these propositions—and the consequences that follow.

Now I don't happen to believe that we should accept these outcomes: it is better to oppose national myths even at the price of disillusion and loss of faith. All the same, national histories and national myths are the necessary and inevitable byproduct of nations. So we need to be careful when distinguishing between the obvious—nations exist—and the constructed: the beliefs that nations tend to have about themselves.

Indeed, nations come all too readily to the idea that they have rights *qua* nations, by analogy with the rights that individuals claim for themselves. But it cannot be that simple. For a nation to have rights or obligations, those same claims and duties must be true of individuals as well as collectivities. If a nation has a right "to be free," so must all its separate citizens and subjects— or else the term "free" is being used in a very distinctive and different sense.

Let me give you an example of a problematic application of the language of individual rights and claims when applied to collectivities. Here I am, living in this country: I am a U.S. citizen. Do I think that this country owes something to its black population? A debt incurred by slavery; by the men and women forced to come here and contribute to the country's prosperity against their will? Yes, I do. Do I think affirmative action was a legitimate strategy towards this end? Yes, I do. And so on.

But do I feel guilty about all this, as a white man? No, I most certainly do not. At the time of the slave trade, and even up to abolition, my forebears lived in poverty in some remote *shtetl* in eastern Belarus. There is no reasonable sense with which they can be held responsible for the America in which I now find myself.

And so I have a civic responsibility, as a citizen; but I feel no moral responsibility for the circumstances I am seeking to alleviate. I am not part of some collective agency called "White America's Crime against Blacks." These may seem subtle distinctions, but in public ethics and public policy they are likely to prove crucial, and not only here in the U.S.

> *I think nations have positive rights, but not negative rights. That*
> *is, the nation doesn't have a right to liberty, which is a negative*
> *right, because that's not coherent. Only an individual can have*

negative rights, which are essentially rights to be left alone: to be free, not to be killed.

But insofar as a nation exists, it has the positive right of welfare, which means that individual people should try to make the nation better. That is, they try to make it exist by virtue of doing things like building roads and railroads and schools and so on. And any individual who claims to belong to a nation has duties to that nation, which are the converse and fulfillment of that nation's positive rights.

So what, then, should intellectuals be talking about when they engage in nation-building or act as advocates for social policies? Is the nation the appropriate unit of judgment and action today?

That's interesting.

The intellectuals most free of the risk of being co-opted for interested parties or purposes are those who start off with loose or nonexistent connections to the nation they happen to find themselves in. I think of Edward Saïd, living in New York but acting intellectually upon the Middle East. I think of Breyten Breytenbach, engaged in African public affairs but very often speaking and writing for non-African audiences.

The starting question for any intellectual has to be this: not what do I think as an American intellectual, a Jewish intellectual or any other tagged participant in a closed debate. The question is: what do I think about problem A or decision B or dilemma C? I may happen to find myself in New York or wherever, but that should not color the terms in which I respond to such concerns.

I have never understood why it is thought so disreputable for someone either to criticize his own country aggressively or to interfere in the affairs of another country. In both cases, surely all that is required is that he knows what he's talking about and has something to contribute. But it's not obvious to me why it would be wrong for, say, a French or English intellectual to write an excoriating piece about Russian domestic policy in a Russian newspaper.

Yes, but Tony, wouldn't such separation from the nation also inhibit you from caring?

If you're not interested in what's happening around you, it's probably because of some other shortcoming, not your failure to identify with the country. I mean, I profoundly do not identify with America, the United States, but I'm deeply interested in what goes on in it, and I care a lot.

How does that work, Tony? Because I do identify profoundly with America. And the reason that I am critical of certain things is that— I think it's because loving something, I want it to be its best self.

What strikes me is how easy it is for you and I to agree, or at any rate, to understand each other, on a range of issues including many things having to do with what's wrong with America, despite the fact that you start off feeling like an American whose country is in need of rediscovering its better self, if I can paraphrase you, and I start off—I don't know where. But not there.

Well, let's try to be programmatic. How do you get to the view from nowhere, assuming that you're right about that and that there is such a place.

John Rawls has this idea in his Theory of Justice *that the way to think about morality is to imagine that you're behind a veil of ignorance, and you know nothing about yourself, even your own talents and your own commitments. And then to begin from there and to try to decide what it is that you would ask for in some kind of collective game. So begins the most respected revision of liberalism in the twentieth century.*

The problem with the Rawlsian search for a liberal Archimedean point is that in order to reach its goals it is constrained to beg some of the very questions that it sets out to answer. The kind of person who is unacquainted with certain crucial aspects of his interests and capacities—and who has to be ignorant in this way in order to serve Rawls's purposes—would seem to me ill-placed to know enough about himself to make morally consistent and intellectually coherent choices. He would be expected to understand the difference between right and wrong and to know what sort of a world someone like him would seek. But in that case, surely he comes to the challenge with a cultural heritage: a way of thinking about self and others and estimating the propriety of his own actions and objectives. These are not value-free perspectives, so the problem of the source of those values remains unresolved.

In the Rawlsian paradigm, such a person is likely to be a northwest European or North American with a certain way of asking and answering questions of this sort, even if deprived of self-knowledge of the more circumstantial kind. The liberalism that predictably results from such a mental experiment has always been vulnerable to the charge that it lacks purchase upon real-world challenges: it neither derives from present circumstances nor responds to past experience.

Perhaps this would not matter if the Rawlsian approach to grounding liberal thought were primarily addressed to persons of a liberal predisposition. But that would be pointless. The test of such a theorem is how effective it is at convincing persons *not* already so disposed. And even then, the question remains of exactly how such liberals should act when dealing with persons and societies that do not correspond to their preferences. On this Rawls is by no means silent, but he is forced to introduce external considerations that cannot be derived from the model itself.

To tell the truth, I prefer the skeptical ethicists of Rawls's generation and a bit later: those for whom the very project of identifying and grounding a universal ethics came to seem at best hopeless, and in any case ultimately pointless. Better to say that there are norms of human behavior which have emerged as both attractive and universalizable; and which are, under reasonable circumstances, enforceable. This is not the same as the neo-relativism of late-generation pragmatists: the ethics that one can enforce are real, and they are better as well as more acceptable than the ethics one would not wish to enforce. But they are attractive in part because people find them acceptable; and in any case, they are probably the best we can hope for if we are in the business of practicing ethics rather than theorizing morals.

> *It sounds as though you're suggesting that an effective intellectual would have to feel at least enough at home in national stories in order to mess around with them. The important debates are actually taking place at the national level.*

I see this as a necessary paradox. No intellectual of any lasting interest can be self-confined to parochial subject matter alone. On the other hand, the world is actually an agglomeration of local spaces, and anyone who purports to float clear of such spaces will have little to say to the daily realities of most people. A French intellectual who had nothing to say about France would sooner or later cease to be audible in France—and even in America his appeal would eventually lapse.

But having once established credibility in a determined context, an intellectual needs to demonstrate that the way in which he or she contributes to local conversation is in principle of interest to people beyond that conversation itself. Otherwise, every policy wonk and newspaper columnist could credibly claim intellectual status.

What does this mean in practice? I would not hesitate to involve myself in American conversations if I felt competent to do so. The reason I get into Middle Eastern issues is not because I think I can influence what's going on in Jerusalem; others are much better placed for that. I see it as my responsibility to try to influence what goes on here in the U.S., since it is in Washington rather than Jerusalem that the problem will be solved. It is *our* American failure to address this subject that worries me. And it is *our* conversation that needs attention.

But there are other American conversations where I would not feel I had anything useful to contribute. I would not feel qualified to involve myself in intra-Christian debates about the responsibilities of believers in a secular state. Of course I have views on that: but I recognize that I stand a long way outside and would be inaudible to the participants.

Likewise, if you—Tim—landed in England today, you might well feel both disposed and qualified to take part in a conversation about British attitudes to Europe or British foreign policy in the Middle East. But you would most likely be adrift and lost in energetic but esoteric discussions concerning relations between England and Scotland. There are certain kinds of conversations where an outsider is at home and may make his mark, and others where he does better to remain silent.

So what is a cosmopolitan intellectual? Someone who lives and writes in Paris, but is not bound by Parisian concerns alone: he is both French and more than French. The same applies to New York intellectuals—who can be strikingly provincial, notwithstanding the implicit cosmopolitanism of their city. It seems to me that many of the people whom I read, particularly in the pages of journals like *Dissent*, are profoundly circumscribed by their parochial roots.

> *How do you get from being the French intellectual to being something else, something larger, whatever that might be? Because as you say, what often tends to happen is that things that resonate at one level are grimly provincial when seen from a distance. And yet at the same time, surely in the twenty-first century, intellectuals are going to have to function beyond a national setting.*
>
> *But it seems to me that there's a problem here. And it's a problem that the twentieth century revealed: the problem of thinking by*

proxies, or thinking—as you sometimes put it—in blocks. If you
start to think in terms of the international working class, say, you
may well have problems. Or if you start to think in terms of the
liberation of the world's poor or the colonized, you may well have
problems. Such attempts to think beyond parochial categories may
be laudable, but few of them have borne lasting fruit.

The bigger your frame of reference, the flimsier your grasp of detail and local knowledge—which is why the best people to ask about what's really going on are usually not the intellectuals but the journalists. You cannot be a "global perspective" sort of person and still hope to maintain regular, on-the-ground knowledge. But it is difficult to keep one's respect for the sort of intellectuals who lack such knowledge: sooner or later, they spin their wheels clear of their own subject matter—if only in search of a perspective that transcends it. In short, people who talk about everything are in danger of losing the ability to talk about anything.

The intellectual has, after all, an input and an output valve. The input valve is reading, seeing, knowing, learning. But the output valve is his audience, in the absence of whom he is simply blowing air. The problem is that there is no such thing as a "global" audience. If you contribute an essay to *The New York Review*, it may be read worldwide; but your real audience is the community of readers who are actively engaged in the particular debate to which you are contributing. It is only in the setting of that debate that the writer has an impact and a lasting significance.

Thus, labels to the contrary notwithstanding, there is no such thing as a "global intellectual": Slavoj Žižek does not actually exist. For the same reason, I have always been skeptical of "world systems theories" and the like. A sociologist like Immanuel Wallerstein may every now and then hit upon a subtle insight. But the terms in which they frame their huge general propositions virtually guarantee that most of the time they will recycle banalities.

Of course, there will always be people disposed to think in such terms, just as there will always be those who do close empirical work. An intellectual by definition is someone temperamentally inclined to rise periodically to the level of general propositions. We can't all be specialists and specialists alone would never suffice to make sense of a complicated world. But it is the middle ground that matters—the space between local detail and global theorem—and this tends even today to be nationally determined. Anyone seriously concerned with changing the world is likely, paradoxically, to be operating in this middle register.

> *Intellectuals who are to matter, even if they're mainly speaking at a national level, are going to have to be addressing problems that weren't international at the time of the Dreyfus Affair. For example, climate change and the unequal distribution of energy resources are inherently international problems that national communities and individuals nevertheless have to deal with.*

But there were a few people, mostly at the end of the nineteenth century, who were starting to talk about comparable matters: with the coming of the machine gun, the laws of war would need attention. Transportation would need closer regulation given the increase of the speed of communications. You couldn't trade with another country if it had a completely different set of criteria for everything from measure to quality to value—and so you had to have agreements. That began or accelerated the process of thinking globally, or internationally as it was then said, when addressing national concerns.

We don't think about the fact that today the railway gauge is almost, not quite, worldwide—there are exceptions for historical reasons. But, you know, were that not so, the cost of an item sent from, say, Canada to Mexico would be two or three times higher because of the effort involved in switching gauges, the time taken, and so on. So there are many ways in which we've simply accepted, from then to now, that we can't think about national interests without thinking internationally. And we can't talk about national policy objectives without thinking beyond the frontiers. But the conversation still takes place within frontiers even now.

Think about Europe today. Kant talked about the single market and the notion of the free movement of goods, the free circulation of money and the free movement of men. But what has turned out to be the case, which was perfectly predictable, of course, is that goods circulate freely, money circulates at the speed of light, virtually—but human beings don't, or at least most of them. An elite clerisy are free to do so, but most people cannot. Most people will think a very long time before giving up their world in, say, Northern France, to move to Luxembourg just because there's a better job there. Even though it's the same currency today, and it's close by fast train, and most of the laws that matter to you are similar. Human beings, even in Europe, live within national frameworks.

*What would you say are the interesting or less interesting,
successful or less successful attempts to cross from a national
conversation to some kind of other conversation? Because we do
seem to be in a kind of fateful moment where yes, what matters is
whether you can change people's minds within a national
conversation carried out within certain national conventions—but
you're unlikely to be effective unless you're drawing on some other
source of knowledge or some other perspective.*

To be a little bit parochial myself, the most important recent shift was the creation of a European identity among the policy makers and educated elite of a large number of countries which had until very recently thought of themselves as functioning chiefly or only in national conversations. Europe is an intellectual creation even though most intellectuals had nothing to do with it.

*My test for the existence of a European national identity is the
existence of a European soccer team or a single European
representation at the Olympics. Things which I don't expect to see
in my lifetime.*

But notice that the concept has been very effectively privatized. In recent years, the London-based Arsenal soccer team kept on winning British competitions while playing utterly glorious football: they were a complete European team. There was not a single English player at one point. And it drew, except for the inevitable Brazilians, on the best European talent across the board. You could operate that at some national level, but you couldn't operate it at a supranational level.

> *You can take Brazilians and Italians and Ukrainians and make an English club soccer team. But you couldn't take a bunch of Englishmen and create a European representation.*

There's an interesting sort of confusion in the English national mind. Teams are bought and sold in a much worse way than even the typical American baseball team—and at the same time, there is a romanticized atavism for the days when on the team you had eleven guys called Smith.

> *English football clubs at this point are a bit like remote castles were a hundred and fifty years ago. If you've made a lot of money in Russia you buy one, because it makes you feel better about yourself.*

> *But here's the difference between America and Europe. At the level of city teams we are the same. You can snap your fingers and create a baseball team, and Americans will get very excited about it, even though the players are from the Dominican Republic, Ecuador and Venezuela. But in America you can actually have an American representation in any international competition, and no one would say Texas or Idaho should send their own teams to the Olympics.*

Of all countries that see themselves still as nations, America is the most invented of all. I mean, it was literally created by choice by a bunch of intellectuals, who described, defined, adjudicated it. But the inventedness of America, paradoxically, makes it much more real to the people who identify with it. Whereas the sheer facticity of a place like France, or Spain, makes it possible actually for many Spaniards or French to disassociate themselves quite actively and radically from any more abstract identification with nation or state—without losing any sense of their identity. They just are French and Spanish. They don't need the flag. They don't even need the national language; they're quite happy to speak English to other people if that's advantageous.

It's a very odd experience for an English person, and I think even more so for a continental European, to come to America and discover the deeply felt national identification of even its most liberal and cosmopolitan citizens— something that is on the whole not the case in Europe. It was once the case that the forms of state-and-nation identification were part of the required civic life. You stood up, as my mother used to, when the Queen came on television. You stood up when the national anthem was played in the cinema, and so on. So these things were the case once—but it's not that they were deeply embedded in what it meant to be a certain national, it's just that they were part of the tradition: like the tartan in Scotland. If you like, they were an invented tradition but perceived as real. The American traditions are now so profoundly embedded that it's very hard to distinguish them from what it means to be American: that is why perfectly reasonable American citizens can get genuinely angry when someone fails to salute the flag or sing the anthem. Such sentiments are unknown in contemporary Europe.

I'm still struggling for a way to get across this barrier of the national to the international. From what you said at the beginning about striving for universalism, I take it that you must see this as desirable, if not always appropriate or possible. And so I wanted to ask you about whether there were, if not values then at least practices that Europeans and Americans ought to be speaking about for export.

*Now the obvious one of these is democracy. The Iraq War—the
moment that you cited and that we've come back to a number
of times—is rather interesting in this regard. Because the Iraq
War was fought by an American government which was not
itself democratically legitimated—a point which no one makes
but which in terms of the theory of war, or the Kantian theory of
war—is of some significance. After all, this is what one would
expect: that it is precisely such a government that is most likely
to go off and fight stupid wars. Meanwhile, though, that same
country, the U.S., was promoting democracy in Ukraine by
taking exit polls in Kiev seriously—which, of course, we didn't
in Miami, which is how Americans got where we are today,
basically.*

Intellectual activity is a little bit like seduction. If you go straight for
your goal, you almost certainly won't succeed. If you want to be someone
who contributes to world historical debates, you almost certainly won't succeed if you start off by contributing to world historical debates. The most
important thing to do is to be talking about the things that have, as we might
put it, world historical resonance but at the level at which you can be influential. If your contribution to the conversation then gets picked up and
becomes part of a larger conversation or part of conversations happening
elsewhere as well, then so be it and so much the better.

So I don't think intellectuals do very well talking about the need for the
world to be democratic, or the need for human rights to be better respected
worldwide. It's not that the statement falls short of the desirable, but it contributes very little to either achieving its goal or adding to the rigor of the
conversation. Whereas the same person, really showing exactly what's defec-
tive about democracy and democracies, sets a much better base for the argument that ours is a democracy that others should be encouraged to emulate.
Merely saying that ours is a democracy or saying that I'm not interested in
ours but I want to help make yours, encourages the response: well, go away

and fix yours and then maybe you'll have a foreign audience, and so on. So in order to be international, we have to be national first.

What should we be caring about today? We are at the end of a very long cycle of improvement. A cycle that began in the late eighteenth century and that notwithstanding everything that's happened since, continued essentially through the 1990s: the steady widening of the circle of countries whose rulers were constrained to accept something like the rule of law. I think that it was overlain from the 1960s onwards by two different but related spreads: of economic and individual freedom. Those two latter developments, which look as though they are related to the first one, are in fact potentially dangerous to it.

I see the present century as one of growing insecurity brought about partly by excessive economic freedom, using the word in a very specific sense, and growing insecurity also brought about by climate change and unpredictable states. We are likely to find ourselves as intellectuals or political philosophers facing a situation in which our chief task is not to imagine better worlds but rather to think how to prevent worse ones. And that's a slightly different sort of situation, where the kind of intellectual who draws big pictures of idealized, improvable situations may not be the person who is most worth listening to.

We may find ourselves asking how we can defend established legal or constitutional or human rights, norms, freedoms, institutions and so on. We will not be asking whether the Iraq War was a good or not good way to bring democracy, freedom, liberty, the market etc. to the Middle East; but rather, was it a prudent undertaking even if it achieved its objectives? Recall the opportunity costs: the lost potential to achieve other things with limited resources.

All this is hard for intellectuals, most of whom imagine themselves defending and advancing large abstractions. But I think the way to defend and advance large abstractions in the generations to come will be to defend and protect institutions and laws and rules and practices which incarnate our best attempt at those large abstractions. And intellectuals who care about these will be the people who matter most.

*When I mentioned democracy before, what I had in mind was not
so much the idea that one ought to be speaking abstractly about
democracy or that one ought to be spreading it but rather that it's
precisely a very tender thing which is made up of a lot of small and
fragile mechanisms and practices. One of which is making sure
that votes are counted.*

*I remember speaking to a Ukrainian friend about the U.S.
presidential elections of 2000. And the Russians were going to send
electoral observers to California and Florida on the rationale that
these were parts of the country which had only recently been
attached and abuses were more likely there. Which I found
laughable. As it turned out, the haughty position I took about our
local practices and their unselfconscious defense by everyone who
would matter from the top to the bottom was completely wrong.
Those elections were, I think, a very good example of an attractive
and even glamorous institution, democracy, having been
hollowed out from the inside while we ignored the details.*

If you look at the history of nations that maximized the virtues that we
associate with democracy, you notice that what came first was constitutional-
ity, rule of law and the separation of powers. Democracy almost always came
last. If by democracy we mean the right of all adults to take part in the choice
of government that's going to rule over them, that came very late—in my
lifetime in some countries that we now think of as great democracies, like
Switzerland, and certainly in my father's lifetime for other European countries like France. So we should not tell ourselves that democracy is the starting point.

Democracy bears the same relationship to a well-ordered liberal society
as an excessively free market does to a successful, well-regulated capitalism.
Mass democracy in an age of mass media means that on the one hand, you
can reveal very quickly that Bush stole the election, but on the other hand,

much of the population doesn't care. He'd have been less able to steal
the election in a more restricted suffrage-based, old-fashioned nineteenth-
century liberal society: the relatively few people actually involved would
have cared much more. So we pay a price for the massification of our liberalism, and we should understand that. That's not an argument for going
back to restricted suffrage or two classes of voters, or whatever it might be—
you know, the informed or the uninformed. But it is an argument for understanding that democracy is not the solution to the problem of unfree
societies.

But wouldn't democracy be a good candidate for a more pessimistic
century? Because it is, I think, best defended as something which
prevents worse systems from coming into being, and best
articulated as mass politics as a way of making sure that people
aren't fooled the same way every time.

The Churchillian dictum that democracy is the worst possible system
except for all the others has some—but limited—truth. Democracy has been
the best short-term defense against undemocratic alternatives, but it is not a
defense against its own genetic shortcomings. The Greeks knew that democracy is not likely to fall to the charms of totalitarianism, authoritarianism or
oligarchy; it's much more likely to fall to a corrupted version of itself.

Democracies corrode quite fast; they corrode linguistically, or rhetorically, if you like—that's the Orwellian point about language. They corrode
because most people don't care very much about them. Notice that the
European Union, whose first parliamentary elections were held in 1979 and
had an average turnout of over sixty-two percent, are now looking to a turnout of less than thirty percent, even though the European Parliament matters
more now and has more power. The difficulty of sustaining voluntary interest in the business of choosing the people who will rule over you is well
attested. And the reason why we need intellectuals, as well as all the good

journalists we can find, is to fill the space that grows between the two parts of democracy: the governed and the governors.

> *There's also the dictum of Göring, which is that in any political system you just claim that you're a victim, and you start a war, and you can get most of the people on your side. Which is much more true than we would like it to be. And it leads to the conclusion, which I think is fairly obvious, that if what you want to do is defend democracy, you have to recognize that wars abroad are one of the great distorting factors. This has been a problem since the beginning, and since Louis Bonaparte—*

It's not accidental that Marx focused on Louis Bonaparte as an instance of the demagogic possibilities of transforming free elections into unfree societies. Marx turned it to his own advantage by arguing that this was a consequence of having a particular kind of electorate, a preindustrial one. But sadly, we've seen that postindustrial electorates are just as vulnerable. It was only a few years ago that people like Michael Mandelbaum were writing books about how democracies never made war and that a world full of democracies would be a safe world!

The Iraq War illustrates precisely the contrary: that a democracy, and particularly an armed democracy, is very easily led into war—so long as it is told stories of the kind that are compatible with its self-image. It can't be told: we're going to make a war of conquest. That runs counter to its capacity to assure itself that what it's doing is right. But tell it that it's going out there to do for others what it was once fortunate enough to do for itself, that it's protecting itself against authoritarian societies about to destroy those very values that make it democratic: then it is readily mobilized for undemocratic objectives, including illegal aggressive war. If a democracy can do that, then there's not much left to distinguish it—back to Göring—from a dictatorship: except its self-justifying narrative of freedom. The latter retains its

value, but it is not much of a defense. It just about meets Churchill's crite-
rion, but not more than that.

*I'm more optimistic than that. I don't think the government which
led the United States into that war was a democratically elected one.
And that has all of the consequences you would expect. Namely, once
you've gotten into power undemocratically, you think of ways of how
you might do it again. And the war was, in fact, the way to get elected
a second time. Bush wouldn't have been competitive for reelection
without the war. It was really the only Republican issue in 2004.*

*First you cheat, then you fight, then you say that the war means
that the other side is illegitimate. So I do think that there is a
connection between democracy and war-fighting, and I do think
that as a first litmus test of what's going on in your country, you
can ask yourself: are we fighting an illegal war of aggression? And
if the answer is yes, then there's a pretty good chance that there
might be some problem with your democratic institutions.*

Democracy is neither a necessary nor a sufficient condition for a good,
open society. I don't want to come across as excessively skeptical about
democracy: as someone having a preference for the aristocratic, liberal societies of the nineteenth century. But I do want to make an (Isaiah) Berlinian
point. We simply have to acknowledge that some earlier non-democratic
societies were in certain respects better than later democracies.

*I agree that constitutionalism and the idea of the rule of law are
anterior both historically and, I think, ethically to democracy. But
in a world where mass politics is already out of the bottle, you have
to have some way of managing it.*

That I accept. But I would say that it would be nice if we were capable
of producing political elites that were not so totally beholden to the uncorked

genie that they could not stand a little clear of it to embody the values of the society that the mass democrats have inherited.

The tendency of mass democracy to produce mediocre politicians is what worries me. The vast majority of the politicians of the free societies of the world today are substandard. Whether you start with Britain and make your way to Israel, or you start with France and make your way to anywhere in Eastern Europe, or you start in America and make your way even to Australia. Politics is not a place where people of autonomy of spirit and breadth of vision tend to go. And I think that that is true even in the case of someone like our present president, Barack Obama, who is proving most adept at what some of us feared would be his salient quality—the desire to be thought reasonable. Not necessarily to compromise but the desire to be thought to compromise. Which makes it very hard to lead.

Can one come up with anything more inspiring, then, Tony? Or is the moral burden on intellectuals to be precisely those who are not inspired?

Well, you know, Cassandra has quite a reputation. It's not so bad to go down fighting as the last person to tell an unpleasant truth.

We remember Cassandra, but no one remembers what her unpleasant truth was.

Fair enough. The unpleasant truth is normally, in most places, that you're being lied to. And the role of the intellectual is to get the truth out. Get the truth out and then explain why it just is the truth. The role of the investigating journalist is to get the truth out; the role of the intellectual is to explain what's gone wrong when the truth has not been got out. I think the danger of thinking of intellectuals as inspirers is that we will ask them for grand narratives again, or for large moral truisms. And the larger the truism and the grander the narrative, the more they'll look like the kind of inspiring intellectual that we think we want. And I don't think we want that.

> *Why wasn't the Iraq War a kind of global Dreyfus Affair? Or at*
> *least an American one?*

Dreyfus was very simple: a matter of truth and lies. That's not quite true of the Iraq War. In order to make the case against it, you have to invoke a certain amount of what you might call contingent considerations: the prudence of precedent, the unwisdom of breaking law if you don't want others to break it, the predictable unlikelihood that any of the claimed good outcomes would actually happen. All of those are very good arguments, but they go beyond simple ethics or issues of fact alone.

The one ethical issue which I think was absolutely clear-cut arose not out of Dreyfusard considerations, but Nurembergian ones. It really is very, very unwise indeed, in the practical ethics of international relations for democracies to make war unprompted—on preemptive grounds—when alternative strategies are available to them. Because that is corrosive, not only of the exemplary quality of democracies—without which they cannot lecture dictatorships—but is also internally corrosive of what democracies are supposed to be about.

> *I would have thought that the crucial point, in the analogy to the*
> *Dreyfus Affair, would be that the American state put about various*
> *lies in the run-up to the war. For example, the lie that Iraqi*
> *authorities had something to do with the attacks of 9/11, and the*
> *lie that Iraq was on the brink of creating a nuclear weapon. These*
> *were lies which were quite consciously used to bring a people to a*
> *state of preparedness to make war.*

When a democracy makes war, it's first got to create a war psychosis, and to create a war psychosis is to risk corroding the values of democracy. You have to lie, you have to exaggerate, you have to distort and so on.

In the twentieth century, America has made war at almost no cost to itself, relative to the costs to others. At the Battle of Stalingrad, the Red Army lost more soldiers than America has lost—soldiers and civilians combined—in all the American wars of the twentieth century. It is difficult for Americans to understand what war means, and therefore remarkably easy for an American political leader to mislead this people into taking a democracy to war.

> *I remember, it was in April 2003, looking through the channels late at night and finding you on the screen. And with a very calm demeanor you were saying things that made total sense, namely that the justification that we had used to enter Iraq could have been used to justify any sort of war. And I had this odd sense that your appearance was exceptional because both in temperament and in content, this was different from what everyone else was doing right at that moment. Then David Brooks came in to disagree, claiming that there was something called "reality," which policy makers responded to, and that they were not seeking logical consistency. Of course at the time the "reality" in question, the supposed threat from Iraq, was an entirely constructed one, which Brooks was helping to construct. Now this description of your calm reason may come across as a compliment . . .*

I'll take it that way.

> *—but what I want to ask is a question about how things went so wrong at that moment. Because if there was a moment when intellectuals ought to have been writing "J'accuse," where they ought to have been trying very hard to reach larger groups of*

people, crystallizing their thoughts if necessary, choosing their
media as necessary, it was in April 2003 as the United States was
getting itself into the mess which so far defines this whole century,
and indeed probably has deprived America of what should have
been its century. You were in the middle of that a bit—could that
have gone a different way?

I'd like to recall a few encounters.

One was during the run-up to the war, when some of us were raising the question of whether or not preemptive war was both necessary and wise. My interlocutor on a television show kept asking: but surely you trust Donald Rumsfeld? He's got so much experience, you're not going to tell me that you've got a better view of national security than Donald Rumsfeld? I remember thinking that this kind of reasoning is terribly dangerous. What we have here is the argument from imputed authority. The secretary of defense must know better because he's in charge. And the whole point of critical intellectual engagement is to say the opposite: if someone is in charge, that puts a special onus upon the rest of us to interrogate them very hard, rather than to back off and say "daddy knows best."

This atmosphere of "they must know better because they're the experts, they're the bosses, they're the big guys, they're the hard men, they're the realists, they've got the inside info, what do we soft moralists know?" was disturbing. Those are the atmospherics of authoritarianism.

The mention of David Brooks recalls a different point, in a different conversation with him, on the Charlie Rose show. It was about what the U.N. could do to solve the Iraq crisis, rather than leaving it to America to just do its own thing. Brooks was arguing very smoothly that the U.N. was useless and couldn't be counted on to do anything forceful. He said: look at how useless it was in the Balkans. I went into some detail at that point about the resolution of the Kosovo crisis and, in particular, the role of international agencies there—in catastrophic situations, I argued, it was still possible for international agencies to do good things, precisely because they were international agencies. And I expected Brooks to come back with: what about this, this and this. Instead, he just said: well, I don't really know anything about that. And changed the subject.

And I remember thinking: you've gone on television, made *ex cathedra* statements against the whole idea of international action to resolve political crises in dangerous places, making a case for America to do its own thing because no one else can; and then when you're pushed on it, you say: well, I don't actually know what I'm talking about. Here we had the public intellectual who now occupies not only prominent television space but also op-ed pages of the most influential newspapers in the English-speaking world: and he knows nothing.

Raymond Aron famously criticized the generation of Sartrian intellectuals who knew nothing about the things they were talking about; but at least they did, after all, know other stuff. Men like Brooks know, literally, nothing. So I encountered in those troubled months a combination of catastrophic acquiescence in authority and plain, old-fashioned dumb ignorance masquerading as commentary. These were the circumstances which allowed a criminal political action to be pushed through the public space with very little opposition.

Something else to remember, though, is that the people who *did* know something just rolled over. I'm thinking of Michael Ignatieff, or David Remnick, or Leon Wieseltier, or Michael Walzer. Instead of asking questions, they all behaved as though the only function of the intellectual was to provide justification for the actions of non-intellectuals. And I just remember being profoundly shocked and also feeling very lonely. Not that I felt comfortable with the isolationists either; I'd been very much in favor of the Balkan intervention and still believe that that was the right thing to do.

Other opponents of the war were the neo-Kissingerians, as it were, who opposed doing stupid things because it's not in our interest. That comes a bit closer to being a legitimate position, but still utterly insufficient. It's not enough to say we should not make idiots of ourselves in places like Vietnam, or Iraq, if the reason you're giving is merely that it's not in our interest. From that premise, you're just as likely to say that we *should* make idiots of ourselves in places like Chile because that is in our interest. So I don't recall reading many essays or articles which shared my own view at the time, certainly not any written by Americans.

> *It seems to me that the first two points might be related to each*
> *other. Namely, journalists' defense of authoritarian epistemology,*
> *let's say, that those in power are presumed to be right, may also be a*
> *self-defense of the journalists themselves and their methods of work.*
> *Because what do many of these journalists have besides their own*
> *authority? And on what is that based aside from contact with*
> *power?*

I think that is a very fair point. Most journalists, and this has something to do with the nature of power and communication today, are as terrified of losing their connected status as they are of being wrong. Yet the idea that the intellectual should think of himself as a transmission belt is of course dangerous because that's exactly what they were in the Soviet Union; the metaphor of the transmission belt is Lenin's. But these guys were frightened—I think you're right—that their standing might be undermined.

Brooks is an interesting case because it's all done with mirrors—there is no expertise. The apparent expertise consists of the capacity to talk glibly each week about any public event in a way that readers have gotten used to thinking of as a sort of enlightened commentary. Thomas Friedman, another prominent contemporary "expert," trades on a slightly different notion of expertise. Notice that pretty much every Friedman column includes a reference to some famous person he's spoken to. So he makes explicit the notion that your expertise is a function of your contacts. As King Abdullah said to me; as the former wife of the undersecretary of state in South Korea's Information Ministry murmured at a dinner party I attended; and so on. It doesn't really matter, actually, who it is. It's the notion of access to something special.

In Friedman's case, access to information is very carefully recalibrated as the acceptable middle ground on any given policy issue. And Friedman's position on the Iraq War was contemptible. Not only did he run along with everyone else, but he actually probably slightly misread the tea leaves and ran along a little too fast on the anti-French, anti-European thing. It was Friedman who ran a column that said that France should be kicked out of the U.N. Security Council for having the chutzpah to oppose the United States on such an important issue.

Investigative journalists like Mark Danner or Seymour Hersh in *The New Yorker* were in a different tradition. Their job is simply to find out what dirt lies underneath the smooth surface of political decisions and political statements. And so it's not accidental that all of the real work of showing what was going on in the first decade of this century was done not by intellectuals, not by mainstream journalists, most certainly not by commentators, but by the guys who dig up dirt: whether it was on the weapons of mass destruction, whether it was on the lies about nuclear fissile material in Iraq, whether it was torture.

The extreme case in the other direction has to be Judith Miller, whose achievement was to legitimize the claim that there were weapons of mass destruction and whose source, Ahmad Chalabi, was someone who not only had an obvious personal vested interest in regime change in Iraq but who then turned out to be an agent of the Iranian secret services.

The last time I saw Judy Miller was at a sort of dinner debate in the Hamptons in, I think, mid-2002, attended by George Soros, prominent journalists, and some other public figures. I spoke about Iraq, at what was then an early stage of the run-up to the Iraq War. Judy Miller put me down in the most contemptuous and categorical way. She was the expert, and I was just a chattering academic. Since George Soros had just said pretty much the same things as me, it was quite striking that I was the object of the attack. But then you don't attack George Soros in the Hamptons; you never know when you might need the money! Then things became rather personal; I tried to respond and a number of people stood up and said in essence, "how can you possibly disagree with Judith Miller?" She has the authority, she has the knowledge and she has the inside sources. The whole experience reproduced the exchanges I described on Charlie Rose—except much less gentlemanly because there were no microphones on.

The only person who came up to me after the Hamptons dinner and said you were right and she was dangerously wrong was Jean-Marie Guéhenno, head of U.N. peacekeeping. He said: I can tell you that everything you said is true, and that everything she said is simply the Washington line filtered through a serviceable journalistic outlet. What was really worrying was that this was a dinner gathering of powerful people: high in the directorate of *The New York Times*, senior producers from public television and others besides. Not one had the courage to support me. In those days Miller was untouchable. And then suddenly, it all comes apart, and no one wants to speak to her anymore.

It seems to me that one of the problems here is that you can't extricate truth from authority when you don't really believe in truth. It struck me that one of the reasons why it was difficult for Iraq to be a kind of global Dreyfus Affair was the American lack of concern for truth as such. ·

This is one of the unfortunate prices we pay for the 1960s: the loss of faith in truth as a sufficient counter to lies. It's not enough to say: she's not telling the truth; you have to say: she's lying because she is connected to an arms manufacturing firm. Or she's lying because her politics are tied to the Zionist lobby, or she's lying because she has a larger plan that she doesn't wish to reveal. What's wrong with her, in short, is not that she lies: everyone lies. Her problem is that she's badly motivated.

Today it takes a very considerable degree of ethical self-confidence to say, as people used to as recently as the Watergate era, that such-and-such a person is a bad politician because he lies. Not because he lies as a spokesman for the arms lobby, or the Israel lobby, or the gun lobby, or whatever it might be—but just because he lies. And if you make that case for honesty today, you're likely to get a raised eyebrow. We all lie, they all lie, goes the reasoning. The question is: is he your liar or my liar?

The historical background to this disturbing loss of moral confidence seems to me in large measure the collapse of the old Left, with all its faults, and the attendant ascendancy of the soft cultural Left. Thus American liberals feel vaguely uncertain about what exactly the ground is that they stand on when they say that they disapprove of something. We're easier with the problem of good and evil if it is unambiguously located in another time (or place); we're more comfortable saying we don't like witch dunking, or we don't like the Gestapo. But we are not always quite clear how we should state our opposition to, e.g., female clitorectomies in East Africa—for fear of giving cultural offense. And that hands huge hostages to those (normally but not always on the right) who, in a much cruder way, think they know exactly what's right and wrong, false and real, and so on. And who are willing to say so in a self-assertive, confident way. The problem of ethical insecurity has kneecapped two generations of liberals.

> *It's a question that dogged Isaiah Berlin, but there was a clear answer to it. Namely, Berlin was a moral realist—he just wasn't a moral reductionist. He thought that these moral concerns were all real; the tragedy of moral life is that they are not commensurable or reducible to any one underlying moral good. But he thought they were all out there and counted and are human values, however ultimately incompatible.*

> *But I think there's another Berlinian point here which is relevant—not having to do with moral pluralism but having to do*

with knowledge. Berlin wrote an essay about political judgment in
which he circled around and then tried to define just what that was
and what it was not. In those years (the 1950s and 1960s), such
considerations had fallen into neglect. For Berlin, political
judgment entailed a sense of reality: the ability to sniff out truth in
a world of intentional obfuscation.

It's part of a larger story that Berlin himself was actively engaged in, which is the problem of thinking politically. We think we know what political theory or political thought or political philosophy are; but actually they are a very subtle, intermediate territory between ethics or philosophy on the one hand, and politics or even policy on the other.

So in American academic scholarship, politics is simply the thing that happens when people engage in public affairs. And what you do is study it, but you don't engage in it. If you must engage in it, you apply to it the sniffily pejorative term "normative" political reasoning, which suggests that you are surreptitiously inserting your own views into the object of study. The activity you just described as "judgment" is actually rather subtle: it requires the establishment of a particular set of rules pertaining to the possible applications of concepts we deploy to make sense of public affairs.

Thus it is easy to show that politicians are inconsistent and fall short of high ideals. But that doesn't address the question of what people should do politically to conform to some set of desirable norms, whether of moral consistency, or of truthfulness, or of practical ethics, or whatever it might be. That is the terrain of political thought. And as John Dunn famously said, it's not easy.

Any engagement with a political decision has to be triangulated through three different questions. One is the consequentialist question. Are we sure that the consequences of a given choice are not dangerous—either directly or as examples and precedents? Even if the Iraq War had paid off beautifully in Bushian terms, it might still—from a consequentialist perspective—have been a rotten idea, encouraging others to act in ways that might not succeed and could have terrible consequences. Thus the mere fact that it succeeded would not be justification alone.

Secondly, there's the realist conversation: what's in it for us? This has to be part of any political decision because politics is, after all, about governance, and it's about creating outcomes which are presumptively in the interest of those who undertook the action. But the thin line separating political realism from moral cynicism is easy to cross—and the price of doing so, over time, is a corrupted public space.

And then the third question must be: is this a good, or right, or just thing to do—independent of both my previous considerations? It is our contemporary inability to keep all three sets of considerations in play (but distinct) that reflects the greater failure of political reasoning.

> *I fear, staying near this example of the Iraq War, that there may be*
> *an underlying problem which makes it difficult for people to*
> *undertake any of those three, let alone all of those three. And that is*
> *a certain disrespect for political thought, or maybe just for logic.*

> *Let me explain: if we're going to make Iraq a democracy, do we*
> *really think that Iraqis are going to vote for our indefinite*
> *occupation of their country? Or do we really think they're going to*
> *vote for us to have their oil resources? If Iraq is a secular state,*
> *should we be knocking it over as part of a campaign against*
> *religious terrorism? Such basic considerations, requiring little*
> *local knowledge, seemed quite absent from the public conversation.*

In my view, the failure to think logically is tied to ideology. Consider communist intellectuals and reformers in the 1960s. Their inability to grasp the scale of the communist catastrophe was in large measure ideologically driven. Blind to the contradictions of what they thought of as "reform" economics, they were neither stupid nor operating in bad faith. But their logical reasoning was subordinated to dogmatic first principles.

Mutatis mutandis, to think that imposing democracy in Baghdad was the necessary and sufficient condition for resolving the dispute between Israelis and Palestinians—an argument one heard again and again—you have to believe an awful lot of impossible things before breakfast, to cite Lewis Carroll. Among them is the view that the world in fact resembles in every respect your abstract construction of it.

Actually, this construction itself consisted of a series of LEGO-like plastic worlds interlocked according to taste: the first described the Arab and Muslim lands as a two-dimensional whole: if you push it in one place, it moves predictably in another. Then came the curious assumption (revealing remarkable ignorance of twentieth-century history) that everyone would be so impressed by the shock and awe of a destructive bombing campaign in Baghdad that they would immediately fall into line many hundreds of miles away; and of course there was the even less plausible assumption that the Israeli-Palestinian conflict was just another Cold War–style issue, with no autonomous or local factors but merely reflecting and subordinate to global forces that America could manipulate at will.

Dialectics. But what's the ideology that imposes itself on logic in America in the early twenty-first century? I have my candidate, which is American nationalism.

American nationalism seems to me never to have gone away. We think we live in a globalized world, but that's because we think economically and not politically. Thus we don't quite know what to do with actions that are so obviously not shaped by globalization or indeed economics. There is an interesting paradox here. The United States is the least globalized of all the developed states. It's the least exposed to the immediate impact of international communications, international movement of peoples, or even the consequences of international shifts in currencies and trade. Although these affect the American economy hugely, most Americans don't actually experience life as international, nor do they immediately connect their personal or local circumstances to transnational developments.

Thus Americans rarely encounter a foreign currency, nor do they consider themselves affected by the dollar's relationship to other currencies. This provincial perspective has inevitable political consequences—what is true of electors is true of their representatives. The United States therefore remains mired in a series of myopic considerations, even though it is still the only world power and exercises huge military leverage across the globe. There is a disjuncture between the domestic politics and the international capacities of the United States which was simply not the case for any of the great powers of the past.

Many Russians and many Chinese are ignorant, I suppose, in much the same way you described Americans as being. The difference is that at the present moment, neither Russia nor China actually has American levels of reach in international affairs. But both, as far as one can tell at a distance, are rather nationalistic.

But how exactly does American nationalism function in practice, and what did it have to do with mistakes like the Iraq War? One thing that strikes me as characteristically nationalist is the confusion over when to be cynical and when to be naïve. Thus one is extraordinarily cynical about everything that is said in Paris, to the point where anyone who believed anything said by President Chirac was beyond the pale—despite the fact that on the whole the man was prudent and cautious, saying many things that turned out to be correct. Meanwhile we accept from Washington propositions and policies which are palpably inane, and emanating from sources and individuals whom we know to be neither intelligent nor reasonable.

American nationalism is very closely associated with the politics of fear: recall the Alien and the Sedition Acts of the 1790s, the Know-Nothings of the nineteenth century, the fear of outsiders that characterized the post–World War I years, McCarthyism and the Bush-Cheney years themselves. All were instances of those moments when American public conversation combines ultra-nationalistic sensitivity to outside influence and offense with a willingness to flout the Constitution, in spirit and letter alike.

When Bush said that we are fighting the terrorists "there" so that we won't have to fight them "here," he was making a very distinctively American political move. It is certainly not a rhetorical trope that makes any sense in Europe, for example. Because "there," whether it's Lebanon, or Gaza, or Baghdad, or Basra, is actually just a short plane ride from the borders of the EU; and what you do there, to "them," has immediate consequences for their fellow Muslims or Arabs or outsiders in Hamburg or the Paris suburbs, in Leicester or Milan. In other words, if we begin a war between Western values and Islamic fundamentalism, in the manner so familiar and self-evident to American commentators, it won't stay conveniently in Baghdad. It is going to reproduce itself thirty kilometers from the Eiffel Tower as well. So the notion of us and them, there and here, which is crucial to American nationalism in its long-established geographical isolation, is utterly absent from the sensibilities of other western countries—which have nationalisms of their own, of course, but which can no longer assume such a hermetic form.

I think that if there is a global trope, or at least in the Western world a general trope, it's the trope of victimhood. People long for that victimhood in ways that would have seemed very strange just twenty years ago.

In the U.S., a lot of the people who are on the right and are voting Republican feel themselves to be victims and for more or less understandable reasons. They may not see themselves in the global economy, as you say, but globalization has really punished them, it has destroyed a certain rural way of life. Walmart has made a mess of rural and semi-rural America. People in the countryside do live worse now than they lived thirty years ago. The American inability to live at the same level of one's parents is much more pronounced in the countryside than it is in the cities. So those people feel like victims, and they have a reason for feeling like victims, and the Republican Party articulates that sense of victimhood for them. Partly it humors them by telling them that they will still one day be rich, and partly it explains why they are not yet rich in terms of the intrusive, costly and inefficient state that Democrats supposedly always build.

And so the gap between the feeling of victimhood of someone in Kansas and the American capacity to project power in the rest of the world is just absolutely enormous. And I think it's that gap which can't be replicated anywhere else.

The suspicion that the elite just doesn't get it is profoundly embedded in American populist resentment. It goes back at least to William Jennings Bryan and the 1896 election. Distance matters in this way, too. In Holland, you will find reference to the fact that those people in Amsterdam don't get it. But those people in Amsterdam are seventy-five miles away at most: whereas the people in Washington or New York or Princeton, or Berkeley for that matter, can be a couple of thousand miles and a couple of thousand light years culturally from the "it" that they don't get.

So there are two senses in which American provincial nationalism feels both remote and uncomprehended. They combine rather elegantly in the fear and dislike of the United Nations: an organization both alien, unfamiliar and somehow very far away (more precisely, in New York).

All that said, the wonderful mystery is that this has never effectively translated into real demagogic politics in the way that it has in most European countries at some point or another. Now partly this could be said to be a consequence of the electoral system. But it also reflects simple geographical realities. Thus, as in England, xenophobia and nationalism have been muted thanks to their sublimation at crucial moments into a conservative party. But in America, sheer size plays a role: everyone is so far away from everyone else that the coherence and organizational energy needed for political demagogy tends to dissipate. All the same, it has on occasions burst through what Marx would have called the outer integument, in the form of Newt Gingrich, or Dick Cheney, Glenn Beck or the Know-Nothings, McCarthyism and so on: managing to do just enough harm to threaten the quality of the republic but not quite enough damage to be seen to be what it really is. Which is a native American fascism.

It does suggest a certain mission for American patriotic intellectuals, which would be the defense of institutions and the defense of the Constitution. And also a certain test of those who claim to be patriots: namely, are they defending institutions or are they rallying around a person who tends to make exceptionalist arguments (or totally bizarre, ignorant arguments in the case of Sarah Palin) about what should happen to those institutions?

American commentators are pretty good at picking up those threats—after the fact. But the key is to identify them at the time and in time. What works against this now is a pervasive culture of fear.

The U.S. is more vulnerable to the exploitation of fear for political ends than any other democracy that I know (with the possible exception of Israel). Tocqueville saw this, so it's not as though I've discovered something original. We occupy a conformist public space. The dissenting traditions of New York are peripheral to this and hardly affect it. As for Washington: that is not a place in which dissent, or indeed intellectual activity of any other kind, is encouraged. There are indeed self-characterized intellectuals in D.C., but most are so mesmerized by the desire for influence that they have long since lost all moral autonomy.

Fear operates in many different ways. It is nothing as straightforward as the old anxiety that the king or the commissar or the police chief will come and get you. It's about the reluctance to transgress one's own community: the fear that has been expressed to me by liberal Jews that they dare not risk being thought anti-Semitic or anti-Israel. The fear of being thought un-American. The fear of breaking with *bien-pensant* academic opinion on anything from political correctness to conventional radical opinions. The fear of being unpopular in a country where popularity is a virtue, first calibrated in junior high school. The fear of standing against the majority in a country where the notion of majority seems to be profoundly enthroned in the idea of legitimacy.

So perhaps we could end with the question of medium, of reaching
people in a conformist society. You have been, in a way, fortunate
in that you've caught what might turn out to be the last gasp of the
kind of classic essayistic medium.

Let me reemphasize the coincidence binding the rise of universal literacy and the advent of mass means of written communication with the emergence of the public intellectual. The typical intellectual from, let us say, the 1890s to the 1940s had literature as a day job. Whether you're looking at Bernard Shaw or Emile Zola, André Gide, Jean-Paul Sartre or Stefan Zweig, these were people who succeeded in translating their literary talent into mass influence. Then, from the 1940s through the 1970s, the intellectuals with comparable access and reach tended to be social scientists of one kind or another: historians or anthropologists, sociologists, sometimes philosophers. This corresponded to the expansion of higher education and the emergence of the university professor as intellectual. In these decades, intellectuals were people whose day job was less likely to be novel writing than college teaching.

The rise of radio dons in 1950s England was another striking shift. It corresponded to the growing fear that mass culture and mass literacy had somehow gone off the rails. Most advanced societies were now universally literate, but the audience for intelligent public debate was actually shrinking—thanks as it seemed to many to television, cinema and material prosperity. Richard Hoggart's *The Uses of Literacy* and some of Raymond Williams's early writings address this point. The fear that you now have a sort of drenched public space for communication but less and less capacity on the part of the educated layman to respond to it became widespread.

This brings us to the third and most recent stage, which is television. The characteristic intellectual of the television age has to be able to simplify. So the intellectual of the 1980s and after is someone able and willing to abbreviate, simplify and target his observations: as a consequence, we have come to identify intellectuals with commentators upon contemporary affairs. This is a very different function and style from that of the intellectual in the age of Zola or even in the age of Sartre and Camus. The internet has only accentuated this.

An intellectual today faces a choice. You can communicate in the kind of journal which came into being in the late nineteenth century: the literary weekly, the political monthly, the scholarly periodical. But then you only reach a like-minded audience that has shrunk domestically—although, to be fair, it has also expanded internationally thanks to the internet. The alternative is to be a "media intellectual." This means targeting your interests and remarks to the steadily shrinking attention span of television debates, blogs, tweets and the like. And—except those rare occasions when a major moral issue arises or there is a crisis—the intellectual has to choose. He can retreat to the world of the thoughtful essay and influence a selected minority; or he can speak to what he hopes is a mass audience but in attenuated and reduced ways. But it is not at all obvious to me that you can do both without sacrificing the quality of your contribution.

*I don't want to finish without discussing a figure who was
extraordinarily important and who certainly was an intellectual,*

but who doesn't easily fall into the categories that we've been using.
And that is the Viennese journalist Karl Kraus, editor of Die
Fackel *and scourge of various political classes for decades.*

Kraus is interesting because of his emphasis on language, because of the sheer coruscating negativity of his critique: using words to tear down veils of delusion and screens of self-mystification. Kraus, for all his unambiguous location in early-twentieth-century Vienna, remains a guide to our own circumstances. As I noted earlier, in contemporary America the only truly effective critics of power are the journalists—particularly investigative journalists. And Kraus was a journalist, first and always.

If you ask who performed the role of the intellectual—speaking truth to power—in George Bush's America, it was certainly not the Michael Ignatieffs; or even—flatter myself as I might—the Tony Judts or assorted other intellectuals seeking to uncover the idiocies of public policy. It was Seymour Hersh, Mark Danner and others: in their modest ways, the Krauses of our age.

Kraus saw this coming a century ago. The more democratic the society, the more limited the influence of genuine intellectuals. The intelligent literary or printed critique of those in authority works best when influence and power are brokered within a restricted circle. Just as Voltaire might approach Friedrich of Prussia, so Zola was without question read by every French politician of his day. But today, intellectuals only succeed if they can bypass or short-circuit conventional access to power and—whether by clever targeting or sheer good fortune—hit a particularly sensitive nodule in the flesh of a decision maker, or public opinion. Beyond such opportunism, the only way to move the public against those in power over it is to reveal scandal, destroy reputation or establish an alternative pole of information. In short, to act like a modern Kraus.

If intellectuals are going to uphold truthfulness as against higher
truth, or, to use a term from the Bush years, against truthiness,
they have to sound *a certain way. They have to be taking care of*

the language in some way. If intellectuals are to survive and
matter, their language must be transparent, as Orwell said.

I think that the intellectual's task is to catch—something which is clearly a talent that not everyone has—the soul of brevity. Say something important, preferably something that goes against the grain of people's beliefs; say it well, so that the audience understands that clarity of exposition is related to truthfulness of content: but make the point in accessible ways. Intellectual obfuscation is self-defeating. There is much to be said for respecting peoples' capacity to grasp a complicated argument by making it clearly. And then? You have to hope that there is still room in the public place for such a contribution: there may not be—the forums for such communications may die; they may already be dying. Certainly most people who pass as intellectuals today can neither write nor communicate with any consistent effect. And this includes some very smart people.

The larger question is whether we're in a political economy where
media have become centralized—even as they appear to become
decentralized, they become centralized—and if that's one of the
reasons why it's hard to get a dissenting point across.

Well, we could ask ourselves that question with respect to what we're doing right now. We have been engaging in a long and serious conversation over the course of months. What are we then going to do with it? We're going to put it into a book. If we are lucky, our book will get reviewed in all the good intellectual journals as well as *The New York Times*—and then, if those reviews are positive, and Penguin is as good as it's supposed to be at selling books, we'll sell (and this would be one hell of an achievement) let's say eighty thousand books in this country. And let's optimistically add a further forty thousand (this is very optimistic) for the rest of the English-speaking market. And then we might do decently across Brazil through continental Europe and so on. In short, if we knock 'em dead, we might hit gross sales of two hundred fifty thousand books across the world. That would be regarded as an altogether remarkable achievement for such a book.

But you could also dismiss such sales as a mere *bagatelle*. Two hundred fifty thousand people, most of whom already agree with us. And many of whom will already know one or both of us and—directly or indirectly—will be pleased to have their views intelligently reflected back at them. You never know, there's a decent chance that one of us—hopefully you—will be invited to discuss the book and its ideas by Charlie Rose. But you know that we will not hit a million or even half a million sales whatever happens. And we should not be ashamed of this because if we had, we'd be in the Stephen King class and would have betrayed our calling.

And so in its way, what we are doing is bizarre. We are engaging in an intellectual exercise that will not have world-shattering consequences and we are doing it in spite of that. Obviously this is the condition of most people who write: throwing a letter into the ocean in the forlorn hope that it will be picked up. But for intellectuals to write and speak in the full knowledge of their limited influence is, at least on first sight, a curiously pointless undertaking. And yet, it's the best that we could hope for.

What, after all, is the alternative? To write some soppy slush about intellectuals for *The New York Times Magazine*? Anything we have to say about relativism or nationalism or intellectual responsibility or even political judgment would certainly be read by millions of people. But it would be edited and distilled and reduced into acceptable midstream generalities. It would be followed by an exchange of letters focusing exclusively upon some superficial, marginal aspect of our exchanges—something I said about Israel or something you said about American nationalism—which condemned us as self-hating Americans or anti-Semitic Jews. And there would be the end of it.

Thus I don't know how to answer your question. The real way to influence the bigger world? I'm rather skeptical about what intellectuals can do. Our best moments come along but rarely: as Aron once said, not everyone gets to have a Dreyfus Affair. But if I'm proud of any of my non-academic contributions, it is still this: during the discussions that led up to the Iraq War I said "no." I said it in a reasonably prominent forum at a time when almost everyone else—including many of my friends and peers—was saying "yes." There were many people who felt as I did; who had the same ideas as me; who could have expressed them no less well—but were in no position to do so. They were not invited onto Charlie Rose, to write op-eds for *The New York Times* or essays for *The New York Review*. I was privileged, and I am proud that I used that privilege as I should.

> *In your book* The Burden of Responsibility *you assert that Camus, despite everything, is a typical French intellectual; that Aron, despite what everyone thought, was a typical French intellectual; and that Blum, although he was a politician, was also a typical French intellectual. And at each point the argument always seemed a bit forced to me. I wonder if what you really wanted to claim was not so much that they were typically* French, *but that they were* intellectuals *because they took responsibility.*

What I wanted to convey about Camus and Blum and Aron was that these were men who stood for France precisely at the time when they were regarded as marginal to the French debate—and as speaking against French interests. I was moving towards the idea that all three men were genuinely independent thinkers in a time and a place where being independent placed you in real danger, as well as consigning you to the margins of your community and to the disdain of your fellow intellectuals.

Maybe I thought this story worth telling because there is a subterranean twentieth-century tale to be told of intellectuals who were forced by circumstances to stand outside and even against their natural community of origin or interest.

9.

THE BANALITY OF GOOD: SOCIAL DEMOCRAT

By the middle of the first decade of the twenty-first century I was a professor at New York University with an established international reputation about to publish a long book on the history of postwar Europe. Upon its completion, I realized—as one often does after the fact—that *Postwar* had become the kind of book I wanted my children to read. What I am now thinking of writing is another book that they could read if the spirit so moved them: *Locomotion*, a history of trains.

The time has come to write about more than just the things one understands; it is just as important if not more so to write about the things one cares about. I had already done a little of that sort of writing, but only with reference to people and ideas: topics I was paid, so to speak, to understand. It took me a little while to convince myself that anyone might be interested in what I had to say about railways.

What I wanted to write was a study of the coming of modern life through the medium of the history of the railway train. And not just modern life, but the fate of modern sociability and collective life in our over-privatized societies. The railway, after all, was a creator of sociability. The coming of the railways facilitated the emergence of what we have come to know as public life: public transport, public places, public access, public buildings and so on. The idea that people who were not obliged to travel in the company of others might choose to do so—if provision was made for status sensibility and physical comfort—was in itself revolutionary. The implications for the emergence of social class (and class distinctions), as well as for our sense of community across distance and time, were huge. It seemed to me that an account of the rise and fall (and, in Europe, the resurrection) of the railway might be an instructive way to think through what has gone wrong in countries like America and Great Britain.

From public policy there is a natural step to the aesthetics of public life: urban planning, building design, the use of public spaces and the like. Why, after all, is the Gare de l'Est in Paris—a transportation hub built in 1856— perfectly functional today, as well as rather pleasing to behold, whereas almost any airport (or gas station) built one hundred years later is already utterly dysfunctional as well as grotesque in appearance? Why do stations built at the height of modernist self-confidence (St. Pancras in London, Centrale in Milan, Hlavní Nádraži in Prague) still appeal both in form and function, whereas Gare Montparnasse, Penn Station or Brussels Central—all the products of the destructive "updating" of the 1960s—fail on both counts? There is something about the durability of the railway, its infrastructure, its penumbra and its uses, that represents and incarnates much that was best and most confident about modernity.

> *You have said that trains formed an integral part of your early years, in a way which binds them to the welfare state that was so formative for you. But surely the link you posit between public services and private benefits is not self-evident? The state doesn't have to furnish these resources in order to be a functional state. It might in contrast be administered by people who maintain that loneliness is an inexhaustible resource for economic growth and that the atomization*

of each of us is for the good of all. That was what the first British
reformers were up against in the nineteenth century, and it is what
we are up against now, in the United States. This is what used to be
called the social question. Is that the right way to talk about it?

Speaking of the social question reminds us that we are not free of it. For Thomas Carlyle, for the liberal reformers of the end of the nineteenth century, for the English Fabians or the American Progressives, the social question was this: how do you manage the human consequences of capitalism? How do you talk not about the laws of economics but about the consequences of economics? Those who asked these questions could be thinking in one of two ways, although many thought in both: prudential and ethical.

The prudential consideration is that of saving capitalism from itself, or from the enemies that it generates. How do you stop capitalism from creating an angry, impoverished, resentful lower class that becomes a source of division or decline? The moral consideration concerned what was once called the condition of the working class. How could workers and their families be helped to live decently without damaging the industry that gave them their means of subsistence?

The basic answer to the social question was planning. I wonder if
we could start with the ethical issue which may be at the origins,
namely, the proposition that the state ought to be engaged in this
sort of thing.

If you asked, what is the intellectual background to post–World War II preferences for planned economies, you would have to begin with two completely different starting points. One would be the liberal, progressive reform era of the 1890s to 1910s, in the United States, in England, in Germany, in France, especially, in Belgium and smaller countries. This began with late-Victorian liberals such as William Beveridge who came to see that the only way to save Victorian society from its own success was by intervening from above through regulatory systems. The other is the 1930s response to the Great Depression, particularly by younger economists—mostly in the States and France, and then some in Eastern Europe, as well—which was to say that only the state could intervene actively against the consequences of economic collapse.

To put it another way: planning is a nineteenth-century proposition, largely realized in the twentieth century. So much of the twentieth century, after all, is the acting out, living out, of nineteenth-century ways of responding to the industrial revolution and the crisis of mass society. Cities in much of western and northern Europe had grown exponentially between say 1830 and 1880. Thus by the late nineteenth century there were cities all across Europe of a size that someone aged fifty could not have imagined in his childhood. The scale of urban increase had far overtaken the scale of state action. And so the idea that the state had better intervene in production and employment grew very fast in the last third of the nineteenth century.

In England, the question was posed first in almost exclusively ethical terms. What do you do with the very large numbers of indigenous, impoverished, disadvantaged, permanently poor people who had moved to industrial cities and without whose labor the flourishing capitalism of the age would have been inconceivable? This was often presented as a religious issue: how should the Anglican Church (and others) respond to the challenge of huge demands for charity and help in industrial cities? It's interesting how many of the people who would later emerge in the early twentieth century as prominent planners, social policy experts, even ministers in Labour or Liberal governments, started out in neo-Christian settlements and charity organizations designed to alleviate poverty.

In Germany, the other major industrial country of the late nineteenth century, the question was posed in prudential terms. How can a conservative state prevent social despair boiling over into political protest? In Wilhelmine Germany, the prudential response was welfare: whether unemployment pay, industrial protection in factories or restrictions on working hours.

If we bring up Prussia or Germany, it seems that we can't avoid
then the question of Marxism and social democracy—because just
as the Prussian state is acting in order to prevent some kind of
revolutionary politics, those who had been practicing revolutionary
politics are then coming to the conclusion that it might be best to
encourage the state to intervene in economic relationships.

The great debate in German social democracy, from Marx's death in 1883 to the outbreak of the First World War in 1914, is the debate over what role the capitalist state could and should perform in alleviating, controlling, and recasting relations between employers and employees. The debates over the Gotha and Erfurt programs of the Social Democratic Party, or between Karl Kautsky and Eduard Bernstein, can be understood within Marxist traditions, as we discussed earlier; but they can also be seen as the socialists' responses, incoherent and fractious, to the same issues that were preoccupying Bismarck and the Catholic Center Party in Germany.

In Germany the socialists come to have doubts about their version
of progress, which is that capitalism is going to create a certain
kind of working class: necessarily large and rebellious. At the same
time, it seems, liberals in Britain and elsewhere were coming to the
conclusion that their version of progress had its own shortfalls.

In England, the debate really is about policy. Here, uniquely, the threat of an insurrectionary working class essentially died in the 1840s. The Chartist movement of that decade is not the beginning of British labor radicalism; it is the end of the story. By the later nineteenth century, the UK could boast a mass proletariat, but already organized and tamed into trade unions and eventually a union-based political party, the Labour Party. The notion that this large labor movement might harbor any revolutionary aspirations was long since moribund. So the center of gravity of conversations about the state and the working class in England are always, as we might put it, reformist.

And already then, in the first decade of the twentieth century, William Beveridge is thinking about what one ought to do or what the state ought to do for this working class. By the 1940s Beveridge will be seen as one of the founders of modern social planning. He is the one who famously distinguished between the welfare state and the warfare state. But his initial preoccupations were with poverty as a moral wrong.

Beveridge, born in 1879, is a product of late Victorian reformist aspirations. Like a number of his contemporaries, he went to Oxford and became embroiled in debates about the problem of prostitution, of child labor, of unemployment, of homelessness and so on. Upon leaving Oxford, Beveridge devoted himself to charitable work aimed at overcoming these pathologies of industrial society; in many cases the word "Christian" figures in the organization to which he and his friends committed their energies. The same was true of his near contemporary Clement Attlee, the future Labour prime minister who was to put Beveridge's ideas into practice.

To see where they were coming from, we need an idea of the history of what we now call social policy in England. The Poor Law of Elizabeth's reign and the Speenhamland system of the 1590s had provided theoretically unrestricted charitable support for the indigent or the helpless, payable from local rates, so long as the beneficiaries were within the district that was obliged to support them. So the poor couldn't be forced into a workhouse or forced to work; they had to be given the means to sustain themselves.

The Poor Law of 1834 mandated *work*. To get relief, you had to go to the local workhouse, and work for a wage lower than that available on the open job market. The intention was to discourage people from taking advantage of poverty relief, and also to make very clear that there was something unworthy about being reduced to this condition. The Poor Law thus distinguished between the so-called deserving and undeserving poor, thereby creating moral categories that did not correspond to economic reality. And indeed it forced people into poverty, since they first had to exhaust their own resources before becoming eligible for public or local assistance. It thus exacerbated the very problem that it was ostensibly intended to treat. From very early on the new Poor Law was regarded as a blot on the face of English society. It stigmatized those whom capitalism had temporarily put out of commission through no fault of their own.

What binds Beveridge and Attlee together and links them eventually to reformers from very different backgrounds was an obsession with reforming the Poor Law.

> *So if it's the Victorian period and the* longue durée *of English*
> *labor history that matters, are the First World War, where the*
> *state gets mobilized, and the Great Depression, where debates about*
> *macroeconomics really begin, less important than we think?*

Most of the intellectual justifications for a welfare state in some basic form were in place before the First World War. Many of the people who were going to be crucial in introducing it after the Second World War were already adult and active in this or related fields before 1914. This holds not only in England but also in Italy (Luigi Einaudi) and France (Raoul Dautry).

There were also significant institutional achievements before the First World War in Germany and in England. The Lloyd George–Asquith governments of 1908 to 1916 introduced a whole series of reforms, essentially pensions and unemployment insurance. Pensions were called the "Lloyd George" well into my lifetime. But such reforms depended upon taxation: how else were these benefits to be paid for? Moreover, in many countries it was only the unprecedentedly expensive war itself which could have brought about the equivalent of a graduated income tax in every major European state, because the taxation and inflation of the war generated the resources that made a welfare state less expensive relative to total government expenditure.

The First World War greatly increased government expenditure, and also the model of government control of the economy, the government direction of labor, the government direction of raw materials, control of incoming and outgoing goods and so on. Moreover, the French tried to stabilize their rapidly tumbling currency and reduce public expenditure; the British went back on the gold standard in the mid-twenties and tried to deflate to overcome the postwar economic crisis. Elsewhere, even those countries which had moved quite far along in a direction of a social welfare state were constrained to keep benefits and payments under strict control. The levels attained shortly after the armistice were not to be exceeded, with only a few local exceptions, for two decades.

If Beveridge is half of this story, the economist John Maynard Keynes is the other. You can argue that Beveridge represents a Victorian Christian sensibility that finds its opening in 1942. But you can't make that sort of argument about Keynes.

Keynes and Beveridge, "planning" and the "new economics," tend to be talked of in the same breath. There's a generational symmetry there, and an overlap in the two policies: full-employment, based on Keynesian fiscal and monetary policy, combined with Beveridgian planning. But we have to be very careful because Keynes came out of a very different tradition. And it's not just because he went to Cambridge whereas Beveridge went to Oxford.

Balliol.

Well, it's King's College, Cambridge, and Balliol College, Oxford,— which are the only colleges that matter in this story, it's true.

Before the First World War, Keynes was a young Cambridge don. His personal relationships were often homosexual and he was closely associated with the emerging Bloomsbury group in London. The self-consciously iconoclastic Stephen sisters—Vanessa Bell and Virginia Woolf—admired him unreservedly. And of course the men of Bloomsbury mostly loved him: not only was he brilliant and witty and attractive, but he was a rapidly rising public figure. During and after World War I he played a high role in the Treasury—where he formed increasingly critical views of British public finances—and then was sent to Versailles to work on the postwar treaty negotiations. Shortly after returning, he wrote his famously critical pamphlet about the treaty and its likely consequences and became an internationally renowned figure. Thus by 1921, still in his thirties and not yet the author of the path-breaking *General Theory*, Keynes was already famous.

And yet, like Beveridge, Keynes was unmistakably a man formed by the previous century. In the first place, and like so many of the best economists of the earlier generations, from Adam Smith to John Stuart Mill, Keynes was primarily a philosopher who happened to deal in economic data. He might just as well have been a philosopher had the circumstances positioned him differently; indeed, in his Cambridge years, he wrote some properly philosophical papers, albeit with a mathematical bent.

As an economist, Keynes always saw himself responding to the nineteenth-century tradition in economic reasoning. Alfred Marshall and the economists who followed J. S. Mill had assumed that the default condition of markets, and therefore of the capitalist economy at large, was stability. Thus instabilities—whether economic depression, or distorted markets, or government interference—were to be expected as part of the natural order of economic and political life; but they did not need to be theorized as part of the necessary nature of economic activity itself.

Even before the First World War, Keynes was beginning to write against this assumption; after the war, he did little else. Over time he came to the position that the default condition of a capitalist economy could not be understood in the absence of instability and the inevitably accompanying inefficiencies. The classical economic assumption, that equilibrium and rational outcomes were the norm, instability and unpredictability the exception, were now reversed.

Moreover, in Keynes's emerging theory, whatever it was that caused instability could not be addressed from within a theory which was unable to take that instability into account. The basic innovation here is comparable to the Gödelian paradox: as we might put it today, you cannot expect systems to resolve themselves without intervention. Thus, not only do markets not self-regulate according to a hypothetically invisible hand, they actually accumulate self-destructive distortions over time.

Keynes's point is an elegantly symmetrical bookend to Adam Smith's claim in *The Theory of Moral Sentiments*. Smith argued that capitalism does not in itself generate the values that make its success possible; it inherits them from the pre-capitalist or non-capitalist world, or else borrows them (so to speak) from the language of religion or ethics. Values such as trust, faith, belief in the reliability of contracts, assumptions that the future will keep faith with past commitments and so on have nothing to do with the logic of markets per se, but they are necessary for their functioning. To this Keynes added the argument that capitalism does not generate the social conditions necessary for its own sustenance.

So Keynes and Beveridge are men of the same era, with comparable but different backgrounds, and addressing related but different problems. Beveridge began from society rather than from the economy: there are certain social goods that only the state can provide and enforce—by legislation, regulation and enforced coordination. Keynes starts from very different concerns, but their approaches dovetail: whereas Beveridge devoted his career to alleviating the social consequences of economic distortion, Keynes spent much of his adult life theorizing the necessary economic circumstances in which Beveridge's policies could be applied to optimal effect.

Let's stay with Keynes for a moment. The First World War
and especially his experience at the treaty negotiations at Versailles

and the little book about the Peace make him what he is. But then
there's the 1936 book, The General Theory, *one of the most*
important texts of the twentieth-century political economy. Would
you stick to the thesis that this is a further development of Keynes's
previous ideas, or are we going to have to discuss the Crash of 1929
and the Great Depression that followed?

Don't underestimate the impact of the 1920s. Keynes was writing quite prolifically then, and some of his writings that would be recast into *The General Theory* were already appearing before the Depression begins. He had well before 1929 rethought, for example, the relationship between monetary policy and the economy. And of course, Keynes was a devastating critic of the gold standard long before countries began coming off it at the Ottawa conference. He saw that attaching themselves to a gold standard deprived states of the ability to devalue currencies as needed.

Moreover, Keynes understood clearly in his own mind well before 1929 that neoclassical economics had no answer to the problem of unemployment. Neoclassical economists, putting it broadly, think that the mass of small decisions made by consumers and producers pursuing their own ends generates a larger rationality at the level of the economy itself. Thus demand and supply find a certain equilibrium and markets are ultimately stable. Apparent social ills such as unemployment are in fact transient forms of economic information permitting the smooth functioning of the economy as a whole.

Keynes's conviction that this was an incomplete description of reality arose primarily from his observations of the British and German unemployment crises of the early 1920s. The neoclassical consensus was for government passivity in the wake of economic problems. Keynes saw already then what others would observe during the Great Depression: the conventional response—deflation, tight budgets and waiting—was no longer tolerable. It wasted too many social and economic resources, and was likely to cause profound political upheaval in the new postwar world. If unemployment was not the necessary price for efficient capital markets, but simply an endemic pathology of market capitalism, then why accept it? This was a question posed in Keynes's writings well before 1929.

The *General Theory* of 1936 puts state, fiscal and monetary power at the center of economic thought—rather than acknowledge them as unappealing excrescences on the body of classical economic theory. This revision of two centuries of economic writing summarized Keynes's own work from the 1920s with the crucial addition of contributions from his students, notably Richard Kahn of Cambridge who came up with the "multiplier": it was thanks to Kahn and others that Keynes convinced himself that governments could indeed intervene countercyclically and to enduring effect. There was no law that mandated acceptance of economic disruption.

Thus Keynes's magnum opus of 1936 completely recast macroeconomic thinking about government policy. And it was this recasting that was important, rather than the theory itself. A new generation of policy makers was now furnished with a language and a logic on which to base the case for state intervention in economic life. Keynes's work was thus as ambitious and influential as a grand narrative of the way capitalism works as any of the great nineteenth-century works which it contradicted.

> *Very little of your account of the challenges to classical liberal economics requires that we look beyond Great Britain at all—and yet, by 1936, certainly there are comparable trends elsewhere, be they corporatism on the Portuguese or the Italian model; or planning within an essentially capitalist economy, as in Poland, where planning starts in 1936 . . .*

Yes, if we confine ourselves to practice and programs, rather than high theory, much of what looks like neo-Keynesian practice in the 1930s seems to be happening in anticipation of Keynes's account of it.

In the interwar years, most young people of any seriousness were looking at alternative ways to respond to economic inefficiency—other than simply throwing up their hands as the left and the right of the nineteenth century had done and say either, it's what's wrong with capitalism, we can do nothing about it; or, it's the price we pay for what's right with capitalism, we can do nothing about it. These were the two essential, conventional positions in both economic and political responses to depression, through 1932. But in Poland, Belgium, France and elsewhere, young people frustrated with left-wing responses were setting up parties or splinter groups of their own, favoring government expenditure and intervention.

Indeed, so widespread was the case for planning and intervention from above that the arguments against them were already under way. Friedrich Hayek was already at work on the case that he would most fully articulate in his 1945 book, *The Road to Serfdom*. In it, he argues that any attempts to intervene in the natural process of the market risk, and indeed, in one version of his account, are guaranteed to produce authoritarian political outcomes. And his reference is always German-speaking Central Europe. Hayek argues that what's wrong with the Labour Party's welfare state, or Keynesian economics, in its policy implications, is that you're going to end up with totalitarianism. It's not that planning might not work economically, but that you'll pay too high a price politically.

Can we pause there for a moment? This has now come up more than once, and the whole Hayekian case seems like a historical misunderstanding that lies close to a debate that is absolutely crucial to the whole century, and indeed to important debates which continue today.

I find the historical origins of Hayek terribly puzzling. He was in Austria, where a conservative, authoritarian Catholic state declared itself in favor of something called corporatism. This was a kind of pose which announced itself as political economy, but it had no political economy. Corporatism was the name of the state ideology, but corporatism in Austria was a partnership between the government and various parts of society. There was very little in the way of interventionist fiscal or monetary policy.

On the contrary, the Austrians were incredibly conventional and strict in fiscal and monetary policy, just as Hayekians would recommend, which is why the country was hit so hard by the Depression and its governments were so helpless. It is also how they built up all their reserves, in foreign currency and gold, which Hitler then took in 1938.

So I have never really understood against what exactly Hayek was reacting. Austria was a politically authoritarian state, but it had no planning at all in a Keynesian sense. The Austrian experience actually seems to disprove *Hayek's argument. If anything a little planning would have helped the Austrian economy, and made local authoritarianism and then Hitler—and all that followed from Hitler—less likely.*

I sympathize. If you read *The Road to Serfdom*, you won't find much enlightenment on that score. But when you set Hayek's writing against Karl Popper's work of the same period, a pattern begins to emerge. What you see is a conflation of two animosities: dislike for the overconfident social democratic urban planning of early 1920s Vienna, and distaste for the Christian Social corporatist models that replaced them on the national level following the reactionary coup of 1934.

In Austria, the Social Democrats and the Christian Socials, by this time gathered up in the governing Fatherland Front, stood for very different constituencies and goals. Thus any ostensible commonalities of rhetoric or program appear far more theoretical than historical. But from Hayek's point of view—and here he agrees with Popper and many other Austrian contemporaries—both were responsible in their different ways for Austria's collapse into the arms of Nazi authoritarianism by 1938.

Hayek is quite explicit on this count: if you begin with welfare policies of any sort—directing individuals, taxing for social ends, engineering the outcomes of market relationships—you will end up with Hitler. Not merely with social democratic housing projects or right-wing subsidies for "honest" winegrowers, but Hitler. Thus, rather than run such a risk, democracies should avoid all forms of intervention which distort the properly apolitical mechanisms of a market economy.

The problem with such arguments, made fifty or even seventy years on, with reference to Hitler and such, is that they ignore so much of the politics of Vienna or Austria in 1934, when democracy there was actually put to an end. These groups who supposedly are similar because of a general tendency towards government intervention are fighting a civil war against each other. And the great achievement, Red Vienna, is being literally destroyed—

Shell by shell—

building by building, by artillery coming down from the hills around Vienna.

This is the political autism of Hayek, manifest in that inability to distinguish the different politics that he didn't like from one another. This initial conflation, pushed forward to the 1980s and 1990s, accounts in a way for the economic policies that we've been living for the last twenty-five years. Hayek returns to favor, "vindicated by history," when in fact his own historical justification for apolitical market economics was entirely wrong.

One of the things which has happened in the meantime, which is less showy than the duel down the decades between Keynes and Hayek, is the displacement of full employment—which for both Keynes and Beveridge was a very important category—by the now-dominant category of economic growth.

The rate of growth of the mature economies was always taken to be

relatively slow. It was understood by the classical and neoclassical economists that rapid economic growth is what happens in backward societies
undergoing rapid transformation. Thus, you would reasonably expect rapid
economic growth in late eighteenth-century England, as it goes from an
agrarian to an industrial base—just as you'd expect it in 1950s Romania, as
you go, admittedly at a rather more forced pace, but not that much more
forced, from a backward, rural society to an at least initially, highly productive primitive industrial society.

The rates of growth in industrializing societies were thus typically 7 or
even 9 percent—pretty much as they are in China today. What this indicates is
that high rates of economic growth do not typically suggest prosperity, stability
or modernity. They were long thought to be transitional features. The typical
rate of growth in late nineteenth-century, early twentieth-century Western
Europe had abated to a fairly steady pace, just as the interest rates were fairly
low and stayed that way. The reason why economic growth rates were so high
in the 1950s, and why economists became besotted with them as a measure of
success and stability, was because of prior economic catastrophe.

That said, we should recall that Keynes's *General Theory* was a theory of
"employment, interest and money." Unemployment was the preoccupation of
the British and the Americans, and in continental Europe of the Belgians. But
employment wasn't actually the theoretical starting point for French or German writing—which was much more concerned with inflation. The way in
which Keynes matters to European policy makers was less about employment
per se than about theorizing the role of government in stabilizing economies by
counter-cyclical measures, such as deficit spending during recession. This
meant not only measures to keep people in jobs, but measures to keep currency stable, and to ensure that interest rates didn't fluctuate wildly and destroy
savings. So employment, which is central to English and American thought, is
not a universal obsession on the continent. Stability is.

German economists are mainly concerned with the vestiges of
hyperinflation, and when they're thinking politically, they're

thinking about the 1920s, but in practice Hitler is quite concerned
with employment. Perhaps this is the moment where we could look
straight on historically at the difference between, say, Keynes circa
1936 and the German Four-Year Plan of the same year.

The fascists and the Nazis assumed that you could mix property-based capitalism on the one hand and government intervention on the other. Industrialists, property owners, large farmers, individual manufacturers, shop owners could be perfectly autonomous, but government could intervene in their relations with their workers, could plan the goods that they produced and determine the prices at which they produced them. There a government could engage, intervene and act, without casting any doubt on the fundamentally capitalist nature of the economic system. That mixture was hard to understand ideologically. So Nazi policy or fascist policy could look pro-capitalist, or anti-capitalist, or neo-Keynesian. It was primarily massive government over-expenditure—"over" in the sense of above resources—to buy off political and social crises at the expense of future stability, or at the expense of future income, unless obtained elsewhere. And Keynes saw that quite early on.

Within Keynesian assumptions, what you're after is the
reestablishment of equilibrium within one system. Whereas on
Hitlerian assumptions, you can only establish equilibrium in some
very distant future, when you've already robbed all of the Jews and
created your racial pastoral utopia in the East.

Equilibrium for Keynes was an objective and indeed a virtue. And that's partly on theoretical grounds, but I would say partly on psychological grounds. The loss of equilibrium that Keynes and his generation experienced with the First World War and the collapse of Edwardian, and therefore Victorian, certainties and security, is the most important informing sentiment in his theoretical writings. Just as it was in his support for the postwar welfare state, which he supported not on economic, much less ideological grounds, but because he understood and anticipated the overwhelming need for security that people would feel after the end of World War II.

Equilibrium was a virtue for Keynes. Government intervention was primarily a way to re-equilibriate the economy. No such concern remotely informs Nazi thinking—where equilibrium is exactly what's destroyed once and for all. You're not interested in balancing the accounts, so to speak, of a complex society; you're simply achieving certain goals—if necessary, at the expense of certain parts of that society, so that the other parts of it will be appreciative of your efforts.

> *Another fundamental difference is something that Hannah Arendt notices, which is that in a stable society of the sort that Keynes is envisioning, people are able to have a private life. This comes across from the very first pages of Zweig's* World of Yesterday, *which is where we began. That's part of what it means to have stability, that you can have a private life—some sphere where you are unconcerned about anything but your own affairs, which in some measure you can predictably arrange. Whereas Hitler was quite consciously trying to make sure that people couldn't think that way ever again.*

That's right. I mean, the notion of wanting to make decent life impossible is precisely absent from anything Keynes could imagine. What Keynes wanted to do was save liberal England from the consequences of its own economic ideology. Well, Hitler is not in the business of saving liberal Germany from anything.

> *The other comparison that might be explored is that between liberal planning and Stalin's Five-Year Plan.*

One needs to excise from the conversation any assumption that planning in its post-World War II forms of the welfare states owed anything to the

Soviet experience. At most you could say that a number of the individuals who—as intellectuals but not as policy makers—favored planning, thought they favored it, in some measure, because they thought that what they saw in the Soviet Union was good, and they thought it was good because Stalin planned.

The history of planning is one of different European societies coming to different conclusions about where and how it is desirable to use the state to pursue these ethical and pragmatic purposes. This very plurality shows how unimportant the Soviet experience actually was: there was only one Soviet model, the Soviets denied the value of pluralism and no European policy makers followed Soviet-style planning unless they had to: and that is the history of postwar Eastern Europe, another story.

The British welfare state as such never planned. There's the Beveridge report of 1942, and there were debates about planning. But what actually emerged were a series of institutions, primarily nationalizations, which were then taken to be necessary and sufficient conditions for a better kind of set of relations between state and society. No one, so to speak, planned the planning. And no one planned the details, either. No one in Britain sat down and planned how much the railways should invest, where cars should be made, how far labor should be discouraged from operating in this area and encouraged, or re-educated, to operate in that area.

That kind of planning is more continental European. Scandinavian economic planning was much more indicative and much less regulatory than the English one, much more concerned with trying to push private investment in certain directions. French planning was centralized and indicative, and so concerned with generating certain kinds of outputs without directly enforcing them. West German socio-economic policies in the postwar years were much more localized, or the encouragement came from localized initiatives. Nationalization mattered much less in West Germany than in Britain. The Italians channeled public money through huge umbrella groups, IRI, ENI and so on, or the Cassa del Mezzogiorno, into particular regional objectives. So "planning" meant lots of different things. But one thing it never meant was modeling yourself on the Soviet model of large-scale, declared, required outcomes.

To see the most basic difference between the Soviet and other cases you have to look at how the policies were generated, as well as at what the politics were. West European plans were all compromises between the perceived technical need to invest in long-run infrastructure and the immediate political wish to buy off consumer discontent. In Eastern Europe, where communism was imposed, you didn't usually have to buy off consumer discontent. You could focus on building up whatever it was your theory told you needed to have lots of—and the fact that it would produce huge consumer unhappiness was a matter of indifference in a closed political system.

The west European compromises were made politically palatable by the American postwar assistance known as the Marshall Plan. If you took the Marshall Plan out of the picture, some European countries, including Britain, would have had real trouble achieving certain public policy objectives without sparking huge political protest. The strikes in France in 1947 are a pretty good indicator of that.

Was the Marshall Plan not an example of brilliant American international political economic planning? And should it not be seen (like planning on the level of a single European economy, which it favored and allowed) not as something which flowed from extreme political models, but as something which is designed to prevent their popularity?

George Marshall had been chief of staff of the U.S. Army during the war, and in 1947 was secretary of state. When Marshall goes to Moscow in March 1947, he stops in European capitals along the way. He knows that the British Labour Party was running out of breath, after two years of hectic legislation. In France each government was weaker than the last, culminating in the collapse of the left-wing coalition in the spring of 1947. In Italy, the communists might have won free elections (those of 1948 were heavily slanted towards the Christian Democrats with papal and American support). In Czechoslovakia, they already had. The communists are doing very well in places like Belgium, and even briefly in Norway.

Western Europe was not at all guaranteed to emerge into the "sunny uplands," to use Churchill's phrase, of the 1950s and 1960s. The immediate postwar boomlet had subsided, and economies were suffering from shortages of goods and of foreign currency. They had no means of buying what they needed if they didn't make it themselves—and most of them didn't. They couldn't borrow dollars, and the dollar was increasingly the international currency. Even those economies like the West German or the Belgian, which were actually starting to recover, were being strangled by a shortage of currency reserves.

Alan Milward argues that Europe was suffering the consequences of its own success: the incipient postwar economic takeoff—particularly the industrial recovery in western Germany and the Low Countries—was creating bottlenecks which in turn were reintroducing unemployment. This was the consequence, of course, of Europe's impoverishment. It was no longer able to fuel its own economic recovery, even at such low levels, and was utterly dependent on foreign currency and imported raw material.

So from one perspective, the Marshall Plan merely opened a blocked valve. But even so, its significance is undiminished. It was—and we forget this—primarily a political, not an economic, response. The view in Washington was that Europe was so lacking in political self-confidence that it would be unable to recover economically and would fall prey either to communist disruption or a reversion to fascism. I emphasize the latter: in the German case especially, observers seriously feared a nostalgic revival in Nazi sympathy.

The idea that you needed to save Europe economically lest it collapse politically was hardly a startling insight. What was new was the idea that the way you could save Western and Central Europe was by making them responsible for their own recovery, but with means that were made available to them. It is a separate debate as to whether this was enlightened self-interest on America's part. This might well be so, both in the short term—because much of the Marshall Plan money came back to the States in the form of expenditure, purchases and so on—or in the long term, because it stabilized Europe and created an important Western ally.

But perhaps this doesn't matter. Whether the Marshall Plan was self-interest, enlightened or otherwise, it was certainly crucially important. It put backbone into Bidault, as one American advisor described it, speaking of the prime minister in France, who seemed to be wobbling helplessly in the face of communist strikes.

With the recovery, in the same moment, the same breath or breathlessness, comes the welfare state.

The legislation to which we refer when we talk of the coming of welfare states begins in most countries in 1944 or 1945, so Marshall is not germane here (though note that the Truman administration mostly favored European welfare reforms as democratic stabilizers). The ideal comes from the Resistance, or from postwar left-wing parties, or indeed from Christian Democracy. The welfare state is not primarily, except in Scandinavia, the work of social democrats.

But I would emphasize again the point I made about planning: there was a common trend by many different variants. From country to country the approach varied, as did the method of financing it. Once it came into operation, the Marshall Plan unquestionably helped cover the initial costs of these welfare states; but we should recall that it only lasted for four years and was not spent for the most part on social services.

Then perhaps a better candidate for a common European reaction to the Marshall Plan would be economic cooperation.

The Marshall Plan involved a system of international payments designed to ensure that beneficiary countries did not simply grab their share and set out to beggar their neighbors. There was a purely notional fund, where you could borrow against a non-existent payments bank and then pay it back with your earnings from trade with another country. It was a very simple system, but it required trade cooperation and discouraged subventions and protectionism.

It is hard to demonstrate the connection—we can hardly rerun postwar history without it to see what might have happened—but I believe it is clear that the mere fact of cooperation at this sort of technical level, albeit enforced by Washington, demonstrated that a continent which had only recently been engaged in mutual destruction could cooperate. And not merely cooperate, but compete and collaborate according to agreed rules and norms. This would have been unthinkable as recently as the 1930s.

Is it right to think of that primarily as a kind of intended side effect of the Marshall Plan, or were there not indeed some Europeans— Frenchmen, Germans, Belgians—

Who had been thinking these—

—things through, ahead of time.

The good news is that there were. The bad news is that many of them had polluted the heritage of economic collaboration because they had been more than willing to accept the terms imposed on them by Nazi and fascist theorists of "European" union.

Thus, some of the men who ran Vichy France would emerge after the war as the major planners of Gaullist France, or Republican France. Some of the bright young economists who were actively involved in the administration of the West German economy in the postwar years had been mid-level economic policy makers in Nazi Germany. Many of the young men around Pierre Mendès-France, or Paul-Henri Spaak in Belgium, or Luigi Einaudi in Italy, had been apolitical economic advisors on trade, on investment, on industry, on agriculture, to fascist or occupied governments during the war.

What had bound these reform-minded innovators had been the cult of European planning that appealed to so many younger bureaucrats in the interwar years. The very word "Europe"—united Europe, the European plan, European economic unity and so on—was slightly suspect for the first ten years after the war because of its association with Nazi rhetoric of a more rational Europe, to replace the democratic Europe of inefficient interwar memory. This rhetoric had reached a peak with the introduction of Hitler's "New Europe" in 1942 as the official basis for collaboration in all occupied countries.

That is one reason why Scandinavians and especially the English were understandably suspicious of glib talk of European unity in the immediate aftermath of Hitler's defeat. The other source of skepticism was the association that "united Europe," "European unity" and such like had with Catholic Europe in particular. All six of the foreign ministers who signed the European Steel and Coal Community, the foundation of institutionalized European economic cooperation, were Catholics: from Italy, France, largely Catholic West Germany and the Benelux countries. This could be—and often was—presented as a Catholic European ploy to rebuild these countries around a sort of neo-corporatist economic collaborative model.

So I'd like to get around to how this history repeats itself as farce, which is now, but first let's say a word about how it repeats itself as tragedy: the 1970s, let's say, when planning is discredited at an intellectual level. How does that come about?

Planning is never fully discredited in France. And it didn't have to be discredited in Germany because there never was "planning" in our sense of the word. The Rhineland economic model and the French indicative planning model were perceived as successful in their respective countries across a broad spectrum of political opinion. And I would say that they are still seen thus today—not least in the light of Anglo-Saxon or Anglo-American experience over the last thirty years. By most international criteria, the standard of living in France and Germany (not to mention other countries whose economies are similarly structured, like the Netherlands or Denmark) strikingly out-distance that of America or Britain. The postwar models simply aren't discredited everywhere; or even where they are partially discredited, they are still present in the different reactions to the financial crisis that we see today.

We do well to recall that it was only a new generation of Anglo-American–inclined economic theorists and policy makers who claimed that planning as such was a failure. Planning—which as we have seen could mean anything, nothing and much in between—lost its monopoly of attraction in England, the U.S. and (for quite different reasons) in Italy and post-communist Europe. Elsewhere, the argument is unresolved, to say the least.

English disillusion with planning was a by-product (not altogether justified) of disillusion with nationalization and the state control of the economy. And that, in turn, stretching a claim that I think is legitimate, was the result of the fact that the achievements of the postwar boom were basically played out by the end of the 1960s. By the 1970s people no longer remembered why you had planning or welfare states in the first place.

The passage of time mattered in another way. The logic of trans-generational welfare states was hard to see in advance. It's one thing to say that we will guarantee that everyone has a job. It's quite a different thing to say that we will guarantee everyone has a pension. This difference comes clear precisely in the 1970s. Fewer people had jobs in that decade and tax revenue was declining, so the growing costs of the social services became a major concern: ever more people were qualifying by age for their long-anticipated benefits. Thus the postwar welfare states collided with the end of the postwar boom they had helped bring about—and the discontents of the 1970s are the outcome.

Just as important is the problem of inflation. Postwar Keynesians were for the most part uninterested in inflation or the related risk of ever-accumulating state debt. They had accepted that full employment was the objective and government expenditure the means—without quite grasping that counter-cyclical policy runs both ways: in good times, you are supposed to cut back. But it's very hard to decrease government expenditure. And so you got increased inflation.

Of course it was not that simple. The origins of the inflation of the 1970s remain in dispute: some were surely external—e.g., the rising oil prices of the decade. But the combination of recession and inflation was disheartening and largely unpredicted. The consequence was that governments appeared to be spending ever larger sums of money to achieve ever fewer objectives.

More broadly, the failure of Soviet planning discredited West European endeavors in the eyes of a new generation of critics. This was the case despite the absence of any historical or logical relationship between the two, and even though west European forms of planning were intended to be, and were, the antidote to communist politics. The interwar myth of Soviet planning success was replaced in the course of the 1970s and '80s by a universally accepted account of socialist planning as utter failure. The implications of this inversion were significant: the failure and the collapse of the Soviet Union undermined not just communism, but a whole progressive narrative of advance and collectivization, in which Soviet planning and western planning were presumptively integrated, at least in the eyes of their admirers.

When that story lost its anchor, much else went adrift.

In your description of both Beveridge and Keynes, you suggest a relationship between economics, ethics and politics. And it seems that what we find in the last quarter of the twentieth century is a renewed belief—which sometimes smacks of the doctrinaire, or even the dogmatic—that you can derive the ethics or politics from the economics.

That's right. Or even if you cannot, it doesn't matter because the core condition of a thriving collectivity is economic output and economic stability and economic growth—and the consequences of that, whether necessary or contingent, are out of your hands.

> *In speaking of the origins of planning, you stressed the prudential*
> *and the ethical considerations. I think a condition for intellectual*
> *influence in these matters was an aesthetic sense. Engels's book on*
> The Condition of the Working Class of England *is very*
> *descriptive. And then, of course, there's a whole genre of Victorian*
> *novel—one thinks of Dickens, but also Elizabeth Gaskell—which*
> *addresses industrialization directly. That literature serves the*
> *function of creating an image of working class suffering, making*
> *society* look *different than it did before.*

The twentieth century saw an echo of that literature in the writing of Upton Sinclair (*The Jungle*), Studs Terkel (*Hard Times*), John Steinbeck (*The Grapes of Wrath*) and others. Note the similarities of approach and theme—in Terkel's case even to the extent of borrowing a Dickensian title.

Today, though we do still experience aesthetic revulsion at poverty, injustice, ill health, our sensibilities are often confined to what we used to call the Third World. We are conscious of poverty and economic injustice—of the sheer *wrongness* of unfair distribution—in places like India, or the slums of Sao Paulo, or in Africa. But we are far less sensitive to comparable maldistributions of resources and life chances in the slums of Chicago, Miami, Detroit, Los Angeles or, indeed, New Orleans.

> *In America, going up in the world means physically moving away*
> *from signs of distress. And so the decline of the city becomes a source*
> *of general decline rather than a stimulus to renewal.*

When Dickens was writing the railway sections of *Little Dorrit*, for example, or when Elizabeth Gaskell was writing *North and South*, both were quite deliberately drawing the attention of their readership back to a social catastrophe which was unfolding before their eyes but from which so many were successfully averting their attention.

We need a similar renewal of attention to what lies under our noses. Today so many of us live in gated communities, physical enclaves that keep one kind of social reality out and also preserve another kind of social reality from intrusion. These enclosed micro-societies reassure their beneficiaries that since they are paying for their own services, they are not responsible for the expenses and demands of the society outside the gates. This makes them reluctant to pay for services and benefits from which they perceive no immediate private gain.

What gets lost here, what is corroded in the distaste for common taxation, is the very idea of society as a terrain of shared responsibilities. Obviously, it's completely disingenuous because when you leave the gated community, you get on the interstate highway, which is a government-provided service that could only possibly be paid for from general taxation and so on. And the police which ultimately guarantee that such pockets of wealth are possible are paid from local taxes.

The decline of the city is crucial here. You're right about that. The rise of the modern city—rather than the medieval town—was exactly contemporary with the rise of the social question. The French geographer Louis Chevalier made the point some fifty years ago: writing of early-nineteenth-century Paris in his *Classes laborieuses et classes dangereuses* (*Working Classes and Dangerous Classes*), he brilliantly demonstrated what happens when a medieval administrative city becomes a modern working class metropolis.

Where once the whole urban community was interdependent, the new industrial center divides its constituent classes. The commercial bourgeoisie who dominate the public life of the town live in growing terror of the very working population on which they depend—but with whom they no longer interact on a daily human basis. The working population become at once the source of wealth and a standing challenge to it. The city splits, held together by common need but also by mutual fear and increasing territorial separation.

Today, we still have the fear and separation—but the sense of common need and shared interest is fast eroding. There are exceptions to that; New York is something of an exception. But the classic city with an upper class, a middle class, a working class and a set of geographical relations which overlay the set of social relations, is largely gone in this country.

> *The city is the place where it's logistically easiest for the state to distribute resources. And the further away from the city you go, the more difficult and expensive it becomes for the state to act, which means that the people who think that they get the least are in fact getting the most. The places, geographically, where people are most disinclined to pay taxes are the ones that are on the dole from the federal government.*

None of the water-starved, western states of the U.S. could survive a year without the American equivalent of what the Europeans think of as regional subsidies. And of course Europeans are no different. Just as Arizona or Wyoming suppose themselves free of governmental intrusion while depending totally upon it, so we have the paradox of Ireland and Slovakia. Between them they were and are among the greatest beneficiaries of regional subsidies from Brussels (financed by the planned or directed economies of France, Germany and the Netherlands) while locally proclaiming the attractions of the free market and minimal regulation.

> *If you told people in South Dakota or Nevada that they are benefiting from the equivalent of the European Union's Regional Development Fund, I'm sure they would be quite upset. But that is, essentially, how the United States works.*

It's worked for quite a long time that way, actually. Imagine the case of the Nebraska corn farmer: of course he benefits hugely from massively distorting subsidies for everything from corn to soybeans to production, as well as from cheap water, cheap gasoline and publicly financed highways. But if he did not benefit from such public largesse, farming (above all family farming) would die; and family farming is a crucial part of America's national identity (this corresponds quite closely to the practice and mythology of French subsidy too, but at least the French acknowledge as much).

The appearance of individual self-reliance is part of the myth of the American frontier. Destroy that or, rather, let it be destroyed, and you destroy part of our roots. This is a defensible and even reasonable political argument—there is no reason in principle why Americans should not pay to maintain whatever they consider most American about their heritage. But as an argument it has nothing to do with capitalism, individualism or the free market. On the contrary, it's an argument for a certain sort of welfare state— not least because of its unquestioned assumption that a certain sort of sustainable individualism requires a good deal of help from the state.

You mentioned the ethical and the prudential sources of social democracy, and I asked you about the aesthetic. It strikes me also that there is a truthfulness question that's important. When we think of Gaskell, or Engels, or Dickens, or Upton Sinclair, we think of certain terms which they introduced which have stuck with us: "hard times," for example. And I wonder if something which is missing today isn't the same willingness or ability of intellectuals to formulate what's actually going on in the economy and in society.

That capacity has come undone in two stages. The first stage, which I would date from the late 1950s, was the self-distancing of intellectuals from a concern with the straightforward, observable injustices of economic life. It seemed as though those observable injustices were rather being overcome, at least in the places intellectuals lived. The focus upon the "down and out in London and Paris," as it might be, seemed almost jejune—you know, "yes,

yes, yes, but it's more complicated than that, the real injustices are," and then something else. Or the real oppression is in the mind, rather than in the unfair distribution of income, or whatever it might be. So left-wing intellectuals became cleverer at finding injustice—and less interested in what seemed rather like the 1930s or, if they were more historically conscious, 1890s style of moral horror at simple economic unfairness and suffering.

More recently, I think we really are the victims of a discursive shift, since the late 1970s, towards economics. Intellectuals don't ask if something is right or wrong, but whether a policy is efficient or inefficient. They don't ask if a measure is good or bad, but whether or not it improves productivity. The reason they do this is not necessarily because they are uninterested in society, but because they have come to assume, rather uncritically, that the point of economic policy is to generate resources. Until you've generated resources, goes the refrain, there's no point having a conversation about distributing them.

This, it seems to me, comes close to a sort of soft blackmail: surely you are not going to be so unrealistic or unworldly or idealistic as to place goals before means? We are accordingly advised that everything begins with economics. But this reduces intellectuals—no less than the workers they are discussing—to rodents on a treadmill. When we talk of increasing productivity or resources, how do we know when to stop? At what point are we sufficiently well-resourced to turn our attention to the distribution of goods? How would we ever know when the time has come to talk about deserts and needs rather than outputs and efficiencies?

The effect of the dominance of economic language in an intellectual culture which was always vulnerable to the authority of "experts" has acted as a brake upon a more morally informed social debate.

Something else strange, I think, happens when intellectuals begin with the economy. And that is, only things which are products are somehow real. And the very nouns that we use have changed, the meaning has changed. If I ask for water at the café down the street, the waiter wants to know which kind of bottled water I want. We all have to drink water. Water is very important. We bathe in it, we want it to be clean. But there is no reason whatsoever for water to be put in bottles. If anything, it's quite harmful. Children's teeth rot for lack of fluoride. You have to use petroleum to make the bottles and you dump oil in the ocean importing water from other continents. And all of this devalues the public good, which is water from the tap, which we had already managed to achieve.

This is a shortcoming of any market economy. Marx observed the fetishization of commodities in the nineteenth century, and he was not the first; Carlyle did as well.

But I do think that it is a particular byproduct of our contemporary cult of privatization: the sense that what is private, what is paid for, is somehow better for just that reason. This is an inversion of a common assumption in the first two thirds of the century, certainly the middle fifty years from the 1930s to the 1980s: that certain goods could only be properly provided on a collective or public basis and were all the better for it.

The transformation of our sensibilities on this account has had all sorts of side effects. When people say, I would rather buy the private product and not be taxed for the public one, it then becomes harder to tax for a public good. This then is a loss for everyone, even the very rich, because the state simply can do certain things better and cheaper than any other entity. The family in the gated community may drink bottled water, but they cook and clean and bathe in public tap water, which no private company would ever find it profitable to provide for them without public guarantees and price supports.

This brings us close to a question which occupied early twentieth-century political economists and social theorists. At what point is it legitimate for a government to simply say that a certain commodity or service is better provided publicly? When is it right to create a natural public monopoly? But since 1980 or so, the question has been posed differently: why should there be any public monopolies? Why should not everything be open to profit? It is that visceral suspicion of any sort of public monopoly in anything that could in principle be rendered private that we live with, or have lived with, for the last twenty-five years. And I don't, by the way, think that it's going to change because of the overhyped crisis in capitalism that we're passing through now. I think what we're going to see more of is the acceptability of government as regulator—but government as monopolizer of certain kinds of goods and services we will not see.

> *Water is a particularly striking example for me because it shows how far you can degenerate civilization and still think that you are progressing by making everything private. The ethic that if you show up somewhere and ask for a drink of water you should be given it is age-old. And the modern version of that, which was prevalent for most of my life in this country, was that there were water fountains in public places. Which are now slowly disappearing.*

The same point holds for other civilizational gains, more recent ones, but which until this last quarter century had also been taken for granted. Americans no longer remember having good public transport, though in many places they once did. In Britain you can see how the privatization of transport changes the society. The Green Line Busses made of me a Londoner, they made of me an English boy, perhaps just as much as school did.

There is nothing like that for a boy in London today. When I was young, I rode the Green Line Busses to school. They were well-tended and pleasant and defined a city with their routes. Today's Green Line Busses are owned and run by "Arriva," the worst of the private companies now responsible for providing train and bus services to British commuters. Their chief purpose appears to be to connect isolated suburbanites with huge shopping malls, often with no reference to the logic of urban geography. There are no cross-London routes at all.

I'd like to push this point back into a more abstract level. It seems to me that in addition to various goods that one could talk about— transport, water, also food, for that matter, or air—there is a basic issue with preserving some categories of economic discourse.

This might be some kind of role for intellectuals who have the Orwellian mission of trying to get terms right, or endorse Aron's idea of preserving the concepts. One category comes to mind since the financial crisis: wealth. If you own a house and that house loses value, you've lost wealth or somebody has lost wealth. Whereas if a finance capital organization makes a bet and loses the bet, it has also lost wealth, as we use the term "wealth" now. Even though there is nothing really attached to it because half of the people making bets, or whatever the percentage would be, have to lose those bets. And bailouts proceeded as though there were no difference between those kinds of wealth, roughly speaking.

Or rather than trying to rescue a word like wealth, one could try to apply a word like planning. It seems to me that finance capitalism gets off a bit easy in its opposition to government planning. After all, finance capitalism is a sort of planning. It's not planning done by one person, and it is organic in a certain way, but it is the way that we allocate capital. And it's not free. The finance sector of the American economy took more than one-third of the corporate profits in 2008. They took 7 percent of wages and salaries.

I would point out, by the way, that if you added to that the rather larger percentage taken by the so-called health-care industry, most of which is, of course, devoted to administering the industry rather than making people well, and subtracted those two from America's economic performance over the last quarter century, the U.S. would be seen to have seriously underper-formed most of the developed world. So a large part of our self-image as an advanced and wealthy society rests upon precisely the distortion you've described.

This raises a debate about risk. A society pays a premium in the form of unfair rewards to people who do nothing for it other than generate paper wealth. The argument for this is that this paper wealth is the formal "grease" beneath the wheels of the real economy. And, so we are told, the only reason people are willing to take the risks involved in generating (or losing) huge amounts of paper wealth is that the rewards are so substantial. There are more complex versions of that argument, but that is its basic form.

Now let us translate that argument into the logic of the casino: which is, after all, what capitalism amounts to at the financial level. Someone bets on a certain outcome. They bet on it either because they have good reason to believe in it, or they wish to believe in it, or they've seen others who they trust bet upon it. They are taking a substantial risk. But the bigger the risk they take in theory, the larger the reward they might recoup.

Imagine if someone walked in and said to the gambler: "you are too big to fail." Or: "we guarantee you that we will absorb X percent of your loss because we, the casino, need you to keep on playing. So please keep on playing with the assurance that your downside is reduced." The argument from risk disappears—and as a result, the casino would soon go out of business.

So let's return to the capital markets: under today's arrangements, the losses of the biggest gamblers are covered sufficiently to ensure that people will, indeed, continue to take the risks but with no downside. Which means the risks they take will be ever less justified. If you don't have to worry about making the wrong decision, then there's a greater chance you will make the wrong decision.

In this sense at least, I am at one with the ultra-marketeers: there is a real threat to the integrity of capitalism if it is too heavily underwritten by government reassurance. We know from experience that state ownership of industrial production can be inefficient because no one worries too much about losing. The proposition has at least as much force in the financial sector.

The gambling comparison is an interesting one not only at the top, at the level of the finance capitalists and the state, but also at the bottom, at the level of society and the businesses and families. That is to say, I think another thing which is happening is that the idea of risk in American society has changed a bit.

Risk, maybe I'm romanticizing, but it used to mean something, like you take a risk because you leave your job to start a business. Or you take a risk because you take a second mortgage on your house in order to invest in a small business. It didn't mean the same thing as just gambling. The housing market in recent years approached a kind of gambling. People were able to acquire things so easily that they were basically just making bets: acting very much like the financial markets themselves, they were purchasing goods they did not need and could not afford on the speculative hope that someone else would relieve them of these goods in the near future.

This coincides with the legitimation of gambling as such. (Which, by the way, strikes me as one of the terms which needs to be preserved, because those who are behind gambling would like to call it "gaming" and make it into something harmless and normal.) But also what happened seems to have required Americans not to understand math. It seems to have required a certain amount of magical thinking about numbers. Which, in some sense, you know, if hundreds of millions of dollars are at stake but they're not yours, it's dangerous in one way. But if tens of thousands of dollars and your life are at stake, that is in a way more dangerous.

I wish I could agree with you about the correlation between American secondary educational incompetence in mathematics and economic illusions. But I think what it really demonstrates is this: the vast majority of human beings today are simply not competent to protect their own interests.

Curiously, this was not at all the case back in the nineteenth century. The kinds of mistakes that people might make to their own detriment were both more straightforward and thus more readily avoided. Assuming you were prudent enough to keep clear of snake-oil salesmen and the outright crook, then the rules about borrowing were so draconian (if only on religious grounds) that many of today's indulgences were simply not available to the common man.

That brings us to gambling. Like debt, it was frowned upon and mostly banned. It was widely and correctly assumed that gambling led to criminality and was thus a social pathology to be avoided. But of course it was also regarded in a long-standing Christian tradition as wrong in itself: money should not beget money.

We could benefit from revisiting that perspective. Whether or not we think gambling is a sin, we can hardly deny that it is a step backwards in social policy: gambling is regressive, selective, indirect taxation. You are basically encouraging the poor to spend money in expectation of wealth, whereas the wealthy, even if they did choose to spend the same amount of money, would not feel the loss.

In its worst form, gambling is now officially encouraged by a number of countries (Britain, Spain) as well as many American states under the guise of public lotteries. Rather than acknowledge the need for certain public facilities—the arts, sport, transport—we now avoid unpopular taxation by covering such expenses from lotteries. Disproportionately, these are played and thus supported by the less-informed and poorer segments of society.

British workers who perhaps have never been inside a theater or an opera or a ballet in their life are now subsidizing out of their proclivity for gambling the cultural activities of a tiny elite whose tax burden has been accordingly reduced. Yet well within living memory the opposite applied: in the social democratic days of the 1940s and 1950s, it was the wealthy and the middle class who were taxed to ensure the availability of libraries and museums for everyone.

This is regression in any sense, encouraged by feckless governments terrified to raise taxes, reluctant to cut services and exploiting the lowest instincts rather than the highest capacities of those who vote for them. I'm perfectly well aware that it's imprudent and ineffective to ban gambling altogether: we know from past experience with alcohol and drugs that such blanket bans can have perverse effects. But it is one thing to acknowledge human imperfection, quite another to exploit it mercilessly as a substitute for social policy.

> *Is modern life really so complicated? What most Americans do is get themselves into lots of credit-card debt. Which if you understood what cumulative interest means, that is, if you had just the most elementary calculus or even just really understood your multiplication tables, maybe you would be able to avoid. The best defense of the working class in general is arithmetic. And that therefore social policy, just looking at it this way, has to include making sure that people can do their own math.*

Well, I certainly believe that. I also believe that in a broader frame, social policy should consist of creating the most educated electorate possible: precisely because the citizenry today are both more exposed to abuse and have more "authority" to abuse themselves than ever before.

But even a well-educated citizenry is not a sufficient protection against an abusive political economy. There has to be a third actor there, beyond the citizen and the economy, which is the government. And the government has to be legitimate: in that it conforms to people's understanding of the basis on which they chose their rulers, and in that its actions correspond to its words.

Once you have that legitimate government, then it seems not only appropriate but actually possible for it to say to people: if you did the math, you'd see that you were being sold a bill of goods. But even if you can't do the math, we're going to tell you that's the case. And we will prohibit you from certain kinds of financial transactions, just as we will prohibit you from driving north on New York City's Fifth Avenue: in your own interest and for the common good.

Here we come to the arguments against the possibility of social democracy, which are of two kinds. One, if you like, structural; the other contingent. The structural argument is that this sense of legitimacy is hard to come by, or even impossible, in a large and diverse country like the United States. Collective trust across generations, occupations, abilities and resources does not come easily to a huge, complex society. So it's not an accident that the most successful social democracies are Norway, Sweden, Denmark, Austria, to some extent Holland, New Zealand etc.: small, homogenous societies.

The contingency argument against the possibility of social democracy says that it was historically possible, but only under circumstances that we cannot reproduce. The combination of the memory of the Great Depression, the experience of fascism, the fear of communism and the postwar boom made social democracy possible, even in quite large societies like France, or West Germany, or Great Britain, or Canada, which is a large society physically if not socially. I don't altogether accept this counterargument—the story was more complicated and the motivations more enduring—but I do respect it.

> *And yet I'm struck by the pickiness of Americans as to when they accept historical arguments and when they don't. So the historical argument that we ought not to have social democracy is taken quite seriously, although the historical argument that social democracy has produced very nice things is not taken seriously.*

> *And I'm also struck by the way that American intellectual life in recent years has become subordinate to European concerns even as prominent American commentators insist that we have soared past Europe. By this I mean that almost all commentary about social policy here in the U.S. sets it in a comparative context: how do we*

fare against Europe? The implication is unavoidable: in certain
respects, at least, we fear that we have entered Europe's shadow.

Almost no one seems to say something like: we're the United States
of America; therefore we ought to be, to borrow a term, a Great
Society. There ought to be a New Deal. Not because social
democracy in Europe is good or bad but because we Americans
could make a wonderful thing ourselves.

From the 1930s to the 1960s, the balance of American social and political argument ran the other way. The default assumption was that if America
could afford to make itself a good society, it should want to do so. Even the
opponents and critics of Johnsonian levels of social investment were mostly
opposing it on, as it were, localized self-interest grounds. If it was too good
for blacks, it was not wanted in the South. If it was too radically redistribu-
tive, it was not wanted by institutions that would be forced to rethink their
recruitment patterns, and so on.

But radical social innovation was not typically opposed on *a priori*
Hayekian grounds, as it might be today. And those who did so incoherently,
like Barry Goldwater, paid a heavy political price. It took twenty years before
the new conservative approach could be integrated into "Reaganism" and
made to look mainstream. Here as so often we encounter an American for-
getfulness about even the very recent American past.

I blame the Left as much as the Right. The Johnsonian rhetoric of collective social purpose, rooted in an American version of Victorian and
Edwardian liberal reformism, sat uncomfortably with the New Left. The latter was much more attracted to self-asserted interests of discrete segments of
society. I would second the contemporary critique of the McGovern-era
Democratic Party: not because it purportedly sought to advance the interests of every hyphenated category you could think of (many of which were in
urgent need of advancing), but because in doing so it undermined its own
rhetorical inheritance and forgot how to speak about the collective society.

The Clintonite welfare reforms of the 1990s were radically at odds with all of the state-centered reforming traditions of both the Anglo-American and the European left-liberal consensus from the 1890s to the 1970s. What they did was reintroduce early industrial notions of a divided citizenry: the citizens who work and the lesser citizens who don't work. Employment thus returns to social policy as the measure of full participation in public affairs: if you don't have a job, you aren't quite a whole citizen. And this was something that three generations of social and economic reformers from the 1910s to the 1960s strove mightily to get away from. Clinton reintroduced exactly that.

> *The politics of hyphenation I think accentuates class divisions.*
> *Feminism, as we've worked it out in this country, serves female*
> *lawyers who make lots of money, it serves female professors, female*
> *university students at some psychological level, maybe—but because*
> *feminism in the United States doesn't begin with maternity leave*
> *and child care, which is the only place I think it could really*
> *sensibly begin for most women, it leaves out the people who are*
> *raising children and especially those who are single mothers.*
> *Likewise the politics of race very successfully, and I'm in favor of*
> *it, brings the black and the Hispanic bourgeoisie into the*
> *institutions of education and then government, and so on. And I'm*
> *sure that's a good thing. But it also separates out the question of*
> *race from the question of class, which is quite a bad thing for many*
> *African Americans.*

American social thought altogether avoids the problem of economically determined social divisions, because Americans find it more comfortable and politically uncontentious to focus on usable divisions of another kind.

But your child-care example is a good one—let us focus upon it for a minute. It's very hard for child care, and more generally for social services designed to facilitate equal opportunity for mothers, to be provided ad hoc, business by business. Any given employer, providing such a resource for his staff, may fear that he is placing himself at an economic disadvantage relative to the person who doesn't provide it. The person who doesn't provide it can either make more money because he doesn't have the cost of providing this service—or he can pay his female workers more money because he's got more cash to hand, allowing them privately, if they can, to find the necessary child care, but meanwhile attracting them away from his lower-paying, social service-providing competitor.

Now in most of Europe, the government provision of tax-paid universal child care gets around this problem. It creates an additional burden upon everyone via taxation, but provides a specific service at no economic cost to a certain class of beneficiaries.

As we well know, there will always be those who take profound offense at the very notion of taxing everyone to benefit some. But it is that very idea which lies at the heart of the modern state. We tax everyone to provide education for some. We tax everyone to provide pensions for some. We tax everyone to provide policemen or firemen from whom, at any given moment, only some people will benefit. We tax to build roads that not everyone will use at the same time. We have (or had) train service to a remote location that seems to benefit the people in that remote location but which together brings all the remote locations into the society, thus making it a better place for everyone.

Now the notion of taxing all to benefit some—or indeed some to benefit all—is absent from the core calculations of American social policy makers. The consequences are clear in the confused reasoning of even the best-intentioned reformers. Take, for example, the feminist line on child care and other facilities from which women might benefit. Rather than suppose that the wider point of the exercise is to revise taxation and social services in such a way as to benefit all, the mainstream feminist position is to seek legislation designed exclusively to advantage women.

It was fallacious in the 1970s for the hyphenated radicals to suppose that pursuing their own interest could be done without affecting the interest of the collectivity as a whole. They echoed, ironically and unconsciously, the very demands of their political opponents. They helped to privatize politics and privatize self-interest.

I'm old-fashioned enough to think that a lot of the American Left is objectively reactionary.

If you want to make an old-fashioned point, you could say this: the fact that so many feminists were themselves drawn from the upper-middle class—where the *only* disadvantage they suffered was precisely that of being female, often no more than a marginal handicap—explains their inability to see that there was a larger class of persons for whom being female was by no means the greatest of their challenges.

Feminism has succeeded in that there are lots of lawyers and businesswomen, and various glass ceilings have been shattered. At that level, it's been a striking success. However, you also have many, many more women at the bottom with families and without men or with economically and socially useless men. They've fallen through the glass floor and are sitting amid the shards and the blood. Their lives, with the long hours of work, the poor or non-existent child care and health care, embody the American sense that anything is possible, but also they reveal very clearly the tragedy of this sort of privatization. And I begin to worry that our American optimism really just serves as a kind of rationalization for not helping people who need help.

The privatization reference is the crucial one. What does "privatization" mean? It removes from the state the capacity and the responsibility for making good the shortcomings in people's lives; it also removes that same set of responsibilities from the conscience of fellow citizens, who no longer feel a shared burden for common dilemmas. All that remains is the charitable impulse derived from an individual sense of guilt towards other suffering individuals.

We have good reason to suppose that this charitable impulse is an ever-less-adequate response to the shortcomings of unequally dispersed resources in wealthy societies. So even if privatization were the economic success claimed for it (and it most decidedly is not), it remains a moral catastrophe in the making.

I'd like to invoke in this context Beveridge's distinction between the warfare state and the welfare state, because it seems that it was warfare in the last, let's say, forty years which made a welfare state or social democracy in the U.S. difficult. The Johnson example is obvious: It was hard to build a Great Society and pay for the Vietnam War. But more recently, after Vietnam, with the development of the all-volunteer army, something very interesting has happened.

The military has itself become a kind of effective welfare organization. That is to say it provides education and upward mobility for lots of people who wouldn't have it otherwise. It also provides state-run hospitals which work rather well—or, at least, did work rather well until the Bush administration cut their funding in the middle of a war so that people couldn't make the argument that I'm making right now.

And so in peacetime the military is a very nice example of state policy which allows upward mobility. But much less so when we're actually fighting a war and sending off these people who are on the margin, and sometimes not even citizens, to die and to kill. At that moment, warfare becomes corporate welfare. The Iraq War redistributed an awful lot of tax money to a very small number of corporate recipients.

In this, as in other respects, the United States sits tangentially to the Western experience as a whole. Elsewhere in the developed West, the warfare states of the early modern and modern era morphed into permanent welfare states. The kinds of government expenditure which would have been unthinkable in peacetime had become unavoidable in wartime—at first during World War I and then definitively after 1939. The things that governments learned that they could do in war they were then obliged to reproduce for peaceful ends. Surprisingly, they found this a remarkably efficient way to achieve their goals, ideological opposition notwithstanding.

America looks rather different, as you say. In the course of what amount to a series of permanent "small wars" dating back to the early 1950s, the U.S. government has borrowed money to fight conflicts it prefers not to acknowledge too openly. The cost of these wars has thus been borne by future generations, either in the form of inflation or else as a charge and limitation on all other public expenditure: welfare and social services above all.

If the warfare state is an acceptable way for conservative Americans to restrict the emergence of welfare politics, this is because war in this country is still not experienced as catastrophe. Vietnam, to be sure, carried social costs: the political class itself was divided, enduring inter-generational cleavages emerged, and foreign policy was stymied for a while by these domestic considerations. But no one to my knowledge argued that this ought to have prompted a rethink of the premises of government and its role in society, the way World War II brought about a political revolution in Great Britain for example.

It is hard to see how this could change. Even at the height of the Iraqi absurdity, a majority of Americans favored huge government expenditure on under-articulated or straightforwardly dishonest military ends, while claiming to believe in reducing taxation across the board, presumably including taxation that was intended to pay for the military expenditure. Americans showed no interest in increasing the role of government in their lives, not realizing that they had just enthusiastically encouraged it to do just that in the most important ways in which government can intervene in their citizens' lives, namely fighting a war. This reveals an American collective cognitive dissonance that is very hard to overcome politically. If there is any cultural reason why the United States will fail to follow the better examples of other Western societies, that will be it.

You've been speaking neutrally about the expressed views of members of American society, which is safer, but their views about the legitimacy of government action arise from American nationalism.

There are two kinds of nationalism. There's the kind of nationalism which says: you and I are both familiar with the postal service and we're also both familiar with our pension plan, and it's the kind of thing that we can talk about on the subway as we're on our way to the office, where neither of us is going to work past seven o'clock because that's the law.

And then there's also the kind of nationalism which says: I pay very few taxes although I'm very rich, and you pay taxes although you're working class, and I am driven to work and you take the bus, and we have very little to talk about—and in any case we never meet. But when something very bad happens, I'm going to find a good patriotic argument why you need to protect my interests and why your children, although not mine, need to kill and die.

Well, let's look at both of these forms of national identification. What strikes me about the latter form is that the reason it either works or doesn't work is cultural rather than political. There are aspects of American cultural assumptions about what it is to be American, what one's expectations as an American might legitimately be, and so on, which are simply very different from what it means to be Dutch. And that would be true even if, as is indeed the case, the two countries are remarkably alike in respect of laws, institutions, economic life and so on.

The cultural difference between Europe and America, and the magic of American nationalism that unites the American rich and poor, is the

American dream. Continental Europeans can generally say with accuracy where they personally rank compared to others in terms of income and are modest in their expectations for retirement. In the U.S. far, far more people believe that they are at the top than actually are, and another large group believes that it will be at the top when they retire. So Americans are much less disposed to look at someone who is very wealthy or very privileged and see injustice: they merely see themselves in some optimistic future incarnation.

Americans think: let's leave the system more or less where it is because I wouldn't want to suffer from high taxes once I became rich. That's a cultural frame of reference that explains a number of things about attitudes toward public expenditure: I won't mind being taxed to pay for a railway system I only occasionally use if I feel that I am being taxed equally with others for a benefit that is in principle shared among us all. I might resent it more if I have the expectation that I will one day be the kind of person who never uses this public facility.

What was brilliant about the construction of welfare states, though, was that the chief beneficiary was the *middle* class (in the European sense of including the professional and skilled elite). It was the middle class whose income was suddenly released because it had access to free schooling and free health care. It was the middle class that gained true private security through public provision of insurance, pensions and the like. The welfare state creates the middle class in that sense, and the middle class then defends the welfare state. Even Margaret Thatcher felt this when she started to talk about privatizing the health service—and discovered that her own middle class voters were the most opposed of all.

The critical part seems to be in creating that middle class in the first place. Without it, you have people who don't want to pay taxes because they want to be rich, and people who don't see the point in paying taxes because they are rich. I see the middle class as being that group which, without enormous wealth, is unconcerned about

*pensions, education, and medical care. By that standard, which is
quite modest really, there is no American middle class.*

*I'm afraid your point about warfare bringing government into our
lives has a stronger formulation. Since the American government is
interventionist abroad if not at home, war creates a certain
perversity. Insisting on fighting wars while refusing to raise taxes
to pay for them was simply a roundabout way of inviting the
Chinese government into our lives. If we're not willing to pay for
our own wars, that means we go into debt to China, with all the
risks to future power and freedom that that entails. It astounded
me that almost no one said this as the Iraq War began.*

There may be an even more profound truth in that. There is a risk that
we are welcoming a kind of Chinese capitalism into American life. The sim-
plest sense in which this is true has been widely noted: China lends the government money, keeps the economy afloat and puts dollars in Americans'
pockets so they can then go out and buy Chinese-made goods.

But there's another dimension. The Chinese government today is
removing itself from economic life except at strategic levels, on the grounds
that maximum economic activity of a certain kind is clearly beneficial in the
short run to China and that regulating it other than for the purposes of keeping out competition would not be in anyone's interests. At the same time it is
an authoritarian state: censorious and repressive. It is an unfree capitalist
society. The United States is not an unfree capitalist society, but the ways in
which Americans conceive of the things they would allow and the things
they would not allow point in a rather similar direction.

Americans would allow the state to do a remarkable range of intrusive
things in order to protect them against "terrorism" or keep threats at a distance. In recent years (and not only in recent years—look at the 1950s, the
1920s or the Alien and Sedition Acts of the 1790s) American citizens have

shown a terrifying unconcern over government abuse of the constitution or repression of rights, so long as they were not themselves directly affected.

But at the same time those same Americans are viscerally opposed to the government playing any role in the economy or their own lives. Although, of course, as we've discussed before, the state intervenes in the economy in a dozen different ways to their advantage, or to someone's advantage, already. There is a sense, in other words, in which Americans are much more disposed, at least, in the logic of their actions to like the idea of Chinese-style capitalism than they are to like the idea of European-style market social democracy. Or is that going too far?

> *Well, it's consistent with a certain nightmare scenario, one which*
> *is made more likely by the use of economic terminology rather than*
> *political terminology. One of the terms that goes unchallenged, and*
> *you've mentioned this as well, is the idea of "global market forces."*
> *Where "global market forces" is more and more a close*
> *approximation of what the Chinese do. Or, worse yet, what they*
> *would like for us to do.*

This takes us back past the social democratic years of the mid-century, to the nineteenth-century agreement between left and right about the market. The notion was that in the final analysis, the market has to be left to its own devices: either because it works for the best in the long run, or else because it must be left to drive itself into the ground if it is ever to be replaced by something better. But this dichotomy is as false today as it was when it dominated "communism vs. capitalism" debates in decades past.

The defect of the all-or-nothing view of global market forces is that it makes it impossible for individual states to operate social policies of their own choosing: of course, for some people this is a desirable and even an intended outcome. We have now become so used to this assumption that the first argument against social democracy—or even simple economic regulation—is that global competition and the struggle for markets renders this impossible.

Following this logic, if Belgium, to pick a random case, decided to arrange its economic and social norms such that its workers were better looked after than the workers of Romania or Sri Lanka, then it would simply lose jobs to Romania and Sri Lanka. So like it or not, European socialism, as the egregious Tom Friedman once put it, would be defeated by Asian capitalism. A prospect that Friedman, a true determinist, rejoiced in—but which, if true, would prove extraordinarily unpleasant for all parties. However, it is not obvious to me that the proposition actually is true. It is certainly not consistent with recent experience.

Think of what happened after 1989. Back then the argument used to be made that Western European social democracy would be wiped out at the hands of Eastern European free market capitalism. The skilled workers of the Czech Republic or Hungary or Poland in any given field would undercut the high wages and other benefits of Western workers: jobs would all be sucked east.

In practice, such a process lasted ten years at most. By that time, those same jobs in Hungary or the Czech Republic were now under threat by cheap competition from Ukraine, Moldova and so on. The reason should have been obvious to the market's own advocates: in an open international economy, given free collective bargaining and freedom of movement, even the cheaper producers would eventually end up paying costs comparable to those of their more expensive western competitors.

The choice—which most of these countries now face—is either consensual regulation on wages, hours, conditions and so forth; or else acceptance of de facto protection. The alternative would be beggar-my-neighbor policies of cutthroat competition and devaluation.

If Belgium started to go under because Sri Lanka was getting its jobs, no Belgian government could simply say we've got no choice but to reduce wage levels to those of Sri Lanka or remove all the wonderful benefits we have because they render us uncompetitive with Sri Lanka. Why? Because politics trumps economics. Any government so compliant with the "necessities" of globalization would be voted out of office at the very next election by a party committed to rejecting them. And so the politics of self-interest in developed countries will work against the presumed economic logic of the global market each time.

And, just as remarkably, note that politics can find a way in economics. The standard of living in most of Western Europe, with the exception of Britain, has only improved since 1989, and that by a great deal. And of course the standard of living in Eastern Europe has improved as well.

> *There's another kind of answer to the argument from "global market forces": that some of the things which seem to be political concessions to the working class or the poor are actually justifiable in purely budgetary or economic terms. One of them is public health care. The state that is responsible for health care is better (as we know) than the private sector at keeping costs down. And because the state is thinking about long-term budgets rather than quarterly profits, the best way to keep costs down is to keep people healthy. So where there is public health care there is intense attention to prevention.*

Avner Offer, the Oxford economist, wrote a very interesting book recently showing that this was true in many other areas too. That in fact, the self-interest of a well-regulated, stable capitalism lay precisely in limiting the consequences of its own success. Only because you do have universal health care can businesses operate efficiently. They can also, for what it's worth, make people redundant without depriving them of a decent level of medical coverage—the equivalent of joblessness with lack of access to health care is something no society should ever accept.

It's also been shown, and illustrated again and again, that societies with extreme forms of dysfunctional income or resource distribution become societies in which eventually the economy is threatened by social imbalance. So that it's not just that it's good for the economy or that it's good for workers, but it's good for some abstraction called capitalism not to push the logic of its own malfunction too far. This was accepted in America for quite a long time. The gaps separating wealthy and poor in the 1970s in this country were not radically out of line with those familiar to the wealthier countries of Western Europe.

Today, they are. The United States exhibits a growing chasm separating the wealthy few from the impoverished or insecure many; between opportunity and its absence, between advantage and dispossession and so on, something that has of course characterized backward and impoverished societies throughout recorded time. What I have just said of the U.S. would be an accurate description of Brazil today, for example, or Nigeria (or, more to the point, China). But it would not be an accurate description of any European society west of Budapest.

> *The odd thing about the moral discourse in contemporary America is that it starts in the wrong place. We should ask what we as a nation want, what a social good is, and then figure out whether the state or the market is better in producing or generating it. Instead, if government is good at something, a strong argument is always presented that this thing is contaminated by its association with government. But what if we really started honestly with the thing itself? Health, for example. Who doesn't like health?*

Money makes goods measurable. It blurs any discussion as to their respective standing in an ethical or normative conversation about social purposes. I think it would serve us all well to "kill all the economists" (to paraphrase Shakespeare): very few of them add to the sum of social or scientific knowledge, but a substantial majority of the profession contributes actively to confusing their fellow citizens about how to think socially. The exceptions are well known, so we could perhaps excuse them.

Your point, however, about social goods is an interesting one. There are two kinds of questions. The first, of course, is simply the problem of determining what constitute social goods. But once you decide what a social good is, there's a different question, which is how is it best delivered. It's perfectly coherent in principle to decide that health is something that all people should have, but that it's best delivered privately in a profit-based market. I don't believe that for a minute, but it is not logically incoherent and is subject to testing.

But what is the most exemplary way to provide something, the way which makes clear that it is a social good? After privatization, what used to be a uniform color for British trains became a kaleidoscope of logos and advertisements. This made it very clear that rail transport was not a public service. Now, whether or not the trains all run on time, and just as efficiently and safely whether private or public, doesn't detract from the fact that what you've lost is a sense of the collective service that we commonly own and in the benefits of which we share. That's one of the things to be taken into account when asking how it should be provided.

> *I think one of the issues in practice is the demonstration that the state can in fact deliver certain goods. And I think a lot of American politics hangs thereby. The Republicans make the argument that the state is unable to deliver. And they prove it by not providing those things or by spoiling them when they do exist, like veterans' hospitals during the Iraq War. Amtrak is another example: a kind of zombie train system which is kept lurching along to demonstrate that public transportation is and must always be dysfunctional.*

I believe that in order to convince people of the need for the state to provide something, you need a crisis: a crisis brought about by the absence of that provision. People in the aggregate will never take it on credit that a service for which they only have occasional need should be made permanently available. Only when it is inconveniently unavailable for *them* can the case be made for universal provision.

The social democracies are among the wealthiest societies in the world today, and not one of them has moved remotely in the direction of anything resembling a return to the German-style authoritarianism that Hayek saw as the price they would pay for handing initiative to the state. So we do know that the two strongest arguments against a state engaged in constructing a good society—that it can't work economically and that it must lead to dictatorship—are simply wrong.

For the sake of argument I would concede that societies which did fall to authoritarianism were often heavily dependent upon the initiative of the state. So we cannot simply dismiss Hayek's case. And, in a similar vein, we must acknowledge the reality of economic constraints. Social democracies can no more spend themselves into utopia than can any other political form. But this is no grounds for dismissing them. It merely confirms that they should be included in any rational discussion of the future of market economies.

Life, liberty and the pursuit of happiness. The people in west European welfare states report higher levels of happiness than we do, and they're certainly healthier and living longer at this point. It's hard to believe that any society actually wants its members to go back to pre-Hobbes: have lives that are solitary, poor, nasty, brutish and short.

The case in America against social democracy, and it is a real argument, has to be around liberty. But even then, there are ways in which American society is unfree because of the absence of certain public goods. And some of them can be uncontroversially provided. Like city parks. You know, if you can't go somewhere safe and sit down when you're tired, you're less free than someone who can.

What Europeans have that Americans have long lacked is security: economic security, physical security, cultural security. In today's increasingly open world, in which neither governments nor individuals can guarantee themselves against competition or threat, security is fast becoming a social good in its own right. How we provide that security, and at what cost to our liberties, is going to be a central question of the new century. The European response is to focus on what we have come to call "social" security; the Anglo-American response has preferred to confine itself to search and seizure. It remains to be seen which will be more effective in the longer run.

Semantically, it's interesting how in American English "social
security" and "national security" are entirely different things.
Whereas in political practice, I'm sure it's the case that people who
feel secure about various aspects of their lives are less threatened by
external shocks. I think Americans are vulnerable to the politics of
terror precisely because it removes the one sense in which they do
think they are secure, namely—

Physically. I think that's absolutely right. We have reentered an age of
fear. Gone is the sense that the skills with which you enter a profession or job
would be the relevant skills for your working lifetime. Gone is the certainty
that you could reasonably expect a comfortable retirement to follow from a
successful working career. All of these demographically, economically, statis-
tically legitimate inferences from present to future—which characterized
American and European life in the postwar decades—have been swept away.

So the age of fear we now live in is fear of an unknown future, as well as
fear of unknown strangers who might come and drop bombs. It's fear that
our government cannot any longer control the circumstances of our lives. It
can't make us a gated community against the world. It's lost control. That
paralysis of fear, which Americans I think experience very deeply, was reinforced by the realization that the one security they thought they had they
now don't. This was why many Americans were willing to throw in their
lot with Bush for eight years: offering support to a government whose
appeal rested exclusively upon the mobilization and the demagogic exploitation of fear.

It seems to me that the resurgence of fear, and the political consequences
it evokes, offer the strongest arguments for social democracy that one could
possibly make: both as a protection for individuals against real or imagined
threats to their security, and as a protection for society against very likely
threats to its cohesion, on the one hand, and to democracy on the other.

Remember that in Europe above all, those who have been most successful in mobilizing such fears—fears of strangers, of immigrants, of economic

uncertainty or violence—are primarily the conventional, old-fashioned demagogic, nationalist, xenophobic politicians. The structure of American public life makes it harder for people like that to get a purchase on the government
as a whole, one of the ways in which the U.S. has been uniquely fortunate.
But the contemporary Republican Party has begun to mobilize just these
fears in recent times and may well ride them back to power.

The twentieth century was not necessarily as we have been taught to see
it. It was not, or not only, the great battle between democracy and fascism, or
communism versus fascism, or left versus right, or freedom versus totalitarianism. My own sense is that for much of the century we were engaged in
implicit or explicit debates over the rise of the state. What sort of state did
free people want? What were they willing to pay for it and what purposes did
they wish it to serve?

In this perspective, the great victors of the twentieth century were the
nineteenth-century liberals whose successors created the welfare state in all
its protean forms. They achieved something which, as late as the 1930s,
seemed almost inconceivable: they forged strong, high-taxing and actively
interventionist democratic and constitutional states which could encompass
complex mass societies without resorting to violence or repression. We
would be foolish to abandon this heritage carelessly.

So the choice we face in the next generation is not capitalism versus
communism, or the end of history versus the return of history, but the politics of social cohesion based around collective purposes versus the erosion
of society by the politics of fear.

*Can a case be made? If that is the question, does it matter what
intellectuals think about it? Is it worth arguing? Our two
preoccupations throughout our conversation have been history and
individuals, the past and the ways people made the past open
morally or intellectually. Is there an opening here? Social
democracy does seem to be a really tricky case in the U.S. Or maybe
generally.*

I mean, even if you look at Europe, the one place where it has come about on a large scale, you could say well, the social democrats made a compromise with the liberals after the First World War, or around the time of the First World War, and then the Christian Democrats made a compromise with the social democrats, or really took up their agenda, after the Second World War, as the Americans, meanwhile, made a compromise with some of the Europeans in the form of the Marshall Plan. Which would suggest that you can't do the whole thing—

Without two world wars.

Without a couple of world wars and a certain divine legitimation from abroad at the end of it. But no one will defeat us in a war fought on our continent, and no one will offer us a Marshall Plan. What we do, whether it's create health care, or sell the country to China, we do to ourselves.

That's not an argument for not trying to make the case. But it is an argument for making the case historically.

The whole story of the United States is one of understandable if misplaced optimism. But much of the grounds for that optimism—for the unique good fortune of America which led Goethe to his famous observation regarding America's luck—are now behind us.

Countries, empires, even the American empire, have histories and these histories have a certain shape to them. Some of what people long took to be deep truths about the United States turn out to be historical chance: combinations of space, time, demographic opportunity and world events. The boom years of American industrial society did not last more than a couple of decades and much the same now turns out to have been true for postwar American consumer society too. If we look at the history of the past two decades we see something quite different: a story of American sociological and economic stagnation camouflaged by extraordinary opportunities for a tiny minority, and which therefore average out as an appearance of continuing growth.

The United States has changed, and it is important that we see that change as opening up possibilities for discussion and improvement rather than closing them off. Where the old optimism and overconfidence once worked to our advantage, it is now a handicap. We are in decline, but burdened with the rhetoric of endless possibility: a dangerous combination, since it encourages inertia.

As I have noted already, the U.S. has been unfortunate in the absence of truly cathartic crisis. Neither the Iraq war of 2003 nor the financial implosion of 2008 have served that function. Americans are confused and angry that so much seems amiss, but not yet frightened enough to do something about it—or produce a political leader capable of moving them in that direction. In some curious ways, it is because we are such an old country—our constitution and institutional arrangements are among the most antiquated of the advanced societies—that we cannot overcome these hurdles.

No intellectual engaging in American public debate will get very far by confining himself to European examples or European questions. So if I were to ask Americans to reflect on the attractions of social democracy *for them*, I would begin with properly American considerations. *Cui bono?* Who benefits from this? The issues of risk, fairness and justice that are typically invoked in America for regressive social policy need to be invoked for progressive social policy.

It's no good saying that it's wrong that America has a bad transport policy or that we should invest more heavily in universal health care: nothing is good in and of itself in this country, not even health and transport. There has to be a story, and it has to be an American story. We need to be able to convince our fellow citizens of the virtues of mass transit or universal health care or indeed of more equitable (i.e., higher) taxation. We need to remake the argument about the nature of the public good.

This is going to be a long road. But it would be irresponsible to pretend that there is any serious alternative.

AFTERWORD

When Tim Snyder first approached me, in December 2008, to propose a series of conversations I was skeptical. Three months after being diagnosed with ALS, I was unsure about my future plans. I had intended to begin work on a new book: an intellectual and cultural history of twentieth-century social thought, which I had been contemplating for some years. But the research involved—not to mention the act of writing itself—was already something that might well prove beyond me. The book itself already existed in my head, and to a substantial extent in my notes. But whether I would ever complete it was unclear.

Moreover, the very concept of such a sustained exchange was unfamiliar to me. Like most public writers, I had been interviewed by the media—but almost always with reference to a book I had published or else to an issue of public affairs. Professor Snyder's proposal was quite different. What he was suggesting was a long series of conversations, recorded and eventually transcribed, which would cover a number of themes that have dominated my work through the years—including the subject matter of my intended book.

We discussed the idea intensely for some time—and I was convinced. In the first place, my neurological disorder was not going to go away and if I wished to continue working as a historian I would need to learn to "talk" my thoughts: amyotrophic lateral sclerosis has no effect on the mind and it is largely painless, so one is free to think. But it paralyzes the limbs: writing becomes at best a secondhand activity. One dictates. This is perfectly efficient, but it does take some adaptation. As an intermediate stage, recorded conversation began to seem a rather practical and even imaginative solution.

But there were other reasons why I agreed to this project. Interviews are one thing, conversations another. You can make something intelligent of even the stupidest question from a journalist; but you cannot have a conversation worth recording with someone who does not know what they are talking about or is unfamiliar with the things that you are trying to convey.

But Professor Snyder, as I already knew, was an unusual case. We are of different generations—we first met when he was still an undergraduate at Brown University and I was visiting there to give a lecture. We also start from very different places: I was born in England and came to this country in middle age; Tim hails from deepest Ohio. And yet we share a remarkable range of common interests and concerns.

Tim Snyder exemplifies something that I have been calling for since 1989: an American generation of scholars of Europe's eastern half. For forty years, from the end of World War II until the fall of communism, the study of Eastern Europe and the Soviet Union in the English-speaking world was largely the affair of refugees from the region. This was not in itself an impediment to first-rate scholarship: thanks to Hitler and Stalin, some of the best minds of our age were expellees or émigrés from Germany, Russia and the lands between. They transformed not only the study of their own countries but the disciplines of economics, political philosophy and much else besides. Anyone who studied the history or politics of the vast swathe of European territories from Vienna to the Urals, from Tallinn to Belgrade, almost inevitably had the good fortune to work under one of these men or women.

But they were a waning resource: retiring for the most part by the mid-1980s, and seemingly irreplaceable. The absence of language teaching in the U.S. (and to a lesser degree in Western Europe), the difficulty of traveling to the communist lands, the impossibility of doing serious research there and perhaps above all the lack of attention to the place in Western universities (resulting in few jobs), had all contributed to discouraging interest among locally born historians.

Despite having no family links or emotional ties to Europe's east, Tim went to Oxford and undertook a doctorate in Polish history—supervised by Timothy Garton Ash and Jerzy Jedlicki and in consultation with Leszek Kołakowski. Over the years he has acquired remarkable facility in the languages of east-central Europe and a familiarity with the countries and the history of the region unmatched in his generation. He has published a unique series of books—of which the most recent, *Bloodlands: Europe Between Hitler and Stalin*, appeared just this year. Moreover, thanks to his first book—*Nationalism, Marxism, and Modern Central Europe: A Biography of Kazimierz Kelles-Krauz (1872-1905)* [1998]—he is familiar not only with the social and political history of the region, but also the history of political thought in central Europe: an even larger topic and more obscure still for most western readers.

If I were going to "talk" the twentieth century, I was clearly going to need someone who was not only able to interrogate me about my own area of expertise but could bring to the conversation a comparable knowledge of the areas in which I claim only indirect familiarity. I have written about central and Eastern Europe at some length. But with the exception of Czech (and German), I cannot claim any knowledge of the region's languages; nor have I done primary research there, despite frequent travels. My own scholarship was initially confined to France before expanding to most of Western Europe and to the history of political ideas. Professor Snyder and I were thus ideally complementary.

We share not only historical interests but political concerns. Despite generational differences, we experienced the post-1989 "locust years" with similar disquiet: first the optimism and hope of the "Velvet Revolution," then the dispiriting smugness of the Clinton years and finally the catastrophic policies and practices of the Bush-Blair era. In foreign policy and domestic policy alike, the decades since the Fall of the Wall seemed to us to have been squandered: in 2009, despite the optimism provoked by the election of Barack Obama, we were both anxious about the future.

What had become of the lessons, memories and achievements of the twentieth century? What remained and what could be done to retrieve them? All around it was assumed—by contemporaries and students alike—that the twentieth century was now behind us: a squalid record, best forgotten, of dictatorship, violence, authoritarian abuse of power and suppressed individual rights. The twenty-first century, it was asserted, would do better—if only because it would be grounded in a minimal state, a "flat world" of globalized advantage to all and unrestricted freedoms for the market.

As our conversations unfolded, two themes emerged. The first was more narrowly "professional": a record of two historians discussing recent history and trying to make some sense of it in retrospect. But a second set of concerns kept intruding: what have we lost in putting the twentieth century behind us? What of the recent past is best left behind us, and what might we hope to retrieve and use in building a better future? These are more engaged debates, in which contemporary concerns and personal preferences necessarily intrude upon academic analysis. They are in that sense less professional, but no less important for that. The result was a remarkably lively series of exchanges: I could not have hoped for better.

This book "talks" the twentieth century. But why a century? It would be tempting to simply dismiss the concept as a convenient cliché, and rework our chronologies according to other considerations: economic innovation, political change or cultural shifts. But this would be a little disingenuous. Precisely because it is a human invention, the arrangement of time by decades or centuries matters in human affairs. People take turning points seriously, as a result of which those turning points acquire some significance.

Sometimes this is a matter of chance: seventeenth-century Englishmen were very conscious of the transition from the sixteenth to seventeenth centuries because it coincided with the death of Elizabeth and accession to the throne of James I—a genuinely significant moment in English political affairs. Much the same was true of 1900. For the English above all—it immediately preceded the death of Victoria, who had ruled for 64 years and given her name to an age—but also for the French, acutely conscious of cultural shifts which collectively formed an era in their own right: the fin-de-siècle.

But even if nothing much happens, these secular milestones almost always form, in retrospect, a reference point. When we speak of the nineteenth century, we know what we are talking about precisely because the era has taken on a distinctive set of qualities—and had done so long before its end. No one supposes that "on or around 1800" the world changed in some measurable way. But by 1860, it was perfectly clear to contemporaries what distinguished their era from that of their eighteenth-century forebears—and these distinctions came to matter in peoples' understanding of their times. We must take them seriously.

So what of the twentieth century? What can we say about it—or is it, as Zhou Enlai is said to have wittily observed of the French Revolution, too soon to tell? We don't have the option of postponing a response, because the twentieth century above all has been labeled, interpreted, invoked and castigated more than any other. The best known recent account of it—by Eric Hobsbawm—describes the "short twentieth century" (from the Russian Revolution of 1917 through the collapse of Communism in 1989) as an "age of extremes." This rather gloomy—or, at any rate, disabused—version of events is echoed in the work of a number of young historians: see as a representative case Mark Mazower, who entitled his account of the European twentieth century *Dark Continent*.

The problem with such otherwise credible summaries of a grim record is precisely that they cleave too closely to the way people experienced the events at the time. The era began with a catastrophic world war and ended in the collapse of most of the belief systems of the age: it can hardly expect fond treatment in retrospect. From the Armenian massacres through Bosnia, from the rise of Stalin to the fall of Hitler, from the western front through Korea, the twentieth century is an unremitting tale of human misfortune and collective suffering from which we have emerged sadder but wiser.

But if we do not start from a narrative of horror? In retrospect but not only in retrospect, the twentieth century saw remarkable improvements in the general condition of humankind. As a direct consequence of medical discoveries, political change and institutional innovation, most people in the world lived longer, healthier lives than anyone could have foreseen in 1900. They were also, strange as it may seem in the light of what I have just written, safer—at least most of the time.

Perhaps this should be thought of as a paradoxical quality of the age: within many established states, life improved dramatically. But because of an unprecedented rise in interstate conflicts, the risks associated with war and occupation increased strikingly. Thus from one perspective, the twentieth century simply continued the improvements and advances on which the nineteenth century congratulated itself. But from another, it was a dispiriting reversion to the international anarchy and violence of the seventeenth century—before the Westphalian settlement (1660) stabilized the international system for two and a half centuries.

The meaning of events as they unfolded for contemporaries looked very different from the way they appear to us now. This may sound obvious, but it is not. The Russian Revolution, and the subsequent expansion of communism to east and west, forged a convincing narrative of necessity in which capitalism was doomed to defeat—whether in the near future or at some unspecified moment to come. Even for those who despaired at such a prospect, it seemed by no means unlikely and its implications gave shape to the age.

This much we can grasp readily enough—1989 is not so far away that we have forgotten how plausible the communist prospect seemed to so many (at least until they experienced it). What we have altogether forgotten is that the most credible alternative to communism in the years between the wars was not the liberal capitalist west but *fascism*—particularly in its Italian form, which emphasized the relationship between authoritarian rule and modernity while abjuring (until 1938) the racism of the Nazi version. By the coming of the Second World War, there were many more people than we now like to think for whom the choice of fascism or communism was the one that mattered—with fascism a strong contender.

Since both forms of totalitarianism are now defunct (institutionally if not intellectually) we have trouble recalling a time when they were far more credible than the constitutional democracies which they jointly despised. Nowhere was it written that the latter would win the battle of hearts and minds, much less wars. In short, while we are right to suppose that the twentieth century was dominated by the threat of violence and ideological extremism, we cannot make sense of it unless we understand that these appealed to many more people than we like to suppose. That liberalism would in time emerge victorious—albeit in large measure thanks to its reconstruction on very different institutional foundations—was one of the truly unexpected developments of the age. Liberalism—like capitalism—proved surprisingly adaptable: why this should have been so is one of the main themes of our book.

To non-historians, it would appear advantageous to have lived through the events one is narrating. The passage of time creates handicaps: material evidence may be scant, the worldview of our protagonists may be alien to us, habitual categories ("Middle Ages," "Dark Ages," "Enlightenment") may mislead more than they explain. Distance too can be a handicap: unfamiliarity with languages and cultures can lead even the most assiduous astray. Montesquieu's Persians may see deeper into a culture than the locals, but they are not infallible.

However, familiarity brings its own dilemmas. The historian may allow biographical insights to color analytical dispassion. We are taught that scholars should stay out of their writing, and on the whole this is prudent advice— witness the consequences when the historian becomes more important (at least in his own eyes) than the history. But we are all products of history and carry with us the prejudices and memories of our own lifetimes, and there are occasions when these may be put to some use.

In my own case, born in 1948, I am a virtual contemporary of the history I have been writing in recent years. I observed at least some of the most interesting events of the past half century firsthand. This does not guarantee an objective perspective or even more reliable information; however, it facilitates a certain freshness of approach. But being there invites a degree of engagement lacking in the detached scholar: I think this is what people mean when they describe my writing as "opinionated."

And why not? A historian (or indeed anyone else) without opinions is not very interesting, and it would be strange indeed if the author of a book about his own time lacked intrusive views on the people and ideas who dominated it. The difference between an opinionated book and one which is distorted by the author's prejudices seems to me this: the former acknowledges the source and nature of his views and makes no pretense at unmitigated objectivity. In my own case, both in *Postwar* and in more recent memoiristic writings, I have taken care to ground my perspective in my time and place of birth—my education, family, class and generation. None of these should be construed as an explanation much less an apology for distinctive interpretations; they are there to provide the reader with a means of assessing and contextualizing them.

No one, of course, is simply a product of their times. My own career sometimes tracks intellectual and academic trends, sometimes runs at a tangent to them. Growing up in a Marxist family I was largely immune to the excessive enthusiasms of my New Left contemporaries. By spending the equivalent of two years in Israel, taken up with Zionism, I was only indirectly affected by some of the wilder enthusiasms of the 1960s. I am grateful to Tim for bringing these variations to light: they were quite obscure to me and indeed I confess I had paid them relatively little attention hitherto.

By studying French history at Cambridge—a hotbed of new scholarship in the history of ideas and English historiography but largely moribund when it came to contemporary European history—I was left to go my own way. As a consequence, I never became part of a "school" in the way of my contemporaries who worked with Sir John Plumb at Cambridge or Richard Cobb in Oxford. I thus became by default what I had always been by affinity: something of an outsider to the professionalizing world of academic history.

There are downsides to this, just as there are disadvantages to joining a socio-academic elite from the outside. One is always a little suspicious of the "insiders," with their bibliographies, methods and inherited practices. This proved more of a disadvantage in America, where professional conformism is valued more highly than it is (or was) in England. I would often be asked at Berkeley and elsewhere what I thought of such-and-such a book which had taken my younger colleagues by storm and would have to admit that I had never heard of it: I never worked my way through "the literature of the field." Conversely, those same colleagues would be taken aback to discover that I was reading political philosophy when my official "slot" was Social History. When I was young, this made me quite insecure, but in middle age it was a point of pride.

Looking back, I am very glad that I stuck with history and rejected the temptation urged upon me by schoolmasters and dons to become a student of literature or politics. Something about history—the emphasis on explaining change through time, and the open-ended character of the subject matter—appealed to me at the age of thirteen and appeals to me still. When I finally got around to writing a narrative history of my own times I was quite convinced that this was the only way to make sense of them, and I remain as convinced as ever.

One of the elderly dons who taught me at Cambridge once upbraided me for my fascination with physical and geological structures (I was at work on the study of socialism in Provence and very taken with the importance of landscape and weather): "Geography," he informed me, "is about maps. History is about chaps." I have never forgotten this, both because it is self-evidently true—we make our own history—but also because it is so palpably false: the setting in which we make that history cannot be taken as given and requires full and affectionate description, in which maps might well play a central role.

Indeed, the distinction map/chap, while self-evidently real, is also misleading. We are all the products of maps, real and metaphorical. The geography of my childhood—the places I went, the things I saw—shaped the person I became no less than my parents or teachers. But the "map" of my youth and adolescence also matters. Its distinctively Jewish but also very

English qualities; the South London of the 1950s—still redolent of Edwardian *mores* and relations, and where place counted for so much (I was from Putney, not neighboring Fulham): without these coordinates, what came later is hard to explain. The Cambridge of the 1960s, with its mix of *noblesse oblige* and meritocratic upward mobility; the academic world of the 1970s, with its unstable compound of decaying Marxism and personalist enthusiasms: all of these are the context for my writings and subsequent trajectory, and anyone interested in making sense of these would probably find that map a serviceable guide.

If I had not written a dozen or so books and hundreds of essays of a deliberately detached character, I might worry that these conversations and reflections were a trifle solipsistic. I have not written an autobiography, though in recent months I have published sketches for a memoir, and I remain quite convinced that the proper default mode for the historian is rhetorical invisibility. But having been encouraged to intrude a little on my own past, I confess that I find it rather helpful in making sense of my contribution to the study of other pasts. I hope that others may feel likewise.

New York, July 5, 2010

WORKS DISCUSSED

Note: This is not a bibliography in the conventional sense, since this book arises from a conversation. It is a list of full references of works to which the authors refer, in accessible editions when possible. The date in brackets is that of original publication.

Agulhon, Maurice. *La République au village: les populations du Var de la Révolution à la Seconde République*. Paris: Plon, 1970.

Annan, Noel. *Our Age: Portrait of a Generation*. London: Weidenfeld & Nicholson, 1990.

Arendt, Hannah. *Eichmann in Jerusalem: A Report on the Banality of Evil*. New York: Penguin Books, 2006 [1963].

___. *The Human Condition*. Chicago: University of Chicago Press, 1998 [1958].

___. *Origins of Totalitarianism*. New York: Harcourt, Brace, Jovanovich, 1951.

Arnold, Matthew. *Culture and Anarchy: An Essay in Political and Social Criticism*. Cambridge: Chadwyck-Healey, 1999 [1869].

Arnold, Matthew. "Dover Beach," in *New Poems*. London: Macmillan and Co., 1867.

Aron, Raymond. *Introduction á la philosophie de l'histoire. Essai sur les limites de l'objectivité historique*. Paris: Gallimard, 1986 [doctoral dissertation, 1938].

Baldwin, Peter, ed. *Reworking the Past: Hitler, the Holocaust, and the Historians' Debate*. Boston: Beacon Press, 1990.

Benda, Julien. *La trahison des clercs*. Introduction by André Lwoff. Paris: B. Grasset, 1977 [1927].

Berlin, Isaiah. "On Political Judgment." *The New York Review of Books*, October 3, 1996.

Beveridge, William. *Full Employment in a Free Society*. London: Allen and Unwin, 1944.

Browning, Christopher R. *Ordinary Men: Reserve Police Battalion 101 and the Final Solution in Poland*. New York: Harper Perennial, 1998 [1992].

Buber-Neumann, Margarete. *Under Two Dictators: Prisoner of Stalin and Hitler.* Translated by Edward Fitzgerald. Introduction by Nikolaus Wachsmann, London: Pimlico, 2008 [1948].

Čapek, Karel. *Talks with T .G. Masaryk.* Translated by Dora Round. Edited by Michael Henry Heim. North Haven, Conn.: Catbird Press, 1995 [1928–1935].

Churchill, Winston. *Boer War: London to Ladysmith via Pretoria and Ian Hamilton's March.* London: Pimlico, 2002 [1900].

___. *Marlborough: His Life and Times.* New York: Scribner, 1968 [1933–1938].

___. *My Early Life: A Roving Commission.* London, 1930.

___. *The World Crisis*, vols. 1–5. New York: Charles Scribner's Sons, 1923–1931.

Davies, Norman. *Europe: A History.* New York: Oxford University Press, 1996.

___. "The New European Century." *The Guardian,* December 3, 2005.

Deutscher, Isaac. *The Non-Jewish Jew and Other Essays.* Oxford: Oxford University Press, 1968.

___. *The Prophet Armed: Trotsky, 1879–1921.* New York: Oxford University Press, 1954.

___. *The Prophet Outcast: Trotsky, 1929–1940.* New York: Oxford University Press, 1963.

___. *The Prophet Unarmed: Trotsky, 1921–1929.* New York: Oxford University Press, 1959.

Dickens, Charles. *Hard Times.* Dover Classics, 2001 [1853].

Eliot, T. S. "The Wasteland," [1922] in *Collected Poems, 1909–1962.* New York: Harcourt Brace & Company, 1963.

Engels, Friedrich. *Anti-Dühring: Herr Eugen Dühring's Revolution in Science.* New York: International Publishers, 1972 [1878].

___. *The Condition of the Working Class in England.* Translated by W. O. Henderson and W. H. Chaloner. Stanford: Stanford University Press, 1968 [1887].

___. *Socialism: Utopian and Scientific.* Translated by Edward Aveling. Westport, Conn.: Greenwood Press, 1977 [1880].

Friedländer, Saul. *The Years of Extermination: Nazi Germany and the Jews, 1939–1945.* New York: Harper Perennial, 2008.

Furet, François. *Le passé d'une illusion.* Paris: Robert Laffont/Calmann-Lévy, 1995.

___. *Penser la Révolution française.* Paris: Gallimard, 2007 [1978].

Garton Ash, Timothy. *The Polish Revolution: Solidarity.* New Haven, Conn.: Yale University Press, 2002 [1983].

Gaskell, Elisabeth. *North and South.* New York, Penguin, 2003 [1855].

Gibbon, Edward. *The Decline and Fall of the Roman Empire.* New York: Modern Library, 1932 [1776–1788].

Ginzburg, Evgeniia. *Into the Whirlwind.* Translated by Paul Stevenson and Manya Harari. London: Collins, Harvill, 1967.

___. *Within the Whirlwind.* Translated by Ian Boland. New York: Harcourt Brace Jovanovich, 1981.

Goldsmith, Oliver. *The Deserted Village.* Introduction by Vona Groarke. Oldcastle, Co. Meath: Gallery Books, 2002 [1770].

Grass, Günther. *Crabwalk.* Translated by Krishna Winston. New York: Harcourt, 2002.

Gross, Jan. *Fear: Anti-Semitism in Poland after Auschwitz: An Essay in Historical Interpretation.* New York: Random House, 2006.

___. *Neighbors: The Destruction of the Jewish Community in Jedwabne, Poland.* Princeton: Princeton University Press, 2001 [2000].

___. *Polish Society Under German Occupation: The Generalgouvernement, 1939–1944.* Princeton: Princeton University Press, 1979.

___. *Revolution from Abroad: The Soviet Conquest of Poland's Western Ukraine and Western Belorussia.* Princeton: Princeton University Press, 2002 [1988].

Grossman, Vasilii Semenovich. "Treblinka Hell," in *The Road.* Translated by Robert Chandler. New York: New York Review of Books, 2010 [1945].

Havel, Václav. "The Power of the Powerless," [1979] in *From Stalinism to Pluralism: A Documentary History of Eastern Europe since 1945.* Edited by Gale Stokes. New York: Oxford University Press, 1996.

Hayek, Friedrich. *The Road to Serfdom.* New York: Routledge, 2001 [1944].

Hobsbawm, Eric J. *The Age of Extremes: The Short Twentieth Century, 1914–1991.* London: Vintage Books, 2006.

___. *The Age of Revolution: 1789–1848.* New York: New American Library, 1962.

___. *Interesting Times: A Twentieth-Century Life.* London: Allen Lane, 2002.

Hoggart, Richard. *The Uses of Literacy.* Introduction by Andrew Goodwin. New Brunswick, N.J.: Transaction Publishers, 1998 [1957].

Hook, Sydney. *Out of Step: An Unquiet Life in the 20th Century.* New York: Harper & Row, 1987.

Hugo, Victor. *Les Châtiments.* Edited by René Journet. Paris: Gallimard, 1998 [1853].

Ingarden, Roman. *Spór o istnienie Świata.* Cracow: Nakł. Polskiej Akademii Umiejętności, 1947.

Judt, Tony. *The Burden of Responsibility: Blum, Camus, Aron, and the French Twentieth Century.* Chicago: University of Chicago Press, 1998.

___. "A Clown in Regal Purple," *History Workshop Journal,* vol. 7, no. 1 (1979).

___. "Could the French Have Won?" Review of *Strange Victory: Hitler's Conquest of France* by Ernest R. May. *The New York Review of Books,* February 22, 2001.

___. "Crimes and Misdemeanors," *The New Republic,* vol. 217, no. 12 (1997).

___. "The Dilemmas of Dissidence," *East European Politics and Societies,* vol. 2, no. 2 (1988).

___. *A Grand Illusion?: An Essay on Europe.* New York: Hill and Wang, 1996.

___. "Israel: The Alternative," *The New York Review of Books,* October 23, 2003.

___. *Marxism and the French Left: Studies in Labor and Politics in France 1830–1982.* Oxford: Clarendon Press, 1986.

___. *Past Imperfect: French Intellectuals, 1944–1956.* Berkeley: University of California Press, 1992.

___. *Postwar: A History of Europe Since 1945.* New York: The Penguin Press, 2005.

___. *Reappraisals: Reflections on the Forgotten Twentieth Century.* New York: The Penguin Press, 2008.

___. *La reconstruction du Parti Socialiste, 1920–26*. Introduction by Annie Kriegel. Paris: Presses de la Fondation nationale des sciences politiques, 1976.

___. *Socialism in Provence, 1871–1914: A Study in the Origins of the Modern French Left*. New York: Cambridge University Press, 1979.

Kafka, Franz. *The Castle*. Translated by Anthea Bell. New York: Oxford University Press, 2009 [1926].

___. *The Trial*. Translated by Mike Mitchell. New York: Oxford University Press, 2009 [1925].

Keegan, John. *The Face of Battle*. New York: Viking Press, 1976.

Kennedy, Paul. *The Rise of the Anglo-German Antagonism, 1860–1914*. London: G. Allen & Unwin, 1980.

Keynes, John Maynard. *The Economic Consequences of the Peace*. London, 1971 [1919].

___. *The General Theory of Employment, Interest, and Money*. London, Macmillan, 1973 [1936].

___. "My Early Beliefs," in *Two Memoirs: Dr. Melchior, A Defeated Enemy, and My Early Beliefs*. Introduction by David Garnett. London: Rupert Hart-Davis, 1949 [1938].

Koestler, Arthur. *Darkness at Noon*. Translated by Daphne Hardy. New York: Bantam Books, 1968 [1940].

___. *The God That Failed*. Edited by Richard Crossman. New York: Harper, 1949.

___. "The Little Flirts of Saint-Germain-des-Prés," in *The Trail of the Dinosaur & Other Essays*. New York: Macmillan, 1955.

___. *Scum of the Earth*. New York: The Macmillan Company, 1941.

___. *Spanish Testament*. London: V. Gollancz Ltd., 1937.

Kołakowski, Leszek. *Main Currents of Marxism: Its Origins, Growth and Dissolution*. Translated by P. S. Falla. New York: Oxford University Press, 1981 [1979].

Kovály, Heda Margolius. *Under a Cruel Star: A Life in Prague, 1941–1968*. New York: Holmes & Meier, 1997 [1973].

Kriegel, Annie. *Aux origines du communisme français: contribution à l'histoire du mouvement ouvrier français*, vols. 1–2. Paris: Mouton, 1964.

___. *Ce que j'ai cru comprendre*. Paris: Robert Laffont, 1991.

Kundera, Milan. *The Book of Laughter and Forgetting*. New York: Knopf, 1980 [1978].

___. "The Tragedy of Central Europe." *New York Review of Books,* April 26, 1984.

Marx, Karl. *Capital: a critique of political economy*, vols. 1–3. Harmondsworth, Eng.: Penguin Books in association with New Left Review, 1976–1981 [1867].

___. *The Civil War in France*. Introduction by Frederick Engels. Chicago: C. H. Herr, 1934 [1871].

___. *The Class Struggles in France, 1848–1850*. New York: International Publishers, 1969 [1850, 1895].

___. *The Eighteenth Brumaire of Louis Bonaparte, with explanatory notes*. New York: International Publishers, 1987 [1852].

___. *Value, Price, and Profit*. Edited by Eleanor Marx Aveling. New York: International Publishers, 1935 [1865].

___. *Wage-labor and Capital*. Introduction by Frederick Engels. Chicago: C. H. Kerr, 1935 [1847].

Marx, Karl, and Friedrich Engels. *The Communist Manifesto: A Modern Edition.* Introduction by Eric Hobsbawm. New York: Verso, 1998 [1848].

Mazower, Mark. *Dark Continent: Europe's Twentieth Century.* New York: Knopf, 1999.

Miłosz, Czesław. *The Captive Mind.* Translated by Jane Zielonko. New York: Vintage Books, 1990 [1953].

Offer, Avner. *The Challenge of Affluence: Self-Control and Well-Being in the United States and Britain since 1950.* New York: Oxford University Press, 2006.

Orwell, George. *Animal Farm.* New York: Harcourt, Brace and Company, 1946 [1945].

———. *Nineteen Eighty-Four.* New York: Plume, 2003 [1949].

———. *Orwell in Spain: The Full Text of Homage to Catalonia, with Associated Articles, Reviews, and Letters.* Edited by Peter Davison. London: Penguin, 2001 [1938].

Rawls, John. *A Theory of Justice.* Cambridge, Mass.: Belknap Press of Harvard University Press, 1999 [1971].

Roy, Claude. *Moi je.* Paris: Gallimard, 1969.

——— *Nous.* Paris: Gallimard, 1972.

Schorske, Carl E. *Fin-de-siècle Vienna: Politics and Culture.* New York: Vintage, 1981.

Sebastian, Mihail. *Journal, 1935–1944.* Translated by Patrick Camiller. Introduction by Radu Ioanid. Chicago: Ivan R. Dee, 2000.

Semprún, Jorge. *Quel beau dimanche.* Paris: B. Grasset, 1980.

Shakespeare, William. *The Winter's Tale.* Edited by Harold Bloom. New York: Bloom's Literary Criticism, 2010 [1623].

Shore, Marci. "Engineering in an Age of Innocence: A Genealogy of Discourse inside the Czechoslovak Writer's Union." *East European Politics and Societies,* vol. 12, no. 3 (1998).

Sinclair, Upton. *The Jungle.* New York: Doubleday, 1906.

Sirinelli, Jean-François. *Génération intellectuelle: khâgneux et normaliens dans l'entre-deux-guerres.* Paris, Fayard, [1988].

Skinner, Quentin. *The Foundations of Modern Political Thought.* New York: Cambridge University Press, 1978.

Snyder, Timothy. *Bloodlands: Europe Between Hitler and Stalin.* New York: Basic Books, 2010.

———. *Nationalism, Marxism, and Modern Central Europe: A Biography of Kazimierz Kelles-Krauz.* Cambridge, Mass.: Harvard University Press, 1998.

Souvarine, Boris. *Stalin: A Critical Survey of Bolshevism.* New York: Alliance Book Corporation, Longmans, Green & Co., 1939 [1935].

Spender, Stephen. *World Within World: The Autobiography of Stephen Spender.* Introduction by John Bayley, New York: Modern Library, 2001 [1951].

Steinbeck, John. *The Grapes of Wrath.* London: Penguin Classics, 1992 [1939].

Taylor, A. J. P. *The Origins of the Second World War.* New York: Simon & Schuster, 1996 [1961].

Terkel, Studs. *Hard Times: An Oral History of the Great Depression.* New York: Pantheon Books, 1970.

Toruńczyk, Barbara. *Rozmowy w Maisons-Laffitte, 1981.* Warsaw: Fundacja Zeszytów Literackich, 2006.

Tyrmand, Leopold. *Dziennik 1954.* London: Polonia Book Fund, 1980.

Wat, Aleksander. "Ja z jednej strony i ja za drugiej strony mego mopsożelaznego piecyka," [1920] in *Aleksander Wat: poezje zebrane.* Edited by Anna Micińska and Jan Zieliński. Cracow, 1992.

Waugh, Evelyn. *Vile Bodies.* New York: The Modern Library, 1933 [1930].

Weissberg-Cybulski, Alexander. *The Accused.* Translated by Edward Fitzgerald. New York: Simon and Schuster, 1951.

Wieseltier, Leon. "What Is Not to Be Done," *The New Republic,* October 27, 2003.

Willis, F. Roy. *France, Germany, and the New Europe, 1945–1963.* Stanford, Calif.: Stanford University Press, 1965.

Zola, Émile. *Émile Zola's J'Accuse: A New Translation with a Critical Introduction by Mark K. Jensen.* Soguel, CA: Bay Side Press, 1992 [1898].

Zweig, Stefan. *The World of Yesterday: An Autobiography by Stefan Zweig.* Lincoln: University of Nebraska Press, 1964 [1943].

INDEX